CANADIAN PR

FOR THE REAL WORLD

CANADIAN PR

FOR THE REAL WORLD

MARYSE CARDIN
KYLIE McMULLAN

PEARSON

Toronto

Vice-President, Editorial Director: Gary Bennett
Acquisitions Editor: Deana Sigut
Marketing Manager: Leigh-Anne Graham
Developmental Editor: Darryl Kamo
Project Manager: Jessica Hellen
Production Services: Sandhya Gola, Cenveo® Publisher Services
Compositor: Cenveo Publisher Services
Permissions Project Manager: Joanne Tang
Photo Permissions Research: Q2a/Bill Smith/Cordes Hoffman
Text Permissions Research: Haydee Hidalgo, Electronic Publishing Services Inc.
Cover Designer: Suzanne Duda
Interior Designer: Anthony Leung
Cover Image: © Ocean/Corbis

Library and Archives Canada Cataloguing in Publication
Cardin, Maryse, author
    Canadian PR for the real world / Maryse Cardin and Kylie McMullan.
Includes index.
ISBN 978-0-13-215480-2 (pbk.)
    1. Public relations—Canada—Textbooks. I. McMullan, Kylie, author
II. Title.
HD59.C366 2013   659.20971   C2013-903279-7

ISBN 978-0-13-215480-2

Brief Contents

About the Authors

Photo by Jan Gates

Maryse Cardin is a PR practitioner and university lecturer. She teaches at Capilano University's School of Communication. Before falling in love with teaching, she was the co-founder of the award-winning agency Turtle & Hare Creative. Maryse has worked on PR campaigns in Asia, Europe, and North America for a multitude of non-profit and corporate clients. She lived for several years in Tokyo where she worked for the Japanese partner of the Worldcom Group, a consortium of PR agencies worldwide. Maryse has a BA in journalism from Concordia University and has earned her Masters degree in Mass Communications from the University of Leicester.

Frame Photography

Kylie McMullan is an Instructor of Public Relations for Simon Fraser University's Continuing Studies Certificate Program. Though she has a strong passion for teaching, Kylie also continues to practise public relations. Kylie has a strong background in public relations and marketing, stemming from her experience both client side, at Johnson & Johnson and Nature's Path Organic Foods, and in agency, working on accounts for clients such as Celestial Seasonings, Happy Planet Juice, Bootlegger, and Sandman Hotels. She also sat on the Board of the Vancouver Chapter of the Canadian Public Relations Society for four years and was the editor of their member newsletter. Kylie has a Masters of Business Administration from Simon Fraser University.

Preface

Public relations is a growing and dynamic field in Canada, one that, as both practitioners and instructors, we are passionate about. Each year, we are excited to see so many young, talented students who want to learn more about the practice of PR and take their place within the profession.

In our classrooms, we are lucky enough to meet and instruct many of these new and emerging practitioners. We wrote *Canadian PR for the Real World* with these students in mind. We wanted this textbook to enhance their understanding and love of the practice and to represent an extension of what we teach in the classroom. We hope it will serve as a reference tool for students long after they graduate and embark on their careers, one that they will refer back to in order to gain clearer insight into a problem or where they will seek, and find, practical guidance.

Above all else, this textbook celebrates public relations in Canada. We sought to make students aware of and to help them appreciate not only the rich history of public relations in Canada, but also the great work that contemporary practitioners produce on behalf of their organizations and clients. Many of the campaigns and projects created by our Canadian colleagues are winning awards and receiving global attention. However, until now, there was no publication capturing their case studies, examples, and testimonies. This textbook serves as an ode to their great work.

WHY WE WROTE THIS BOOK

While this textbook is new and is the first of its kind in Canada, the content is built upon years of practical experience and instruction in public relations programs. It reflects what we have found to be useful content in our own classrooms, as well as the type of material and information our students demanded from us. Our students wanted a practical textbook with content that they can reference and use: PR for the real world. They were also looking for "straight talk" from experienced practitioners, which is why we included **Practitioner Interviews** with PR professionals from coast to coast.

In this textbook, we have also included an **After-Class PR Advice** section, which provides professional advice and answers to many of the real-world questions our students are so curious about, such as entry-level salaries, job search tips, and networking strategies. At the end of each chapter, we have included a visual summary of the chapter content. These summaries serve as at-a-glance refreshers for busy students and are a helpful tool for students who have an aptitude for visual learning.

WHY THIS BOOK IS NEEDED

The publication of *Canadian PR for the Real World* represents a milestone in the history of public relations in Canada. It is the first textbook to examine the unique practice of public relations in its many forms within our borders and to recognize Canadian public relations practitioners. Not only do we in Canada have a rich public relations history that students should be made aware of, but there are many differences between the PR industries in Canada and the United States. However, when we started our teaching careers, we were dismayed to find that the only PR textbooks available on the market were American, providing only U.S. examples and case studies. While the markets do have similarities, we wanted students to understand the unique aspects of the Canadian market and Canada's distinctive cultural environment, as well as the differences between Canadian and U.S. legal and professional associations. We have even included a section on Canadian law and how it affects public relations.

CHAPTER ORGANIZATION

Chapter 1: Public Relations in Canada. In this chapter we define public relations and introduce the practice of PR in Canada. We look at strategic thinking and the RACE formula. We also look at a practitioner's typical day and at prospects in the industry. Importantly, we explore the role of ethics and the law in PR.

Chapter 2: Influencing Public Opinion: The Foundation of PR Then and Now. Here we look at public opinion, propaganda, attitudes and beliefs, influencers, and the factors of persuasion. We also look at the history of PR in the United States and Canada.

Chapter 3: Corporate Social Responsibility, Cause PR, and Environmental PR. In this chapter we discuss the importance of corporate social responsibility, examine matching causes to organizations, and look at the practice of environmental public relations.

Chapter 4: The Public Relations Plan. In this section we start to look at practical applications of public relations, starting with the formulation of an effective PR plan.

Chapter 5: Writing for PR. This chapter provides a comprehensive overview of writing for public relations, covering writing basics, key messages, news values, the media kit, media releases, speeches, and other PR materials.

Chapter 6: Media Relations. This is a practical step-by-step look at how to conduct media relations. This chapter also provides an overview of the role of the journalist and the media landscape in Canada.

Chapter 7: Social Media. While social media may be changing some components of communications, many of the basics remain the same. We look at what has changed and how to effectively communicate through social media.

Chapter 8: Media Training. This chapter provides the rationale and techniques behind media training spokespersons.

Chapter 9: Internal Communications. While many students believe that public relations is primarily externally directed, in this chapter we examine effective communication with an internal audience.

Chapter 10: Special Events Management. This chapter examines the various types of events, the special events plan, and PR practitioners' roles and responsibilities in managing special events.

Chapter 11: Issues Management and Crisis Communications. This chapter provides an overview of techniques for prevention of, preparation for, and response to issues and crises.

Chapter 12: Other Areas of Specialization. This chapter introduces students to investor relations, public affairs, and international and multicultural public relations, including conducting PR in Quebec and in other French-speaking communities.

REAL-WORLD EXAMPLES

The first edition of *Canadian PR for the Real World* provides timely, real-world case studies and examples from across the country. Some of these interesting and instructive examples include:

- The Occupy Wall Street movement and its influence on public opinion as it spread across Canada
- Best Buy Canada's internal communications plan during the 2010 Vancouver Olympics
- The special events management for the Juno Awards
- The Saskatchewan Roughriders' and Canadian Blood Services' Bleed Green campaign
- Tourism New Zealand's Canadian social media campaign
- Issues and crisis management around the collapse of the BC Place stadium roof and the Maple Leaf Foods product recall

SUPPLEMENTS

- **Instructor's Manual** This comprehensive guide contains a lecture outline of each chapter, descriptions of the discussion boxes, answers to the cases and exercises, and additional suggested group and individual exercises.
- **PowerPoint Slides** The PowerPoint slides feature key points and figures and tables from each chapter.
- **CourseSmart** CourseSmart goes beyond traditional expectations, providing instant, online access to the textbooks and course materials you need at a lower cost for students. And even as students save money, you can save time and hassle with a digital eTextbook that allows you to search for the most relevant content at the very

moment you need it. Whether it's evaluating textbooks or creating lecture notes to help students with difficult concepts, CourseSmart can make life a little easier. See how when you visit www.coursesmart.com/instructors.

GRATITUDES

Behind every book, there is a team of supporters who work diligently and encourage quietly, but receive little recognition. Even so, they are instrumental to the completion of the project. We would like to take a moment to acknowledge some of the major contributors to our textbook.

We are deeply appreciative to the publishing team at Pearson Canada. Nick Durie, former Acquisitions Editor, believed in this textbook and its importance to PR students in Canada and signed us on. Nick championed the project and provided vision, solutions, support, and encouragement when times got tough. We would not be here at the finish line without him. This book could not have been completed without a lot of hand-holding from our Senior Developmental Editor extraordinaire, Darryl Kamo. His patience and dedication to the project were outstanding. Thank you, Darryl.

We also thank the rest of the talented team: Deana Sigut, acquisitions editor; Jessica Hellen, in-house project manager; Marcia Gallego, copy editor; the team at Cenveo, including Sandhya Gola; and finally, Leigh-Anne Graham, marketing manager.

We are also indebted to all the PR practitioners who shared information with us and joined our mission to help foster the next generation of Canadian PR practitioners.

We would like to thank all the academic reviewers who took the time to review our manuscript and offer insight. A special thank you to Terri Smolar, academic and former member of the CPRS National Council on Education, for sharing valuable information on areas of practice to include in the textbook.

Many thanks also to our industry colleagues, former bosses, mentors, and teachers who helped us learn the profession and develop our expertise.

Kylie would also like to thank Mike Newall, Richard McMullan, and Chelsea McMullan for their unconditional love and support throughout the writing of this textbook. She owes a special thanks to her mother, Heather McMullan. Kylie would also like to thank Peter Walton, Fawn Mulcahy, and her colleagues at Simon Fraser University. It's because of their encouragement that she has the best job in the world: teaching.

Maryse thanks her husband, Robert Gibbens, and her daughter, Eloise, for their love and for sharing her with this textbook. Her work is better because of them. A heartfelt thank you goes to her parents, André and Yvaine Cardin, for believing in her. Many thanks are extended to her colleagues at Capilano University's School of Communication for their professional support.

Finally, thanks to you, the instructors and the students who look to continue the long tradition of exemplary public relations in Canada.

Maryse Cardin
Kylie McMullan

REVIEWERS

David Eames, Seneca College
Pamela Hart, Simon Fraser University
Elizabeth Hirst, McGill University
Marina Jaffey, Camosun College
Amelia Kennedy, University of Victoria
Stephanie Koonar, Langara College
Jennifer Leonard, Humber College
Chen-Yu James Liu, Assiniboine Community College
Amy MacArthur, Crandall University
Albert Mastromartino, Fleming College
Julianne McCaffrey, Cambrian College
Ed McHugh, Nova Scotia Community College
Deborah McKenzie, Seneca College
Kevin O'Doherty, George Brown College
Kathy Patterson, St. Lawrence College
Andrea Petruzella, Algonquin College
Teresa Sturgess, Northern Alberta Institute of Technology
Danielle van Dreunen, St. Lawrence College
Cynthia Wrate, Camosun College

Contents

CANADIAN PR

FOR THE REAL WORLD

Chapter 1
Public Relations in Canada

The Heart Truth public relations campaign effectively raised awareness among Canadian women about heart disease and stroke. Source: Edelman PR

LEARNING OBJECTIVES

1. Explain what public relations means to you and what the job entails.

2. Understand what it means to think strategically in public relations and how to approach a campaign, including the steps of the public relations process.

3. Describe a typical day and the role of a public relations practitioner.

4. Understand the importance of ethics and the law in public relations.

5. Explain why evaluation is an important component of public relations and describe two ways to measure a campaign's success.

The Heart Truth Campaign: Changing How Women Think about Heart Disease and Stroke

When the Heart and Stroke Foundation launched The Heart Truth campaign in 2008, research showed that most women thought of heart disease and stroke as a "man's disease." In fact, heart disease and stroke are leading causes of death of women over the age of 35. To change the public's perception of women's risk for heart disease and stroke, The Heart Truth campaign was launched with the objective of putting a female face on the issue.

The challenge facing the Heart and Stroke Foundation was to break through all the health-related messaging Canadian women receive daily and raise awareness of the disease among women. Working with the Heart and Stroke Foundation, Edelman—the PR agency for The Heart Truth campaign—had to strategically find a way to get their important message heard. One of the ways the team tackled this problem was by joining with well-known Canadian celebrities and fashion designers, whose involvement in the campaign has helped open new channels to reach women with heart health–related messages. Similar programs in the United States had used this model before and were viewed to be successful.

The Heart Truth campaign is a national, bilingual, integrated awareness campaign that reaches Canadian women with a message that could save their lives. While the campaign is led by traditional PR, including social media and community outreach, it is supported by advertising. The Heart Truth Facebook page serves up heart-healthy recipes, tips, and support, while the campaign website, thehearttruth.ca, includes information about heart disease and stroke, online tools, and community action kits, as well as a quiz women can take to evaluate their risk of heart disease. Print and online ads showcase the campaign, along with public service announcements on the radio and TV.

The signature event for the campaign, however, is the annual The Heart Truth Fashion Show featuring Canadian celebrities and designers. A media relations program leverages the fashion show to deliver health messaging to women through the media. A **LiveStream** of the show is also broadcast on the campaign's website and Facebook page.

The campaign is evaluated every year and the results are impressive. To date, The Heart Truth campaign has generated over 2,131 media stories, leading to more than 462.7 million media impressions. The Heart Truth Facebook community engages more than 32,000 fans. In addition, awareness is up dramatically with women over 35, as measured by the independent research firm Harris/Decima. In a survey the firm conducted before the campaign started, 33 per cent of women knew that heart disease was the leading killer of women over 35. As of April 2012, this number had risen to 59 per cent.

Welcome to the wonderful world of public relations! As a profession, public relations is dynamic, ever changing, and rewarding. The purpose of this textbook is to help familiarize you with the key terms, skills, and concepts that you will need to succeed in PR. You have seen how powerful PR can be from the opening vignette on the Heart Truth campaign. In this case, the PR team was able to help Canadian women understand that heart disease is a serious threat to their health. Throughout the chapter we will refer back to this opening vignette, explaining the terms and the concepts you have read there.

In this opening chapter, we will define public relations and provide a broad overview of what it encompasses before getting into more specific topics in the following chapters. As you make your way through this opening chapter, you will take away three main concepts. First, you will gain a sound understanding of public relations, an idea of the misconceptions surrounding it, and a grounding in what it can achieve. You will also be exposed to what a typical day in the industry looks like. Second, you will understand what is considered ethical behaviour in public relations and how ethics is a guiding principle of the profession. In this section, you will also review the laws that may affect your work in PR. Finally, you will read about evaluation techniques PR practitioners use to measure the success of their campaigns.

Understanding Public Relations

The Heart Truth campaign is one example of PR work, but there are many other case studies that represent what public relations is about and the activities that PR practitioners conduct, such as the following:

- A media conference is organized by an artisan cheesemaker because bacteria are found in its cheese, causing a product recall.
- A cosmetic manufacturer hosts a special event to launch a new lipstick.
- A pop singer is hired as a company's spokesperson and performs at an event.
- A nonprofit organization delivering meals to people living with AIDS sends out a newsletter to prospective donors.
- An airline flies travel journalists and bloggers to its new Asian destination.
- A lunch reception with a guest speaker is organized for politicians by a teachers union.
- The vice president of communications at a bank advises the chief executive officer (CEO) on the organization's reputation in the local community.

Now, take a moment to consider what the term *public relations* means to you. This is an important first step because there are many different opinions about what public relations is, a variety of definitions, and many misconceptions surrounding the profession. PR practitioners often encounter individuals, including other marketing professionals, who are not sure what the work of public relations entails.

When thinking of public relations, many students might envision Samantha Jones, the sassy public relations practitioner from the TV series *Sex and the City*. While she definitely made the job seem fun and exciting, the show did not represent the day-to-day reality of PR. Or students might register for a public relations program because they are attracted to one aspect of it but do not necessarily have an overall understanding of the industry. The most commonly known aspects of public relations are that it involves writing, planning special events, and working with people. And while PR does involve these activities, that does not begin to do justice to this complex, dynamic, and very strategic profession. We begin our understanding of PR by looking at some of its many definitions.

DEFINITION OF PUBLIC RELATIONS ❶

While there are many different definitions, in its simplest form, public relations is about communicating and building relationships with external and internal stakeholders. Let us consider the example mentioned above regarding the nonprofit organization. The nonprofit sends out a newsletter to communicate with its donors, keeping them informed about its latest initiatives to provide meals to people living with AIDS. With the newsletter, it also aims to maintain a close relationship with its donors, hoping to stay top of mind with them and generate more donations in the future.

The Canadian Public Relations Society (CPRS), one of the supporting professional associations available to PR practitioners and students across Canada, defines public relations in the following way: "Public relations is the strategic management of relationships between an organization and its diverse publics, through the use of communication, to achieve mutual understanding, realize organizational goals, and serve the public interest."[1]

As the CPRS definition states, PR practitioners build and manage relationships with publics. They act as a bridge between an organization and the target audiences it is trying to reach. PR professionals help the organization understand what audiences think and help the public understand the organization. They act as an intermediary to help them in communicating to each other. They build and maintain long-term relationships that are mutually beneficial, while supporting the organization in meeting its goals. The Heart Truth PR team, both in-house and in the agency, was the bridge between the Heart and Stroke Foundation and Canadian women at risk of heart disease. By helping the foundation understand how and in what ways to communicate to these women, the communications team helped the foundation achieve its goals. Figure 1.1 illustrates how the PR practitioner acts as the bridge between an organization and its target audiences.

Figure 1.1 "The Bridge"
The PR practitioner acts as a bridge between an organization and its target audiences.

While PR professionals support organizations, they also need to keep in mind what is best for society as a whole by acting ethically and in ways that will benefit communities. This sentiment is echoed in the definition of PR provided by Denny Griswold, the founder of *Public Relations News*, the first PR newsletter: "Public relations is the management function which evaluates public attitudes, identifies the policies and procedures of an individual or an organization with the public interest, and plans and executes a program of action to earn public understanding and acceptance."[2]

PROSPECTS OF THE PR INDUSTRY

There has never been a better time to embark on a career in public relations. The future of the industry looks bright, and PR professionals are in high demand. PR has been classified as one of the top 50 careers, and the number of jobs in this industry is expected to grow over the next decade.[3]

In addition, the industry stays strong in both good economies and poor ones. PR is thought to be nearly recession-proof because organizations need public relations to deliver key messages not only when there is good news to share but also when times are turbulent.

Even as other marketing functions are experiencing some softening, public relations is growing in popularity. For example, although spending on advertising is on the decline, organizations as a whole are spending more on public relations. Advertising spending fell by 8 per cent in 2009, while PR spending increased by 3 per cent in the same year.[4] In more good news for the industry, a survey of more than 200 Canadian small businesses conducted by BizLaunch revealed that 43 per cent of respondents believed PR was their most important marketing tool. According to Andrew Patricio, co-owner and head trainer at BizLaunch, "Small businesses, in particular, are turning to PR because media exposure is more effective than advertising at building a brand and credibility."[5]

MISCONCEPTIONS ABOUT PUBLIC RELATIONS

Despite the growing popularity of the profession and industry, many misconceptions about public relations still exist. Television shows like *The Hills* and *Sex and the City* portray public relations as a glamorous field with parties where people have a glass of Cristal champagne in one hand and bark orders into the iPhone they hold in the other. Even the CBC's radio drama about a public relations agency, *Trust Inc.*, portrays a dazzling world of backstabbing, crises, and romance. Such portrayals are perpetuated because PR practitioners *are* sometimes involved in glamorous events, such as the Heart Truth Fashion Show. What a lot of people don't see, however, is the blood, sweat, and tears and many unglamorous tasks that go on behind the scenes in order to launch such an event.

To confuse the public further, disparaging terms, such as *spin doctor* or *flack*, have been used to describe practitioners. These expressions insinuate that PR practitioners manipulate and bend the truth, if not outright lie, on behalf of their organizations and clients.

Samantha Jones, a character in the TV series *Sex and the City,* made PR look fun, but the show did not portray the realities of working in this industry.
Source: © Andy Myatt/ Alamy

These media images and terms have done nothing to help the public understand or respect the functions of public relations. A top Canadian practitioner laments "the misconception that public relations is about blowing up balloons or at its worst lying and misguiding the public." Another practitioner notes, "When people tell me they need some 'good' PR it just makes me cringe. Because I know they don't really mean PR—they mean they want their image polished in the media. PR is one of the most misrepresented professions I know of."[6]

Public relations practitioners often talk about their own need of PR, or how the industry must enlighten the public about the benefits that effective public relations contributes to the achievement of organizational goals.

PR AND MARKETING

The difference between PR and other elements of marketing, such as advertising, is often misunderstood. In marketing and advertising, the goal is to convince customers of the benefits of a product or service. While PR may try to do this as well, it has the broader task of building relationships with and communicating to all stakeholders. In PR, we often try to convince media or publics to spread our message or tell our story. If we were to conduct PR to launch a new restaurant, for example, one of the tactics we might employ is media relations. This would entail writing **media materials**, or written materials that are distributed to the media, outlining the benefits and unique features of the restaurant and contacting restaurant reviewers to invite them to a launch event or to visit the restaurant and write a review. Our objective would be to generate **media coverage** or **earned media**—a positive restaurant review in the newspaper in order to influence patrons to come to the restaurant. Earned media is generated without content being purchased. With earned media, there are no guarantees that coverage will occur, or if it does, what the size or tone of the

The Heart Truth campaign delivered its message through both paid and earned media.
Source: Edelman PR

coverage will be. In advertising, an ad would be designed and space would be bought in the newspaper for the ad to run. When an ad is purchased, there is an agreement that it will be a specific size or length and run on a specific page or station. This is also called **paid media**, where promotional content is purchased.

Think about the difference between an ad for a restaurant and a restaurant review. Which would be more likely to grab your attention? Which would you be more likely to trust? In a nutshell, that is the difference between advertising and public relations.

PR can be conducted on its own, but as we saw with the Heart Truth campaign at the beginning of the chapter, it is most powerful when it is part of an **integrated marketing** campaign. This means that many or all marketing programs, which might include advertising, direct mail, and public relations, work together to create one overall **campaign**, or planned course of action, using the same unified messaging. The Heart Truth campaign incorporated social media relations, media relations, online and print advertising, and special events. Each of these tactics communicated the same messages to women: that heart disease affects women like them and that they may be at risk. In another example, Tropicana conducted an integrated marketing campaign to promote its juice with its campaign Brighter Mornings for Brighter Days. As part of this campaign, the company floated a giant illuminated helium balloon in Inuvik, Northwest Territories, to bring "sunshine" to the town after weeks of winter darkness and featured the campaign in TV advertising, social media, media sponsorship, and special events.

Increasingly, PR practitioners are called upon to play a larger marketing role and to take on promotional marketing tasks. Marketing is composed of four Ps: price, promotion, product, and place. Public relations typically does not contribute to the Ps of price, product, and place, but often contributes to the P of promotion. Promotion is often defined as **marketing communications** and can include everything from design to creating ads, writing copy, creating direct mail pieces, and preparing materials such as banners and booths for trade and consumer shows.

Strategic Thinking and the PR Process ❷

The most important asset that PR practitioners bring to the table is their ability to apply strategic thinking to a business problem or need. **Strategic thinking** is the thought process that drives the direction of the PR campaign. PR professionals seek innovative and creative ways to help organizations communicate in order to achieve their objectives. That includes planning and making decisions regarding how and why a campaign is carried out. To build a career in public relations, you need to start thinking like a PR professional. Anyone can learn the tactics of PR such as how to organize a special event or write a blog. The true challenge is to identify a problem or a need an organization faces and then to decide on the best course of action and the tactics required.

A communications process has been developed to help practitioners approach a campaign in a methodological and strategic way. This process involves formulas that enable PR professionals to strategically plan and implement a campaign by breaking it down into distinctive steps. While there are many different formulas that achieve the same results, the one that is most commonly used in Canada and that is recommended by CPRS is the RACE formula, developed in 1963 by John Marston in his book *The Nature of Public Relations*.

The letters in the acronym RACE are an easy way for PR practitioners to understand and to remember the four steps that go into planning and implementing a campaign. They are as follows:

R: research

A: analysis

C: communication

E: evaluation

Let us examine each step.

Step 1: Research A PR practitioner conducts research before undertaking planning or **implementation**. This is to help ensure that smart decisions are made and that campaigns are based on solid information rather than assumptions. The communications plan is then based on this information. Research can involve everything from conducting a questionnaire or focus group to speaking to journalists to get their opinion on a certain topic or doing online research. Sometimes a research company will need to be hired to provide their expertise and services in order get more in-depth, statistically valid research. See Chapter 4 for more information on research.

Step 2: Analysis In the analysis stage, a PR practitioner looks at all the elements of a campaign, such as target audiences, objectives, key messages, and tactics. We will look at the elements that go into this crucial step later in this chapter. In this step, the PR practitioner drafts a PR plan detailing all the actions or tactics that will be conducted. The plan is like a road map. It guides the way in terms of what steps need to be taken and when to take them. The plan needs to be very clear about what the campaign is trying to accomplish and what the objectives are. If you are not clear about what you are doing, how can you evaluate whether or not you've been successful?

Step 3: Communication In this step, the PR professional puts the plan into action, implementing the campaign and tactics and following a **timeline** (the chronological order in which actions are carried out) to ensure that every activity is undertaken and completed within a specified timeframe and that **deadlines** (the time by which an activity or campaign must be completed) are met.

Step 4: Evaluation In the **evaluation** stage it is time to reflect on and measure the success of the campaign. This involves looking at the results generated by the tactics and determining whether the campaign achieved everything it set out to do. The PR practitioner will determine if the campaign was successful and look at whether any lessons can be learned from mistakes. There are always things to learn from each campaign, even successful ones. Evaluation is covered in more detail later in this chapter.

STEP 2 IN MORE DETAIL: THE FAB FOUR OF PR

Step 2 of the process, the analysis, is an extremely important step, which we cover in detail in Chapter 4. For now, let us look at the four elements that make up the analysis. We like to call these four elements the Fab Four of PR. They are

1. Target audiences: Who you are trying to reach?

2. Objectives: What you are trying to accomplish?

3. Key messages: What you are trying to say?

4. Tactics: How you will do it? The tactics employed in public relations are the means by which PR practitioners put these objectives into practice; it is how they achieve their goals.

Target Audiences and Stakeholders: Who You Are Trying to Reach

To recap, public relations helps organizations meet their objectives and communicate with their **target audiences**—the people and organizations with whom they aim to communicate. These audiences can be very specific (for example, mothers who buy organic baby food in Halifax) or more general (such as Canadians who vote for the Liberal Party). Target audiences can also be stakeholders. **Stakeholders** are publics that an organization is accountable to, such as employees, board members, or investors. In the opening vignette we saw that the target audience of the Heart Truth campaign was Canadian women, especially those over the age of 35.

The more an organization knows about its target audiences, the better. This can include information on such details as their income level, what they do in their leisure time, and which media they consume. These data enable practitioners to tailor their campaign to their target audiences, meaning that each campaign is specifically designed with the particular audience in mind.

Audiences are also divided into internal or external categories. Examples of internal audiences are employees, union members, board members, and management. Examples of external audiences include media, the municipal government, consumers, and donors. Figure 1.2 illustrates target audiences.

As an example, in its public relations campaign, the Early Psychosis Initiative—a program to help identify and treat young people suffering from mental disorders such as schizophrenia—aimed to communicate with the following external target audiences:

High school students
College and university students

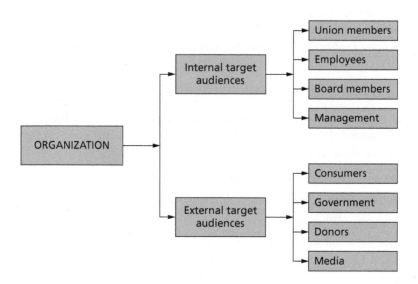

Figure 1.2 Internal and External Target Audiences

Family members of young people showing symptoms of psychosis

Friends of young people showing symptoms of psychosis

You will find more information on the Early Psychosis Initiative in a case study at the end of this chapter.

Objectives: What Can Be Achieved with PR

As we have seen, public relations plays a prominent role in management, and its practitioners counsel the heads of organizations. PR also wields considerable influence in terms of an organization's reputation. It has the power to solve problems, build a solid reputation, and help make a business achieve its targets.

Public relations is powerful and effective. It can bring a host of benefits to an organization and play an important role in assisting organizations to meet their overall **objectives**—or goals or targets—with both internal and external audiences. In the Heart Truth campaign, for example, the main objective was to raise awareness with women about heart disease.

Other objectives that can be achieved with PR include the following:

Raising the profile of organizations with their target audiences

Raising awareness of products and services

Educating the public on important issues

Building relationships and engaging target audiences

Helping pass laws and regulations

Attracting new clients

Attracting investors

Raising funds and donations for nonprofits and charitable organizations

Attracting and retaining employees

Recruiting volunteers, leads, and contacts

Building a strong and trustworthy relationship with the community

Combatting rumours

Navigating an issue or crisis such as a product recall or a strike

The BC Principals' and Vice-Principals' Association (BCPVPA) formulates a yearly public relations plan in which all of its objectives are outlined. Objectives have included raising awareness of the important role that principals play in schools, attracting new members to the association, maintaining the reputation of the BCPVPA as the most trusted and respected voice in public education, and informing members about breaking educational issues.

Key Messages: What You Want to Say

Key messages are the basis for all communication. To craft an effective key message, the practitioner must begin with a clear understanding of what an organization wants to

"Is there such a thing
as over communicating?"

Source: Cartoonresource/Shutterstock

communicate to its target audiences. Each key message encapsulates a simple idea that the company wants its audience to know. The simpler the key message, the better.

The importance of knowing your target audiences in order to decide which messages will resonate with them cannot be emphasized enough. Key messages are used as the basis for all written materials, including speeches, websites, and media materials. An example of a key message for a company whose main differentiator is being family owned might be "family owned and operated." A key message for an organic cotton company might be "always organic." These companies would ensure that their key messages were included throughout all their communications pieces, whether it be a speech, an ad, or a news release. The more repetition a key message receives, the more it will stick in the audience's mind.

The general rule of thumb is to have three key messages. Three is a number that is easy for the brain to process and absorb. There is an adage in PR that only *you* care about the fourth key message. There can be overall key messages for an organization, specific ones for certain publics, key messages for crisis situations, or even messages that are crafted for a special circumstance or event.

Public Relations Tactics: How You Will Do It

Not until the target audiences, objectives, and key messages have been clearly defined is the decision made regarding which **tactics**, or actions, will be the most effective. As we mentioned earlier, each PR campaign is unique and is specifically tailored to the audiences and designed to meet specific objectives. Some of the tactics employed in public relations include the following:

Writing: creating a myriad of written materials, such as media materials, websites, annual reports, and speeches

Social media: working with the tools of social media, such as Facebook, and contacting bloggers

Media relations: working with print (newspapers, magazines) and broadcast (television, radio) journalists to generate media coverage (stories)

Media training: preparing **spokespersons**, or people who represent the company in the public sphere, to speak to the media

Marketing public relations: using PR to meet marketing goals

Special event management: organizing events such as product launches, fundraisers, or trade shows

Issues and crisis management: dealing with situations that can affect an organization's reputation

Investor relations: communicating and working with the organization's investors

Government relations: communicating and working with all levels of government, from the municipal to the federal, to **advocate** for, or support, an organization or an issue

Nonprofit PR: communicating for nonprofit organizations

Fundraising: generating funds and communicating with the organization's donors

Aboriginal relations: communicating with this specific target audience

Community relations: building relationships with the local community

Internal communication: working on internal audience relations

Strategic consulting: providing advice, direction, plans, and strategy to organizations and working with management

These tactics are explained in more much detail in later chapters. Figure 1.3 summarizes the RACE formula.

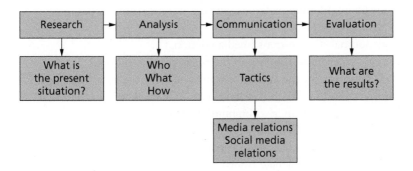

Figure 1.3 The RACE Formula

The RACE formula is an easy way to remember the four steps that go into planning and implementing a PR campaign.

A Typical Day in PR [3]

It's 8 a.m. You arrive at your busy downtown public relations agency and check your email. You see an urgent email from your manager asking you to draft a press release that a client needs by the end of the day. You make a note of it and then scan the media coverage on all your clients, as well as reviewing the news to see if there are any issues that might affect them. At 10 a.m., you spend two hours on media relations, pitching real estate reporters on a new project for one of your clients who is a developer. At noon, you eat at your desk while researching background information in order to help you draft the release your client needs. By 2 p.m., you've sent it to your manager for approval. At 3 p.m., you have a meeting in the boardroom to brainstorm ideas for a new holiday campaign for one of your clients who is launching a Christmas tea. Before you leave at 5 p.m., you log your hours in your timesheet and pack up your bag to head home.

PR is a high-energy, dynamic career, and to be successful in it requires many skills. Long hours tend to be the norm. A PR professional juggles a full workload and is an ace at multi-tasking because many projects advance simultaneously. In addition, many tasks present themselves without warning, such as media calls or breaking issues. A practitioner may perform some or all of the following activities in a typical day:

Write media information materials (writing and media relations)
Chair a meeting (project management)
Answer a journalist's questions (media relations)
Train a spokesperson to conduct an interview (media training)
Craft a PR strategy for the launch of a new product or service (drafting a PR plan)
Organize a trade show booth (special events management)
Represent an organization at a community event (community relations)
Write a proposal (new business acquisition)
Manage a breaking issue (issues and crisis management)
Email information to a blogger (social media relations)
Update the organization's website and Facebook page (social media relations)
Draft and send a letter to an MLA (government relations)
Write a company employee newsletter (internal communications)

To illustrate this point, think about the Heart Truth campaign and the large number of tasks that the PR team conducted to achieve the level of success that they did. Think about the number of hours that had to be spent writing the website, the media materials, and the Facebook page. Think of all the time spent researching and writing the plan. Think of all the meetings that took place and all the journalists that were contacted. Think of the coordination needed to secure celebrities to take part in the fashion show, and all the planning that went into the event itself. Think of all this and you will still see only a fraction of the effort, time, and talent that went into this campaign.

TYPES OF PUBLIC RELATIONS JOBS

PR practitioners' skill sets are appropriate for a variety of jobs, and PR professionals are highly sought by many kinds of employers. PR practitioners can find employment in various aspects of the profession, including community relations, corporate communications, public affairs, investor relations, or government lobbying. PR people work for nonprofit organizations, charities, and art groups. While some practitioners work in many industries over their careers, others have expertise in a specific field. One practitioner may own an agency that caters exclusively to the horse breeding industry, while another may specialize in entertainment, health care, law, fashion, or restaurant publicity. Some PR professionals promote books and authors, and others work for unions, in not-for-profit, or in high tech. There are also public relations practitioners working for governments in departments of public affairs and for organizations such as the United Nations.

Public relations offers numerous career opportunities in a variety of organizations. Practitioners tend to work either in-house (in an organization itself) or in an agency setting, and because public relations skills are highly transferable, there are no limits to the kinds of work that these professionals can do. Figure 1.4 illustrates the wide variety of industries that have PR positions. Figure 1.5 provides examples of PR job titles.

CORPORATE	PUBLISHING
NONPROFIT ORGANIZATIONS	LAW
FILM AND MUSIC INDUSTRY	ANIMATION
FASHION	HIGH TECH
LOCAL, PROVINCIAL, AND FEDERAL GOVERNMENTS	MEDIA (TELEVISION, RADIO, NEWSPAPERS, MAGAZINES)
HEALTH CARE	SPORTS
HOSPITALITY	FESTIVALS AND OTHER COMMUNITY EVENTS
BANKING	PROFESSIONAL ASSOCIATIONS

Figure 1.4   Examples of Industries in which PR Practitioners Work

VICE PRESIDENT OF COMMUNICATIONS	DIRECTOR OF SOCIAL MEDIA
DIRECTOR OF CORPORATE COMMUNICATIONS	SOCIAL MEDIA MANAGER
COMMUNICATIONS STRATEGIST	NEWSLETTER EDITOR
DIRECTOR OF CONSUMER AFFAIRS	DIRECTOR OF MARKETING
COMMUNICATIONS SPECIALIST	DIRECTOR OF INVESTOR RELATIONS
PUBLIC RELATIONS CONSULTANT	FUNDRAISING OR DONOR
COMMUNICATIONS MANAGER	RELATIONS MANAGER
ACCOUNT EXECUTIVE	SPECIAL EVENTS MANAGER
COORDINATOR	SPECIAL EVENTS COORDINATOR
MARKETING AND COMMUNICATIONS COORDINATOR	COMMUNITY RELATIONS MANAGER
PR MANAGER	GOVERNMENT PUBLIC AFFAIRS
MEDIA RELATIONS MANAGER	MANAGER

Figure 1.5 **Examples of Job Titles that PR Practitioners Hold**

ADVICE TO NEW PRACTITIONERS

Professional Support

- Think of joining one of Canada's professional PR associations. Some of the associations are for general PR work, such as the International Association of Business Communicators (IABC) and the Canadian Public Relations Society (CPRS). Others are more specialized, such as the Canadian Investor Relations Institute (CIRI) and the Canadian Society of Professional Event Planners (CanSPEP). These groups have regular meetings with guest speakers and are a good place to meet PR practitioners and other students. The American Marketing Association (AMA) also has chapters in several Canadian cities that are attended by PR professionals. Some associations offer special student discounts for membership.

- Volunteer for a PR association: join one of their committees or write for their newsletter. It is a great way to gain professional experience and make connections in the industry.

- Take advantage of the mentorship programs some associations offer. An experienced practitioner can help guide you in your career path.

- Later in your career, consider obtaining professional accreditation from CPRS. This is a certification program that demonstrates your professional capabilities. It lets employers and colleagues know that you have achieved a high level of competency in the profession. And you get to put APR (Accredited in Public Relations) after your name.

Ethics and the Law: Guiding Principles of Public Relations ④

Public relations can be very powerful. Performed well, PR can influence the way people think and the actions they take, whether they are voting for a political party, supporting a cause, or trusting a company. PR professionals also provide information to journalists that results in media coverage, which the public might read and trust. Because of their influence over public opinion, it is of the utmost importance that PR practitioners are honest and practise moral behaviour—that they act ethically in all that they do. It is just as critical that they follow the law and regulations that affect the different parts of their practice.

ETHICS AND PR

Ethics, our sense of knowing and doing what is right, is especially important to public relations. Unlike some other professions, public relations is conducted in full view of the public. Most of our contact with people is on the record, written in statements and media materials, recorded in the media, and distributed in the community, not to mention the fact that these materials may now live forever in the digital world. Transparency, honesty, and integrity build our credibility as practitioners and that of the organizations we represent.

The Canadian Centre for Ethics and Corporate Policy defines ethics as the guiding principles by which people make decisions and conduct their lives: "Business ethics involves applying ethical principles to the activities of business and to the relationships between businesses and various stakeholders."[7]

Regrettably, public relations does not possess the most sparkling of reputations. Some past events raise questions about the credibility of PR professionals. A survey of the Canadian public found that PR ranked among the three least trusted professions, with only 38 per cent of people surveyed trusting its practitioners.[8] According to one commentator,

The credibility of public relations has occasionally been affected adversely by conscious efforts of some individuals to engage in "public-relations exercises" in an effort to obscure facts or even mislead public opinion. Responsible public relations, however, is concerned with communicating factual information, with full disclosure of sources and open discussion of all aspects of controversial issues.[9]

Professional associations lead the way in efforts to turn this reputation around. Foremost among these efforts is the creation of codes of conduct for their members, which outline systems of ethical behaviour for PR professionals. Various associations have developed codes of conduct, including the Canadian Public Relations Society (CPRS; see Figure 1.6), the International Association of Business Communicators (IABC), the Global Alliance for Public Relations and Communication Management (GA), and the International Public Relations Association (IPRA). These are voluntary terms, which the members accept. There is no enforcement, except for the occasional reversal of membership.

Some practices conducted in the PR industry are considered unethical and are against the professional codes of conduct. Such unethical activities might include disguising a PR campaign to look like a community-based grassroots movement (sometimes called *astroturfing*), concealing who the PR professionals represent, establishing fake blogs (known as *flogging*), or paying bloggers for reviews (sometimes known as *pay-for-play*).

As PR professionals sit at the management table and advise the top echelons of organizations about how to proceed and what to communicate, they must be the ones advocating on behalf of truth and accuracy. It is always in the long-term interest of organizations and practitioners to do the right thing. While unethical behaviour might work in the short term, it usually comes back to bite the organization.

In addition, PR professionals work on many issues and in crisis situations where credibility factors into how an audience will receive and engage with the message and the organization. If trust is not established as an ongoing principle, it will be nearly impossible to manage an issue or crisis effectively because the messages won't be believed. The values PR people bring to the table and the high standards they apply to their work contribute to building ongoing credibility.

The good news is that ethical behaviour not only represents the right thing to do but is also a smart career move. Research demonstrates that a strong sense of ethics can help advance a public relations professional's career.[10] Your reputation will follow you throughout your career so you want to invest in it, and that includes working for organizations that follow ethical practices. It is not just the credibility of the organization that is on the line, but also the credibility of the PR professional themselves: "Representing clients who are considered morally objectionable can also call into question the ethics of a firm or practitioner. In the criminal justice system, even the guilty are entitled to representation. However, representing all clients and causes, regardless of their moral status in society, can have serious consequences."[11]

Canadian Public
Relations Society

Source: Canadian Public Relations Society

A member shall practice public relations according to the highest professional standards.

Members shall conduct their professional lives in a manner that does not conflict with the public interest and the dignity of the individual, with respect for the rights of the public as contained in the Constitution of Canada and the Charter of Rights and Freedoms.

A member shall deal fairly and honestly with the communications media and the public.

Members shall neither propose nor act to improperly influence the communications media, government bodies or the legislative process. Improper influence may include conferring gifts, privileges or benefits to influence decisions

A member shall practice the highest standards of honesty, accuracy, integrity and truth, and shall not knowingly disseminate false or misleading information.

Members shall not make extravagant claims or unfair comparisons, nor assume credit for ideas and words not their own.

Members shall not engage in professional or personal conduct that will bring discredit to themselves, the Society or the practice of public relations.

A member shall deal fairly with past or present employers/clients, fellow practitioners and members of other professions.

Members shall not intentionally damage another practitioner's practice or professional reputation. Members shall understand, respect and abide by the ethical codes of other professions with whose members they may work from time to time.

Members shall be prepared to disclose the names of their employers or clients for whom public communications are made and refrain from associating themselves with anyone who would not respect such policy.

Members shall be prepared to disclose publicly the names of their employers or clients on whose behalf public communications is made. Members shall not associate themselves with anyone claiming to represent one interest, or professing to be independent or unbiased, but who actually serves another or an undisclosed interest.

Figure 1.6   CPRS Code of Professional Standards *(Continued)*

Source: Code of Professional Standards. Used with permission.

A member shall protect the confidences of present, former and prospective employers/clients.

Members shall not use or disclose confidential information obtained from past or present employers/clients without the expressed permission of the employers/clients or an order of a court of law.

A member shall not represent conflicting or competing interests without the expressed consent of those concerned, given after a full disclosure of the facts.

Members shall not permit personal or other professional interests to conflict with those of an employer/client without fully disclosing such interests to everyone involved.

A member shall not guarantee specified results beyond the member's capacity to achieve.

Members shall personally accept no fees, commissions, gifts or any other considerations for professional services from anyone except employers or clients for whom the services were specifically performed.

Figure 1.6 *(Continued)*

PR AND THE LAW

PR practitioners are not lawyers and as such are not expected to be familiar with every aspect of the law. However, they must be aware of the areas of the practice where legal issues arise in order to avoid legal pitfalls for themselves and their organizations. This is especially important for investor relations, where the regulations are abundant and complicated, and the consequences for not following them are severe.

It is important to note that the legal areas we outline do not concern criminal law where a person can be arrested, but rather civil law where the consequences can include being sued. As noted by Marko Vesely, a top Canadian media lawyer at the law firm of Lawson Lundell LLP, it is uncommon for PR people to be sued. However, it can and does happen. A review of court cases in Canada revealed several such cases.

Marko Vesely provides this suggestion to young practitioners:

> Anyone involved in public relations should have at least an elementary grasp of the legal rules that apply to the dissemination of information. It is often said that a little knowledge can be a dangerous thing. But knowing enough about the law to pause and reflect, and if appropriate, seek legal advice, before going forward with a potentially risky project can often prevent embarrassment and the substantial cost and inconvenience of defending a lawsuit.[12]

The following are the areas of law most likely to affect practitioners and their work in many disciplines within PR, such as media relations, social media relations, special events management, government relations, and investor relations. This overview, however, is not meant to substitute for professional legal advice.

Defamation Law

Defamation is a statement about individuals or organizations that can damage their reputation and lower them in the esteem of others in the community. This law covers both printed statements (known as *libel*) and oral statements (known as *slander*).[13]

It is important to note that in cases of defamation, "the intended meaning of the speaker is not relevant. Rather, the test is what meaning would be attributed to the words by a reasonable reader or listener. As a result, a publisher may be found liable for a statement which appears innocent, but which may carry a defamatory imputation."[14]

In several Canadian cases, public relations practitioners and the organizations they represent have been sued for defamation.[15] In one such case, a biotechnology company hired a PR agency to conduct a campaign about how its product was safer than that of the competition. As part of the campaign, the agency sent a letter to the media with claims about the competitor's product that turned out to be untrue. A radio station ran the story on the air and also on the Internet. The competitor sued both the biotechnology company and the PR agency for defamation, arguing that the story was false.[16] Although officials at the PR agency explained that they had not meant harm and had made a factual mistake, the law of defamation is not based on intentions.

An interesting new area of defamation law involves the Internet and social media. Since information can now be distributed globally with these tools, an organization can now be sued in a foreign country. This means that an organization would be exposed to the defamation laws of other countries, which may be more likely to proceed with legal action than in Canada.[17]

What It Means for PR Practitioners PR professionals must pay careful attention to the information that they release, whether in writing or orally. They have to be certain that what they write is true and comes from reputable sources. The materials they write might include media materials and all social media tools. Spokespersons must also be careful of the statements they make to the media or during public speeches.

It is essential to get all information in writing and double-check each fact. Defamation is the area that most often gets practitioners into trouble. Some PR practitioners have especially sensitive material reviewed by a defamation lawyer before distributing it.

The law also provides organizations with protection from what journalists or bloggers may say or write about them. Perhaps an organization has been defamed in a story, or the way it has been portrayed is false and damaging to its reputation. In these cases, the organization may decide to bring the media outlet to court. Obviously, this is a serious decision that should not be taken lightly. Not only are court cases time-consuming and costly, but taking legal action will destroy the organization's relationship with the media outlet. Furthermore, recent changes in defamation law have provided journalists with a lot more leeway in terms of the mistakes they are allowed to make. This holds implications for PR practitioners, as seen in a recent court case described in PR practitioner Alan Fryer's blog:

> A good public relations person will always respond in an effective and timely way to media requests for information, reaction or interviews. The reality is many don't. And now ineffective or untimely response can severely limit or negate a company's legal options when it comes to a damaging report in the media. The potential damage to your clients' reputations can be enormous and permanent.
>
> What happened to a major Canadian retailer recently could happen to your clients if they fail to respond effectively to a media story. A recently aired news report strongly

suggested that an employee of the retailer created a safety hazard by tampering with a customer's property, in order to sell him a replacement part he didn't need.

That claim may or may not be true—there's simply no way to prove it. However, the reporter did reach out to the company for comment. The head of PR then took three whole days to get back to the reporter and then responded with a written statement that did not adequately address the issue. By the time the report appeared online the company went into full damage control and demanded the story be pulled. But it was too late; the story was out there.

After the report aired, the company served notice of its intention to sue for damages. When the media lawyer presented the retailer's legal team with the sequence of events—which made clear the untimely and ineffective response of the PR person—the retailer backed down.

The company realized—after they were reminded of it by the media lawyer—that they had handed the broadcaster a defense that would likely get the case thrown out.

The journalist had exercised responsible journalism by giving the company more than enough time to respond. Because the company—through its PR person—chose not to, the reputational damage was done and the company was denied any legal recourse.[18]

Source: "A good public relations person will always respond in an ..." (appr 192 words) January 6, 2011. Used by permission.

Copyright Law

This area of the law seeks to protect owners of original work from having their work used without their authorization. The Copyright Act protects literary, dramatic, musical, and artistic works internationally, typically for the author's lifetime plus 50 years after his or her death.[19]

PR practitioners must ensure they have proper approval before using any photographs, writing, or art in a campaign. In one case, a public relations agency was sued for using, without permission, the photo of an internationally known water skier in a brochure for a children's summer camp.[20] In another, the Eatons Centre in Toronto was sued for tying red Christmas ribbons on artwork, created by the Canadian artist Michael Snow, which hung at the mall. Through the lawsuit, the artist was able to force the Eaton's Centre to take the ribbons off his work.[21]

What It Means for PR Practitioners It is vital that PR professionals obtain permission in writing from any artist, writer, or photographer whose work they wish to reproduce and distribute to the public. In some cases, permission may be granted to use the work such as a photograph in a brochure. Before using the work in other ways, the practitioner would have to obtain further permission. As we saw in the case of the Eaton's Centre, PR professional must also be careful to seek permission before making any modifications to works of art for special events.

Some works fall within what is called the public domain. This means that they are not subject to copyright and anyone can use them without seeking permission.

Trademark Law

A trademark is a mark such as a symbol, word, or design that distinguishes one organization's product or service from another's.[22] Once a trademark is registered with the

Canadian Intellectual Property Office, it provides the owner with the exclusive right to use it in Canada for 15 years. The symbol™ or ® is generally placed after the mark as evidence of ownership.

What It Means for PR Practitioners Generally, PR practitioners' role is to ensure that their organization's trademarks are not being used without permission or infringed upon by others. They also ensure that trademarks are being used correctly by those who have received permission, on banners, for instance, or in the media. If you are partnering with another organization such as a charity for a campaign, make sure you follow their logo standards and apply the proper trademarks when mentioning them.

Invasion of Privacy Law

Individuals have the right to keep certain information about themselves from being made public. In Canada, there is not one law that protects against the invasion of privacy; instead, it is addressed under several different statutes and areas of the law.[23]

What It Means for PR Practitioners Practitioners must be careful not to infringe on the right of individuals to their privacy, when writing an employee newsletter, for example, or posting photos on an organization's social media site. It is important to get individuals to sign a **release**, which gives permission to use photos and text that are personal in nature. PR professionals need to be especially careful not to distribute information that is embarrassing or offensive.

PRACTITIONER INTERVIEW

Kristin Ann Janishefski: PR for Fashion and Lifestyle Eco Products

Kristin Ann Janishefski is the owner of the Vanguard PR, an agency with offices in Vancouver and Los Angeles that specializes in eco fashion and lifestyle products. The Vanguard PR is a full-service PR agency offering clients the gamut of PR tactics and strategies, including media relations, social media relations, and special event management. Prior to opening her own agency, Kristin Ann worked in-house for a fashion corporation as well as for other PR agencies.

Question: How did you start your career in PR?

Answer: My PR career started at a boutique agency in Los Angeles, which I worked at while I was in fashion marketing school at the Fashion Institute of Design and Merchandising.

Starting off at a boutique PR agency really enabled me to learn so much and learn directly from the owner of the company. I was able to get really hands-on with clients and work with accounts that I would not have been able to work with if I started at a bigger agency, which would have probably had me filing papers. This also really helped me develop a "thick skin" when it came to connecting with and pitching the media, because I actually called and talked to the media on a day-to-day basis (which most assistants in bigger agencies don't get to do), so it helped to develop my confidence along the way.

Question: What kind of PR work do you do?

Answer: I have worked in a number of different PR arenas throughout my career, including fitness,

(Continued)

Kristin Ann Janishefski: PR for Fashion and Lifestyle Eco Products

celebrity, entertainment, beauty, design, food, and fashion, but my real passion lies within the eco/sustainable realm. The Vanguard PR has a specific focus on all areas of the eco/sustainable arena, from working with organic beverages to eco fashion designers and ethically produced accessory lines to planet-friendly yogis! I think that it's very important to find what you are good at and what you are passionate about and our agency combines both of those elements. When I started the agency, I wanted to really tap into a niche market and something that no one was doing at the time (and really still isn't) so that is why the Vanguard is an eco/sustainable-focused PR agency.

Question: What aspects of the profession motivate you?

Answer: When you are passionate about what you do, you find motivation in the smallest details of your work. I am a really creative person, so this field is really a perfect fit for me. Every day is an opportunity to do something exciting. I can create unique client opportunities and media opportunities. It is so important that you never feel "bored" or "stuck" in your job.

I think that another huge motivating factor is the type of clients that we work with. For the most part, these are not huge corporations. Most of the clients are those who have an incredibly unique vision and are still at the "beginning" stages of their collection or who have never worked with PR before. The fact that I worked with a designer at the beginning stages and first season of their collection and have been with them for over four years and seen them in the pages of some of the biggest magazines in the world is an incredible motivating factor.

Question: What are the most important skills you need in this field?

Answer: I'm a firm believer that a positive attitude can get you anywhere you want in life. Days in PR can be filled with ups and downs, but you have to be able to find that balance in every opportunity so that your emotions don't get the best of you. A "thick skin" is essential! You get hung up on, yelled at, and told to never contact someone again, but you have to learn to just let it roll off your shoulders.

Other than that, the actual "skills" that you need are a great ability to communicate (in person, on the phone, via email) and communicate effectively. Writing skills that capture someone's attention are essential, organization is key (there are so many different things that, go on daily in the Vanguard PR office that, if you are not highly organized, you will get left behind), and I believe that one of the most essential skills you need in PR is the ability to find a personal and real connection with someone.

Question: What is it really like to work in this field?

Answer: I recently read a report that PR was rated one of the most stressful jobs in the country, and I believe it! Thankfully, I do a ton of yoga and am able to find a life–work balance, which is so key in this industry. Yes, there are times when you are working 12+ hours a day, for weeks upon weeks when you are prepping for fashion weeks, but you have to keep in mind the end goal and why you got into this industry. PR is a field where you are granted a lot of unique opportunities and insight, and for those that think it's all "glitz, glitter, and fun parties" … it's not. You work extremely hard. If you do your research, if you know your client, and you know the media you are pitching, and overall if you take the time to understand the industry and keep on top of trends (both in business and beyond), you will make it.

Municipal Laws

Municipal laws are the legislation and codes that municipalities enforce on a local level, such as taxation, zoning, and planning.[24]

What It Means for PR Practitioners It is important to know municipal regulations especially when planning events. Practitioners need to know what permits are needed in their own cities. For instance, a municipality may have fire codes dictating the number of people who can be in a building.

A fundraising event for the Children's Wish Foundation was once brought to a halt because the organizers forgot to obtain a liquor licence. Police visited the event and forced organizers to stop serving alcohol—a major disaster, since the fundraiser was a wine tasting. Fortunately, this happened early in the evening and it was still possible to obtain a liquor licence. Wine flowed freely again after a 30-minute halt, saving the fundraiser.

The Canadian Code of Advertising Standards

The Canadian Code of Advertising Standards, overseen by Advertising Standards Canada (ASC), a nonprofit organization, outlines what you can and cannot say in advertising in Canada. "The Code sets the criteria for acceptable advertising and forms the basis upon which advertising is evaluated in response to consumer, trade, or special interest group complaints."[25] The Code has 14 clauses that deal with such topics as accuracy and clarity.[26]

What It Means for PR Practitioners While the name of the code makes it sound like it is outside the scope of PR, it is, in fact, very relevant to the profession. Janet Feasby of ASC says that while it is uncommon, they do receive some complaints about media releases.[27] That is because the ASC broadly defines advertising in the following way: "'Advertising' and 'advertisement(s)' are defined as any message (the content of which is controlled directly or indirectly by the advertiser) expressed in any language and communicated in any medium (except those listed under Exclusions) to Canadians with the intent to influence their choice, opinion or behaviour."[28] This means that an individual or organization can contact ASC and make an official complaint about the content of PR materials.

Securities Law

Securities law comprises a complex body of legislation and administrative rules that regulate Canada's capital markets.[29] There are very strict and detailed rules regarding what information can and/or must be disclosed by publicly traded organizations.

What It Means for PR Practitioners This area of specialization for PR practitioners, called *investor relations*, is extremely complicated, with many laws and regulations. It is advisable for PR professionals to work with a lawyer if they are not sure what they are doing, as this area can involve serious legal issues. "Information must be handled and disclosed in just the right way. This is an area that you definitely don't want to try at home," cautions Marko Vesely.[30]

As we have mentioned before, investor relations practitioners have their own professional association, the Canadian Investor Relations Institute (CIRI). This group provides guidance to its members and publishes information on what practitioners are allowed and not allowed to disclose to the public.[31]

Lobbying Law

Lobbying activities are regulated federally by the Lobbying Act. Several provinces also have implemented lobbying legislation.[32] Lobbyists must be registered with the Office of the Commissioner of Lobbying of Canada. Failure to comply with the Act's registration requirements may result in criminal penalties. Lobbyists are also required to disclose information about their work, including the nature of their lobbying activities and the names of their clients.[33]

What It Means for PR Practitioners This area is of pertinence to PR practitioners who practise government relations and who are paid to lobby government officials. They must follow strict guidelines as outlined in the Lobbying Act. See Chapter 12 for more information on lobbying and government relations.

Contract Law

A contract generally refers to a written document that records an agreement between two parties. However, some contracts can be oral. The terms of the contract are enforceable within the law.[34]

What It Means for PR Practitioners PR practitioners enter into a variety of different contracts, ranging from employment contracts that outline the terms and conditions of their work to nondisclosure agreements in which they agree to keep certain information confidential.

Hate Speech Laws

Canada has specific laws that forbid any speech or writing that can incite hatred. It is illegal to make comments that are derogatory toward a person's colour, race, religion, ethnic origin, or sexual orientation.[35]

What It Means for PR Practitioners We want to assume that PR practitioners would never undertake any action or release any information that is hateful, bigoted, or racist. It is not only unethical but also criminal. But just to be clear: saying or writing these things is illegal and can lead to fines, arrest, and even imprisonment.

Thinking Like a PR Practitioner

1. Cite three things that PR practitioners can do to ensure that their PR work is ethical.

2. Are there any industries in which you would not work because they are against your personal ethics?

3. Cite a reason why PR practitioners need to know some of the areas of the law that can affect their practice.

4. Explain the law of defamation and how it relates to PR work.

Public Relations and Evaluation ⑤

One of the hottest topics in public relations is evaluation and measurement. PR practitioners agonize over the best **metrics**, or measurement, to use. Clients want to understand how they will know that their campaign has been worth the money they have spent, and senior managers want to better understand how to prove **return on investment (ROI)**—the results versus the amount of money they invested in the campaign.

As we saw in the Heart Truth case study, there are many ways to measure a campaign, including the number of stories that appear in the media; **impressions**, or number of viewers or readers who will see the coverage; Facebook likes; and increases in awareness, to name a few. But what is the right measure? This depends on the goals of the organization. For example, some organizations might be interested in the number of impressions, while others will want to measure only positive impressions. Some organizations want to know if the campaign has increased sales, and some want to measure customer loyalty. A PR practitioner organizing a special event may want to use event attendance as a measurement tool. A social media campaign may measure the number of conversations and visits to a website. Let's look at a few commonly used metrics in more detail.

AWARENESS STUDIES

It is important to outline how a campaign will be measured before starting to execute. This way, you can plan for the evaluation in your campaign. For example, if you want to measure awareness, you'll need to conduct an awareness study prior to launching the campaign, so that you'll have a benchmark to measure it against after the campaign. In order to measure awareness, typically you would need to hire a research company to conduct a pre-campaign and a post-campaign survey to see if awareness increased following the campaign. That is exactly what was done in the Heart Truth campaign.

For longer campaigns, the organization may choose to do several additional surveys throughout the campaign to see if the strategy and tactics are effective at raising awareness. If the surveys are showing little success, the organization will be able to adjust the tactics to deliver better results.

AD VALUE

Another way the value of PR is measured is through ad value. **Ad value** tries to establish what it would have cost an organization to purchase the media it obtained from public relations. For example, if a quarter-page ad in the *Moncton Free Press* costs $250, then the value of a quarter-page article on an organization would be $250.

Ad value is often criticized for not properly representing PR value. This is because it does not take into account the increased credibility that a third-party endorsement, especially from a trusted journalist or celebrity, lends to an organization, or the better placement a news article has compared to an ad. This is why a different measure, called PR value, was developed.

PR VALUE

With **PR value**, the ad value is multiplied by three in order to take into account the higher value of PR. Thus, the PR value of coverage from the *Moncton Free Press* would be $750 ($250 × 3).

$$\text{AD VALUE} \times 3 = \text{PR VALUE}$$

In addition to PR value, there are other evaluation tools that PR practitioners employ to measure the success of campaigns. One of these tools is the RACE formula, which we described earlier. Again, the RACE formula is used by CPRS in evaluating submissions for its PR awards. CPRS evaluates each section of a campaign, including research, analysis, communication, and evaluation. The society asks practitioners to show how the research and analysis that went into a campaign drove the communications plan leading to the results demonstrated through the evaluation. The RACE formula is also a good lens for practitioners to evaluate their own work. After a campaign, it is the best practice to have a team debrief to examine if the research helped the team to take the correct course of action and produce the desired results.

MEDIA IMPRESSIONS

Media impressions are calculated by looking at the overall number of people who may have heard the story through the media. For instance, the PR team will study how many people heard the story on the radio, read about it in the newspaper, saw it on the evening news, and read it on a blog. These numbers are calculated by obtaining the circulation, viewership, audience numbers, or subscription numbers of a certain media outlet. If, for example, a story appeared in a national magazine, which has a subscription of 50,000 people, and on a local radio station, which has a listenership of 25,000 people, we would say that there were 75,000 media impressions generated in the PR campaign. One of the metrics used to measure the success of the Heart Truth campaign was media impressions. The campaign has generated the impressive number of over 362 million media impressions. In some campaigns, only positive impressions are calculated. This means that if the story that ran in the magazine included negative comments on the organization, these impressions would not be counted.

ESTABLISHING INDUSTRY STANDARDS

As you can see, there are many different ways to measure success. The profession has attempted to create industry standards so that all practitioners will use the same measurement tool for the same tactic. Recently, the International Association for the Measurement and Evaluation of Communication (AMEC) developed the Barcelona Principles of Measurement, which aims to establish an international standard. Locally, CPRS has created a media relations measurement tool called the Media Relations Rating Points (MRP). This system awards points based on coverage length and tone. The goal of CPRS is to make this the industry standard in Canada.

Firms also can be hired to conduct campaign measurement on behalf of practitioners. For example, research firms such as Harris/Decima, which was hired by the Heart and Stroke Foundation, can measure awareness levels. Media analysis firms like Cision can evaluate media coverage and social media coverage.

Thinking Like a PR Practitioner

1. Explain the difference between ad value and PR value and describe how each is measured.

2. Which metrics were used to measure the success of the Heart Truth campaign in the opening vignette?

CASE STUDY EARLY PSYCHOSIS INITIATIVE

As we mentioned earlier in this chapter, the Early Psychosis Initiative (EPI) aimed to educate young people and other target audiences about the first signs of psychosis. Getting this message out to young people was particularly important because the longer psychosis goes without diagnosis and treatment, the worse it becomes.

The objectives of the campaign were to drive interest and referrals to the EPI program, promote the benefits of early assessment and treatment for psychosis, raise awareness of the age when early signs of psychosis are most likely to occur, and educate the public about the early signs of psychosis.

A public relations campaign was launched to reach target audiences. A poster and postcard campaign was created using young people affected by the early signs of psychosis depicted in different scenarios. The PR team developed the concept, wrote the text, and organized the photo shoot, while a professional design firm, the Image Foundation, designed the posters. Forty-four thousand posters and postcards were distributed and hung in over 200 locations, including community centres, colleges, universities, high schools, and transit shelters, as well as other areas where young people go, such as coffee shops. Slides of the posters were also screened in cinemas before movies that appealed to the target audiences. A media relations component was implemented with a doctor who was trained as a spokesperson. The doctor appeared in television news segments and radio talk shows, as well as in newspaper interviews on behalf of the organization. A social media initiative was also conducted with a new website and information distributed in forums and chat rooms. Results included a 100 per cent increase in referrals to the program, as well as a substantial increase in patients being seen.

Questions

1. What other tactics could be employed to reach this target audience?

2. How was success evaluated in this campaign? Name one other measurement tool that could have been used.

"Matt used to be the life of the party."

Matt, age 18, waiter

"Now nobody wants to talk to him because of his strange ideas."

Psychosis is a treatable medical condition that affects thinking and perception. Three out of 100 people will get it.

Worried about yourself or a friend?

Visit www.hopevancouver.com or call us at 604-225-2211 for confidential help.

Vancouver CoastalHealth

Source: Maryse Cardin

This poster was created as part of the PR campaign to communicate with the target audiences of the Early Psychosis Initiative.

AUTHOR'S OWN EXPERIENCE

Yves Veggie Cuisine Media Relations Campaign

Yves Veggie Cuisine is the leading Canadian brand of prepared vegetarian ready-to-eat foods such as veggie dogs and burgers. The food manufacturer's products are sold across the country in supermarkets and natural food stores. The company enlisted us to help raise awareness of their products and brand with a mainstream audience. The products were already popular with a vegetarian audience, yet Yves Veggie Cuisine wanted to grow its market share with meat eaters looking for easy-to-prepare healthy alternatives.

Our strategy included conducting a national television campaign targeted at an audience of mainstream consumers. To bring the products to life and make them interesting to television audiences, we hired a chef who could cook with the products live on air. The chef had a lively personality but no television experience. We conducted media-training sessions in a test kitchen to prepare him, bringing in cameras to allow him to watch himself and learn from what he watched.

We broke down the recipes into several parts and had the chef determine what he would say in each segment. The chef not only had to explain the recipes, but also convey the key messages of the company in each interview.

We then contacted morning television shows across Canada and successfully pitched the story to several producers. The chef went on a media tour across the country, stopping at major cities to do local morning television shows, as well as national television talk shows.

Introduction to PR

prospects
- typical day
- positions
- industries

misconceptions
- spin
- glamour
parties

definition
- bridge
- relationships
- communication

ethics
- professional
standards
associations
code
reputation

strategic thinking

law
- municipal
- invasion privacy
- lobbying
- securities
- ASC code
- trademark
- copyright
- contract
- defamation
- hate speech

- analysis **RACE** - evaluation
- research
media impressions
ad value
 PR value

marketing
- ads
- integrated
- PR

- communication
key messages
objectives
target audiences
tactics
measurement
 success
RDI
awareness

Key Terms

ad value The assessment of the value of PR coverage by determining what it would have cost to purchase an ad of the same size.

advocate To push for a certain issue or provide support to an organization.

campaign An overall planned course of action.

deadline The time by which a tactic or campaign must be completed.

earned media Media coverage that has been earned through public relations instead of being purchased.

evaluation The judgment of the results and the worth of a campaign.

implementation Executing a plan and putting tactics into practice.

impressions The number of people who may have seen a story in the media and in social media outlets.

integrated marketing Many or all marketing activities working together to ensure consistency of messaging.

key messages Concise main points and thoughts to communicate with target audiences. These messages are elaborated in all communication vehicles, such as speeches, media materials, and social media initiatives.

LiveStream A video delivered or streamed live over the Internet.

marketing communications A public relations role that combines elements of traditional marketing with PR.

media coverage Stories covered by media outlets that are sometimes generated by media relations.

media materials Written documents, such as press releases, backgrounders, or fact sheets, that outline story ideas and information and that are distributed to the media.

metrics Tools or techniques to measure a campaign that can help PR professionals see if they are meeting their objectives.

objectives The desired results of a PR initiative or campaign and the goals to be achieved in the future, usually within a specific timeline.

paid media Media placements that are purchased, such as advertorials or ads.

PR value Capturing the value of PR coverage by determining what it would have cost to purchase an ad of the same size and then multiplying the ad value by three to account for intangibles such as increased credibility.

release A document that describes the information, text, or photo an organization plans to use and make public. It is signed by the individual who is granting permission.

return on investment (ROI) A measure of whether a campaign is profitable. ROI looks at the cost of a program and compares it to the results.

spokesperson A person who speaks on behalf of an organization.

stakeholders The publics to whom an organization is accountable.

strategic thinking The thought process that enables PR practitioners to assess situations and deliver business solutions.

tactics The activities or actions taken to accomplish objectives.

target audiences The publics and groups a PR campaign is trying to reach and for whom the key messages are designed. These publics can be affected by or interested in an organization.

timeline The chronological order in which the plan is implemented and the different tactics are carried out.

Weblinks

Barcelona Declaration of Measurement Principles
http://amecorg.com/2012/06/barcelona-declaration-of-measurement-principles/

Canadian Centre for Ethics and Corporate Policy
www.ethicscentre.ca/EN/index.cfm

Canadian Investor Relations Institute (CIRI)
www.ciri.org/Home.aspx

Canadian Public Relations Society (CPRS)
www.cprs.ca/

Global Alliance for Public Relations and Communication Management (GA)
www.globalalliancepr.org

International Association of Business Communicators (IABC) Canada
www.canada.iabc.com

International Association for the Measurement and Evaluation of Communication (AMEC)
http://amecorg.com/

International Public Relations Association (IPRA)
www.ipra.org

ISO 26000, Guidance on Social Responsibility
isotc.iso.org/livelink/livelink/fetch/2000/2122/830949/3934883/3935096/home.html?nodeid=4451259&vernum=0

Media Relations Rating Points (MRP)
www.cprs.ca/membership/mrp.aspx

PR in Canada
www.princanada.com

Endnotes

1. "Definition," Canadian Public Relations Society. Accessed February 25, 2013, http://www.cprs .ca/uploads/PR_Definition.pdf

2. J. Grunig and T. Hunt, *Managing Public Relations*. Austin, TX: Holt, Rinehart and Winston, 1984.

3. "Public Relations Specialist," *U.S. News & World Report*. Accessed February 23, 2013, http:// www.usnews.com/money/careers/articles/2009/12/28/public-relations-specialist.html

4. A. McMullen, "Spreading the Word for Business, PR Industry Proves to Be 'Almost Recession-Proof,'" *Financial Post*, February 2, 2010. Accessed February 25, 2013, http://www2.canada .com/edmontonjournal/news/business/story.html?id=1750c2f9-b6c0-48b9-b1ce-904fa9207d72

5. Ibid.

6. Amy Thurlow, "'I Just Say I'm in Advertising': A Public Relations Identity Crisis?" *Canadian Journal of Communications*, vol. 34 (2009), 245–283.

7. "What Are Ethics and How Do They Relate to Business Conduct?" Canadian Centre for Ethics and Corporate Policy. Accessed February 25, 2013, http://www.ethicscentre.ca/en/ resources/faq.cfm#1

8. Canadian Press/Leger Marketing, *How Canadians Perceive Various Professions*. Accessed February 25, 2013, http://www.rnantnu.ca/Portals/0/Documents/News/trusted_pros.pdf

9. *The Canadian Encyclopedia.com*, s.v. "Public Relations." Accessed February 25, 2013, http:// www.thecanadianencyclopedia.com/index.cfm?PgNm=TCE&Params=A1ARTA0006551

10. Shannon A. Bowen, "Ethics and Public Relations," Institute for Public Relations. Accessed February 25, 2013, http://www.instituteforpr.org/essential_knowledge/detail/ethics_and_ public_relations

11. R.M. Devin, "Rescuing PR's Reputation," *Communication World*, vol. 24, no. 4 (2007), 34.

12. Marko Vesely, interview with the author.

13. Raymond Brown, *The Law of Defamation in Canada* (2nd ed.). Toronto: Carswell, 2009.

14. Allen Linden and Bruce Feldthusen, *Canadian Tort Law* (9th ed.). Markham, ON: LexisNexisCanada, 2011, p. 779.

15. *Sullivan Entertainment Group Inc. v. Butler* (2004) 69 OR (3d) 354 (Ont. Sup. Ct.); *Janssen-Ortho Inc. v. Amgen Canada* (2005) 256 DLR (4th) 407 (Ont. CA).

16. *Janssen-Ortho Inc. v. Amgen Canada* (2005) 256 DLR (4th) 407 (Ont. CA).

17. *Berezovsky v. Michaels et al.* [2000] UKHL 25.

18. Alan Fryer, "Public Relations and the Law," *Alan's Blog*, January 6, 2011. Accessed February 25, 2013, http://www.alanfryermedia.com/category/media-public-relations/

19. David Vaver, *Intellectual Property Law* (2nd ed.). Toronto: Irwin Law, 2011, pp. 55 and 694.

20. *Athans v. Canadian Adventure Camps* (1977) 80 DLR (3d) 583.

21. Vaver, *Intellectual Property Law*, p. 209.

22. Ibid., p. 704.

23. Robert Martin, *Media Law* (2nd ed.). Toronto: Irwin Law, 2003, p. 211.

24. Denis Le May and John Eaton, *Essential Sources of Canadian Law / Les références essentielles en droit canadien*. Toronto: Irwin Law, 2009, p. 73.

25. Advertising Standards Canada, "The *Canadian Code of Advertising Standards*." Accessed February 25, 2013, http://www.adstandards.com/en/Standards/canCodeOfAdStandards.aspx

26. Advertising Standards Canada, "The 14 Clauses of the *Canadian Code of Advertising Standards*." Accessed February 25, 2013, http://www.adstandards.com/en/Standards/the14Clauses.aspx

27. Janet Feasby, interview with the author.

28. Advertising Standards Canada, "The *Canadian Code of Advertising Standards*."

29. Jeffrey G. MacIntosh and Christopher C. Nicholls, *Securities Law*. Toronto: Irwin Law, 2002, p. 1.

30. Marko Vesely, interview with the author.

31. Canadian Investor Relations Institute, *Standards and Guidance for Disclosure and Model Disclosure Policy* (4th ed.). Accessed February 25, 2013, http://www.ciri.org/NewsPublications/PublicationPurchase.aspx?publicationID=53d18c5d-018f-4a32-aaf1-880d979a2813

32. Office of the Commissioner of Lobbying of Canada, "Lobbying Legislation in Canada: www.ocl-cal.gc.ca/eic/site/012.nsf/eng/00543.html

33. Craig Forcese and Aaron Freeman, *The Laws of Government* (2nd ed.). Toronto: Irwin Law, 2011, p. 469.

34. John McCamus, *The Law of Contracts*. Toronto: Irwin Law, 2005, p. 1.

35. *Criminal Code*, R.S.C. 1985, c. C-46, ss. 318, 319, 320.

In-House or Public Relations Agency

Generally, public relations specialists work either in an agency or a consultancy, or in-house as an employee of an organization. Some people will spend their entire career in one setting, while others will switch from one to another. It tends to be more common for practitioners to go from agency work to in-house positions, although the opposite also takes place.

PR agencies: Practitioners work in public relations agencies or consultancies, which vary in size from a one- to three-person shop, to a medium-sized local agency of ten to twenty employees, to a global conglomerate like Ketchum or Hill+Knowlton Strategies.

Advantages of working in a PR firm:

- Fast-moving, dynamic environment
- Many chances for advancement and promotions
- Opportunity to work with many clients in different industries
- Always learning something new
- Never boring: no two days are ever the same
- Switching jobs: agencies tend to hire people who have worked in other agencies
- Creativity is welcomed and rewarded

Challenges:

- Long hours, long weeks
- Difficulties in managing schedule as clients have many unexpected, last-minute needs with breaking issues
- Entry-level salaries tend to be lower than in-house
- Difficult to be an expert about several industries simultaneously
- Constant multi-tasking
- Can be stressful
- Must keep the client happy in order to keep the account

In-house: A number of companies, associations, nonprofits, and government agencies have in-house PR professionals either working solo or within the communication or marketing departments. For instance, each Fairmont Hotel has its own in-house PR specialist.

Advantages of working in-house:

- Entry-level salaries tend to be higher
- Opportunity to become an expert in your field
- Control over budgets and resource allocation
- Shorter hours
- Ability to manage the external PR agency
- Opportunities for advancement, reaching the top echelons of the organization

Challenges:

- Less diversity in your work
- Less freedom
- Less creativity
- Fewer opportunities to gain exposure to a wide range of industries and projects

Chapter 2
Influencing Public Opinion:
The Foundation of PR Then and Now

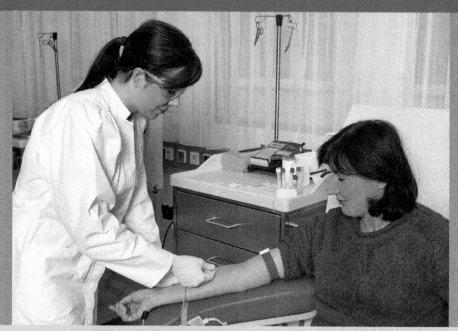

To generate donations during the slow summer months, the Saskatchewan chapter of Canadian Blood Services used the Roughriders' popularity to their advantage. They persuaded the public to give blood. Source: Saskatchewan Roughriders Football Club

LEARNING OBJECTIVES

❶ Explain public opinion and why it is important to the practice of public relations.

❷ Describe the various tactics that influence public opinion and explain how they are used.

❸ Outline the contributions to the profession of key people in public relations history.

❹ Explain why the public's perception of PR practitioners might be negative and what PR practitioners can do to counteract this view.

Bleed Green: Convincing the Public to Donate Blood

Summer is traditionally a slow month for blood donations in Canada. Summer vacations and busy schedules mean that regular blood donors stop coming, causing a dramatic drop in the number of donations. According to Bonnie Monteith, manager of public affairs for Canadian Blood Services, "The months of our campaign, summer and early fall, are most challenging because people are enjoying outdoor pursuits and are typically away on vacation. Blood donation is not a 'top of mind' activity—even for our regular, committed donors." To try to counteract the drop in donations, Canadian Blood Services is aiming to convince a new audience to become blood donors during these key months.

The organization found a unique way to combat its summer collection challenges in Saskatchewan. It created a partnership with the Saskatchewan Roughriders football team and launched the Bleed Green campaign during the football season. (The team's predominant colour is green.) Riders fans ("Rider Nation") are famous for being the most devoted in the league. The goal was to convince these fans to show their loyalty and give blood, or as the name of the campaign suggests, "bleed green."

Bleed Green was launched with a media conference that featured Riders players and **spokespersons**—individuals representing the organization to the public or media—from both organizations. The Riders mascot showed the media a bag of "green blood," creating an interesting photo opportunity. Posters were distributed throughout the province and flyers were handed out to fans and game-day attendees. Former donation recipients who had been saved by blood donations, including two-year-old twins who had needed transfusions at birth, participated in pregame events.

Social media tactics were also employed throughout the campaign, with the Facebook pages of both organizations seeing their hits rise significantly. Media coverage was generated in all provincial media outlets, as well as in community newspapers, which ran stories about Bleed Green blood donors in their communities.

The Bleed Green campaign raised awareness of the importance of blood donation during the summer months while influencing public opinion about being a blood donor and generating action. The first year of the campaign was so successful—fan donations saved 2100 lives—that the two groups partnered again for a second year. Of the campaign, Monteith notes, "The Riders are the number one brand in Saskatchewan. There is no question their committed fans were inspired by the organization's involvement and dedication to this initiative. They used that sense of 'nation' to answer the call to donate."

As this opening vignette illustrates, public relations can influence an audience in favour of a certain action. In this case, the campaign shaped public opinion in favour of donating blood. The Saskatchewan chapter of Canadian Blood Services increased the number of blood donations in its greatest time of need by connecting the act of donating blood with showing loyalty to the Roughriders in the public's mind. The organization was able to influence this audience, or public, into giving blood.

At its core, public relations is dedicated to doing just that: influencing public opinion. That is the overall objective of almost everything we do. We want the public to either think in a certain way or take a certain course of action. We want to raise awareness in our target audiences about our organization and influence their decisions. Whether we are trying to convince an audience to vote for a political candidate, attend a fundraiser, or make a new lip gloss popular, we are aiming to influence public opinion.

Influencing public opinion can be achieved only through setting clearly defined objectives, applying strategic thinking, and having a deep understanding of the target audiences. As we have seen in Chapter 1, public relations is not just about executing tactics such as organizing an event or writing a media release. Public relations practitioners are skilled thinkers who base their work on research, audience insight, and strategy. Shaping public opinion is the foundation of everything that they do.

From the early days of the profession, influencing the public has been vital to achieving results. The founders of PR devoted themselves to understanding how to modify people's attitudes or behaviour in favour of their organization. Some practitioners today believe that PR as a profession has become too distanced from its roots and is failing to meet its potential because practitioners are simply executing tactics instead of focusing on the larger overall strategies behind influencing public opinion.[1] In this social media era, with the lines between advertising and public relations blurring, the future prosperity of the profession will depend on developing strategy rather than just executing tactics. That is where the true value of public relations lies. However, in order to influence the future, we need to learn from our past.

In this chapter we are going to define public opinion and review some of the thinking around influencing it. As we discuss public opinion, we will also examine the positive and negative perceptions that the public has about PR itself. Finally, we will review the history of PR and learn about the pioneers in this field who shaped the profession's practice of influencing public opinion. Have you ever wondered why we write press releases or hold press conferences? Many of the strategies early practitioners developed are still being used today. It is important that we understand the profession's beginnings and key influences in order to better understand public relations and explain the reasoning behind some of the practices employed today. This knowledge will make us stronger, more professional practitioners.

Traditionally, teaching of the history of PR has concentrated on American examples. However, although PR as we understand it today may have started in the United States, it quickly moved across the border into Canada, where it developed its own nuances. Since this is a Canadian textbook, we have taken special care to research and feature the Canadian history of PR. We have also focused on the history of women in PR, as women now make up the majority of the profession. Women in PR history have been largely ignored in other textbooks, which is a shame, as they have contributed much to the profession.

Public Opinion: What It Is and How It Is Shaped ❶

Public opinion is defined as a prevailing opinion or a popularly held belief. When a certain percentage of the population thinks the same way, this perception becomes public opinion. It is often challenging to change public opinion, because once a belief is commonly held, a feedback loop occurs, with mainstream media feeding popular opinion back to the public and thereby reinforcing the belief.

Public opinion is important to any democracy. A thriving democracy depends on having vibrant, multi-voiced media that deliver quality information to the public so that they can form their opinion on a variety of topics. Politicians monitor the media and public opinion polls closely to ensure that the political winds are not changing and leaving them behind. This has always been the case. Even in much earlier times, kings had to ensure their subjects were not becoming weary of their rule. In Latin, the expression *vox populi, vox Dei* means "the voice of the people is the voice of God."[2]

Though it can be difficult to change public opinion, it is subject to shifts. In fact, it is continuously evolving as new information is introduced to the public and as cultures adapt. In the 1950s, the mainstream consensus on topics such as race relations or a woman's place in the home and workforce, for example, was very different from commonly held beliefs today. Public opinion can also vary by country and culture. A popularly held belief in Belize might be seen as ludicrous in South Africa and vice versa. Public opinion's modifiable nature keeps PR practitioners employed because they are able to help organizations either strengthen or change people's mindsets. In the case of Canadian Blood Services, the organization was able to convince Riders fans of the need to give blood.

Organizations are not the only ones who monitor and attempt to influence public opinion. Governments across the globe also measure public opinion and then find ways to influence it to have their message accepted favourably by the public. The Canadian

---

ADVICE TO NEW PRACTITIONERS

With Power Comes Responsibility

Think for a moment of the responsibilities that come with the ability and power to influence public opinion. Think also of the consequences. As a PR practitioner, you play a role in forming the ideas and opinions of your target audiences. Use this power with the utmost respect, as your accountability lies not only with your organization but also with your target audiences. The PR practitioner is the bridge between the organization and the public and must be the advocate for both.

Always keep in mind both the welfare of your organization and the common good.

Remember to be truthful and transparent at all times.

government regularly conducts PR campaigns to persuade the public to take a specified action, whether it is to vote, practise emergency preparedness, or take precautions for food safety. For example, when the World Health Organization sent out an alert that the H1N1 pandemic was going global, the Canadian government acted quickly to convince Canadians to be vaccinated. It conducted public opinion research to determine what Canadians knew about the virus and how they felt about the vaccine. The government then used the research results as a basis to draft key messages and decide on the best tactics to persuade the public to get vaccinated.[3]

The PR teams of politicians also continuously keep their fingers on the pulse of public opinion and try to influence it. They need to know what the public is thinking so they can develop the strategy to generate public support, whether they want to get their candidate elected or get a policy approved.

Public opinion is a powerful force in many spheres. It has a huge influence on many aspects of our lives, from music to fashion, the arts, and literature. Trends or fads are the result of public opinion. The organics industry is the perfect example of this. What was once viewed as a product segmentation that was of interest to only a small cohort mostly made up of hippies became a multi-billion-dollar industry after more mainstream consumers decided that buying organic was important for their health and the environment. Knowing this, the question becomes how do public relations practitioners influence public opinion to benefit their organizations or clients?

HOW PUBLIC OPINION IS FORMED

In order to influence public opinion, we first need to understand how it is formed. We will look at how to influence public opinion later in the chapter.

Studies have shown that public opinion is influenced by many factors. It starts with individuals preferences, attitudes, and beliefs, as well as the information they possess on a certain topic. For a belief to become public opinion, individuals must share their views with others and convince them of their merit. The opinions of people in positions of leadership, such as the prime minister or a celebrity, will often be influential in persuading the public to adopt a certain viewpoint. These leaders are sometimes considered **opinion leaders,** but an opinion leader can be anyone who has more knowledge or is more vested in a particular issue, causing others to look to them to help form their opinion. The sharing of opinion is typically facilitated by the mass media. Finally, when a large percentage of the community agrees with a particular viewpoint, it becomes public opinion.[4]

Let us examine one of the most important factors in this equation: attitudes. We all have attitudes about almost everything in life, including people, places, things, ideas, and actions.[5] Our attitudes are based on a large number of factors, such as personal and childhood experiences, social and economic conditions, race, religion, and even our parents' beliefs.[6] As John R. Zaller explains in his book *The Nature and Origins of Mass Opinion*, "Citizens are more than passive receivers of whatever

Many people look to opinion leaders such as politician Justin Trudeau or celebrity Lisa Ray to form their opinions.

Source: © Stephanie Gunther/Alamy

Source: Getty Images

media communications they encounter. They possess a variety of interests, values, and experiences that may greatly affect their willingness to accept—or alternatively, their resolve to resist—persuasive influences."[7]

Why is it important to know about attitudes? Because the audiences that you will try to influence in your career in public relations will have attitudes of their own, and only by knowing what those attitudes are can you hope to either strengthen or change them.

Some attitudes are next to impossible to change. While weak attitudes are flexible and can be changed quite easily by **persuasive messages**, strong attitudes tend to be inflexible and entrenched.[8] Weak attitudes tend to be on subjects that someone knows little about or is not affected by very much. For example, you may have a weak attitude toward dog leash bylaws if you don't own a pet. You could be easily swayed one way or another. However, you might have a strong attitude about this issue if you have been bitten by an off-leash dog or if you are a dog owner who enjoys walking your dog off-leash. PR practitioners need to know the strengths of the attitudes that their target audiences have before they can try to influence them. There are some attitudes that a PR practitioner can hope to influence, while there are others that, no matter how good the campaign, will never be changed. And you need to know the difference.

Target audiences will typically already have an opinion on your product, organization, or message, unless they have never heard about it at all. Your ability to persuade your target audience or change their mind depends on what their attitude is and how strong it is to begin with. You are more likely to be able to change their attitude if it is uncommitted. Your messaging can also help to **crystallize an attitude**.[9] This means that the target audience is already prone to support your message but you are strengthening their belief.

In the example of the Bleed Green campaign from the opening vignette, it was possible for Canadian Blood Services to convince some Riders fans to give blood because these fans either already had a favourable attitude toward blood donation or did not have an opinion either way. Or these fans might have found blood donation slightly distasteful but were convinced of the need because of the campaign. However, it would be virtually impossible to persuade individuals who have strong attitudes or religious views against giving blood, whether or not the Riders are involved. If the target audience has a strong attitude against your cause, you may be unable to sway them in any way. On the other hand, if they only slightly dislike the concept, you may convince them that it is worth giving it a second chance.

To recap, there are three basic positions that a target audience can hold about your organization or cause. PR practitioners need to know the position in order to strategically devise a plan to influence their audience's opinion. The three positions are the following:

1. The audience likes the organization or cause and is a proponent of it. This can range from individuals liking it a little to being huge fans.

2. The audience dislikes it and is against it. Again, this can range from slightly disliking it to hating it intensely.

3. The audience is neutral and has no opinion on the organization or cause.

Thinking Like a PR Practitioner

1. Give an example of a recent media event that was the result of a change in public opinion. Describe what contributed to the shift in thinking.

2. Explain why public opinion is just as important to organizations as it is to governments.

How PR Practitioners Work with Public Opinion ❷

PR practitioners use public opinion to assist them with their work in two primary ways. The first involves conducting surveys and then using public opinion information as a media angle. The second involves measuring public opinion at the beginning of a campaign and then measuring it again during and at the end of the campaign to see whether it has been influenced. Let us look at both in more detail.

Kenneth Evans is senior vice president at APEX Public Relations, a full-service PR agency in Toronto. He has worked on several national campaigns for major banks, which employed public opinion polls to generate media coverage. Here is how it was done. Every year the banks compete to generate media coverage during RRSP season, hoping to influence their target audiences to visit their bank and buy financial products. Evans says that all the major banks conduct public opinion polls on the saving habits of Canadians. The polls are intended to uncover public opinion around saving habits, concern about the economy, and so forth. The answers obtained are then used to provide stories and angles in media relations. "The media coverage is intended to boost their brand and share of voice in media coverage," says Evans.[10] In this case, the objective was to encourage individuals to buy financial products. It was not to change the opinions that the survey uncovered.

In the second way, the objective is to change public opinion itself. PR practitioners conduct public opinion research at the beginning of a campaign and then conduct it again during and at the end of the campaign to see whether their work has had any effect on influencing public opinion. Evans worked on such a campaign for a health care client in order to raise awareness and acceptance of a naturopathic option by patient groups. The objective of the campaign was to increase public awareness and acceptance by 10 per cent over two years. Through an extensive national campaign that included media relations and social media, the objective was met.[11]

Public opinion can be measured through different types of research, the most common of which is the public opinion poll (see the following Advice to New Practitioners box). These types of polls are conducted by professional research firms. However, PR practitioners must be able to interpret the results and make decisions based on them. In the H1N1 example we examined earlier, the government first had to know what the public thought about the H1N1 vaccine before it could figure out what to say to Canadians to convince them to be vaccinated.

TECHNIQUES FOR INFLUENCING PUBLIC OPINION

Several techniques are used to influence individuals and sway public opinion. One that is commonly used by PR practitioners has been practised for more than 2300 years. The Greek philosopher Aristotle believed that individuals could be influenced through three arguments: their reason (*logos*), their ethics (*ethos*), or their emotion (*pathos*).[12] PR practitioners should rely on as many of these arguments as they can in order to persuade as many people in their audience as possible.

When calling on reason, PR professionals use facts in their messaging to appeal to their target audiences. When evoking ethics in their argument, PR practitioners need to make sure their readers or listeners trust them; if they do not, they will not be moved by an ethical appeal. For emotional persuasion, a good tactic is to tell a story.[13] For example, telling a story of an abandoned or abused puppy in a media release can be a compelling way to raise funds for the SPCA. The Bleed Green campaign was so successful because it used all

The Canadian Blood Services appealed to fan loyalty in order to persuade Roughriders fans to become blood donors.

Source: Saskatchewan Roughrider Football Club Inc.

three arguments to persuade Riders fans to give blood. The campaign used reason (giving blood saves lives), ethics (Canadian Blood Services is a trustworthy organization), and emotion (appealing to fan loyalty and featuring the stories of individuals, such as the two-year-old twins, who were saved by blood donations.)

Influencers and Ordinary Individuals

Identifying and then using influential individuals is another technique used by PR practitioners. Certain individuals are more influential than others and are called **influencers**. Members of the public are more apt to listen to people whom they trust, such as experts like doctors or government officials, or whom they admire, such as celebrities. The opening vignette is a good example of identifying influencers and working with them to shape public opinion on a certain subject. The Canadian Blood Services were able to turn fan loyalty to the Saskatchewan Roughriders into blood donations.

There are various types of influencers. In his book *The Tipping Point*, Malcolm Gladwell identifies three groups that are particularly influential: connectors, mavens, and salesmen.[14] *Connectors* are people who have many connections and have a talent for building connections between people. They are the people who will tell you about their real estate agent, doctor, or lawyer and make an introduction. *Mavens* cultivate knowledge rather than connections. They are the people who you go to for a restaurant recommendation or a stock tip. *Salesmen* are incredibly persuasive and adept at objection handling.[15] They can sell anything to anyone. Hiring or finding these types of personalities and influencers and bringing them on board a campaign makes it easier to persuade an audience. Influencers play different roles in campaigns, such as working as spokespeople or **brand ambassadors**. Brand ambassadors are stakeholders who are loyal to the organization and let others know about it.

Influencers are not the only ones who hold sway over others. Some individuals are influenced by other ordinary people just like them who would not be considered persuasive. Research shows that individuals with weak attitudes are easily influenced by like-minded peers.[16]

Finger on the Pulse: Tracking Public Opinion

Now that you know more about public opinion, you might wonder how organizations gauge what people are thinking. It is not always as easy as you might think. Public opinion polls and focus groups can be expensive, and people do not always tell surveyors what they actually believe and sometimes do not even know how to articulate those beliefs. It often takes a professional research firm to come up with results that can be trusted.

Some ways you can gauge public opinion include the following:

- Public opinion polls: These are conducted by specialized research firms and are based on surveys given to a certain percentage of the population. They are often conducted by telephone or online. Surveys are useful tools to find out what a statistically representative group thinks about a topic. The downside is that it is hard to gain deep insights from a survey.

- Focus groups: Focus groups involve getting a group of people in a room and having discussions on topics that are of interest to the researcher. A skilled moderator can guide the discussion and ask probing questions, getting a level of interaction that is not possible from a poll. Focus groups can be costly and time-consuming, but they are better than surveys at finding the underlying beliefs or reasons around why people behave the way they do. Focus groups are also good for testing new creative ideas or concepts.

- Environmental scans: Many practitioners will scan the media (newspapers, radio, TV, magazines, Facebook, Google, Twitter) to locate articles and posts on particular topics that might affect their company or clients. These environmental scans help provide information on changes in public opinion or new developments that might affect how the public views a particular topic.

Thinking Like a PR Practitioner

1. Describe the ways PR practitioners work with public opinion and give an example of when you would use each one.

2. Outline Aristotle's three ways to persuade and give examples of when you might employ each.

The History of PR and the First Practitioners to Influence Public Opinion ❸

Influencing public opinion is not new in public relations. It has been done from the very beginnings of the profession. Although PR practitioners have been around as long as there has been public opinion, several key players shaped public relations into what it is today.

In this section we will explore the history of PR in both the United States and Canada. We will look at the factors that shaped PR into the profession as we know it. Reviewing this history helps us better understand the evolution of PR. Some components of the practice have changed and some are almost identical to the way PR was practised in the early days. For instance, we may now use social media and new technologies in our work, but PR remains grounded in influencing public opinion.

Public relations started in the United States and came to Canada about 25 years later.[17] The U.S. practice had a definite influence on how the profession developed in Canada. Many of the early practitioners in this country were originally members of American PR associations or cut their teeth working in the United States.[18]

In this section we will also examine the role women had on the profession. While much has been written about men—especially American men—as the early pioneers of PR, women also played a significant role in the development of the profession and should not be overlooked. In *Women in Public Relations: How Gender Influences Practice*, the authors write that "little historical evidence of women's contributions to public relations exists."[19] This is a large omission, especially since women now make up the majority of practitioners in the PR profession.[20] For this reason, we have included a separate section on some of the first women PR professionals.

EARLY U.S. PRACTITIONERS

Ivy Lee, Edward Bernays, and Arthur Page are widely regarded as the early founders of the public relations industry. They shaped the public's perception of what public relations is and formed the profession into what it is today. These founding fathers added both good and bad to the industry's beginning. They made businesses more conscious of their public reputation and thus more likely to practise corporate social responsibility. In addition, they convinced business leaders to be more accessible to the media and provided reporters with greater access to information. However, they were also accused of manipulating public opinion through sometimes dishonest or calculating practices. Unlike today, in the early years of PR there were no ethical guidelines set out by associations. There were no rules guiding behaviour. This period can be thought of as the Wild West of PR.

Ivy Lee was one of the early pioneers of PR. He developed many of the practices still used today.

Source: © Everett Collection Historical/ Alamy

Ivy Lee

One of PR's founding fathers, Ivy Lee is credited with convincing corporations that they needed to be mindful of public opinion.[21] Having graduated from Princeton in journalism, Lee quickly became disenchanted with the profession. At the time, the media were very hostile to business, and by extension so was the public. The early 1900s was a time of **muckraking journalism**, a style of investigative journalism whose aim was to expose corporate evils. Lee, who was pro-business, had nothing but disdain for how companies were portrayed in the press.[22]

In 1906, coal-mining executives hired the former journalist to help them sway the public opinion away from the striking trade unions. Lee recognized that public opinion was something to be feared. He also found that the public responded well to facts and figures.[23] A proponent of public relations being a dialogue rather than a monologue, Lee believed businesses should listen to the public and then respond to their concerns.[24]

During the coal company's campaign, Lee was the first to draft what is now known as the "press release" to tell the coal company's side of the story.[25] The press release was controversial when it began. Journalists accused those who used press releases of being "space grabbers" because they were trying to get free space in publications for their messages. Some journalists even tried to boycott the press release. Lee could not understand the media's resistance, saying that any journalist who didn't use the information in his releases should be "convicted of stupidity."[26] In addition to developing the press release, Lee is credited with being the first to practise crisis communications as we know it today.[27]

In 1914, Lee's widely regarded, principled approach to public relations changed when he was hired by the powerful Rockefeller family. The Rockefellers reached out to him to improve public opinion after striking miners at a Rockefeller mine in Colorado and their families were murdered by hit men hired by the company. Lee spread lies about the strikers among the papers and sent out a press release accusing an elderly union organizer called "Mother Jones" of being a prostitute. Lee earned the nickname "Poison Ivy" for these antics and later testified to a congressional inquiry, "'What is a fact?' The effort to state an absolute fact is simply an attempt to give you my interpretation of the facts."[28] Though Lee's reputation had been damaged, he did manage to improve the Rockefellers' image by publicizing their philanthropy and humanizing them through photo ops. Once a hated dynasty, the Rockefellers today are known for their generosity.[29]

Edward Bernays

While Ivy Lee was interested in swaying public opinion through educating the public, Edward Bernays was interested in persuading them.[30] Bernays is credited with taking PR from its publicist roots under Lee to a more strategic function that used psychology to alter people's behaviour.[31]

Edward Bernays was hired by American Tobacco to remove the stigma around women smoking.
Source: © Bettmann/CORBIS

A nephew of Sigmund Freud and born in Germany, Edward Bernays was engaged in the psychology of marketing.[32] Like Lee, Bernays was a journalist. Bernays moved to the United States as an infant and had his first glimpse of the power of persuasion when he was involved with a play that educated the public about the spread of syphilis in families.

During the First World War, President Woodrow Wilson recruited Bernays to be part of a committee to convince Americans that their country's involvement in the war was justified. One of the psychological findings that Bernays exploited during this time was that people would rather put their confidence behind someone they trusted than research the facts themselves. To support this theory, he put together a group of "four-minute men"[33]—respected community leaders who would give speeches in public places in support of the war effort. This idea that the masses should follow the lead of the elite was telling of Bernays's opinion about the public's ability to make rational decisions. So prominent was his belief that people needed to be led, instead of trusted to think for themselves, that Bernays once claimed, "The conscious and intelligent manipulation of the organized habits and opinions of the masses is an important element in democratic society."[34]

Bernays was comfortable using propaganda tactics and manipulation to sway audiences. He once stated, "The secret of successful manipulation was in understanding the motivations of people and in using research to identify the messages most likely to produce the attitudes and behaviors desired by an organization."[35] One of Bernays's most famous PR campaigns was for American Tobacco, which wanted to grow its market share by getting women to smoke more cigarettes.[36] At the time, smoking cigarettes in public was considered taboo for women. In order to break this social proscription, Bernays organized a group of debutantes to smoke while marching in a parade down Fifth Avenue.[37] He had his secretary contact the women anonymously, so that they wouldn't feel that they were being used for a commercial purpose. This PR stunt garnered a lot of media coverage, causing smoking to be associated with an act of social defiance and women's liberation. It was so successful, in fact, that decades later, Virginia Slims used the same spirit in their tagline, "You've come a long way, baby."[38]

Arthur Page

In 1927, Arthur Page became a PR officer at AT&T, where he worked until 1946.[39] He was the first PR officer to be employed by a U.S. company. He was also the first PR practitioner to serve on the board of directors of a public company.[40] Page claimed that the majority of a corporation's reputation was based on what it did and only a fraction was based on what it said, and thus he promoted positive corporate actions.[41] Page has been credited with being the father of corporate transparency.

AMERICAN WOMEN IN PR

The first instances of women working professionally in public relations coincided with the entry of women into the workforce in general in the 1930s and 1940s. Often women got their start working in newspapers or as secretaries and assistants at PR agencies, while others got into the field by working in teams with their husbands.[42]

Doris Fleischman

From the start, PR was a profession that attracted many women. In her 1939 book, *Careers for Women: A Practical Guide to Opportunity for Women in American Business*, Doris Fleischman wrote that the PR profession held many opportunities for women, and she encouraged them to make it their career choice. Fleischman was the first woman to make her living as a PR practitioner. She wrote that the field was new and wide open and that women could be key in its development.[43] Fleischman was known for the strategic thinking she brought to campaigns. She was originally a journalist before she joined Edward Bernays's PR agency in 1919. She later married him. As one researcher described Fleischman, "Her perseverance made her a trailblazer for women aspiring to careers in public relations in the twentieth century."[44]

Eleanor Roosevelt

Starting in the early 1930s, Eleanor Roosevelt, the wife of President Franklin D. Roosevelt, became the equivalent of a full-time PR practitioner. She used many public relations tactics to build awareness and support for her husband's political issues. This included holding her own media conferences, acting as spokesperson, touring the country, writing newspaper columns, and hosting radio and television programs.[45] The first 350 media

Eleanor Roosevelt helped build awareness and support for her husband's political agenda.
Source: Carolyn M Carpenter/Shutterstock

conferences she organized were exclusively for women journalists. Her goal for these press conferences was twofold: to publicize issues of relevance and interest to women, and to support women journalists. She continued her work after her husband's death.

Anne Williams Wheaton

In 1957, Anne Williams Wheaton became the first woman to hold the position of associate **press secretary** to a U.S. president. She worked for President Dwight Eisenhower organizing media conferences and acting as spokesperson. Her position was so high profile that it brought national attention to women's growing influence in PR.[46] She was very popular with the journalists covering the White House, who affectionately called her "our Annie."[47]

Denora Griswold

Denora Griswold was the founder and editor of the first-ever industry newsletter. Her publication, *Public Relations News*, which is still published today, covered PR issues, trends, and breaking news. The idea for the publication came to her in 1944, at a time when PR was still new and there were no more than 25 corporate PR departments in the United States.[48] Griswold also ran her own PR agency, which she co-owned with her husband.

PRACTITIONER INTERVIEW

Marcella Munro: Managing a Public Opinion Campaign

Marcella Munro is principal at Earnscliffe Strategy Group, an agency that specializes in government relations, research, policy analysis, and strategic communications, with offices in Ottawa, Toronto, Edmonton, and Vancouver. Munro has worked on a wide variety of campaigns for clients, including pharmaceutical companies, environmental organizations, nonprofit nongovernmental organizations (NGOs), telecommunications companies, and real estate development companies. Her background is in journalism and political communications.

Question: What do you need to know about public opinion before starting a campaign?

Answer: High-quality public opinion is a critical tool in public campaigning. Through this research, you can find out not only where the public stands on any given issue you may be working on, but also what messages you can use to best communicate your issue or side of the debate.

Question: Which tools do you use most often to find out about public opinion?

Answer: Focus groups are generally the best starting point for any public opinion campaign. Good ones will help capture the public mood for you on any given issue, and can also help you hone in on particularly important populations as the campaign progresses. A well-done focus group can help you shape the questions you need to answer for the public, and it can also help you figure out what pitfalls may exist in the overall story you want to tell. In terms of a straight snapshot of public opinion, polling is the most obvious tool and the one that gets the most attention in the media.

(Continued)

Marcella Munro: Managing a Public Opinion Campaign

There are many kinds of polling, of course. These days, we find a combination of live phoning and online polling to be the most accurate.

Question: How does knowing what the public thinks influence the direction of your campaign?

Answer: In a word, it's critical. The essence of good public policy is that it bears relation to how the public views any given issue. The politicians are, of course, more sensitive to this than anyone. Their very jobs depend on being on the side of public opinion, at least as much as they can.

When we are undertaking a campaign effort on a public policy issue on behalf of a client, we want to ensure that we are putting our best foot forward, so to speak. You can't do that unless you know what the public thinks. To engage the public, to try and get them to act on or shift their views on an issue, you need to know first what they think.

Question: How do you influence public opinion?

Answer: Public opinion on any given issue isn't static—it changes for a wide variety of reasons over time. Job number one is to figure out where the public stands on the issue at hand and engage them in a dialogue to give them more information that may be relevant to shaping their views. In the end that's what it is, after all—a dialogue. We are extremely lucky these days in that we have such sophisticated tools to do these kinds of campaigns. The Internet and social media tools allow us to talk to very specific groups of people on issues they actually want to engage with, and allow for a real-time conversation and, most importantly, an ability to track those conversations. There are also new tools like telephone town hall technology, allowing the ability to create a phone-in show where, again, you can target specific groups of people by demographic or by location for direct engagement. So these are all amazing tools for furthering a dialogue.

Question: Do you think it is always possible to change public opinion? What about in cases when the public is against your organization or position?

Answer: Obviously, some issues are more challenging than others. The most important thing is to do the research, know where the public stands, and, especially in the age of the Internet, be prepared to engage directly. I think it's always possible to change the narrative of a debate on an issue, but it takes resources and a commitment to really have that back-and-forth conversation. Especially in Canada, where we have a strong democratic tradition, people who are engaged in public policy issues generally want more information, not less. And that is the first key to unlocking a discussion that can change minds.

THE HISTORY OF PR IN CANADA

Many of the PR practitioners who shaped the profession as we know it in Canada have continued to practise until recently. These individuals, whom you will meet shortly, developed the way we do our work in this country. They also started the professional associations that support and guide us and developed the ethical standards we follow. These Canadian pioneers were the first to realize the importance of PR education and of training the next generation of practitioners, and were instrumental in creating PR programs in universities and colleges. We have a lot to be grateful to these practitioners for, which is why we are now going to examine the history of PR in Canada.

As we mentioned earlier in the chapter, it is believed that the Canadian PR industry came approximately 25 years after the U.S. industry.[49] The main reasons for the later development in Canada was the lack of money for national PR programs and, as one PR practitioner described it in 1953, the absence of "crusading public relations leaders to help educate business."[50]

The development of the industry took a different direction in Canada than it did in the United States. Whereas in the United States the first PR efforts were corporate, in Canada the government took the lead.[51] The government began employing PR tactics long before public relations was even known as such and before there was an established profession. Although it would be years before public relations was defined, the earliest case of a PR campaign in Canada is considered to be found in the writings of Samuel de Champlain in the early 1600s, in which he encouraged French settlers to move to this country.[52] Jump ahead to the mid- to late 1800s, and the government once again used PR tactics to meet its immigration objectives. The immigration initiatives of Clifford Sifton, the minister of the interior, have been lauded as one of the most effective and earliest public relations campaigns in Canada.[53] Sifton used a score of tactics still employed today to attract more than 2 million immigrants to Canada between 1896 and 1911. This included launching a speaking tour, where spokespersons appeared at community events in the United States; distributing pamphlets; and bringing hundreds of American media, as well as members of the British government, to visit Canada in the hopes that they would influence potential settlers to head for Canada.[54]

EARLY CORPORATE PR

Public relations as a paid occupation started in Canada around the 1890s. By the early 1900s, some corporations had begun conducting PR. These included the Canadian Pacific Railway, the Bell Telephone Company of Canada, and the Royal Bank. Some of the tactics they used included media relations and media tours, advocacy advertising, community relations, special event sponsorship, and internal communication with employees. For example, Bell launched its first employee newsletter, *The Blue Bell*, in 1921.[55]

The Second World War was the training ground for many of Canada's early PR practitioners. The government recruited journalists and advertising executives for its public information units, such as the Wartime Information Board.[56] There they practised a wide range of PR functions to influence the Canadian public during this crucial time. In fact, Canadian government PR units were recognized at the time as some of the best in all the Allied forces.[57]

Many of the PR practitioners of the 1950s and 1960s first worked for information units in the Canadian army and later took this knowledge into civilian affairs. After the Second World War, public relations as a profession took off in Canada,[58] growing in direct correlation with the Canadian economy.[59]

One of Canada's most famous politicians of that time was a skilful PR master. William Lyon Mackenzie King, who served as Canadian prime minister between 1921 and 1948,

Prime Minister Mackenzie King was skilled at media relations.
Source: © Ivan Vdovin/Alamy

was noted for his media relations skills and developed strong relationships with several key members of the Canadian Parliamentary Press Gallery. A former journalist, King had a solid understanding of media relations techniques, which he used to his political advantage. Interestingly, prior to becoming prime minister, he was hired by Rockefeller to work on a campaign alongside Ivy Lee. In fact, he was considered a much better PR practitioner than the famous Lee.[60]

As mentioned earlier, some of the founders of CPRS were part of U.S. professional organizations that were operating in Canada before we had our own.[61] The first Canadian groups were created by practitioners who had been meeting informally over lunch. In 1948, the Canadian Public Relations Society was formed in Montreal and the Public Relations Association of Ontario was created in Toronto. The groups merged in 1953.[62] Around this time, PR became more of an established profession, with guidelines and structure, and support for PR practitioners was established.

EARLY CANADIAN PRACTITIONERS

Like the United States, Canada has a rich history of characters who shaped the PR profession, including George Ham, Jimmy Cowan, and Lou Cahill.

George Ham

George Ham was a former journalist who joined the Canadian Pacific Railway in 1891, where he pioneered media relations, wrote media materials, acted as spokesperson, and gave speeches. He was an early supporter of women journalists and one of the first corporate PR practitioners to give them recognition. He organized media tours exclusively for female journalists, providing them with their own car. He was described as a master at his job.[63]

Jimmy Cowan

In 1930, Jimmy Cowan was the first Canadian to open a PR agency. Cowan was a Toronto-based journalist originally from Shakespeare, Ontario.[64] Cowan advised both corporations and politicians, including President Franklin D. Roosevelt.[65]

Lou Cahill

Lou Cahill has the distinction of having founded the oldest PR agency still operating in Canada. He started OEB International in St. Catharines, Ontario, in 1936.[66] This PR agency is now called Enterprise Canada and has offices in three cities.

Jack Donoghue

Jack Donoghue was an early practitioner who started his career during the Second World War. He went on to work in public relations for the Canadian government and later spent several years conducting corporate PR in an agency. He is the author of the book *PR: Fifty Years in the Field*, which provides an interesting overview of the history of PR in Canada.[67]

Gordon Hulme

Gordon Hulme worked for the Shawinigan Water and Power Company in Montreal, a corporation that established a PR role within the organization early on. Hulme was instrumental in the formation of CPRS, after serving as area vice president for the American group, the National Association of Public Relations Counsel.[68]

John H. Yocom

CPRS calls John Yocom one of Canada's greatest practitioners, both for his expertise and for his support to others in the field. He was a key member of this professional association and served as its president for many years. He co-founded the accreditation examinations in Canada and was an early supporter of PR education, developing and teaching courses at several Ontario universities and colleges. Originally a journalist, he became general manager of public affairs for the British American Oil Company in the early 1960s.[69]

Munro Brown

Munro Brown, a journalist at *The Gazette* newspaper in Montreal, began practising PR in the 1930s, first at a publishing company and then at the Bank of Montreal, where he established the PR department. He was one of the first corporate practitioners in the mid-1940s to conduct PR research to assess public opinion and make strategic decisions based on the results.[70]

WOMEN IN PR IN CANADA

While many of the first practitioners in Canada were men, women quickly joined them and have left their own legacy.

Ruth Hammond

Ruth Hammond was one of the first women to found her own PR agency. She began her career in journalism at the *Toronto Star* before switching to public relations. In the 1950s, she conducted campaigns for numerous nonprofit organizations, including the Canadian Cancer Society, Girl Guides of Canada, and the United Way. She was instrumental in developing an accreditation system with John Yocom and introducing PR courses in postsecondary institutions.[71]

Hilda Wilson

When Hilda Wilson was told that she could not have the manager's job in the PR department of her company because she was a woman, she took that as her cue to leave and open her own agency, Investor Relations Canada Ltd., specializing in financial and consumer education PR. *Marketing* magazine named Wilson one of the top ten most influential marketers in Canadian history, saying, "At a time when PR was exclusively a male domain, she opened it up to women."[72]

Thinking Like a PR Practitioner

1. Think of an example of a recent media event and describe how it might have been influenced by one of the founders of public relations.

2. Identify three positive contributions and two negative contributions to PR made by the founders of public relations.

The Public's Opinion of Public Relations ❹

As discussed in the previous section, the founders of public relations relied on newspapers and mainstream media to help them influence public opinion. This is because the media are key in both agenda setting and shaping the public's beliefs on a topic.[73] Knowing how to leverage the media's influence can help your client or company sway public opinion in its favour. However, PR practitioners have traditionally struggled to promote their own profession in the public's eyes. Both historically and today, various negative attitudes toward PR practitioners have permeated the mainstream media. These negative attitudes centre on the perception that PR practitioners are spin doctors who twist the truth in order to make bad things companies do seem, if not good, less harmful than they are.

The old saying that "a shoemaker's wife goes barefoot" applies to public relations and public opinion. While PR practitioners work hard to manage the public's perception of their clients, as an industry they are not doing a great job of gaining the public's trust. As Brenda J. Wrigley, an associate professor of PR at the University of Syracuse, states, "PR has a PR problem. We have to get our own house in order before we go around advising corporations what to do. We are advocates and there's no shame in that as long as it's grounded in ethics and values."[74] Lack of public education is one reason that PR does not always have a stellar reputation. Other factors include the way that PR professionals are portrayed in the media and some unethical tactics that a minority of practitioners have engaged in, such as spin, propaganda, and astroturfing. Let us look at these in more detail.

PR AND MEDIA PORTRAYAL

Studies have shown that PR practitioners are often negatively portrayed in the media. In fact, the phrases "public relations gimmick" and "public relations nightmare" are even used in negative news stories that have nothing to do with public relations.[75] The media also sometimes portray the PR profession as trying "to thwart and subvert democratic decision making."[76] This framing by the media affects the profession's credibility.

Part of the perception problem stems from journalists' long-standing suspicion of PR practitioners. PR people are viewed as intermediaries, blocking journalists from speaking directly to an organization. The case of Christy Clark's PR director is a perfect example. When Christy Clark became premier of British Columbia, a PR director was assigned to help change the public's opinion of her. In her first week on the job, Sara MacIntyre fought with local media when she refused to let journalists ask the premier questions.[77] Caught on video, the exchange went viral on the web and led to MacIntyre being dubbed by *The Globe and Mail* "Canadian TV's newest villain."[78] In her efforts to influence how the premier was portrayed in the media, MacIntyre created a PR disaster. This case demonstrates that PR practitioners must sometimes walk a fine line. On one side is their relationship with journalists, and on the other, with their organization.

Christy Clark's PR director did more harm than good when she refused to let the press ask Clark questions. The exchange with the media was caught on tape and went viral.

Source: Punit Paranjpe/Newscom

Furthermore, whereas journalists are expected to tell a story from many angles, PR practitioners tell their client's story from the angle that suits their interests,[79] creating tension between the media and communicators. PR practitioners are hired to help the public see their clients in the best light, and so their neutrality is questioned. This is fine. PR people are not paid to be impartial, but they do need to be honest. As Jim Lukaszewski, founder of the Lukaszewski Group, a PR firm in White Plains, notes, "If you really simplify things, as for example a reporter does, and say, 'Well look, what do you need a public relations person for anyway? Just tell me the truth and I'll convey that to the public,' … there's some issues with something as simple as that, 'cause many ideas that matter have some complexity and need some explanation."[80]

PROPAGANDA

Some members of the public accuse PR practitioners of **propaganda**. What is the difference between influencing public opinion and outright propaganda? In John Fisher's article "Public Relations and War," he quotes *The Encyclopedia of Public Relations*, which says propaganda and public relations "stem from a common desire to affect the attitudes and perceptions held by people ... to shift opinion and beliefs in a desired direction."[81]

Propaganda usually has a kernel of truth but is so exaggerated that it is no longer true. Propaganda aims to evoke strong emotions such as patriotism in order to manipulate the public and is usually associated with religion, politics, or war.[82] Conversely, public relations should be about telling a story that is based on fact. As Jim Hoggan, founder of the PR agency Hoggan & Associates, writes on his blog, "There is a line between public relations and propaganda—or there should be. And there is a difference between using your skills, in good faith, to rescue a battered reputation and using them to twist the truth."[83] Hoggan & Associates is so committed to this principle that they offer office space to the blog DeSmogBlog, which outs the PR tactics used by companies and the government to put doubt in the public's mind about the reality of climate change.[84]

If PR practitioners find that they are having to exaggerate or twist the truth to tell their client's or organization's story in a compelling way, they need to re-evaluate whether they want to be associated with that organization.

SPIN AND ASTROTURFING

Two other practices that have harmed the reputation of PR are spin and astroturfing. Before exploring them, however, we would like to emphasize that in our professional experience we have found these practices to be extremely rare and have observed that the majority of PR practitioners follow the highest professional standards.

Let's look at spin first. In 2006, Finance Minister Jim Flaherty announced the federal government's plan to tax income trusts. This announcement was a sharp reversal from the Harper government's previous policy on taxing this popular investment vehicle. In the press release announcing the change, which would affect the retirement plans of many Canadians, the **lead**, or the most important message in the story, was buried, with a headline that stated, "Canada's New Government Announces Tax Fairness Plan."[85] The headline and press release lead was designed to distract from the real news that affected Canadians: that income trusts would be taxed. This is now considered a prime example of political spin.[86]

Is there any word in the English language that brings up more negative connotations than *spin*? It conjures up images of dishonest politicians or scandalous celebrities bending the truth to make themselves look better. But what is spin exactly? Are all PR professionals spin doctors? *Safire's New Political Dictionary* defines **spin** as "the deliberate shading of news perception; attempted control of political reaction."[87] Many PR professionals find the term *spin* insulting, especially when it is used as a blanket explanation of what PR practitioners do. Defenders of the profession argue that most PR practitioners are portraying their clients or organizations in an honest manner, albeit in their best light. They argue that as in the court of law, where everyone has the right to a defence lawyer, in the court of public opinion everyone has the right to defend themselves as best they can, through PR and media training.

The press from Finance Minister Jim Flaherty's office release announcing the taxation of income trusts was criticized for being political spin.
Source: © Aaron Burns/ Alamy

Media training is often criticized for enabling spin because it teaches spokespeople how to deliver their key messages no matter what questions are asked of them. Good spokespeople are able to satisfy the question while weaving in their key points. Poorly trained spokespeople deliver at times hilarious, at other times frustrating, interviews in which they completely ignore whatever is asked of them and simply jump into their messaging. During her leadership race in 2004, Belinda Stronach was interviewed by the CBC in Halifax and paid no attention to her interviewer's questions on the economy, giving long-winded answers that emphasized her key messages but that were in no way related to the questions.[88] This type of interview annoys both journalists and listeners and gives the impression that the spokespeople are hiding the truth. Well-trained spokespeople will answer the question but bridge into the key message. See Chapter 8 for more information on media training.

Another grey-area tactic is **astroturfing**, in which a fake grassroots coalition or citizens' group is set up for corporate or political interests to hide behind. In Canada, one of the most famous examples of astroturfing is by the Calgary-based Friends of Science (FoS).[89] This advocacy group argues that climate change is not caused by human outputs. FoS runs political attack ads against climate change initiatives, posts web videos, sponsors speakers across the country, and submits anti–climate change op-eds, among other tactics. Accused of being closely tied to the Alberta oil patch, FoS has been linked to the general manager of the public relations firm Fleishman-Hillard.[90] Many PR practitioners believe that putting out messaging on behalf of a client without revealing that client's real identity is unethical. Furthermore, it goes against the ethical standards outlined by the professional associations. Astroturfing is discussed further in Chapter 12.

PUBLIC RELATIONS' MORAL COMPASS

The reputation of PR is based upon the ethical behaviour of all its practitioners. As they say, one bad apple can spoil the bunch. When the unethical behaviour of one practitioner makes the news, it affects the entire industry and harms our reputation. After all, the public does not usually hear about us when we have done good work that brings benefits to both our organization and the public. That is because our work is done behind the scenes. The only stories the public hears about are the negative ones.

It is the responsibility of all PR practitioners to educate the public about what we do. The profession needs to build both the media's and the public's trust. In order to create a better public perception of the practice of PR, practitioners need to follow strict codes of conduct in ethical behaviour, as outlined by professional organizations such as CPRS, discussed in Chapter 1. It is in the PR practitioner's best interest to follow these ethical guidelines, not only because the reputation of the industry is at stake but also because the media will work only with PR practitioners they trust. If practitioners get a reputation for being dishonest or spinning, it will be difficult for them to get their clients coverage in the future.

While there are many black and white ethical rules in public relations, such as not to lie, steal, or misrepresent the facts, many of the decisions we must make fall within areas of ethical ambiguity. In many of the ethical decisions you will make as a PR practitioner you will need to consult your own moral compass. For example, while some people would never want to do public relations for a company that harms the environment, such as a mining or oil company, others might not have a problem with this. A vegetarian might refuse to do public relations for a meat processor like Maple Leaf Foods, whereas others might jump at the opportunity to work for them. PR people represent clients in the court of public opinion. In the course of this work, they may be forced to confront their own opinion of their client or employer. See Chapter 1 for more information on ethics and PR.

Thinking Like a PR Practitioner

1. How valid do you think the negative perceptions of PR are? How would you defend the profession to a critic?

2. What is your definition of *spin*? Do you believe it is a fair term to be used in describing public relations?

GARNERING PUBLIC OPINION TO HELP WITH NEGOTIATIONS: THE NLMA

The Newfoundland and Labrador Medical Association (NLMA) is the bargaining agent for the 1200 practising physicians in Newfoundland and Labrador. When salary negotiations with the provincial government broke down in March 2010, the NLMA knew it needed public opinion on its side to force the government back to the table. The association also needed to improve the reputation of physicians and of the association, which was under attack after then premier Danny Williams criticized the NLMA in the media. In response to these needs, the association implemented a public relations and advertising campaign.

Publicly opposing the premier was a major challenge, given his unrivalled popularity. Research showed 93 per cent satisfaction with his government, the highest level ever recorded in Atlantic Canada in more than 20 years of tracking. The NLMA had to take a different tactic and avoid being seen as directly opposing the premier.

Additional research showed that the residents of the province thought that one of the most important issues facing the health care system was the shortage of doctors. When asked what the provincial government could do to strengthen the health system, the number-one answer was that the government should increase the number of doctors.

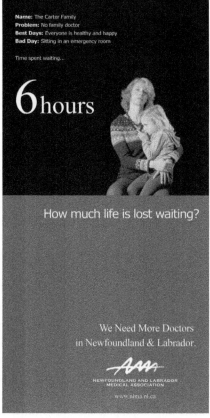

Source: Newfoundland and Labrador Medical Association

The NLMA's communications team decided to focus its campaign on this issue. The campaign had three objectives:

1. Inform the public about significant patient wait times and the need for more doctors.

2. Pressure the government to resume talks and resolve the negotiation's impasse.

3. Achieve a contract settlement and a new memorandum of agreement for physicians.

The campaign began with media relations tactics three to four weeks before ads were broadcast on television, radio, and newspapers to create context for the ads in the public's minds.

Although each person in the province will have a requirement for health care services at some point, the NLMA chose to target adults aged 25 to 54. This group is more likely to bear the emotional impact and logistical responsibility of dealing with sickness and disease in their children and their aging parents.

To have maximum impact, the same messaging was used for both media relations and the ads. The NLMA identified potential areas of medicine to serve as scenarios for the ads, with a focus on identifying medical services that have historically generated media interest and are known to have excessive wait times and/or physician shortages.

It was also important that the scenarios presented in each ad resonated with people and focused on areas of medical service that affect a large number of people. Therefore, the ads depicted a variety of patient demographics, making them applicable to a broad audience. The NLMA worked with physicians to identify realistic patient scenarios. Each ad was developed using a consistent template that presented a patient, described his or her disease or condition, and outlined its impact on the individual's quality of life. The ad then presented the number of days the patient was waiting to see a physician, while posing the question "How much life is lost waiting?" The ads concluded with the statement "We need more doctors in Newfoundland and Labrador." To ensure consistency and repetition, the campaign used this template for TV, radio, and print and social media. Thus, over a short period of time, the public saw many different ads, but all with the same underlying message.

The campaign was launched with six news conferences, which garnered significant earned media coverage. The environment was then ripe for the ad campaign to begin. In fact, the ads themselves generated extensive media coverage on CBC TV, on CBC Radio, and in Newfoundland's leading newspaper, *The Telegram*. The ads also generated blog posts and letters to the editor. CBC Radio even dedicated a full one-hour call-in program to the topic.

The campaign had not even run its course before the government resumed talks and the impasse in negotiations was resolved. The NLMA met all its objectives and a new memorandum of agreement was achieved.

Questions

1. Explain why the NLMA decided to sway public opinion in its favour.

2. Discuss the issue the campaign focused on in order to influence public opinion.

The Snacking Habits of Canadians

The Hain Celestial Group is one of the world's leading natural foods companies. The organization was launching a new line of healthy snacks such as granola bars, sweet potato chips with olive oil, and cookies, and it was our job to get the word out in Canada.

To raise awareness of these new snacks with a target audience of consumers interested in healthy eating, we decided to conduct a media relations campaign. We had to develop a story that would be of interest to journalists and help us generate media coverage. We decided to conduct public opinion research and look into the snacking habits of Canadians. We also wanted to know if they were interested in eating better-for-you options instead of less nutritious mainstream snacks.

To find out, we conducted an informal online survey with Canadians. We say "informal" because we did not use the services of a professional research firm. Once we had collected a few hundred answers, we analyzed them. The survey revealed that a large percentage of Canadians were interested in eating healthy snacks if they tasted just as good as traditional ones. That's the story that we delivered in our key messages and in the media release. The media release also announced the launch of the new products but positioned them within a larger story about snacking.

The media release was picked up by journalists across the country, resulting in media stories in newspapers in many cities, including Toronto and Vancouver. See Chapter 6 for more information on media relations and generating media coverage.

public opinion

early practitioners

- men   • Canada
- women   • US

attitudes & beliefs

- 3 positions of audiences
  - neutral
  - for
  - against

factors of persuasion

- propaganda
- influencers

public's opinion of PR

- spin
- reputation

measurement

- opinion polls
- research
- media relations
- angles
- stories

Key Terms

astroturfing Creating a fake grassroots organization for the purpose of misleading the public.

brand ambassadors People who are loyal to a brand and tell their peers about it. These people can be employees, may be paid in kind, or may simply be fans of the brand.

crystallize an attitude A communication strategy designed to strengthen an existing belief.

influencers People who are influential and whose opinion is trusted.

lead The most important and attention-grabbing information in a story.

muckraking journalism A style of investigative journalism that exposed the wrongdoings of people or companies.

opinion leader Someone to whom others look in order to help form their opinion on a particular topic.

persuasive message A communication designed to influence an audience.

press secretary A person who works for a public figure and handles his or her public relations.

propaganda Biased information disseminated to promote a position.

public opinion A prevailing opinion or a popularly held belief.

spin A negative term, sometimes used to describe what PR practitioners do, to denote taking a negative story and twisting the truth so that it seems more positive.

spokesperson A person who represents an organization to the public or media.

Weblinks

CBC's Spin Cycles
www.cbc.ca/news/background/spincycles/

DeSmogBlog
www.desmogblog.com

Internal Communications: It's Not Rocket Science!
http://novascotia.ca/cns/pubs/ItsNotRocketScience.pdf

The PR Coach
www.theprcoach.com/internal-communications/

Strategic Communications: An 8-Step Process for Creating Effective Internal
Communications Plans
www.stratcommunications.com/media/cushycms/Resources_83_2776689510.pdf

Endnotes

1. David Wolf, "Bernays' Propaganda Holds a Message for Modern PR," *Media: Asia's Media and Marketing Newspaper*, October 8, 2009, 18.

2. Thomas J. Roach, "Managing Public Opinion: The Best Strategy Is Not to Shut It Down but Keep It Informed," *Rock Products*. Accessed February 27, 2013, http://www.rockproducts.com/index.php/key-issues/community-relations/10306-managing-public-opinion.html

3. Public Works and Government Services Canada, *Annual Report 2009–2010*. Accessed July 3, 2012, http://www.tpsgc-pwgsc.gc.ca/rop-por/rapports-reports/2009-2010/introduction-eng.html#intro3

4. V. Price, *Public Opinion*. Newbury Park, CA: Sage, 1992.

5. S.T. Fiske, D.T. Gilbert, and G. Lindsey, *Handbook of Social Psychology* (5th ed.). Hoboken, NJ: John Wiley & Sons, 2010.

6. J.R. Zaller, *The Nature and Origins of Mass Opinion*. Cambridge: Cambridge University Press, 1992, p. 22.

7. Ibid.

8. Jon A. Krosnick and Wendy R. Smith, *"Attitude Strength."* Accessed February 18, 2013, http://comm.stanford.edu/faculty/krosnick/docs/1994/1994%20Attitude%20strength.pdf

9. Ibid.

10. Kenneth Evans, interview with the author.

11. Ibid.

12. "Three Argumentative Appeals," *Paradigm Online Writing Assistant*. Accessed February 18, 2013, http://www.powa.org/index.php/convince/three-argumentative-appeals

13. Ibid.

14. Malcolm Gladwell, *The Tipping Point: How Little Things Can Make a Big Difference*. New York: Little, Brown, 2002.

15. Ibid.

16. Duncan J. Watts and Peter Sheridan Dodds, "Influentials, Networks, and Public Opinion Formation," *Journal of Consumer Research*, December 2007, 441–458.

17. Ira Basen, "Spin Cycles: A Century of Spin: Episode 1," *CBC News*, January 19, 2007. Accessed February 18, 2013, http://www.cbc.ca/news/background/spincycles/index-episode1.html

18. Peter Johansen, "Professionalisation, Building Respectability, and the Birth of the Canadian Public Relations Society," *Journalism Studies*, vol. 2, no. 1 (2001), 55–71.

19. Larissa A. Grunig, Linda Childers Hon, and Elizabeth L. Toth, *Women in Public Relations: How Gender Influences Practice*. New York: Guildford Press, 2001, p. 189.

20. Russell Working, "Women Dominate the PR Industry: Why?" Ragan Communications, December 28, 2010. Accessed July 4, 2012, http://www.ragan.com/PublicRelations/Articles/Women_dominate_the_PR_industry_Why_42373.aspx

21. "Rise of the Image Men," *The Economist*, December 16, 2010. Accessed February 18, 2013, http://www.economist.com/node/17722733

22. Ira Basen, "Spin Cycles: A Century of Spin: Reporter's Interview Transcript: Stuart Ewen on Ivy Lee," *CBC News*, January 19, 2007. Accessed February 18, 2013, http://www.cbc.ca/news/background/spincycles/transcript-ewen-lee.html

23. "Rise of the Image Men."

24. Basen, "Spin Cycles: A Century of Spin: Reporter's Interview Transcript: Stuart Ewen on Ivy Lee."

25. "Rise of the Image Men."

26. Ira Basen, "Spin Cycles: The Spindustrial Revolution: Episode 2," *CBC News*, January 25, 2007. Accessed February 18, 2013, http://www.cbc.ca/news/background/spincycles/index-episode2.html

27. Basen, "Spin Cycles: A Century of Spin: Episode 1."

28. "Rise of the Image Men."

29. Ira Basen, "Spin Cycles: A Century of Spin: Reporter's Interview Transcript: Fraser Seitel," *CBC News*, January 19, 2007. Accessed February 18, 2013, http://www.cbc.ca/news/background/spincycles/transcript-seitel.html

30. Basen, "Spin Cycles: A Century of Spin: Episode 1."

31. Ira Basen, "Spin Cycles: A Century of Spin: Reporter's Interview Transcript: Larry Tye," *CBC News*, January 19, 2007. Accessed February 18, 2013, http://www.cbc.ca/news/background/spincycles/transcript-tye.html

32. Mark Ritson, "30 Seconds On … 'Fathers' of Marketing," *Marketing*, October 21, 2009, 22.

33. "Rise of the Image Men."

34. Ibid.

35. John R. Fisher, "Public Relations and War: Socially Responsible or Unethical," *Journal of International Business Disciplines*, vol. 4, no. 1 (November 2009), 54–67.

36. Basen, "Spin Cycles: A Century of Spin: Reporter's Interview Transcript: Larry Tye."

37. Ibid.

38. Basen, "Spin Cycles: A Century of Spin: Episode 1."

39. Ira Basen, "Spin Cycles: A Century of Spin: Reporter's Interview Transcript: Chet Burger," *CBC News*, January 19, 2007. Accessed February 18, 2013, http://www.cbc.ca/news/background/spincycles/transcript-burger.html

40. "Background and History," The Arthur W. Page Society. Accessed February 18, 2013, http://www.awpagesociety.com/about/background-history/

41. Basen, "Spin Cycles: A Century of Spin: Reporter's Interview Transcript: Chet Burger."

42. Jaimee Moore, "Women in Public Relations: Our Past, Present, and Future." MA thesis, University of North Texas, 2000.

43. D. Fleischman (ed.), *Careers for Women: A Practical Guide to Opportunity for Women in American Business.* New York: Garden City Publishing Co., 1939.

44. Moore, "Women in Public Relations: Our Past, Present, and Future."

45. Suzannah Patterson, "Examining the Role of Women in the Development of Public Relations," *Public Relations Journal*, vol. 3, no. 1 (2009).

46. "Anne W. Wheaton, 68, an Eisenhower Aide; Named Associate Press Secretary in 1957 after Reporting Career," *New York Times*, March 25, 1977. Accessed July 4, 2012, http://select.nytimes.com/gst/abstract.html?res=F50711FC3A5F167493C4AB1788D85F438785F9

47. Ibid.

48. Patterson, "Examining the Role of Women in the Development of Public Relations."

49. Basen, "Spin Cycles: A Century of Spin: Episode 1."

50. Merle Emms, "The Origins of Public Relations as an Occupation in Canada." MA thesis, Department of Communication, Concordia University, 1995, p. 163.

51. Johansen, "Professionalisation, Building Respectability, and the Birth of the Canadian Public Relations Society."

52. Ibid.

53. Emms, "The Origins of Public Relations as an Occupation in Canada."

54. *The Canadian Encyclopedia.com*, s.v. "Public Relations." Accessed July 4, 2012, http://www.thecanadianencyclopedia.com/articles/public-relations

55. Emms, "The Origins of Public Relations as an Occupation in Canada."

56. Jack Donoghue, *PR: Fifty Years in the Field.* Toronto: Dundurn Press, 1993.

57. Ibid.

58. Basen, "Spin Cycles: A Century of Spin: Episode 1."

59. *The Canadian Encyclopedia.com*, s.v. "Public Relations."

60. Mark Bourrie, "The Myth of the 'Gagged Clam': William Lyon Mackenzie King's Press Relations," *Global Media Journal—Canadian Edition*, vol. 3, no. 2 (2010), 13–30.

61. Johansen, "Professionalisation, Building Respectability, and the Birth of the Canadian Public Relations Society."

62. *The Canadian Encyclopedia.com*, s.v. "Public Relations."

63. Emms, "The Origins of Public Relations as an Occupation in Canada."

64. Basen, "Spin Cycles: A Century of Spin: Episode 1."

65. "Public Relations in Canada. James A Cowan: 1901–1978," Toronto Seminars, April 26, 2011. Accessed July 4, 2012, http://www.seminars-toronto.com/public%20relations%20in%20 Canada.htm

66. Johansen, "Professionalisation, Building Respectability, and the Birth of the Canadian Public Relations Society."

67. Donoghue, *PR: Fifty Years in the Field.*

68. Johansen, "Professionalisation, Building Respectability, and the Birth of the Canadian Public Relations Society."

69. "Public Relations Profile Collection," Canadian Public Relations Society. Accessed July 4, 2102, http://www.cprs.ca/foundation/yocom.aspx

70. Emms, "The Origins of Public Relations as an Occupation in Canada."

71. "Public Relations Profile Collection."

72. Ibid.

73. Candace White and Joosulk Park, "Public Perceptions of Public Relations," *Public Relations Review*, vol. 36, no. 4 (November 2010), 319–324.

74. Timothy L. O'Brien, "Spinning Frenzy: P.R.'s Bad Press," *New York Times*, February 13, 2005. Accessed February 5, 2013, http://www.nytimes.com/2005/02/13/business/yourmoney/13flak. html?_r=0

75. White and Park, "Public Perceptions of Public Relations."

76. Josh Greenberg, Graham Knight, and Elizabeth Westersund, "Spinning Climate Change: Corporate and NGO Public Relations Strategies in Canada and the United States," *International Communication Gazette*, vol. 73, no. 1–2 (2011), 65–82.

77. "Premier's Director of Communications Says No Video," *GlobalTV*. Accessed April 10, 2012, http://www.globaltvbc.com/video/premiers+director+of+communications+says+no/video .html?v=2210194834&p=1&s=dd&fb_source=message#news+hour

78. "Clark's New Communications Director Spars with Media," *Thetyee.ca*, March 21, 2012. Accessed July 3, 2012, http://thetyee.ca/Video/2012/03/21/Sara-McIntyre-Spars/

79. Basen, "Spin Cycles: A Century of Spin: Episode 1."

80. Ira Basen, "Spin Cycles: The Spindustrial Revolution: Reporter's Interview transcript: Jim Lukaszewski," *CBC News*, January 25, 2007. Accessed February 5, 2013, http://www.cbc.ca/ news/background/spincycles/index-episode2.html

81. Fisher, "Public Relations and War: Socially Responsible or Unethical."

82. Ibid.

83. Greenberg, Knight, and Westersund, "Spinning Climate Change," p. 75.

84. Ibid.

85. Ira Basen, "Spin Cycles: Calling Dr. Spin: Episode 3," *CBC News*, February 2, 2007. Accessed February 5, 2013, http://www.cbc.ca/news/background/spincycles/index-episode3.html

86. Ibid.

87. "Spin," *NPR.org*, November 4, 2002. Accessed February 5, 2013, http://www.npr.org/programs/ morning/features/patc/spin/

88. Ira Basen, "Spin Cycles: The Spindustrial Revolution: Episode 2."

89. Greenberg, Knight, and Westersund, "Spinning Climate Change."

90. Ibid.

Women in PR

Many women are drawn to the public relations industry, even though public relations has historically been a male-dominated field. In fact, women now outnumber men in the PR profession by 40 percent.[1] They also make up the majority of students in PR programs in Canada.

Even with this increase of women within the profession, men still hold many of the more senior positions and subsequently command larger salaries.[2] One theory of why this gender discrimination takes place is that many CEOs and executives are men and seek the counsel of other men.[3] As more women take their place at the executive table, we hope to see more female practitioners move in greater numbers from execution roles to strategic ones. Amelia Reigstad is a PR practitioner and the owner of Crosspoint Communications. Reigstad conducted research about gender in PR in Canada for her master's degree in media, communications, and public relations. Here she speaks about some of her findings:

Q: Why do you think there are so many more women than men studying PR?

A: Women have an interest in business but feel that the industry is too male-dominated. Some don't necessary excel at accounting, etc., but do at communications, so there is a natural fit with public relations. Many fields are traditionally "male," so there is a natural progression for females into PR. There is still a misconception as to what public relations is due to stereotypes in the media. Men are much more likely to say they are enrolled in a communications program than a public relations program. Family influence also plays a role.

Q: What do women bring to the table?

A: Women bring communication skills, organizational skills, and a "mother"-type persona toward an organization, and they are typically multi-taskers and good listeners. My research also showed that different communication styles, traditional qualities, and personality traits of men and women within the public relations industry influence the practice of public relations that leads to a feminized profession and predominantly female industry.

Q: Are there PR specializations that attract more men than women?

A: I didn't cover this too much in depth but what I did discover was that women identify themselves as working in PR, whereas men identify themselves more so with the sector that they are doing PR for.

Q: What are some of the interesting findings you came across in your research?

A: The findings mentioned above, as well as the fact that men seem to be entering the industry through other forms of education. For example, they may do a business degree but have strong writing skills so they end up working for a PR firm or they have a graphic design background and end up working in the PR department of a nonprofit. Men are entering the industry in a different way than women. I also discovered that misconception surrounding the public relations industry continues to be present, and the role and responsibilities of a PR practitioner are not clear. Stereotypes in the media are reflected in society, and this provides a tainted view of the industry and contributes to limited enrolment of men in university public relations programs.

Q: Are men still making more money than women? Is that likely to change?

A: Yes, it's an age-old thing and hierarchy still exists to some extent. Men still make more money than women in top positions because women drop out of the race to focus on raising a family. It is linked to career vs. family. It was determined that in like positions, men are not afraid to ask for what they want, whereas women tend to avoid asking for what they want financially, and this is linked to the difference in communication styles between men and women.

Q: How do you see the future of PR for women?

A: I believe that public relations will always be an industry that women have a knack for, but through my research it was determined that, because of the rise of social media, arts/creativity, and technology, the field will neutralize eventually, since PR is exploding as an avenue to use artistry and technology. I feel that for women, it is possible to have a career and a family if employers continue to offer job schemes, part-time and flexible working options, mentorship, and recognition.[4]

Endnotes

1. Michael Sebastian, "In the PR World, Men Still Earn More than Women," *Ragen's PR Daily*, March 3, 2011. Accessed March 6, 2013, http://www.prdaily.com/Main/Articles/In_the_PR_world_men_still_earn_more_than_women_7411.aspx#

2. Ibid.

3. *IABC Velvet Ghetto Summary Report*, 1986. Accessed March 6, 2013, http://www.iabc.com/researchfoundation/pdf/VelvetGhetto.pdf

4. Charlotte Sherry, "Women, Leadership, and the PR World," *PR Week*, October 24, 2012. Accessed March 6, 2013, http://www.prweekus.com/women-leadership-and-the-pr-world/article/265021/?goback=.gde_4092391_member_178555956

Chapter 3
Corporate Social Responsibility, Cause PR, and Environmental PR

The Canadian Pacific Holiday Train visits 150 communities across North America. Everywhere it stops, it generates holiday cheer, media coverage, donations for food banks, and goodwill for CP. Source: Newscom

LEARNING OBJECTIVES

❶ Explain corporate social responsibility and the public relations practitioner's involvement in it.

❷ Describe the various ways PR practitioners might be involved in cause PR.

❸ Explain the challenges of telling the environmental story.

❹ Define greenwashing and explain how it hurts all companies in the environmental space.

Community Relations at Its Best: Canadian Pacific's Holiday Train

Like Santa's elves, in the three weeks leading up to Christmas, Canadian Pacific (CP) employees are busy at work. However, instead of building toys for good girls and boys, the company is running its annual Holiday Train community relations program, which raises money and food donations for food banks across the United States and Canada.

CP runs a North American transcontinental railway. To operate, it needs the support of many communities across the continent. To build relationships and engage with these residents, CP wanted to create a community relations program that both met a need and made sense with the organization's business. Beginning in 1999, the company launched the CP Holiday Train program, which today runs two trains, covered in festive lights and decorations, through more than 150 communities. In each community, the train stops and hosts a concert on the train's specially converted boxcar stage in order to raise donations for local food banks. All donations remain in that community for local distribution.

With a target audience of residents and elected representatives of the municipalities where CP conducts business, this program is also dear to the hearts of CP employees. Many of the company's employees live and work in the targeted communities and are proud to be able to support their food banks during the holiday season. Planning for the program typically begins in early March with a handful of employee leaders and is executed in late November and early December by hundreds of dedicated CP employees across North America.

As a community relations campaign, the program allows CP leaders to engage with 150 communities and meet mayors, councillors, emergency responders, business owners, and residents. It also provides the opportunity to strengthen current relationships. The campaign is a partnership between the community and the company. CP brings the train, and the local community organizes each event and makes it its own. This type of event also builds goodwill for the company in each city, allowing it to mitigate any community concerns, enhance business development planning, and ensure a unified approach between the railway and community if there were ever an accident or a negative incident.

CP also uses these holiday events to engage the media, issuing several press releases and media advisories throughout the campaign. "The Holiday Train generates money, food, and, most importantly, raises awareness that hunger remains a problem for millions of people across North America, all the while inspiring us to give back in our own communities," says Mark Seland, general manager of communications and public affairs for CP.

The company's media team rallies behind this event and calls hundreds of media outlets, including radio, TV, and print. In 2011, the media relations efforts resulted in over a thousand news stories about the campaign. Social media programs were integrated into the campaign in 2009 and the Holiday Train Facebook page now boasts more than twelve thousand active followers. The Holiday Train team tweets and blogs as the train travels the rails each year.

Perhaps most importantly, the positive impact of the campaign is undeniable. In 13 years, the Holiday Train campaign has resulted in donations of more than $6.4 million and close to 2.6 million pounds of food collected for those in need in the participating communities. These impressive results prove that with the right approach to community relations, everybody has a reason to believe in Christmas miracles.

As we saw in Chapter 2, part of the reason PR practitioners sometimes struggle with a bad reputation is that some individuals have the misconception that PR professionals work only for evil corporations with deep pockets who have something to hide through "spin." Nothing could be further from the truth. First, many organizations are good corporate citizens, deliver needed goods and services, and provide jobs across the country. Second, many PR practitioners choose to either work for or offer their services as volunteers for good causes and **nonprofit organizations** that they believe in. Nonprofit organizations are organizations that do not generate a profit and are created to meet societal or charitable objectives. Art galleries, film festivals, hospitals, and foundations all need PR people to assist them in promoting their good works.

As we also saw in Chapter 2, PR practitioners play a role in convincing companies to increase their transparency or societal contributions. Part of public relations' contribution to the public dialogue is its role in convincing organizations of the need to practise greater corporate social responsibility and in helping nonprofit organizations get their stories out and raise their profile. As we saw in the opening vignette about the CP Holiday Train, PR practitioners also help their organizations let people know about their charitable endeavours and raise awareness about the ways the public can contribute to the causes they support. The more people know, the more they can help. The efforts of CP's PR team to get the word out through media relations and social media relations enable more monetary and food donations to be raised for the communities the train serves.

PR practitioners play an important role in promoting corporate social responsibility within their organization. PR practitioners can help educate their internal audiences about the rewards of following a triple bottom line that supports people, profits, and the planet. In addition to promoting ethical and transparent actions within an organization, some PR practitioners might find it rewarding to work for a nonprofit in **cause PR** or to work on environmental PR. Cause PR is public relations conducted for social, environmental, or charitable reasons. Many PR agencies will take on a portion of clients that are charitable or environmental organizations **pro bono**, or without charge, in order to give back to the community.

In this chapter, we will examine corporate social responsibility and the role that PR plays in it. We will also look at cause PR and environmental PR and examine some of the issues facing PR practitioners who work in these fields.

Corporate Social Responsibility ❶

Corporate social responsibility (CSR), an organization's responsibility toward people and the planet, is increasingly seen as an important part of doing business. Not only is it the right thing to do, but it helps corporations engage in a positive way with their target audiences. People are more apt to support organizations that contribute to their communities and the causes that are important to them. Building its relationship with the communities its trains rolls through is an important objective of the CP Holiday Train. By bringing a festive holiday display to each town, as well as raising funds and food donations for those communities, CP hopes to gain community support and good-will toward the organization.

According to the Canadian Centre for Ethics and Corporate Policy, CSR directs how a company or organization interacts with all its stakeholders, whether they are sharehold-ers, employees, or community members.[1]

CSR involves how an organization comports itself in all areas, including environmen-tal sustainability, working conditions, human rights, and labour practices. It also involves being a good corporate citizen and making a commitment to contribute to the economic well-being, environmental preservation, and social sustainability of communities.[2]

CSR is growing in importance in Canada and around the globe, as is exemplified by the recently launched ISO26000, an international standard providing guidelines for social responsibility, created by the International Organization for Standardization. The rationale for the new standard was that "the need for organizations in both public and private sectors to behave in a socially responsible way is becoming a generalized requirement of society."[3]

As we will see in the next section, PR practitioners play a key role in helping com-panies identify needs and then plan and execute their CSR initiatives.

THE ROLE PR PLAYS IN CSR

What does CSR mean for PR professionals, and what role does public relations play in assisting organizations in practising or encouraging them to adopt CSR?

Public relations increasingly plays a role in advising organizations on the best CSR strategies and on methods of communicating to their target audiences what they are doing. As we saw in the opening vignette, CP's PR team is instrumental in organizing and getting the word out about the Holiday Train community relations initiative. They do this by employing a series of tactics, including media relations and social media relations.

Professional PR associations offer opportunities for their members to learn about this growing aspect of PR. IABC, for example, holds conferences on communicating CSR and has formed a social responsibility committee. An online service, CSRWire.ca, also distributes media information materials focusing exclusively on this topic.

In-house practitioners and PR agencies are increasingly choosing to focus on CSR as an area of expertise. The PR agency Environmental Communications Options special-izes in organizations working with environmental issues, while Nimbyist Communications works with nonprofits and community groups. Both cause PR and environmental PR, which will be discussed later in the chapter, are elements of CSR.

MATCHING THE CAUSE TO THE ORGANIZATION

CSR is best practised when an organization gets involved with a cause or community group that resonates with its target audiences, takes advantage of its strengths, or aligns with its strategic priorities. The CP Holiday Train is a perfect example: by organizing a train-focused event to bring holiday cheer and to raise money and food donations in

In partnering with the B.C. government to increase high-speed Internet access in rural communities, Telus played to its strengths.
Source: Ken Straiton/Newscom

many of the communities it serves throughout the year, CP strengthens its bond with the residents in these communities. Another good example is Telus, which in 2011 partnered with the B.C. government to increase high-speed Internet access in rural communities across the province.[4] This partnership leveraged Telus's strengths and made sense from a strategic perspective. Telus built relationships with the government, developed infrastructure to better service its customers, and reinforced its position as an industry leader.

PR practitioners are experts at understanding messaging that appeals to their audiences. They can help organizations in their support of a cause that connects with their stakeholders. L'Oréal Canada, for example, is a sponsor of Business for the Arts (BFTA), a Canadian association for business leaders who support the arts. "We are in the business of beauty and well-being," says Javier San Juan, president and CEO of L'Oréal Canada, which has been a BFTA sponsor for two years. "Art is part of that. It's a natural fit."[5]

Sometimes companies want to garner goodwill among their customers or the public through the "halo effect" a charity offers. This halo effect occurs when the good feelings the public feels for one organization, such as a charity, spreads to a company that associates with the charitable cause. To create the halo effect, companies conduct public relations around their own charitable actions, their association with a nonprofit organization, or a sponsorship.

When deciding which initiatives to support, companies often determine what appeals to a demographic they would like to reach and what makes sense for their industry (see Figure 3.1). Think about the CP Holiday Train: a festive train that raises funds and food donations for the very communities it serves is the perfect initiative for a train company. Another example is food companies that donate excess inventory to food banks. Not only is this convenient for the companies, as excess inventory is a cost of doing business, but it has a great outcome for the food bank.

Organization	Example of a Supported Charity/Cause
Bell	Mental Health
Telus	JDRF (Telus Walk to Cure Diabetes)
RBC	Toronto International Film Festival
CP Rail	Food Banks
CIBC	Canadian Breast Cancer Foundation (CIBC Run for the Cure)
Tim Hortons	Tim Horton Children's Foundation
McDonald's	Ronald McDonald House
Money Mart	Easter Seals (Money Mart Easter Seals 24 Hour Relay)
Petro-Canada	Olympics and Paralympics
Home Hardware	Special Olympics

Figure 3.1 Corporations and Examples of the Charities and Causes They Support

You might rightly ask, what's in it for the companies that spend so much time and energy on CSR and the reporting that comes out of it? Higher profits, for one thing. A Harvard study found that companies that are good corporate citizens outperform other companies on the stock market.[6] Just as ethical behaviour is good for the public relations professional, CSR benefits organizations in many ways, helping their bottom line with better earnings and attracting quality employees who are loyal and committed.[7] L'Oréal reports that its support of the BFTA has seen its financial numbers go up across the board.[8] CSR is a win–win for everyone. The Holiday Train not only helps the communities where it stops, it helps CP.

COMMUNICATING CSR TO TARGET AUDIENCES

If the first step is matching an organization to the appropriate cause, the second is ensuring that target audiences become aware of what the organization is doing. It is important to deliver CSR information to the stakeholders and make the information relevant to them. Again, consider how well the CP Holiday Train and the PR campaign do this.

Tonya Frizzell, manager of employee communications with Vancity Credit Union, communicates the organization's social responsibility efforts through an integrated annual report to its target audiences of members and employees. Frizzell explains,

> Corporate social responsibility is not an add-on. It's part of our brand and our value proposition. We tie specific products to specific causes. Our Visa cards, for example, support the enviro fund. In general, though, by choosing to do business with a local, values-based organization like Vancity, members are indirectly benefiting the community because the more successful Vancity is, the more we can give back to communities.[9]

CSR is a part of Vancity Credit Union's value proposition.
Source: LianeM/Shutterstock

The tactics used to communicate these messages with Vancity members and employees include an accountability report that features both financial results and the organization's social and environmental performance, online initiatives, and media relations.

In order to measure and report on their CSR initiatives, corporations will often publish an annual **CSR report**, a document that is much like a fiscal annual report. In it the company outlines the environmental and social programs it is involved in and the progress it has made. One of the most famous CSR reports is Apple's annual supplier responsibility progress report. In it, Apple reports on audits of its supply chain regarding priorities such as safe working conditions, employee rights, and environmental compliance. As Apple shows, it is okay to admit that compliance is not 100 per cent and instead to show positive intent and progress. The public understands that changing behaviour is a work-in-progress and appreciates a high level of transparency.

One way that organizations support the community and good causes is through sponsorship. This can involve either funds or goods in-kind. When issuing **in-kind donations**, a company donates its products or services instead of money. The right sponsorship opportunity can increase awareness and goodwill among consumers and build morale among employees. PR practitioners are often key in helping an organization decide which groups it will sponsor and in getting the word out.

It is PR practitioners' job to help organizations benefit from charitable partnerships by letting customers, the media, and the public know about their good works. They can do this by posting information on the company's website, using social media, conducting media relations, holding press conferences, or putting the charity in its advertising. As the online newsletter *O'Dwyer's* states on the PR benefits of sponsorship,

Imagine your president standing next to the president of Memorial Sloan-Kettering [a cancer centre] to announce a major new project. The doctor tells how serious a problem is, how many people will get a particular kind of cancer, and what Memorial Sloan-Kettering hopes to accomplish with the research trust funded by your company. Your president then tells why your employees, stockholders and customers are proud to be helping anti-cancer research. If the world's top cancer doctor ends with tips on ways to prevent that type of cancer, how many of the world's top newspapers and stations will not at least run something?[10]

Obviously, cancer sponsorship isn't right for every company, but for some, such as a sunscreen producer or another manufacturer of a product that prevents or treats cancer, this type of partnership could be a perfect fit.

CRITICISM OF CSR

CSR is not without its critics, mostly because of companies who overhype their CSR or who engage in CSR only after a crisis. The public wants to know that CSR efforts are sincere. Companies should not just participate in CSR because it is the trendy thing to do and so they can capitalize on it. Stakeholders can see through such motives and might even be put off by them. The danger is that a company will look as if it is throwing money at a cause even though it doesn't really care about it or because the organization has been accused of malpractice. Sometimes organizations sponsor events or make donations to causes as part of their issues management in an attempt to "make things right" but neglect to address the root issue. For example, after being accused of unfair labour practices, Wal-Mart donated $500,000 in scholarships to minority students.[11] Yet consumers might wonder what Wal-Mart has done to change its labour standards. Similarly, many consumers might doubt the sincerity of a tobacco company sponsoring lung cancer prevention organizations. This is why it is important to choose a cause that the organization cares about and that makes sense for your organization's goals, industry, and audience. However, even when you strategically select the CSR cause your organization will support, this does not mean that the company will be above reproach.

In this section we will examine two examples of organizations that were on the one hand applauded for their efforts and on the other criticized for contributing to the problem in the first place. These cases demonstrate the importance of thinking about any potential backlash from target audiences before starting a CSR public relations campaign. See Chapter 11 for more information on this topic.

The first case we will examine is that of the Dove Campaign for Real Beauty. In this case, the organization did not sponsor an ongoing CSR initiative but started its own. The company realized that its products were getting lost in a sea of competing beauty products.[12] After learning that many women were unhappy with their appearance and weight, the company launched the Dove Campaign for Real Beauty,[13] first in England and later in Canada and the United States. The objective of the campaign was to garner media interest and generate broadcast and print coverage. In addition to an advertising campaign, the company launched a website and asked women to participate in a dialogue about beauty. It also created a self-esteem fund to raise money for the National Eating Disorder Information Centre in Canada. In regards to its PR objectives, the campaign delivered. It was featured in many media sources, from *Good Morning America* to *Ellen*, *Oprah*, and *The Globe and Mail*. This all sounds good, but there is more to the story. Not all the media coverage or perception of the campaign has been positive. Some have cited hypocrisy on part of Dove, whose parent company, Unilever, also owns Axe body spray, which shows the opposite of real women in its ads. The ads feature sexy young women throwing themselves at men who wear Axe. Unilever is accused of helping build the self-esteem of women with one brand while harming it with another, something that the PR team at Dove had to take into consideration.

The second example is an in-kind donation. Coca-Cola Canada publicizes its donation of Minute Maid fruit juice to the Breakfast Clubs of Canada. The Breakfast Clubs benefit from the juice donation, and it costs Coca-Cola less to donate the product than to make a cash donation. Coca-Cola Canada also partners with ParticipACTION and has committed $10 million over ten years in order to get kids active.[14] This partnership is logical from a targeting perspective, as Coca-Cola products are sold to families. Coca-Cola receives a halo effect from moms who support efforts to get children to exercise more. This sponsorship is also strategic because the growth in childhood obesity has become a hot-button topic and soft drink companies like Coca-Cola have come under fire. By promoting healthy lifestyles among kids and working to counteract the effects of high-calorie soft drinks, Coca-Cola is trying to protect itself from criticism on this issue. However, some might accuse Coca-Cola of only helping to counteract a problem that it is contributing to through its sugary beverages targeted at youth. When evaluating sponsorship opportunities, PR practitioners must try to anticipate how they will be viewed by various groups and weigh the potential downside with the upside before making a decision to go ahead with a campaign.

Cause PR ❷

Many PR practitioners find meaningful careers working on cause PR. They may work on behalf of nonprofit organizations, community groups, social movements, or for-profit organizations that have strong ties to important causes. Lending your skills to organizations that practise good works that you believe in, as either an employee or a volunteer, is truly rewarding. Just like investor or government relations, which we will examine in Chapter 12, cause PR, especially at a nonprofit, is a specialized skill. While many of the fundamentals remain the same as in other types of public relations, there are some key differences. In this section, we will look at these differences, as well as at ways corporations can leverage their charitable support. We will also look at the Occupy Wall Street protests as an example of a social movement initiative that generated ample media coverage.

Nonprofit, or not-for-profit, organizations are those that do not generate a profit but instead contribute to society through services or funds. Working for a nonprofit

Communicating CSR

- Make sure that the cause matches the target audiences of the organization. The audiences must care about it for it to be effective.
- Don't practise CSR silently. Let your key audiences know what you are doing. Better yet, find a way to involve them.

- Make sure that the organization will not be seen by its target audiences as practising CSR solely for the positive headlines. It must be an initiative that the organization truly supports and that brings benefits to others.

Thinking Like a PR Practitioner

1. How can you evaluate if a cause is a good match for an organization?
2. What would be a good match for the Toronto International Film Festival (www.tiff.net); for Canada's immigration museum, Pier 21 (www.pier21.ca); and for Birks jewellers (www.birks.com)?
3. How can you involve target audiences in an organization's CSR program?

organization can be extremely rewarding and a valuable learning experience. PR practitioners work for a range of nonprofit organizations, including charities, professional associations, and foundations.

In many ways, conducting public relations for nonprofits is similar to managing it for any other organization. However, there are some key differences, such as potentially smaller budgets and a different audience. Because nonprofits are often small and want to keep overhead low, the public relations budget is usually not as large as in other organizations. In addition, a negative perception can be created if a nonprofit is seen to be spending frivolously, so campaigns and events must be cost efficient. There are some exceptions, however—art galleries and theatres will often throw lavish fundraisers and black-tie events.

Another difference can be the audiences that a nonprofit organization is targeting. PR campaigns for nonprofits are typically not selling goods but rather asking audiences to buy into an organization by supporting it with their money or their time. Volunteers are another major audience of many nonprofits, one that it is important to engage and motivate. Volunteers' concerns are different from those of consumers, as they want to feel a connection to the cause and to be convinced of how the donation of their time will generate results. The public also expects more from nonprofits than from companies. The public wants to feel good about where they are donating their hours or money.

Another audience that PR practitioners who work for nonprofits must also consider is organizations that partner with them for their CSR initiatives. Nonprofit PR practitioners often help such companies or sponsor them leverage their contribution through media relations in order to create a strong partnership and solidify future donations. Nonprofits will often put the name of their partners and sponsors on their website and advertisements, mention them in their social media and news releases, or name events after them, such as the CIBC Run for the Cure or the Telus Walk to Cure Diabetes. They might also agree to have a joint press conference with the company to announce the sponsorship or provide the company with quotes and photos for their press releases.

The Obakki Foundation provides one example of how PR is helping a foundation raise awareness of its work. Obakki is a global fashion design house based in Canada that launched the Obakki Foundation. One of the first projects of the foundation was focused on was helping three orphanages and 150 orphans in Cameroon. The children were asked three questions: What makes you happy? What makes you sad? What makes you afraid? Their answers were then incorporated into a limited-edition line of clothing—T-shirts, scarves, bags, and children's wear. All proceeds of this campaign went back to the orphanage, helping to bring a teacher, a nurse, a kitchen, and other services to the children. The children were also shown the power and value of their words in helping themselves and their communities. Obakki uses many social media tools, such as Twitter, Facebook, and a blog, to spread the word about the foundation and its fundraising campaigns.

OCCUPY WALL STREET

Occupy Wall Street is an interesting example of how PR can put a cause, in this case a social movement, on the map. In 2011, the Occupy Wall Street movement took North America by storm and garnered a large amount of media coverage. As the movement spread from city to city, in both the United States and Canada, the protesters captured the media's imagination and showed a certain degree of media savvy. In just two months, between September 17 and November 17, 2011, Google News counted 60,800 mentions of Occupy Wall Street.[15] A great example of cause PR, a portion of the movement's success was due to the fact that the protesters were authentic and embraced controversy.[16]

Occupy Wall Street helped demonstrate that large amounts of money are not needed to generate a lot of media coverage. In Canada, the Occupy movement spread to cities including Edmonton, Victoria, and Ottawa. However, eventually the unorganized nature of the movement, which had given it authenticity, became a hindrance as support for the cause waned in cities like Vancouver, where two drug overdoses occurred in or near the Occupy campground in front of the Vancouver Art Gallery. Because the movement lacked clear demands or objectives, the public began to lose interest and the story eventually faded.

Environmental PR ❸

Ever since Rachel Carson's book *Silent Spring* helped launch the environmental movement, North Americans have been increasingly aware of consumerism's effect on the environment.[17] Corporations are keen to communicate their environmental efforts to their target

Occupy protests came to parks and galleries across Canada in 2011, including St. James Park in Toronto.

Source: © Paul McKinnon/Alamy

audiences, whether or not they are legitimate, as we will see later in this section. As going green becomes increasingly important to the public, more and more organizations are eager to be seen as environmentally responsible. Films like *An Inconvenient Truth* are creating greater awareness among the public about environmental concerns such as climate change and are increasing support for these issues, and many PR practitioners are using their skills to help the crusade. Just as with general CSR, PR practitioners are key in helping their organizations to be greener and letting others know about it.

Thinking Like a PR Practitioner

1. Give an example of a nonprofit organization that has garnered many positive media impressions and explain why it has. Contrast it with an organization you believe has garnered little or negative publicity.

2. Find an example of a charity that has a corporate sponsor and explain how it has helped raise awareness for its sponsor.

Groups like the David Suzuki Foundation use PR practitioners to help get their message out, increase donations, and change behaviour. The objectives of these groups are to increase awareness and action around environmental issues. The David Suzuki Foundation maintains an active website, issues media releases regularly, has a blog, and publishes books to get the word out.

Another example of environmental PR work is provided by Satwant Kaur, a Canadian who has carved out an international career for herself in PR. She is presently regional information officer, Asia Pacific, for the United Nations Environment Programme (UNEP). Says Kaur about her work, "At the United Nations I get to use my natural skills as a communicator to serve a cause bigger than myself. In particular, I am passionate about raising environmental awareness amongst young people."[18]

Satwant works on a wide range of campaigns to raise awareness of environmental issues, from organizing climate talks for youth to generating support for climate deals and coordinating tree-planting campaigns in schools. Satwant works closely with the media, whether print, broadcast, or community-based, to reach out to the public. She also does a substantial amount of writing, including media materials, web copy, fliers, and brochures. To further promote her message she organizes special events, such as multi-city press launches of major reports, press conferences, and training and workshops for the media. She organizes yearly youth meetings and an annual consultation with social organizations such as women's groups, farmers' organizations, and indigenous groups in the region. She relies heavily on the latest scientifically backed information to raise awareness of issues and publicizes the latest findings on specific areas with recommendations on what governments can do to tackle the issues.[19]

ISSUES FACING ENVIRONMENTAL PR ❹

Students interested in conducting PR in the environmental space need to be aware of a few issues. Embarking on an environmental PR campaign without this awareness could

ADVICE TO NEW PRACTITIONERS

Doing PR for Good Causes

There are so many good causes competing for a limited amount of attention, funds, and support. As a PR practitioner you can really make a difference by helping a group stand out.

- Make your story timely. Give journalists and individuals a reason to care about your cause now. Make sure that your story has as many news values as possible to garner interest. (See Chapters 5 and 6 for information on news values.)

- It is common for PR agencies to give some of their time for free to nonprofits. If you are working in-house, find an agency that is willing to do some pro bono work to help your organization.

- When working with a smaller budget, be extra creative. A small budget does not mean that you cannot achieve big results.

lead to failure in communicating to target audiences or to backlash against the organization. The first issue is that environmental stories are often challenging to communicate and can be confusing to the public. The second is that some organizations actively try to discredit environmental issues such as climate change. The third issue is that some organizations engage in greenwashing—purposely lying or exaggerating their environmental claims—which leads to increased suspicion among the public.

Challenging Stories

Although PR practitioners in environmental groups like UNEP and the David Suzuki Foundation spend a lot of time and resources raising awareness of issues, the fact remains that many people are still confused about the issues and their severity, which makes conducting communications for environmental groups challenging.

This confusion results in part because scientists' explanations of climate change can be hard to understand. Scientists use precise methods of measuring climate change, such as the extinction of coral reefs and the melting of ice caps, and for many people these measurements can be abstract and hard to visualize. Most people see climate change through a social lens.[20] They want to know about the impact for them, their families, and their communities. When environmental groups try to educate the public on the science, they can come across as confusing, or worse, condescending.[21]

What this means for PR practitioners is that they need to paint a picture that people can relate to. If they work in PR for a nonprofit or government group trying to explain the science of environmental issues to target audiences, they need to communicate the information in ways that make sense and that enable audiences to take action if needed. They should ask, "Why does this matter to my target audience?" and then communicate why it is important to them.

Jim Hoggan's firm, Hoggan & Associates, created a document to help communicators tell the environmental story. In it they recommend acknowledging the complexity of sustainability, highlighting hope and change instead of using scare tactics, and using themes of community and interconnectivity. They also recommend emphasizing small, manageable actions audiences can take, because large tasks can be overwhelming except to the most committed environmentalists.[22]

Discrediting of Environmental Problems

Another issue that PR practitioners need to be aware of is that the public may be confused about environmental issues not only because the science and the story are complicated, but also because other PR practitioners are working for organizations trying to confuse the public on the issue of climate change.

Some PR practitioners, acting on behalf of organizations in industries where increased environmental scrutiny would be harmful, use **front groups** and junk science to discredit the climate change theory. A front group is an activist organization that is created to hide

Vincent Power: Communicating CSR for Sears

Vincent Power is divisional vice president of corporate affairs and communications for Sears. He looks after all external and internal communications for the retailer, including media relations, annual reports, community relations, shareholder meetings, special events, the intranet, and key messages. Sears was ranked as one of Canada's top 50 corporate citizens by *Corporate Knights* magazine.

Question: What are some examples of CSR initiatives that Sears conducts?

Answer: At Sears we have what we call the 4P approach: people—how we treat our employees; products—where we buy and source our products respecting human rights; planet—the environmental impact that we have; and partners—our community partners.

Question: Can you please elaborate?

Answer: For people, we conduct an annual survey with our employees asking them about their experience working at Sears and then use the results to make Sears a better place to work. For products, we have a code of vendor conduct with which we require our suppliers to comply in order to make products for Sears, and this code covers areas of fairness and human rights. We evaluate supplier adherence to the code with both internal and third-party audits. For the planet, we have a goal of a 50 per cent reduction in our carbon footprint by 2020, and we are well on our way to meeting it. That includes everything from reducing the energy used for lighting to upgrading our heating, ventilation, and cooling systems. For partners, we embrace a few meaningful causes that we believe both our customers and associates would find appropriate and these are centred around support for kids and their families.

Question: How do you communicate your CSR initiatives?

Answer: Externally, with media relations, media events, special events, and our website Sears.ca. Internally, through our intranet as well as video messages from our CEO that are distributed in all our stores for our associates to see. Retail employees have varied hours, so it is challenging to communicate with all of them at once. Communicating with our employees is key. They are the ones engaging face to face with our customers. Our CSR results, especially community relations, are directly related to how involved our managers and associates are. We are more than what we sell. Our community engagement on a local level is what differentiates Sears.

Question: What is an example of a campaign?

Answer: We sponsor a cycling ride from Vancouver to Halifax every year. About 24 to 50 cyclists cross the country, raising funds for the fight against children's cancer. It is an area that receives much less funding than adult cancers. This event is called the Sears National Kids Cancer Ride. The riders stop in Sears stores along the way to meet with Canadians. On the first day, we hold an event where the cyclists dip their back wheel in the Pacific Ocean before departing. We invite local media to attend, as we do when they reach Halifax and dip their front wheels into the Atlantic. We also invite children from the local hospitals we visit coast to coast to come out and meet with the cyclists if they are well enough to do so.

the organization(s) funding the group. When journalists put spokespeople from the front groups into their stories, it appears that there is more debate within the scientific community on climate change than there actually is. In Chapter 2, we looked at one of these front groups, Friends of Science, which has been accused of being tied to the oil industry.

When confusion is created, paralysis sets in, since the public does not know what to do, or if they should do anything at all. The use of PR to create confusion has come under attack even by those within the PR industry, such as Jim Hoggan. On CBC's *Spin Cycles*, Jim Hoggan explains,

> I think climate change is a very serious problem, and when public relations people engage in an exercise in trying to slow down changes in public policy and the development of clean technology by business by confusing the public around the science around climate change, that it is a crime. And it is something that I think people in my industry that are doing this should take responsibility for. To have confusion, public confusion, as the objective of your communications campaign is fundamentally unethical.[23]

Greenwashing: It's Not Easy Being Green

Another issue facing environmental PR is **greenwashing**, whereby some companies, in their rush to jump on the green bandwagon, try to deceive customers into believing they are eco-friendly when they are not. PR practitioners need to be aware of this issue because they may face skepticism from target audiences when conducting a PR campaign.

As the environment has become an increasing concern for consumers, companies have clamoured to declare their "green" status. The term *greenwashing*, a play on *whitewashing*, was coined by a New York activist who criticized hotels that claimed to be eco-conscious by not washing their customers' towels every day when in fact they were motivated by saving money, not saving the planet.[24] It's no wonder that people have a hard time distinguishing between what is authentic and what is marketing when it comes to all things green. Even Earth Day, which you would think would be above reproach, was launched in 1970 with the help of a U.S. senator and an advertising executive. The ad man chose the name Earth Day because it sounded like "birthday" and he launched it on his on own birthday, April 22.[25]

In Canada, the environmental movement became mainstream in 1971, when Environment Canada was founded.[26] After this, consumer behaviour started to change based on new information on the environment, forcing companies to also adapt. For example, phosphates in laundry detergent and leaded gas were phased out.[27]

Canadian audiences care about the environment. A 2009 survey of over 5300 Canadians on their views on climate change revealed that 93 per cent of Canadians feel that climate change should be made a priority and 72 per cent believe that climate change is real.[28] The survey also found that 83 per cent believe that companies' sustainability claims are based less on results and more on the desire for good public relations. Given the importance Canadians put on the issue of climate change and the low faith they put in companies' environmental claims, PR practitioners could do more to convince their organizations to increase their environmental efforts in an authentic and measurable way.

Most companies still have a long way to go in their sustainability efforts. Yet, to read most corporations' media releases you would believe that they are all single-handedly saving the earth from pollution. Georg Kell, from the United Nations Global Compact, which promotes sustainability, says that of the 1000 organizations in the compact, only about 15 per cent are practising what they preach.[29] However, even though most of us want to do what's best for the planet, navigating the environmental implications of consumerism can be tricky.[30]

We all know that walking is better for the environment than driving, but not all decisions are as straightforward. Think of the questions consumers must ponder when deciding what is best for the environment. Is it better to buy corn-based biodegradable materials, or are the genetically modified organisms (GMOs) used to grow that corn worse for the environment than nonbiodegradable materials? Is local, nonorganic produce or imported, organic produce better for the environment?

Because of this confusion, PR practitioners and their organizations are sometimes able to deceive the public by declaring themselves green when they are not. This is completely unethical and has ramifications for both opportunistic organizations and the ones that are actually well intentioned. If the public is skeptical about the authenticity of green products, they might not be willing to pay a premium for sustainable products and practices because they assume that they are being lied to anyway. Furthermore, companies that claim to be environmentally friendly often come under heavy scrutiny as a result of the public's interest in the company's motives.[31] People want to support companies that are actually motivated by sustainability. Moreover, the better an organization's PR claims it to be, the more consumers will punish the company if it is proven to be a fraud. The higher the pedestal, the greater the fall. This is why PR practitioners must be careful when bragging about their green accomplishments. They should let their actions speak louder than their words when proclaiming their sustainability.[32]

Although PR practitioners must consider a variety of issues when working on campaigns in CSR, cause PR, and environmental PR, they can make a real difference. They can help their organizations become better corporate citizens as well as help get the word out and increase support for important environmental and social causes. As we have examined in earlier chapters, PR can be very powerful and, when practised ethically, can make a positive difference in the world.

Thinking Like a PR Practitioner

1. Explain the difficulties a PR practitioner might face in telling the environmental story and suggest potential solutions. Find an example of an organization that tells the environmen- tal story in a clear, compelling way. Describe what the organization does well.

2. Define *greenwashing* and explain its implications for environmental public relations.

HALTON REGION USES FEATHERED FRIENDS TO DELIVER A SUSTAINABILITY MESSAGE

In 2011, the Halton Region Health Department (HRHD) realized it had a problem. The HRHD is responsible for promoting and protecting health and preventing disease. However, the community's rapid growth was leading to lower air quality, which would continue to deteriorate as the region expanded. Halton, Ontario, includes the city of Burlington and the towns of Halton Hills, Milton, and Oakville. As a result of this worsening air

A Farewell to Featherwagons teaches children in Halton about air pollution.
Source: Regional Municipality of Halton

quality and the associated health risks, the HRHD decided to conduct an education and awareness campaign among the region's most vulnerable population: its children.

The Canadian Medical Association (CMA) found that in 2008 around 21,000 Canadians died from side effects of air pollution. To educate regional children about the hazards of poor air quality and how they could alter their behaviour to protect their environment, the HRHD opted to create a picture book that explained air pollution to children and their caregivers, as opposed to a more traditional education campaign.

The HRHD's illustrated storybook, A *Farewell to Featherwagons*, uses stories, activities, and tips to teach children how they can make a difference. Once Halton's PR team created and self-published the book, the next challenge was to publicize it to the target audiences.

The primary audience for this book is four- to eight-year-old children and their caregivers. Approximately 150,000 children live in Halton. The team decided that the best way to reach these children was through schools, libraries, and daycare centres. The secondary audiences included media, bloggers, and elected officials—all groups that could help raise awareness of the book.

A launch event for the book was organized at a local childcare centre to coincide with Clean Air Day. The team also developed posters, bookmarks, and stickers to distribute at community events.

In the HRHD's communication plan, the department outlined specific goals and targets. The goals of the campaign included generating 3 positive articles in the local press, increasing traffic to the webpage by 50 visits, generating 8 tweets, and distributing 2000 copies of the self-published book. Based on these evaluation criteria, the campaign was a resounding success. In addition to garnering both local and international coverage, 8 blog posts, and 15 tweets and retweets, visits to the website increased by 2000. Furthermore, 2500 copies of the storybook were distributed.

Questions

1. If Halton Region had wanted to obtain a sponsor to cover the costs of the book, what kind of organization would have been a good match?

2. This was a very local community PR campaign. If this book had been published by Environment Canada and was targeting children across the country, discuss how the PR campaign would have been different.

AUTHOR'S OWN EXPERIENCE

Giving Back

PR skills are highly valued and much in demand. If you are interested in contributing to your community or doing good works, you could not have picked a better career. Think of all those important causes that can use your help. Many nonprofits are small enterprises with a limited number of staff who have to do everything themselves. They often don't have the time, the knowledge, or the resources to do PR. That's where you can step in and help. You have so much to offer: writing skills, knowledge of using social media, special event management, and PR plans are in high demand. You can make a huge difference. You can actually help a group raise funds, attract volunteers, or get grants.

Over the course of my career I have regularly provided free services to groups that needed my assistance. While I have done paid work for them, I much prefer to offer my services pro bono when I can. Unless the nonprofit is large and well funded, these groups tend to be strapped for cash, and I found it stressful to think that I was drawing from their valuable budget.

One of the tactics that I often provided free of charge was a training session to teach nonprofit groups how to do their own ongoing PR and media relations. I also provided media training where I taught their spokespersons how to be media savvy. (See Chapter 8 for information on media training.) One year, I conducted a media-training session for the actors at the Vancouver Fringe Festival. What fun! Another time, it was for the directors of the Cinderella Project. And yet another training session was for the Kidney Foundation, attended by all their regional representatives. These were the people on the front lines, conducting media interviews in their communities. They left my session knowing how to garner attention for their cause and get their message across to kidney patients, the people who can most benefit from their services.

environmental PR

- pro
- anti
- greenwashing

- career
- society

contribution

CSR &
Cause PR

- Occupy Wall Street

socially conscious PR

- PR for nonprofits

partnerships
challenges
differences

role of PR

- matching cause to organization

Key Terms

cause PR PR efforts that are conducted for social, charitable, and environmental reasons.

corporate social responsibility (CSR) An organization's responsibility toward its community and the planet, and its overall corporate citizenship. CSR can include many elements, such as a company's waste management, the number of women and minorities on its board, measures taken to avoid or decrease pollution, and the organization's social and charitable contributions.

CSR report A document that is released on a consistent basis (quarterly, annually, etc.) that informs an organization's stakeholders of its CSR goals and its performance in meeting these goals.

front groups Activist groups that are formed to hide the identity of their main beneficiary.

greenwashing The attempt to make companies that are not environmentally friendly seem as though they are.

in-kind donation A donation of products or services instead of money.

nonprofit organizations (or not-for-profits) Organizations created for social or charitable reasons in which all revenues earned must be used by the organizations and not distributed as profits.

pro bono Work that is done for the public good without pay or compensation.

Weblinks

Apple's Supplier Responsibility Progress Report
www.apple.com/supplierresponsibility/reports.html

Coca-Cola Canada's Live Positively Campaign
www.livepositively.ca/who-cares/sogoParticipaction/index.jsp

David Suzuki Foundation
www.davidsuzuki.org/

Dove Campaign for Real Beauty Case Study
psucomm473.blogspot.ca/2007/03/dove-campaign-for-real-beauty-case.html

Environmental Communications Options
ecostrategy.ca

Greenpeace Canada Press Center
www.greenpeace.org/canada/en/Press-Center/

Hoggan Shared Values, Canadians and Sustainability Survey
hoggan.com/shared-values-canadians-sustainability-survey-general-public

Obakki Foundation
obakkifoundation.org

United Nations Environment Programme (UNEP)
www.unep.org

Endnotes

1. "Business Ethics FAQs," Canadian Centre for Ethics and Corporate Policy. Accessed February 21, 2013, http://www.ethicscentre.ca/EN/resources/faq.cfm

2. "Principles for Global Corporate Responsibility," Bench-marks.org. Accessed February 21, 2013, http://bench-marks.org/glossary.shtml

3. "Social Responsibility," International Organization for Standardization. Accessed February 21, 2013, http://isotc.iso.org/livelink/livelink/fetch/2000/2122/830949/3934883/3935096/home .html?nodeid=4451259&vernum=0/

4. "Strategic Collaborations," Ministry of Citizens' Services and Open Government, Government of British Columbia. Accessed February 21, 2013, http://www.cio.gov.bc.ca/cio/networkbc/ strategic_collaborations/index.page

5. C. Adams, "Paying More than Lip Service to 'Giving Back,'" *PR In Canada*, October 22, 2008. Accessed February 21, 2013, http://www.princanada.com/paying-more-than-lip-service-to-giving-back

6. Stephen J. Dubner, "Is Good Corporate Citizenship Also Good for the Bottom Line?" Freakonomics Radio, April 18, 2012. Accessed February 21, 2013, http://www.freakonomics .com/2012/04/19/is-good-corporate-citizenship-also-good-for-the-bottom-line/

7. J.D. Costa, "The Upside of Ethics," *Marketing*, October 2, 2006. Accessed February 21, 2013, http://www.marketingmag.ca/news/marketer-news/the-upside-of-ethics-19935

8. Adams, "Paying More than Lip Service to 'Giving Back.'"

9. Tonya Frizzell, interview with the author.

10. Ronald N. Levy, "Sponsorship: What's In It for You?" *Public Relations Quarterly*, September 22, 2004. Accessed February 21, 2013, http://web.ebscohost.com.proxy.lib.sfu.ca/bsi/detail?vid=5&sid=77732158-5638-4fa3-99e6-192537882a70%40sessionmgr10&hid=20&bdata=JnNpdGU9YnNpLWxpdmUmc2NvcGU9c2l0ZQ%3d%3d#db=bth&AN=15783302

11. Ibid.

12. Melinda Broadbeck and Erin Evans, "Dove Campaign for Real Beauty Case Study," Public Relations Problems and Cases blog, March 5, 2007. Accessed February 21, 2013, http://psucomm473.blogspot.ca/2007/03/dove-campaign-for-real-beauty-case.html

13. Ibid.

14. "Live Positively," Coca-Cola. Accessed February 21, 2013, http://www.livepositively.ca/who-cares/sogoParticipaction/index.jsp

15. Ed Cafasso, "Power to the People: Lessons from Occupy Wall Street," *The Public Relations Strategist*, January 10, 2012. Accessed February 21, 2013, http://www.prsa.org/Intelligence/TheStrategist/Articles/view/9549/1042/Power_to_the_People_Lessons_from_Occupy_Wall_Stree

16. Ronn Torossian, "Why Did Occupy Wall Street Protestors Occupy So Much Media Attention? They Understand PR...," *Digital Journal*, April 13, 2012. Accessed February 21, 2013, http://digitaljournal.com/blog/16161

17. Terry O'Reilly, "Green Marketing," *The Age of Persuasion*, CBC Radio, April 17, 2011. Accessed February 21, 2013, http://www.cbc.ca/ageofpersuasion/episode/season-5/2011/01/08/its-not-easy-being-green-green-marketing/

18. "Satwant Kaur," United Nations Careers. Accessed February 21, 2013, https://careers.un.org/lbw/home.aspx?viewtype=VP&PID=353

19. Satwant Kaur, interview with the author.

20. Jungmi Jun, "How Climate Change Organizations Utilize Websites for Public Relations," *Public Relations Review*, vol. 37, no. 3 (September 2011), 245–249.

21. Ibid.

22. Edward Wachtman, "Discovering the Sustainability Story: Fall–Winter 2005–2006," Hoggan and Associates, Communicating Sustainability, 2006. Accessed February 21, 2013, http://www.hoggan.com/sites/default/files/Hoggan%20SUSTAINABILITY%20Storytelling%202006%20(1).pdf

23. Ira Basen, "Spin Cycles: Spinning in the 21st Century: Episode 6," CBC News, February 23, 2007. Accessed February 21, 2013, http://www.cbc.ca/news/background/spincycles/index-episode6.html

24. O'Reilly, "Green Marketing."

25. Ibid.

26. Ibid.

27. "Shared Values, Canadians and Sustainability: Survey of the General Public," Hoggan and Associates, April 2009. Accessed February 21, 2013, http://hoggan.com/shared-values-canadians-sustainability-survey-general-public

28. Ibid.

29. Dubner, "Is Good Corporate Citizenship Also Good for the Bottom Line?"

30. O'Reilly, "Green Marketing."

31. Ibid.

32. Ibid.

Time Matters

Tick-tock. PR is all about time. In agencies, we sell our time to clients in 15-minute increments. (Ah, the pleasure of time sheets!) Every project has a timeline with a start date and an end date. We know when a project is due. Deadlines are a daily, and in crunch time, an hourly affair.

We are assessed and judged by our ability to meet deadlines and to show up on time for meetings or at the start of the day. Our ability to manage campaigns—on time—brings us success, promotions, and accolades. So being on time makes good career sense.

Think of the messages you are sending when you are late: "I don't care enough to be on time," "This is not important," "So what if you are here waiting for me? My time is more precious than yours."

If your manager or boss cannot trust you to show up on time, how is he or she going to trust you to do good work? Being punctual builds trust. It shows that you respect your commitments and that you value your time and the other person's. Punctuality demonstrates integrity and shows that you are a person who follows through on your commitments.

There are times when extraordinary circumstances may get in the way of your being punctual. You are probably going to miss some deadlines. That is life. But when that happens, let your client or manager know beforehand. Maybe someone can help you finish on time, or maybe your deadline can be extended. Don't miss it without giving the key stakeholders a heads-up. And if you are going to be late to a meeting, call. It is always appreciated.

Chapter 4
The Public Relations Plan

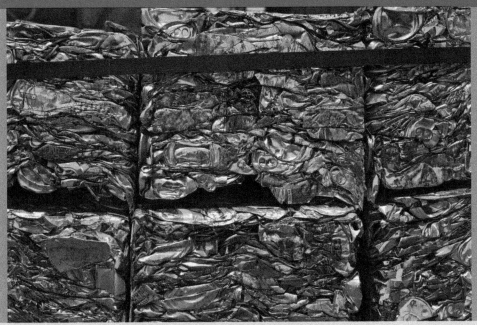

The Alberta Beverage Container Recycling Corporation launched the Don't Be a Tosser campaign to reduce the number of bottles and cans in landfills. Source: Huguette Roe/Shutterstock

LEARNING OBJECTIVES

1. Explain the role that the PR plan plays.

2. Summarize research methodologies and explain how gathered information applies to PR.

3. Understand how to analyze a PR problem and devise a PR plan to address it.

4. Explain the breakdown of a PR budget.

5. Understand how to generate creative ideas to enhance PR plans.

The PR Plan: Don't Be a Tosser

In 2008, Albertans threw over 340 million bottles, cans, and juice boxes into the trash, which ended up in provincial landfills. This discovery was disappointing, since research indicated that Albertans were getting the message about the need to recycle their empties. When surveyed, Albertans disclosed that they knew that recycling containers was the right thing to do, but their behaviour demonstrated the exact opposite. The Alberta Beverage Container Recycling Corporation (ABCRC) decided that action needed to be taken and hired the communications agency Trigger to help solve the problem. Trigger's challenge was to create a public relations plan and campaign that would motivate consumers to recycle more beverage containers and increase the recycling rate from 70.4 per cent to 75 per cent in 2009.

ABCRC's own research identified the prime non-recycling offenders as males aged 18 to 25. They became the target audience of the campaign. The objective was to persuade the public—especially the target males—that it was socially unacceptable to throw empties into the trash. In getting the message across to this group, Trigger knew that any preaching would fall on deaf ears and that peer pressure would be far more effective. As a key message, Trigger developed the rallying cry "Don't Be a Tosser," a phrase with humorous language that the target audience could embrace as its own and that emphasized personal responsibility.

Trigger worked with ABCRC, which involved stakeholders such as the Alberta Bottle Depot Association, the Alberta Beverage Container Management Board, and the Alberta Soft Drink Council, to develop a creative campaign that would challenge the status quo with regards to recycling empties.

A central tactic that was planned and implemented was a website to create awareness and empower young people to call out friends who tossed empties into the garbage (dontbeatosser.com). On the homepage, an estimated tally of empties sent to Alberta's landfills since the website launched ran continuously. The social networking feature of this website comprised a Tosser Gallery, where people could post photos of and make comments about non-recyclers.

To get people to visit the website, street teams went out to photograph non-recyclers caught in the act and—with their permission—posted their photos on the site. They handed participants cards with the dontbeatosser.com URL and encouraged them to visit the site and tell their friends about it. The campaign also used marketing communications tactics, including advertising on television, on the radio, and in newspapers, in addition to digital display ads on male-targeted websites, such as sports sites.

Two nontraditional contests were held to generate content for the website. The first was a back-to-school contest open to postsecondary students. The theme was "turn your mountain of empties into a mountain getaway." The student who returned the most recyclable containers would win a weekend ski trip for 21. The contest was facilitated online, where students could enter their totals. Trigger set up booths at ten university and college campuses across Alberta during frosh weeks to promote the contest.

The second contest corresponded with the 2009 Grey Cup Festival in Calgary—an event attended by 150,000 people, many of whom fit the target demographic. The PR team tapped into the spirit of the Canadian Football League (CFL) tradition by hosting a "Show Us Your Best End-Zone Dance" contest. They set up two booths at the four-day Grey Cup Festival, with each booth simulating an end zone with a recycling bin in the middle. Participants pretended they were CFL stars who had just scored a touchdown and showed-off their best end-zone celebratory dance, spiking an empty beverage container into a recycling bin instead of a football.

Each dance was recorded and instantaneously uploaded to dontbeatosser.com. Friends and family were encouraged to vote for the best dancers, and the top ten became finalists for the prize—a 46-inch flat-screen TV. Calgary Stampeder Jeremaine Copeland chose the final winner. The contest was promoted through posters and postcards encouraging festival-goers to vote online, and by street teams handing out Don't Be a Tosser toques, hundreds of which were worn to the game.

Media relations was also conducted, with creative media information kits sent to local news outlets. The media kits included a branded recycled, reusable grocery bag, along with a branded T-shirt, toque, bottled water, and black and yellow jellybeans.

In the end, the campaign exceeded its objectives. Recycling rates jumped 11.7 per cent to 82.1 per cent, and visits to the website were up by 92 per cent. Post-campaign research also indicated that 88 per cent of individuals agreed that the program had encouraged them to recycle their empties. The campaign was considered such a success that it continued into the following year.

This opening vignette demonstrates the strength of a campaign that is strategically planned and based on solid research. The prime target audience was identified as males 18 to 25, the group least likely to recycle and therefore the demographic most in need of targeting. The rest of the campaign was carefully planned and tailored to this target audience. The key message, "Don't Be a Tosser," was crafted to be appealing to the young male demographic, as were the tactics, such as the digital ads on sports websites. It was the careful planning of this campaign that enabled it to be so successful.

In this chapter we will outline the key components of effective PR planning and emphasize that PR planning must be based on solid information that is gathered through research. We will detail how plans are broken down into several components of strategic information and learn how creativity can bring added value to a PR plan and strengthen the overall campaign.

PR Plans Defined ❶

When creating any PR campaign, whether a Don't Be a Tosser campaign or a product launch, it is imperative to start with a solid plan. No matter the industry or the type of PR, the plan is always the first step.

"Now give us your spontaneous response."

Source: Cartoonresource/Shutterstock

A **public relations plan** is a written document that outlines all the strategies and tactics that will be implemented over a defined period of time. It also provides the rationale for the proposed actions. In other words, a PR plan outlines what you want to achieve and the steps you will take to get there. As one practitioner puts it, the plan is like a road map showing the direction to success. It also outlines the markers along the path that will help you know that you are headed in the right direction. As Lewis Carroll wrote, "If you don't know where you're going, any road will do." In public relations, it is important to know the objectives you are reaching toward and the path that will get you there.

Think about it this way: if you do not have a clearly identified direction before you start any initiative, how will you be able to judge when you have achieved success or whether you have achieved it at all? It is only by establishing what your objectives are at the beginning that you will be able to measure the effectiveness of your public relations work at the end. The public relations plan also enables you to prove to managers or clients that you have been successful in the tasks assigned to you and demonstrate that the results achieved match the objectives stated at the beginning of a campaign. In this way, the PR plan serves as a contract between you and your client or superiors. If they sign off on the plan, everyone is aligned on exactly what will be delivered. Their sign-off ensures there are no surprises.

In the planning process, practitioners brainstorm and develop strategic solutions to the PR problems or challenges that their organizations face. A PR plan enables integrated, well-thought-out, strategic action. Without a plan, actions are ad hoc, without any clear direction, and reactive instead of proactive. A plan keeps you organized and lets you know what the next step is. It is the backbone of the entire public relations program.

The scope of a plan can be broad or narrow. Some plans outline an entire year, or even two or three, and encompass all the initiatives that will be conducted during that time. Other plans are limited in scope and are drafted to come up with solutions to a specific challenge that has suddenly arisen, such as an issue or a crisis. The time frame might be as limited as a couple of weeks.

RESEARCH ❷

A well-crafted PR plan must be based on information and data that are relevant and accurate. This data must be based on solid research. Research can be likened to doing your homework. Before writing a school essay, you must conduct background research in order to support your hypothesis. Likewise, a PR practitioner must have research-backed knowledge to make the right decisions. Through research, you identify your target audiences and gain insight into what is important to them. Research can also identify the environmental factors that might affect your campaign. The opening vignette on the Don't Be a Tosser campaign illustrates a campaign with a solid footing in research. Research was conducted to identify the primary target audience as males between the ages of 18 and 25 and to outline their interests and preferred ways to be communicated to. All public relations plans must begin with the same level of diligence.

In his book *Primer of Public Relations Research*, Don Stacks explains the importance of PR research:

> Without research, practitioners are left to "fly by the seats of their pants"; that is, they are reduced to taking, at best, educated guesses regarding the problem and potential intervention programs, and thus run a greater risk of being unable to predict outcomes accurately. Without research the practitioner cannot assess where a public relations program begins, how it evolves, or what the end product will be.[1]

What is research exactly? At its core, research is the process of asking questions and finding the answers to those questions. In the example of the Don't Be a Tosser campaign, some of the questions that research helped to answer included: What are the recycling rates before and after the campaign? Who recycles the most and who recycles the least? Where is recycling done? What prevents some people from recycling? The answers to these questions influenced the PR team's strategy and the plan for the campaign.

The research that must be conducted prior to drafting a PR plan will differ depending on the objectives. The types of questions that PR practitioners need to research are varied and might include the following:

What do our employees think of our newsletter?
What is the reputation of our organization in the community?
Would this type of special event be of interest to our investors?
What do journalists think of this issue?
What are our competitors doing in their PR programs?
What kind of media coverage has appeared about this topic in the past?

How many people voted for a political candidate in the latest election?
Are consumers aware of all the products and services that we offer?
Who is an expert on this topic that I can quote in a media release?

Though you may already have an inkling as to the answers to these questions, only through research will you obtain a true understanding. Sometimes our gut feelings are confirmed, but other times the research results prove us wrong. Either way, we need to have the supporting data in order to make a case to our client or our superiors to support our plan.

You may be wondering, "How do I get the data I need?" In some instances, PR practitioners conduct the research themselves or hire a professional research firm to do it on their behalf. That could include a survey or an environmental scan. (See the section on methodologies below.) When research is conducted from scratch like this, it is called **primary research**.

The advantage to using professional research firms is that they have quick access to large numbers of people for questionnaires and focus groups, as well as the expertise to generate reliable research results. Using a professional research firm also allows you to ask the exact questions you would like to ask. The disadvantage to using one is that it can be very costly. Professional research can cost tens of thousands of dollars. The project budget will determine if this route is an option.

In other instances, the PR practitioner might use the results of other people's research. This is called **secondary research**. In secondary research, PR practitioners use research or sources that are already available to conduct their research. This might include research published in books or magazines or other companies' survey results. Secondary research is often inexpensive, but it might not be directly applicable to your specific problem. You might have to use it as a reference and infer its application to your situation or audience. For example, if you were doing a campaign for restaurants in Whitehorse, you might not be able to find specific secondary source statistics on restaurant patronage in Whitehorse, but you may be able to infer that they are similar to the general statistics for Canadian restaurant patronage.

METHODOLOGIES

In order to answer the determined questions, research employs structured research methods, or **methodologies**. Methodology refers to the way in which the research is conducted and how the data are collected. There are several research methods, and selecting the best one is part of the decision-making process. Some methods are better suited for surveying large numbers of people, and others are better for getting more specific details from a smaller group. Some methods tell you a little information about a lot of people, while others give you a lot more information and insight about fewer people. Another factor in deciding which research method to pursue is the available budget. The methods most frequently used in public relations are explored in the following sections. Figure 4.1 lists all the methodologies we will explore, both primary and secondary.

Primary research	Secondary research
Surveys	News articles
Questionnaires	Research reports
Interviews	Statistics Canada publications
Focus groups	Websites
Communication audits	Other companies' research
Environmental scan	
Media content analysis	
Informal sounding	
Competitor analysis	

Figure 4.1   Methodologies Used by PR Practitioners

PRACTITIONER INTERVIEW

John Willis: Research and Planning at Strategic Communications

John Willis is director of campaigns and research at Strategic Communications. He has worked on campaigns for UNICEF, Greenpeace International, and Oxfam. His areas of expertise include public affairs and public opinion research.

Question: What advice can you give us for conducting research?

Answer: The real key factor is that you set up research methods to gain insight from beyond your usual suspects. Key informants in your own organization or the clients are very important as a starting point, but leaving it at that is a recipe for failure. True knowledge comes at the limit of what you already know. Innovation is usually something that arises from external pressures— so bring them on.

For a public relations person who has done their planning well, it will be starkly obvious who the nonusual suspects are. They are key audiences without whom you cannot reach your objectives and who typically are not part of your daily dialogue. Often it is only the PR

practitioner who speaks with and listens to those stakeholders. Be proud and confident that this is your job.

Question: How important is research to the planning process?

Answer: It is very, very important. Planners must defeat their own assumptions in order to be free to do what is required to achieve the objectives. Research is that step. But it can be costly and time-consuming. But I should also say that many research tools are getting cheaper these days, so don't lose heart—online testing can be very powerful and very fast.

If you do not have the budget or the time, one way to deal with this problem is to mock up the research. In other words, do your best to assemble whatever you think you know in an objective description of the context and the landscape on which you are going to operate. What do your audiences want and where can they be found? What messages are most likely to cut through, and why?

(Continued)

John Willis: Research and Planning at Strategic Communications

This will at least give you a good handle on whether you are being careful or foolish in your assumptions. When you do this type of mock-up, consider a range of sources of data—social media, news media, existing (past) market or opinion research, and your own interviews with key informants.

As a communicator, your job is to understand the existing narratives and how they relate to the behaviour of key actors and stakeholders—knowledge and insight do not arise from one single specialized source.

Question: How can research help us determine which tactics will work with which key audiences?

Answer: It is best to do actual research with that audience. You determine tactics by the role and strategic value of audiences, not the other way around. Do not let tactics lead the plan regardless of whether the organization really wants to run "breakthrough" ads or launch a cool website with a wicked widget. Don't get suckered into letting the tactic determine the strategy. For every objective there is an audience, for every audience a channel, for every channel a tactic or suite of tactics. Keep it straight.

Also, very important these days: think interaction, engagement, dialogue—open up and listen to audiences in order to encourage them to open up and listen to you. Do not hammer them with so-called clever ads and messages that you think are cool, funny, flip, and transgressive unless you have very good solid research showing that this is what they respond to. Most people are sick to death of being marketed to, but they will never tire of being treated with respect and listened to. And it makes for better outcomes.

Question: Do you have any advice on other aspects of the planning process?

Answer: Get clear on your objectives and make sure they relate in a coherent way to the goals of the program/client/campaign for which your communication plan is an element. Work over the statement of objectives until it is a SMART list of bullets (specific, measurable, achievable, realistic, time-limited).

The second step is to have a strategic definition of audiences or people who need to be engaged. Strategic in this context means that any group or person who is going to be reached by the communications strategy has a role in achieving the program's goals and your objectives. This needs to be written down, with an indication of what their specific role is (are they learning something? are they taking action? making a decision? talking to others and passing on a message?).

Surveys

Surveys are a data collection method where individuals are asked questions. These individuals are meant to represent a larger section or be a representative sample of the population. Surveys determine opinions, attitudes, satisfaction levels, and impressions of a general public. Research for the Don't Be a Tosser campaign was conducted with a survey in which Albertans were asked about their recycling habits. The research identified that the group least likely to recycle was males 18 to 25 years old, so the campaign targeted this group.

In another example of how surveys are employed, an internal communications practitioner might survey employees to see how they like to receive company information.

Political polls are a leading type of survey. Surveys can be administered in written format, verbally in person or by telephone, or online. Surveys work best for easy-to-answer, clear, straightforward questions. Surveys are not the method to use for exploratory research or to understand nuanced positions.

When writing surveys, practitioners need to be very careful in how they pose the questions. Survey results can be affected by leading or biased questions. Asking leading questions such as "Do you love movies?" or "Do you hate movies?" could generate very different responses than "How do you feel about movies?" Also, anonymity will encourage respondents to give their honest opinions. Social pressure is powerful. If people think they are going to look bad, they might answer in a way that reflects positively on themselves. For example, in a questionnaire about the environment, like the one used in the Don't Be a Tosser campaign, many people wouldn't want to admit to a surveyor or a group that they don't recycle. However, if they are able to answer questions in a way that's completely anonymous, such as through an online survey, they might be inclined to answer honestly.

There are many free online survey sites that can help PR practitioners conduct quick and easy surveys. An example of such a service is SurveyMonkey. These services work best if you know all the email addresses for the audience you want to survey. For example, if you are a volunteer at an association and would like to conduct a quick, inexpensive survey of what members think of the educational events, a free online survey can do the trick.

Research results of surveys can be used in different ways. In addition to enabling practitioners to make strategic decisions, they can also be used to generate media coverage. As we examined in Chapter 2, the Hain Celestial Group PR team conducted an online survey on the snacking habits of Canadians. The research provided interesting angles to highlight in a media release, as part of a larger media relations campaign.

When to use surveys: When you want to collect directional data from a large number of people but do not need to get into the specifics. Surveys are better for broad, easy-to-answer questions. Surveys are the tools that will tell you how many people think a certain way or to identify a demographic that might need more convincing on a certain subject.

Questionnaires

The term **questionnaire** is often used synonymously with the term *survey* but can also refer to one type of survey consisting of a series of paper-format written questions that are used to gather information.

When to use questionnaires: When the information you seek is easily understandable with fairly short, written answers and can be collected in paper format.

Interviews

An **interview** is a research method where verbal questions are asked and information is obtained from an individual on a one-on-one basis. Interviews are conducted in person or by telephone. They are more casual than surveys and questionnaires, and they enable the interviewer to be flexible with questions and to get more in-depth information on certain topics. For example, exit interviews, which are conducted when employees leave an organization to find out why they are leaving and their candid thoughts on the organization, are a type of interview.

When to use interviews: When you need to gather information from fewer individuals but want to get into more detail and when you want to speak to each individual personally. Interviews can be especially useful for internal communications.

Focus Groups

A **focus group** is a group of individuals who are brought together and, as in an interview, are asked about their opinions and beliefs regarding certain topics or products. The conversation is led by a moderator who poses a series of questions. The conversation is captured on video. Focus groups are generally held on the premises of firms that specialize in conducting them. They take place in specially designed rooms with one-way mirrors, so that PR practitioners can watch the participants without being seen. A political party might use a focus group to find out what voters think about its party messaging. Yves Veggie Cuisine's media relations campaign, which was explored in Chapter 1, used research results derived from focus groups. Several insights were obtained about what mainstream consumers wanted in meat alternatives from focus groups in which individuals tasted new soy-based foods and discussed their opinions about them.

An advantage of the focus group is that the moderator interacts with the participants and the participants interact with one another, eliciting valuable input that would not come out in an interview. Another advantage is that PR practitioners can see nonverbal responses, such as smiles or frowns, which provide a great source of information.[2]

When to use focus groups: When you want to get into more detail about a certain topic or to see people's reactions to it. Focus groups are good when you want to explore ambiguous topics that would be hard to get people's perspective on from a survey or when you want to get both verbal and nonverbal reactions to a creative product, such as a television ad or a poster.

Communications Audits

A **communications audit** is a research method that is employed to evaluate the effectiveness of the public relations program within an organization. It assesses how well an organization carries out its PR practices, what works, and what does not. It also determines what steps are needed to make improvements. Generally, a communications audit involves having stakeholders review all the communications pieces put out by an organization for a set period of time, including newsletters, business cards, the website, and so on. When looked at as a whole, trends or patterns may be spotted that are missed when each piece is seen in isolation. For instance, a leading Canadian bank carried out a communications audit to determine what employees thought of its newsletter and identified what adjustments needed to be made to make the newsletter more popular.

Communications audits also enable practitioners to identify any brewing issues: "Traditionally, a ship's captain was always the last person to find out that his crew intended to mutiny. Communication audits identify the symptoms of discontent, before either customers or employees storm the bridge. They are an organization's early warning system."[3]

When to use communications audits: When you want to determine the success of a program, know what target audiences are thinking, or discover any communications problems. Communications audits also help communicators evaluate whether the various communications tactics are consistent and on message.

Environmental Scan

An **environmental scan** is a research tool that looks at everything that has been written or said about a particular topic to gauge public perception, including news articles, blogs, online comments, and tweets. It can be conducted on its own or as part of a communications audit.

ADVICE TO NEW PRACTITIONERS

Communications Audits

Katita Stark is a leading PR practitioner who has expertise in communications audits. She has conducted them for a whole range of organizations, including both corporations and nonprofits. She has this advice to provide on communications audits:

Question: What are the reasons to have a communications audit?

Answer: There are various reasons you may want to conduct an audit. The most important reason is that the process provides one with specific outcomes for the strategic direction in the development of a communications plan. Often what triggers a call for an audit is a merger/acquisition, new management, change in an organization from government to private or private to public, crises or issues, staff morale, or anything that bespeaks change. In addition, the audit is an excellent management tool that provides measurable benchmarks for communications programs, provides "due diligence" evidence for continuing or introducing programs, and often, valuable data for recommendations for all areas of an organization.

Question: How do you start a communications audit?

Answer: We start with a strategic planning session with senior management to determine the goals, scope, target audiences, issues, schedule, and development of an "audit task force." This task force is chosen from a variety of job levels and functions, and it is this internal representation that we report to during the process and with whom we plan the details of the process. The outcomes provide us with further direction on the development of the questions, whether it's for an internal or combined internal and external communications audit. We create questions that are the same for all audiences, then adapt a few extra for that specific audience—for example, for media versus board of directors. Then we begin the process by interviewing key senior executives to identify what they consider the communications challenges and target audiences. From that information, we can refine what we question the employees and the external audiences.

Question: How do you conduct the interviews?

Answer: People who are interviewed are told up front that they were chosen at random, that we have been given more names than we interview so no one knows whom we interview, and that the interviews are confidential. If further reassurance is needed we tell them that this is a communications review (*review* can be less threatening than the word *audit*), not a job review, and no names or job functions are attributed to any comments. And, especially for internal interviews, we ask for double the numbers we need to ensure random choice and anonymity. Certainly the variety of interview techniques used varies from focus groups to online questionnaires, but we prefer to concentrate on the one-on-one interviews with open-ended questions as that is often where the "meat" of the information is gathered with many suggestions volunteered on "righting the wrong." In addition, there is an extensive review of communications tools and tactics to assess what is working and what isn't or what needs to be adapted or introduced.

Question: What can be discovered with the interviews?

Answer: Once the interviews are clustered, tabulated, and summarized, you find that there are several key trends and recommendations that will form the strategic direction for the formulation of a communications plan. At this point, the audit probably confirms some of the communications problems that you have informally discovered, but there are often surprises as to what is considered most important. There may also be an "aha" moment in an interview or interviews that suggests something that you hadn't thought of or didn't deem important. Whatever the results, it is important to have noted at the beginning of the audit, with a letter about the process from the CEO, that you will communicate in summary the audit results to your audiences and then tell them what you're going to do about them.

When to use environmental scans: When you want to get a sense of what all the different audiences, from journalists to consumers, are thinking or saying about your organization. This can help a PR practitioner decide what to communicate or identify brewing issues that might require action.

Media Content Analysis

Media content analysis is a type of research that involves studying media coverage of an organization or a topic in traditional media, such as newspaper articles or television news segments, as well as social media. Both the quality and quantity of the media coverage are analyzed. The analysis may include looking at how the organization is positioned within the media story and the inclusion and prominence of specific key messages.

When to use media content analysis: When you want to know how your story is playing out in the media, what messages are getting through, and which journalists are advocates and which are critics.

Informal Sounding

An **informal sounding** is a casual conversation held with members of the target audience to get their perspective. An informal sounding is a type of interview. Informal soundings can also be held with journalists to find out if a certain topic is considered newsworthy.

A good example of an informal sounding is the one Vancouver Coastal Health used when it wanted to organize a special event to thank its volunteers. Not sure of the type of activities the volunteers would prefer, the majority of whom were retirees between the ages of 65 and 85, the organization conducted an informal sounding by contacting several individuals to ask their preference. The process uncovered unexpected intelligence. The organization learned that the senior volunteers enjoyed activities during the day, not in the evenings, in addition to preferring to go out at their own convenience instead of on a set date. Based on this information, the volunteers were offered a selection of special events to thank them. The events they could choose from included an afternoon tea with an orchestra and a dance at a top local hotel, or two tickets to visit a botanical garden at a time of their choosing.

When to use informal sounding: When you need quick, informal, and inexpensive information to help you to proceed. It will either confirm what you know or provide you with fresh insight.

Competitor Analysis

A **competitor analysis** is a type of research that identifies competitors and investigates their strengths and weaknesses. This enables organizations to determine how they can differentiate themselves and identify opportunities and threats. A competitor analysis involves looking at how the other organizations position themselves by examining their websites; their social media initiatives, including Facebook, Twitter, Pinterest, and blogs; their media information materials; and any media coverage they have received. It can also include visiting stores to look at their products and testing them. In one example, as part of a competitor analysis for the launch of a new soymilk, the PR team attended a food trade show to learn about all the other soymilks on the market and to taste them.

Sometimes organizations order a media clipping service that clips their competitors' coverage in addition to their own. This provides insight on competitor campaigns, messaging, and volume and tone of coverage.

When to use competitor analysis: When you need to find out about the market and about the competition. Competitor analysis provides insight into the competition's positioning, campaigns, and media activities and allows you to ensure that you differentiate your organization from the others.

Secondary Research

Not all research needs to be conducted from scratch. A PR practitioner can legitimately use other people's research findings. As discussed above, this is called secondary research. Secondary research sources can include libraries, journals, articles, government agencies such as Statistics Canada, and various Internet sources. It is obviously much quicker and less expensive to uncover previously conducted research. The key here is to ensure that it is obtained from a legitimate and trustworthy source. You will be basing many of your decisions on this research, or in some cases, presenting this information to your target audiences; therefore, it needs to be dependable.

When to use secondary research: When it is available and reliable and can be easily applied to your organization and challenge. You may choose to use secondary sources when you do not have the budget or the time to conduct your own research. Secondary research is useful when you are looking for information on industry trends or need quotes for media materials.

PR Plan Components ❸

Once research has been conducted, the next step is to put on your strategic thinking cap and draft the public relations plan. Drafting the plan is an important step in any campaign and should not be rushed or skipped. As noted above, the PR plan is like a map that provides directions for getting to your objectives. The PR plan lays out how to get to a desired end result. It also can be used to ensure that everyone is aligned in terms of the process, messaging, and budget prior to implementation. As the Don't Be a Tosser campaign illustrates, the PR plan is essential to creating a successful campaign. A lot of work went into the planning of this campaign before any action was taken. It is tempting, especially when the timelines are tight, to jump right into a campaign, but taking the time to plan all the steps well is always necessary. Writing the plan allows you to be strategic and outline what needs to be done throughout the campaign.

A comprehensive plan includes ten strategic components, which we will examine in this section:

1. Situation analysis
2. Research summary
3. Objectives
4. Target audiences
5. Key messages
6. Strategies
7. Tactics

8. Timeline
9. Budget
10. Evaluation and measurement

1. SITUATION ANALYSIS

Before you proceed in any direction, it is important to know exactly where you are. A **situation analysis** is the first component of a PR plan. It is the introduction and sets the tone for the entire plan, putting it in perspective. It provides information on the operating environment, where the organization stands, and its strengths and weaknesses. In addition, it outlines the challenges or opportunities and explains how public relations will address them. A situation analysis might explain the perceived communications problem and then describe the actual problem, which might be different.[4] Sometimes, through your research, you will find that the issue is different from what it was assumed to be. The situation analysis may also provide information on the market, industry, and competition. In the Don't Be a Tosser campaign, the situation analysis would have described the recycling situation in Alberta and the needs that the ABCRC had.

2. RESEARCH SUMMARY

This section includes a summary of the information that was gathered during the research phase, which we discussed earlier in this chapter. It highlights the main findings and conclusions, using the research findings to provide the rationale for the decisions that are outlined in the plan. Solid research was conducted prior to the start of the Don't Be a Tosser campaign. The key research results, those of most concern to the PR campaign, would have been highlighted in the PR plan.

3. OBJECTIVES

As we noted in Chapter 1, PR objectives are the specific goals that your organization wants to achieve with its campaign. These objectives must be specific enough so that you are able to determine at the end of the campaign whether you have met them or made some progress toward achieving them. For that to happen, the objectives must be attainable within a specific amount of time. (See Chapter 1 for more information on objectives.)

Objectives should follow the SMART principle.[5] The SMART principle is a model for ensuring that your objectives are meaningful. SMART stands for specific, measurable, achievable, relevant, and time-bound.[6] Let's look at each letter in more detail:

Specific: The objective should be clear and unambiguous.

Measurable: The objective should be able to be measured objectively at the end of the campaign. Everyone should agree what success will look like.

Raising donations	Improving the corporate image
Influencing new legislation or public policy	Increasing visits to the website
Attracting new volunteers	Recruiting employees
Educating the public on a certain issue	Raising awareness of a new product

Figure 4.2 Examples of Objectives

Achievable: There's no point in having an objective that can never be attained with the campaign's resources. While the objective can stretch the team's skills, they should be confident that they will be able to attain the goal.

Relevant: The objective needs to be relevant to the organization and its situation.

Time-bound: There should be a clear deadline for when the objective will be achieved.[7]

An example of an objective that follows the SMART principle is, "Our company will increase the number of bloggers who follow us on Twitter to 20 by December 2."

The main objective of the Don't Be a Tosser campaign was to increase the percentage of containers that were recycled during the year. For the launch of Linacare, a skincare line, (see below), the objectives included raising awareness of the new line, generating media coverage, and encouraging spas and boutiques to carry the products. Figure 4.2 provides examples of objectives.

4. TARGET AUDIENCES

The target audiences section is the fourth component of a PR plan. This section outlines the groups and individuals that you are trying to reach with your campaign. You must identify the main groups that are important to your organization and with whom you want to communicate. That includes both internal audiences, such as employees or board members, and external audiences, such as customers, stockholders, and community members. In the case of the Don't Be a Tosser campaign, the main target audience was males from the ages of 18 to 25. The decision to target this group was made based on the research results that indicated that they were the group least likely to recycle.

In order to successfully communicate with the audiences, a PR practitioner must know them well—or as well as possible given resource and time constraints. Some organizations that have deep pockets conduct substantial research into their target audiences and understand a lot about them. They know, for instance, how much money they make, how many times a year they buy a product, where they went to school, how many children they have, what kinds of cars they drive, the television programs they watch, and their musical preferences.

Target audiences can be broken down into general groups, such as consumers, Canadian voters, or mothers. They can also be very specific, such as mothers working full time in Ottawa with children in daycare. Again, the more specific you can be, the easier

Customers	Local community
Government agencies	Stockholders
Employees	Board of directors
Healthcare providers	Investment community
Competition	Analysts
Business associates	Labour unions
Investors	Regulatory authorities
Media	Suppliers

Figure 4.3 Examples of Target Audiences for a Corporation

it is to make decisions regarding the messaging for that audience and the tactics that will have the highest chance of success. Figure 4.3 provides examples of audiences that a corporation could target, while Figure 4.4 provides this information for a nonprofit organization.

Linacare is a Canadian skincare line that is sold exclusively in spas and in specialized boutiques. The cream was originally developed by a physician for his patients with kidney disease, a condition that makes the skin extremely dry, chapped, and itchy. The moisturizer is therefore very hydrating, works well on aging skin, and is helpful for skin conditions like eczema. When Linacare was launched across Canada, its four target audiences were

1. Women who buy expensive face creams
2. Women or members of their family who have extremely dry skin or eczema
3. Journalists at lifestyle and fashion publications
4. Managers and owners of spas

5. KEY MESSAGES

The next component of a plan is to establish key messages. This means deciding what you want to say to each target audience. The messaging may be the same or it may be different for each target audience; what is important to one group may not be important to another.

Clients - the people who use the services	Other non-profits that might lend support
Community members	Donors
Neighbours	Contributors of in-kind services
Public officials	Media
Government agencies	Employees
Volunteers	Suppliers

Figure 4.4 Examples of Target Audiences for a Nonprofit Organization

A key message is simply the information about your organization that is most likely to appeal to the target audience and that will encourage them to take action as outlined in your objectives. Key messages must be clear. You want to leave your audience in absolutely no doubt about what you are telling them. A key message is the most memorable, motivating, and competitive thing we can say about the organization. However, the key message must be believable. In our opening case study, the key message was "Don't Be a Tosser." It was specifically developed to appeal to the primary target audience, males 18 to 25 years old. Key messages are addressed in Chapters 1, 5, and 6.

6. STRATEGIES

Strategies are the specific approaches you will implement to accomplish your objectives. They articulate the big-picture items that need to be accomplished to deliver on the objectives—the general actions you will execute to reach your goals. For example, a strategy can be to use the media as a conduit to reach target audiences or to communicate the value of something to your target audience. In the case of the Don't Be a Tosser campaign, the strategy was to convince 18- to 25-year-old males to recycle.

7. TACTICS

Tactics are the specific action items that you will implement to reach your target audiences and meet your objectives. You might think of each strategy as an umbrella, with several tactics underneath it. They are the tangible steps you take to achieve results—the details of what you described in your strategies. If, for example, you had a strategy of targeting new mothers through the media, tactics could include sending media materials to editors of parenting magazines or developing relationships with "mommy bloggers."

It is not uncommon for junior PR practitioners to confuse strategies with tactics. Lew MacDonald is a communications officer with the B.C. Nurses' Union. He uses a war analogy to explain the difference between strategies and tactics. According to MacDonald, the strategy should explain *how* the objective (i.e., winning the battle) will be achieved. Tactics, on the other hand, describe *what* kinds of weapons or technology will be used to achieve the objective. He says that a strategy to use against an opponent might be one of "divide and conquer," and the tactic used to implement this strategy would be the dissemination of misinformation that promotes mistrust within the enemy's ranks, which in turn demoralizes or weakens them.

The decision to choose one tactic over another is based on several considerations, including budget (can you afford to do it?), timeliness (do you have enough time to do it?), and staff (are there enough people to accomplish this?).

It may seem exciting to perform an attention-grabbing stunt, but is it realistic? There is, of course, an element of risk in PR. You can never be 100 per cent sure that a tactic will be successful, no matter how strategically you have planned it. Even if tactics fail, this doesn't necessarily mean the strategy was wrong. You might just need to implement

Internal communications (chapter 9)	Investor relations (chapter 12)
Community relations (chapter 12)	Public affairs (chapter 12)
Media relations (chapter 6)	Special events management (chapter 10)
Media training (chapter 8)	Social media relations (chapter 7)
PR Writing (chapter 5)	Issues and crisis management (chapter 11)

Figure 4.5 Examples of Tactics

a more effective tactic under the same strategy. However, with careful planning, you put the chances on your side that the tactics will generate the results you want.

The Don't Be a Tosser campaign contained numerous tactics to accomplish the strategies and objectives, including media relations, social media relations, and marketing communications. Figure 4.5 outlines examples of broad tactics used in public relations that we will cover in this textbook and notes which chapter explains each tactic.

8. TIMELINE

In PR, you must be a good project manager and consistently meet deadlines; therefore, your plan must also include a timeline. A timeline is a detailed account of when every element of your campaign will be conducted, with a beginning and end date. It will spell out your important deadlines and key milestones. The timeline can be short, with execution in a few days or weeks, or longer, up to two or three years for some plans. The Don't Be a Tosser campaign was conducted over a one-year period.

The timeline in your plan may sometimes be very broad—for example, you might suggest sending out media kits in November. Other times your timelines will be very specific, such as "on November 10 at 7:10 p.m. we will kick off the event with an opening speech." The more specific you can be in terms of timing and dates within your plan, the better. Figure 4.6 shows an example of a timeline for the implementation of media relations.

Project Timeline									
	Team Lead	12–Oct					12–Nov	12–Dec	Completed
		w/o Oct 1	w/o Oct 8	w/o Oct 15	w/o Oct 22	w/o Oct 29			
Drafting Media Materials									
Draft media ralease	Carmen	■							
Draft backgrounder	Carmen		■						
Draft fact sheet	Mike		■						
Conducting Media Relations									
Create media list	Carmen		■						
Send out email pitch	Carmen			■	■				
Conduct media callbacks	Mike				■	■			
Evaluation									
Collect press clippings	Carmen						■	■	
Prepare client report	Kylie							■	

Figure 4.6 Example of a Timeline for Implementing Media Relations

9. BUDGET ❹

Public relations is a business practice, and like all sound business practices it involves budgeting. A budget is the entire amount of money that is available to plan and implement a campaign. Knowing how to calculate an estimate and stay on budget during a campaign is an essential skill. This holds true whether you are working at a PR agency and must manage a client's budget or you are working in-house and have a yearly budget to respect.

You may have the best idea in the world for your campaign, but the first question you will be asked is how much it will cost. In some cases, you will be told how much money an organization has to spend. You will need to come up with a plan to fit that amount. In other circumstances, you are asked to come up with a budget for consideration. That can be tricky, especially if you have no idea how little or how much money an organization plans to spend. You may do all the calculations only to discover that the client cannot afford it. In that case, you must go back to the drawing board to either change the program or find ways to make it more affordable.

There are two components in calculating a budget. The first is a sum of the hard costs or out-of-pocket expenses, which includes all the items or services you buy or rent (printing, location rentals) and the vendors or subcontractors you hire (photographers, designers). You must collect price estimates for all of them. Out-of-pocket expenses are calculated by making a detailed list of all the costs in your campaign and adding them up.

The second element of the budget is the cost of hiring the practitioners who will do the work. These are called the fees. This component is applicable to your budget only if your organization will be hiring a PR agency to conduct some or all of the work. Practitioners working at PR agencies calculate how much time a campaign will take, multiply that number by their hourly rate, and come up with a fee budget as part of the PR plan they submit to their client.

PR agencies sell their time as their main source of revenue. That is how they make their money, so hours are carefully calculated. Employees of PR agencies keep track of their time in 15-minute increments and record the information on timesheets. Hourly rates range from $75 per hour for junior coordinators to $500 per hour for agency principals. Fees budgets are calculated by breaking down a plan into every component and then estimating how many hours each will take.

The overall budget for a campaign is calculated by adding the out-of-pocket expenses and the fees budget (if applicable). Figure 4.7 shows the calculation of a fees budget for the management of a special event. Figure 4.8 shows the calculation of an out-of-pocket expenses budget for a special event.

10. EVALUATION AND MEASUREMENT

The final component of a PR plan is the explanation of how you will evaluate your results. Chapter 1 contains information on evaluation and measurement. What must be emphasized is that the decision on how to measure success must be made *before* embarking on the campaign. In the evaluation and measurement phase, you will evaluate your

Writing invitation	1 hour
Distribution of invitation to guests	2 hours
Writing and editing media release	2 hours
Distribution of media release to media	1 hour
Creation of media database	2 hours
Follow-up with media	10 hours
Meeting with caterers	3 hours
Organizing event logistics	15 hours
On-site event set-up and break-down	15 hours
Event attendance	3 hours
Client meetings	5 hours
Total	**59 hours**

The number of hours is multiplied by the hourly rate:

59 hours x $120/hour = $7080 fees budget

Figure 4.7 Special Event Fees Budget

Event Budget		
Item	**Description**	**Cost**
Costumes		$600
Flowers	Table arrangements, corsages	$500
Town car	For dignitaries	$200
Venue		$3,000
Catering		$4,000
Goodie bags	Macaroons for each guest	$200
Sound system	Mic, speakers	$500
Music	Live band	$1,000
Cake	Red velvet	$600
Wine	Red/white/cocktails	$2,000
Sparkling wine	For when people arrive and for the toast	$500
Non-alcoholic beverages		$300
Invitations	Invites, postage	$500
Thank-you cards	Cards, postage	$500
Misc		$500
Total		**$14,900**

Figure 4.8 Special Event Expenses Budget

results against your objectives to see whether you have accomplished them. For example, measurement may involve an analysis of the quality of media coverage you have generated in a campaign or the number of new volunteers that were recruited.

The Don't Be a Tosser campaign was evaluated in several ways. One evaluation was done by comparing container return rates before and after the campaign. Return rates increased by 11.7 per cent after the campaign. They were calculated by comparing weekly sales volumes in Alberta reported by all the beverage brands against actual unit numbers of beverage containers recycled. Also, in a survey, individuals were asked if they had been encouraged to recycle because of the campaign and 88 per cent agreed.

Thinking Like a PR Practitioner

1. Evaluate the tactics that were implemented in the Don't be a Tosser campaign.
2. Devise additional tactics for this campaign.
3. Create a PR plan for the Canadian Gas Association (www.cga.ca) that includes all ten components.

The Added Value of Creativity [5]

As we have just discussed, all sound public relations practice is based on a detailed plan that has its footing in research and strategic thinking. An additional element to devising successful PR plans is creativity. This is the part where you come up with ideas to really make your program sing, capture the attention of your target audience, and stand out from the competition. Creativity is highly valued in the industry and is the attribute most praised in PR awards.

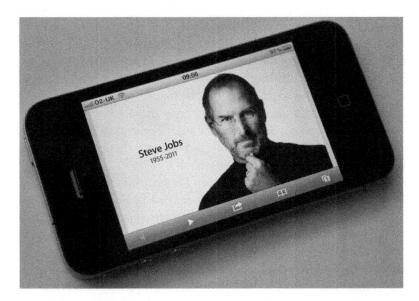

Industry visionary Steve Jobs was known for his creativity.
Source: © David Levenson/Alamy

The Don't Be a Tosser campaign won several industry awards because it was considered highly creative, in addition to meeting its objectives. This campaign bubbled over with fun and unique ideas. They included using peer pressure to encourage young men to recycle. The campaign asked the audience to identify friends who didn't recycle and post photos of them online. The end-zone dance at the Grey Cup Festival was also brilliant. Instead of spiking a football, participants spiked an empty beverage container. The best dance was judged by Calgary Stampeder Jeremaine Copeland, adding excitement to the program.

What is creativity exactly? It is not uncommon for students to lack confidence in their creativity and to believe that creativity is the mark of great artists like Pablo Picasso or industry visionaries like Steve Jobs. While these individuals demonstrated creativity that was off the charts and is known as "Big C" creativity, all of us have creative potential. The ways that we use creativity in our everyday lives and careers is known as "Little c" creativity.[8] We all possess this type of creativity to a lesser or greater degree. In fact, more important than the amount of creativity we are born with is our desire to work to strengthen and develop it. In other words, how much effort we put in and how motivated we are is more important than how much raw ability we have.[9] It is believed that individuals reach their full creative potential only after ten years of hard work and commitment to their field.[10] That means that, as a PR practitioner, you will only keep getting more strategic and creative with time.

Creativity is considered a form of problem solving. It is the capacity to come up with ideas to address challenges. Creativity is the ability to identify problems and generate multiple solutions and ideas. Creativity also involves having the courage to do things differently and take risks.[11] The ideas do not have to be revolutionary to be considered creative, but they must be novel, and more importantly, appropriate to the situation and context.[12] In other words, the ideas have to be realistic and practical.

Creativity comes into the plan once all the strategic pieces have been put together. Now is the time to explore new and unexpected ideas. Ask yourself what you can add to your program to make it more interesting and add a "wow" factor. These novel ideas must enhance the campaign, not detract from it—they must bring added value. Andy Green, in his book *Creativity in Public Relations*, describes it this way: "The mark of an outstanding creative practitioner is to analyse the situation coolly and to assess what is required—and only then, crucially, to decide what added value is needed."[13]

Creative ideas can add value to every element of a PR campaign. Creativity can be applied to an overall theme for a campaign, such as that of Don't Be a Tosser in the opening vignette. All the tactics employed, such as the contests, played up this creative theme.

Creativity can also be found in a single tactic. A good example of a novel tactic is the Iron Watermelon Carving Competition that the National Watermelon Promotion Board held to raise awareness of its fruit. Culinary students competed for the grand title by carving original serving vessels out of watermelons. Creativity can also be expressed in media information kits. For the launch of a new conditioner called Fast Food, AG Hair Cosmetics sent journalists custom-designed pizza boxes each containing a product sample and a media release.

GENERATING IDEAS

PR students often want to know where more experienced practitioners get their ideas. However, when you start working in PR you realize that there is an endless stream of ideas just waiting to pop up and be noticed. Ideas are in abundance, but they do not come on their own. You need to take time and make space to be creative. In fact, too little time and too much pressure to perform can kill creativity. The following are some techniques PR practitioners use to get their creative juices flowing and come up with those award-winning campaigns. The secret is to come up with as many ideas as you can. Only later do you judge which ones are good and which ones will not work. Andy Green compares coming up with creative ideas to turning on the hot water tap. In his analogy, the judgment process is likened to turning on the cold water tap. If you try to be creative and judge your ideas at the same time, you end up with tepid water.[14]

Get Inspired

You do not have to invent a concept from scratch to be creative. You can find inspiration all around you which can spark a brainwave. Movies, books, music, fashion, trends, design, art, magazines, food and restaurants, technology, nature, spirituality, and social media can all be sources of endless ideas. You can also look at case studies and at PR campaigns held in other markets to generate ideas. Or, you can recycle past campaigns and build on them to give them a fresh new vibe.

Conduct Brainstorming Sessions

A brainstorming session is a technique for generating creative ideas and solutions. In a **brainstorm**, a group of people get together and are given a specific topic to investigate. They spontaneously come up with ideas, with participants thinking of new concepts and building on the ideas of others. The important rule about a brainstorming session is to be open to all the ideas that are generated and to not judge them. Evaluating the ideas takes place at a later stage in the process. During the session, your goal is to have a positive flow of ideas, and assessing each one would put an end to that. Agencies are famous for holding brainstorming campaigns to come up with fun and unusual ideas. During these sessions all employees are invited to participate. It is likely that Trigger, the agency that planned and implemented Don't Be a Tosser, first started the process with a brainstorming session.

Create a Mind Map

A mind map is a technique, developed by British academic Tony Buzan, that allows you to have a brainstorming session on your own. This method of generating ideas involves drawing a type of diagram around a key word. Mind maps can be very effective in helping you come up with all kinds of ideas and concepts—many of which you probably did not even know you had until you saw them on the mind map.

Let It Go

One of the best ways to generate new ideas is to simply stop trying. Once you have filled in all the blanks in your strategy, take a pause, go do something else, and let your subconscious do the work. Go for a walk. Take a shower. The solutions and ideas may come to you unexpectedly. A well-known, award-winning PR practitioner often had flashes of insight during her after-work swim.

Evaluate Ideas

After you have come up with a whole slew of ideas, now is the time to assess them. As we mentioned before, assessing them too early in the process can kill creativity. However, eventually you do need to weed out the ideas that won't work for your specific needs. Use your evaluative skills to determine if the ideas have any merit and can be implemented. Once you've shortlisted your ideas so that only the best ones are left, you can begin creating a case to share with your manager or client for why you should implement an idea. As you work through your argument and gather information on the costs involved with the idea, you might discover other roadblocks that will make it difficult to execute. If you decide an idea won't work, you can go back to another one of your shortlisted ideas and try making a case for it until you settle on the one that makes the most sense for your organization and objectives.

CASE STUDY A STRATEGIC AND CREATIVE CAMPAIGN: LOCALS KNOW

A great example of a public relations campaign that was planned both strategically and creatively is one that was conducted by the Canadian Tourism Commission and the PR agency DDB. The Locals Know campaign encouraged Canadians to travel locally. They were to get ideas on where to go from other Canadians, who were encouraged to upload their favourite travel secrets on the campaign website (www.localsknow.ca).

The Canadian Tourism Commission's PR campaign encouraged Canadians to share their favourite secret travel spots.
Source: Stephen B. Goodwin/Shutterstock

The problem to be solved in this case, or the main objective of the campaign, was to encourage Canadians to travel within their own country and therefore keep their travel dollars in Canada.

The tactics of media relations, social media relations, and marketing communications were implemented to raise awareness of the campaign and drive traffic to the website from both locals and potential tourists. Media releases were distributed to journalists. The marketing communications tactics included ads that showed an intriguing scene, followed by the question "Where is this?" in order to encourage people to visit the website to get the answer.[15] Further increasing the campaign's profile, Canadians who posted travel spots also uploaded the information on their personal social media networks.

Case Study Continued >

In addition to targeting consumers, the campaign spoke to the travel industry and included business-to-business tactics. Canadian travel industry organizations such as airlines and travel agencies were able to upload travel information and packages to match the destinations that were featured. This created industry engagement and increased visitor revenue.

Canadians really took to this campaign, and the results exceeded all expectations. Over 4000 travel spots were uploaded, and almost 500,000 people visited the website. Media coverage included 130 articles. Furthermore, Locals Know was rated by Forbes.com as one of the top travel campaigns in the world.[16] The campaign is credited with generating $705.9 million in tourism revenue for Canada.[17]

Questions:

1. Give examples of four research questions that would be pertinent to this campaign.
2. Conduct a brainstorming session and come up with three creative tactics that would bring added value to this campaign.

AUTHOR'S OWN EXPERIENCE

Creative Ideas Come and Go

A question that students often ask me is if I ever worry that someone will steal my ideas. The answer is a resounding no. Stealing ideas in this industry is extremely rare since most practitioners are very ethical. However, even if someone did, I know I would think of others that are just as good. There is an abundance of ideas just waiting to be discovered. I also believe that ideas are to be shared. Give them freely to clients, industry contacts, or friends and you will get them back tenfold when you need them. I've had brilliant ideas given to me from unexpected sources. I once held a brainstorming session with family members when I had a mental block. Surprisingly, my father—who knows nothing about PR—was the one who came up with the campaign concept for the launch of a new airline menu.

I've also had ideas that never went anywhere. They seemed good at the time but on further reflection were just not very practical. Other times, my clients did not have the stomach to risk trying something unconventional. In those cases, we came up with an alternative plan and the campaigns met their objectives anyway.

Sometimes an idea needs to wait until its time has come. When an idea comes to you, record it so you won't forget. You never know when it will come in handy. A colleague once shared an idea for a creative media kit that he had been waiting for two years to use on the right campaign. It involved sending journalists a pair of sunglasses and inviting them to a restaurant's sunny terrace. When it was finally implemented, it was a big hit with the media.

At our agency, we tried to demonstrate creativity not only in our planning and execution of campaigns, but also in our pitches to new clients. We wrote strategic new business proposals and then asked ourselves what we could do to make them more interesting so they'd stand out from the competition. In one case we wore custom-made baseball uniforms to pitch an animation studio that produced a baseball cartoon. At another pitch, we took a bottle of juice made by the client we coveted and replaced the label with one that we designed with our proposal on it. We wanted to show potential clients the kind of creative thinking we could bring to the table. In both instances, we got the business.

tactics
- writing
- media relations
- special events
- social media

integral
- support
campaigns
- research
- methods
surveys
focus groups
environmental scans

PR Planning

- road map
measure
evaluation
- success

plan
- components
objectives
target audience
messages

strategic
- thinking
- management
- decisions

- value added
creativity
- techniques
inspiration
mind map
brainstorm

Key Terms

brainstorm A creativity-generating technique in which a group of people come up with ideas and build upon them.

communications audit A research method to determine the effectiveness of the public relations programs of an organization.

competitor analysis An investigation of the strengths and weaknesses of the competition.

environmental scan Collecting and analyzing internal and external sources to identify public perception on a particular topic.

focus group A group of individuals representing a target audience who are brought together and asked questions by a moderator.

informal sounding A casual conversation held with members of the target audience to determine their thoughts or feelings on a certain topic.

interview A research method in which verbal questions are asked of individuals.

media content analysis The study of media coverage that an organization or topic has received.

methodologies Techniques used to conduct research and collect data. In PR they involve such methods as surveys, interviews, and media coverage analysis.

primary research Conducting new, first-hand research.

public relations plan A written document that outlines all the actions you will be taking and the rationale for them over a predetermined period of time.

questionnaire A research method using written questions to gather information from individuals.

secondary research Conducting research by using pre-existing materials, such as research reports.

situation analysis The first section of a PR plan, which outlines the challenge(s) facing an organization and all the factors that influence it.

strategies The articulation of the specific actions that will be undertaken to achieve an objective.

survey A data-collection method in which individuals are asked predetermined questions. A small group is surveyed and their answers are considered to be a representative sample of the larger population.

Weblinks

Andy Green (Creativity in PR)
www.andygreencreativity.com/

Brainstorming Sessions
www.mindtools.com/brainstm.html
www.businessweek.com/innovate/content/jul2006/id20060726_517774.htm

Ipsos Reid
www.ipsos.ca

Mind Maps
www.mindtools.com/pages/article/newISS_01.htm
www.usingmindmaps.com

Nanos Research
www.nanosresearch.com

Sharp Suits
http://sharpsuits.net

Strategic Communications
www.stratcom.ca

SurveyMonkey
www.surveymonkey.com

Endnotes

1. D.W. Stacks, *Primer of Public Relations Research*. New York: Guilford Press, 2011, p. 4.

2. D.W. Stewart, P.N. Shamdasani, and D.W. Rook, *Focus Groups: Theory and Practice*. Thousand Oaks, CA: Sage, 2007, p. 42.

3. O. Hargie and D. Tourish, *Handbook of Communication Audits for Organisations*. London: Routledge, 2007, p. 4.

4. Larry M. Litwin and Jacob C. Farbman, "Public Relations Planning". Accessed March 4, 2013, http://www.jakefarbman.com/other/PR%20Planning%20PRSA%20Institute%20043007.pdf

5. The Government of Saskatchewan, *Setting SMART Objectives*. Accessed February 20, 2013, http://www.employeeservices.gov.sk.ca/ISWP/smartobjectives?Anc=97fdb7a3-656c-475e-ac4f-0eb54d5e3338&Pa=cca90bef-7f6e-44e4-92ce-2323e0889c45

6. Ibid.

7. Ibid.

8. A. Tan, *Creativity: A Handbook for Teachers*. Singapore: World Scientific Publishing, 2007.

9. R.S. Nickerson, "Enhancing Creativity." In R.J. Sternberg (ed.), *Handbook of Creativity* (pp. 392–430). Cambridge: Cambridge University Press, 1999.

10. D.K. Simonton, *Genius, Creativity and Leadership: Historiometric Inquiries*. Cambridge: Harvard University Press, 1984.

11. Nickerson, "Enhancing Creativity."

12. M. Runco, "Creativity," *Annual Review of Psychology*, vol. 55 (2004), 657–687.

13. A. Green, *Creativity in Public Relations*. London: Kogan Page, 2010. p. 9.

14. Ibid.

15. "CTC 'Locals Know,'" YouTube. Accessed March 4, 2013, http://www.youtube.com/watch?v=ZRCCBAzbFjo

16. "CTC Campaign Outstrips Expectations: More than Two Million Page Views and 450,000 Site Visitors, Boosts Industry Across Canada," Industry Canada. Accessed March 4, 2013, http://www.ic.gc.ca/eic/site/ich-epi.nsf/eng/02048.html

17. "CTC's Successful Locals Know Campaign Wraps Up," Canadian Tourism Commission. Accessed March 4, 2013, http://en-corporate.canada.travel/content/ctc_news/ctc%E2%80%99s-successful-locals-know-ad-campaign-wraps

Expand Your Horizons by Relocating

After graduating from university, Jessica Lam decided to relocate to improve her chances of landing her dream job. "I looked at my local market and saw how few jobs there were in public relations. It was a smaller pool here, so I was competing for every position with people who had years of experience. I went where the head offices are, where they have the bigger budgets."

Jessica headed to Toronto for a few years before relocating to Hong Kong. "It was a lot easier in a bigger market to find an interesting position. If Vancouver had five openings at one time in communications, Toronto had 50, and Hong Kong had even more." Once back in her hometown, agencies that would not meet with her after graduation now interviewed her. "My experience in different markets made me a much more attractive candidate. It opened the doors for the interviews," she said.

Moving to a new city or country may not be an option for everyone, but if you are willing to relocate, it can do wonders for your PR career. That holds true whether you are just starting out or you are looking for opportunities for advancement. Within Canada, generally the larger the city, the more PR jobs there are available. Similarly, some international markets such as London or New York have more PR positions than Canadian cities do.

There are countless examples of Canadian PR practitioners finding success overseas. Satwant Kaur relocated to Asia after university in Montreal and now works in public affairs at the United Nations Environment Programme in Thailand. Ema Tanaka specialized in tourism public relations after moving to New Zealand and landing a job in media relations at Tourism New Zealand. Another practitioner who had a mid-level position here did stints in agencies in L.A., New York, and Hong Kong before returning to Canada at the level of vice president. One of the co-authors of this textbook herself was given her first public relations position in Tokyo.

Chapter 5
Writing for PR

We're in your neighbourhood.

Atlantic Path is the **largest cancer research study** ever conducted in Atlantic Canada. If you are between 35 and 69, we need you to volunteer. Book an appointment today.

We're only a click away – and in the heart of Sydney at 335 George Street. Go to www.atlanticpath.ca and complete the web form in the "Volunteer" section or call 1-877-285-7284.

Atlantic
PATH PARTNERSHIP FOR TOMORROW'S HEALTH
For the Benefit of Future Generations

www.atlanticpath.ca

The PR campaign for Atlantic PATH aimed to recruit 30,000 volunteers. Source: Quantum Communications

LEARNING OBJECTIVES

❶ Explain the importance of defining the audience and key messages prior to writing any communications materials.

❷ Outline the different news hooks and explain why they are important to PR writing.

❸ Describe the purpose of a media kit and its components.

❹ Outline the role of research in public relations writing.

The Writing That Supports a Big Campaign

The Atlantic Partnership for Tomorrow's Health, or Atlantic PATH, is the Atlantic component of the Canadian Partnership for the Tomorrow Project, which is the largest study of its kind ever undertaken in Canada. The mandate of this national study is to investigate how genetics, the environment, lifestyle, and behaviour correlate with cancer. The research aims to examine why some people develop cancer and others do not. To do this it will follow the health of 300,000 people in British Columbia, Alberta, Ontario, Quebec, and Atlantic Canada for 30 years.

The owner of the agency Quantum Communications in Halifax, donalee Moulton, headed the communications team for Atlantic PATH. A wide spectrum of PR materials was developed and drafted in order to meet the campaign objectives of recruiting 30,000 Atlantic Canadians, aged 18 to 69, to participate in the study and to raise awareness of its importance to their future health. The objectives were particularly important because Atlantic Canada has the highest cancer rates in the country. One in three Atlantic Canadians will be diagnosed with cancer during their lifetime.

The written components of the campaign included the following:

- Media materials for distribution to journalists in order to generate media coverage
- Revised web copy for the updated website
- Marketing communications materials, including ads for TV, print, radio, and online media
- Posters and postcards for distribution in the community
- **Email blasts** (emails sent at the same time to a large mailing list) sent to former and potential participants
- An e-newsletter for distribution to stakeholders and supporters as needed

All the written PR materials mentioned above were integrated to be consistent and communicate the same themes and key messages. Furthermore, they were all based on the two key messages that donalee describes as follows:

1. "This study is vital to the health of all Atlantic Canadians. It will help researchers find out why some people develop cancer and others don't, so that we can find new ways of preventing this disease. It will also help us find ways of spotting cancer earlier, when it can be easier to treat."

2. "This research is particularly important for Atlantic Canada, which has the highest rates of cancer in the country. Every year, more than 13,400 Atlantic Canadians are diagnosed with cancer and 6300 die from it. The disease touches everyone living in the region, either personally or through family and friends."

As donalee explains about the campaign, "The pressure to inform Atlantic Canadians and recruit volunteers was great, and as a result, there was intense demand to create written materials, distribute them, and show results. This was both daunting and exhilarating. The enormity of the goal—30,000 volunteers in four provinces in a little over two years—also forced us to put on our creative thinking caps."

The results? Atlantic PATH led the country in recruitment efforts and garnered national media coverage for its recruitment and awareness efforts. This accomplishment would not have been possible without the expertly written materials donalee's team prepared.

There are two skills that PR practitioners need in order to really stand out in this competitive field. They need to be excellent writers and they need to be good at media relations.

Strength in these two areas will set young practitioners apart from their peers as they build their reputation in the industry. In this chapter we will cover the first of these important assets, PR writing. (We cover media relations later in this textbook.) As you saw in the opening vignette on Atlantic PATH, a PR campaign can involve a large number of different written materials. In PR, writing is not an infrequent task. PR is much like the profession of journalism, in that writing is a routine task and we must be prepared to draft materials on many different topics. Furthermore, in addition to the traditional media materials that we must be competent at writing, such as media releases and newsletters, we are now also expected to produce social media materials, such as Facebook and Twitter posts or blogs.

Despite the fact that writing is so vital to the public relations profession, numerous studies have shown that employers of recent PR graduates are underwhelmed by entry-level practitioners' writing ability.[1] Some lament that this is because more people are entering the field who were not initially trained as journalists, as was traditionally the case. However, it does not have to be this way. With proper instruction, any PR professional can write with the same competence as a trained journalist.

A great writing style is something that is hard to teach. It takes much practice and a desire to develop and strengthen one's writing skills. One of the best ways to improve is to read as much and as many different materials as you can. When you read something that grabs your attention, try to learn from it. Dissect it to tease out why it caught your interest. What made it flow well? What made it an interesting read? Read the newspaper. Know what is current and what is newsworthy. Notice which headlines are compelling. This will make you a better writer and a better PR practitioner.

The objective of this chapter is to describe the various pieces that are critical in public relations and to outline the conventions and principles of each piece. We will cover basics that are applicable to many types of PR writing. We will also look at a variety of written materials that PR practitioners are expected to produce, such as speeches, web copy, social media copy, opinion editorials, annual reports, internal communication materials, and marketing communication materials. Since writing material, such as media releases for journalists to repurpose in their publications, is a big part of what we do and is a specialized type of writing, we will explore it in more detail than the sections on other written materials.

PR Writing 101 ❶

As we noted in Chapter 2, the overall goal of public relations is to influence public opinion. We want our target audiences to take a specific course of action, whether it is telling their friends to visit a restaurant or voting for a political candidate. Influencing public opinion is also the overall goal of everything that we write in public relations. For instance, if we were to write an employee newsletter, all the writing in it would be intended to influence our target audience, employees, in a certain way. The objective could be to raise employee morale, increase job satisfaction, reinforce company policies, or build loyalty. All the items in this newsletter would be carefully selected and then written in a persuasive or educational way. The language would be carefully chosen to include certain elements, such as Aristotle's arguments (see Chapter 2), and to convey empathy with the audience.

"The one thing on your resume that concerns me is you misspelled your last name."

Source: Cartoonresource/Shutterstock

Another important point is that as the PR practitioner you are not for the most part writing in your own voice on behalf of yourself. You will often be **ghost writing** the materials. This means that you will be authoring them on someone else's behalf, such as your organization, CEO, client, or supervisor. Your name will not appear in the byline or anywhere on the piece, and you are expected to write in a style that is fitting to the person or organization.

To have any credibility with your target audiences, all written pieces must be technically flawless. Taking care with grammar and spelling and avoiding writing in clichés will help your writing tremendously. Proofread everything three times! We do not have the space in this textbook to cover basic spelling and grammar, other than to say that they are of the utmost importance. Any mistakes will distract the reader from your writing and could call your credibility into question. If you are unsure of your skills in these areas, there are many great grammar and writing books available. A wonderful reference is *The Canadian Press Stylebook*. This is the stylebook used by most news organizations in Canada. Most PR agencies will have copies of this vital reference book in their offices to guide their writing.

Writing for public relations is a particular skill that blends journalism with marketing. It is very different from any other marketing communication functions. The writing of media materials cannot be overly "adsy" or use lots of flowery language or adjectives. This means that while you want to convey your organization's key messages in the piece, the content must be factual, not opinion based. Media releases, fact sheets, and backgrounders, especially, must be of newspaper quality.

PR practitioners must create pieces that are clear and direct and that deliver a deliberate message to a specific audience. The PR practitioner must also be a versatile writer and be able to switch from writing a media release to composing a speech and then writing a blog post, sometimes all in one afternoon. In fact, the diversity of writing expected from a PR practitioner has probably never been greater.[2] From tweets and blog posts to media releases and opinion editorials, the PR practitioner is expected to be proficient at drafting engaging, appropriate content for each.[3] No matter what the piece is, though, there are some basics that apply to all of them, such as establishing the audience and developing the key messages. We have already studied these elements in Chapters 2 and 4, but we will examine them once more because they are so vital to PR writing.

TARGET AUDIENCES

It cannot be emphasized enough that, before any action is taken in PR, three basics need to be researched and defined. These are target audiences, objectives, and key messages. Let us look at each to understand how they apply to PR writing.

When writing for public relations it is important to establish your target audience. The **audience** is the end user to whom you want to deliver your message. Often there will be more than one audience. The PR practitioner should then separate the audience into (1) a primary audience, the main target; (2) the secondary audience, an important audience but not the bull's eye target; and sometimes even (3) a tertiary audience.

It helps to know as much about the audience as possible before starting to create the materials. The PR practitioner will want to do some research on and cater to the audiences' demographics, geographics, and psychographics, as well as their base knowledge of the company or cause. All of these factors will help inform the level of writing, style, and background information that will need to be provided. For example, if you are writing a speech for the CEO to deliver to his company's employees, you will not have to include the level of background company information that you would if the speech were being written for the local chamber of commerce. In the Atlantic PATH example featured in the opening vignette, various PR materials were written for different target audiences. For example, the media materials were produced for journalists and their publications' audiences, while the quarterly e-newsletter was written for stakeholders and supporters.

OBJECTIVES

After establishing who the audience is, the PR practitioner must outline his or her communications objectives. Is the objective to reassure, motivate, educate, or entertain the audience? Is the objective to get the audience to do or buy something? Or is it to reaffirm or change their opinion? If you were writing a speech for a politician to deliver to her supporters, your objective might be to persuade the audience to donate to the campaign. However, if you were writing a newsletter for company employees, your objective might be to build loyalty to the company and to motivate them. The end goal will also inform the flow of your writing and the information you choose to include. The objectives of the Atlantic PATH campaign were to recruit research participants and raise awareness of the importance of the research to Atlantic Canadians' health.

KEY MESSAGES

Prior to writing any PR piece, PR practitioners should develop their key messages. **Key messages** are the main ideas the PR practitioner wants to communicate to the audience.[4] When considering a key message, the PR practitioner should think, "If the reader remembers only one thing from this piece, what would I want it to be?" Key messages should guide the writing and be front and centre throughout the piece. It is important, though, that the PR practitioner doesn't try to inject too many key messages into one piece, as there is a risk that the audience will become confused or not remember the most salient points. There should never be more than three key messages in any communication. This can take discipline on the PR practitioner's part. Often when we are part of an organization, we begin to think every message is important and we want to communicate too much to the audience. It takes effort to be mindful of what we communicate and to choose only the most relevant messages.

Key messages are short sound bites. A long, convoluted sound bite will be hard to communicate and hard for your audience to understand and remember. Though an organization's key messages are always evolving and will change over time, consistency is also important.[5] If you are communicating on behalf of an upscale jewellery store, the key message that you communicate in all your pieces might be around fine craftsmanship. While the wording of this key message might change over several years, its essence will remain the same. Through repeating this key message in all your communication pieces,

---

ADVICE TO NEW PRACTITIONERS

Learning to Write

Look carefully at how editors, your manager, or clients amend and edit your writing. Don't take it personally when your writing is critiqued. Instead, see it as an opportunity to learn and improve.

Develop a thick skin if you can. Your work will continually be edited by someone else. Everyone will have a preference for the best way to express a thought. Many times you'll have to adapt your style to your manager's or client's writing style.

Practise. Then practise some more.

Care about the quality of your words—and chose them carefully. More words doesn't mean

better. In fact, it is usually the sign of a weaker writer. Being able to write clearly but concisely takes skill and practice.

Always get the final draft of documents approved by your manager or client before they go out to the public. If possible, get the approval in writing.

Be curious. Read the work of others and try to figure out what was done well and what could be improved.

you will reinforce it with your audience. This is exactly what was done in the Atlantic PATH example that we studied in the opening vignette. The key messages were written first and then all of the numerous PR materials, from media materials to web copy, were written to encompass them.

Media Materials ❷

Writing media materials is a skill that many PR practitioners must practise. These materials must be written in a specific way, always keeping journalists and editors in mind. This is why so many journalists become successful PR practitioners—they understand writing for the media. There is a particular way to write media materials and certain guidelines that should be followed. Typically, media materials are written to facilitate media relations efforts. The concept of conducting media relations is explored in Chapter 6. Here we will focus specifically on writing for the media.

NEWS VALUES

When writing media materials, it is important to identify the news values that you are going to use in your materials. **News values**, or news hooks, as they are also called, are the angle that makes something newsworthy. A media release without a news hook is really just an ad. As we have examined, media coverage is called "earned" media because you've done something interesting to earn the publicity. As Robert Stephens, founder of the Geek Squad, says, "advertising is tax you pay for being unremarkable."[6] Advertising is sometimes referred to as "paid" media, because organizations must pay for the ad or promotional piece.

In order for information in a media release to be of interest to journalists and used in a news story, it needs to follow news conventions.

Generally employed news values include the following:

Immediacy[7]: When something is timely, it becomes more newsworthy. Something that took place recently is generally considered more newsworthy than something that happened a long time ago. The same is true with products. Products that have been recently launched are typically more newsworthy than older products. Another way to use the immediacy news hook is to tie your release or pitch to a trendy or timely topic.[8] For example, around Earth Day would be a good time to send a release on an organization's new environmental initiative.

Locality[9]: An event that takes place close to a publication's readers or viewers is more relevant to them. This is why there are community and regional newspapers—because people care about news that happens in their area. PR practitioners sometimes try to use locality by employing the **hometown release**. This type of release is targeted to the specific community or town. For example, if your client won a major award, you might consider including his or her hometown community newspaper in the distribution of the release.

Human interest: Everyone loves a heartwarming story. Stories of dogs rescuing children or good Samaritans making a difference in their community often receive coverage. This news hook is the basis for "hometown hero" segments in the news.

Conflict[10]: Usually PR practitioners want to stay away from the conflict news hook, because this often signifies a negative news story such as a crisis. However, used strategically, conflict can be a useful tool for the practitioner. For example, the CEO of an organic company may want to publicly debate GMOs, thus employing the conflict news hook, in order to raise awareness about the company and the issue.

Novelty[11]: When something is odd or unusual, it is more likely to be newsworthy. When employing this news hook, PR practitioners usually stage a stunt. Richard Branson is the king of the media stunt. When Virgin Atlantic launched in Canada, Branson and his colleagues mooned the crowd, showing off the company's name written across their bums.[12] Another company that received a lot of coverage using the unusual news hook is the Hans Brinker Budget Hotel in Amsterdam. It made headlines when it launched an advertising campaign telling the world how bad it was; the owner decided he wanted to stop guests from complaining by lowering their expectations.[13] The hotel's ads let the world know about its terrible service, uncleanliness, and rat infestation.[14] It even ran a stunt where it put flags with the hotel's name on it in dog poo around the hotel.[15] This counterintuitive marketing campaign received international media coverage and boosted the number of visitors to the hotel.

Peril: Fear or danger can attract the media's interest. This news hook might include stories about the importance of keeping fit to avoid cardiovascular problems or about a firefighter who saved the lives of a family trapped in a burning house.

Violence: This news hook explains why wars and crime make the news. Violence is naturally interesting to the public.

Celebrity: People, companies, or landmarks that are famous are newsworthy. When a celebrity does anything, it is suddenly more interesting than when you or I do it. Tabloid magazines publish pictures of celebrities like Drake or Celine Dion doing even mundane tasks, such as grocery shopping or walking in the park—because people are interested in their lives, they make the news. Celebrity doesn't pertain only to people, either. A company or cause can be famous as well. For example, Apple computers receive much more media attention than small businesses because many people know Apple and are interested in the announcements the company makes.

Other elements that lend a newsworthy note to stories but are not news hooks include children, crime, money, animals, royalty, religion, and sex. Adding any of these components to a story can assist in increasing the attention it receives.

The Atlantic PATH campaign examined in the opening vignette contained several news values. It had locality, as volunteers were being recruited in Atlantic Canada and the issue affected this population. It had immediacy, as the campaign was being launched and volunteers were needed right away. It had novelty, as it was the first such large-scale research conducted in Canada and the first to seek so many volunteers. It also had peril, as Atlantic Canada has the highest rate of cancer in the country and this study was important to the future health of the region's residents.

The Duchess of Cambridge, the former Kate Middleton, is inherently newsworthy because she encompasses the news hook of celebrity and the added interest of royalty.

Source: © Tal Cohen/Alamy

THE MEDIA KIT ^❸

A **media kit** can take many forms, but at its simplest it is a folder or PDF with information on a product or company. Sometimes companies will build more elaborate media kits that come in beautiful, branded boxes, or that are themed. For example, for the launch of Sarah Jessica Parker's perfume, Lovely, the Canadian media team put their media materials in a hat box that contained a teacup monogrammed with the initials SJP and a sachet of tea that was specially formulated to smell like the perfume. Other companies put their media kit on a jump drive with all the media materials available electronically and loaded with ready-to-use images. Photos are an important component of a media kit because they allow PR practitioners to put forward their best images and packaging shots, and for many publications, particularly those with smaller staffs, being provided with high-quality images saves time and makes it easy for them to cover the story.

The purpose of a media kit is to make it simple for the media to cover an organization, product, or event because all the information they might need is in one place. The components of a media kit may include all or some of the following pieces:

- Media release
- Media advisory
- Photos
- Backgrounder
- Biography
- Fact sheet

Clothing retailer Roots regularly posts media information and media kit materials on its website. The information ranges from new store openings to celebrity designers joining the firm.

In this section we will examine the written components of the media kit.

Media Release

There are many different written tools that a PR practitioner can use to garner coverage, but none is as prevalent as the **media release** (also called a *news release* or *press release*; we use these terms interchangeably in the text). The media release is a document that announces the news about the story at the heart of a campaign. It is widely used, and for good reason. The media release is a cost-effective and efficient way to send information to the media. When used appropriately, the media release can generate a lot of coverage for very little cost.

The media release should be written like a news article. The sign of a great media release is that it can be published word-for-word in a newspaper—although that is not its goal. The goal of the media release is to inform the media of your organization's or client's news, such as a new product launch or initiative, and to provide them with information that will make them interested in publicizing that news to their audience.

PR practitioners also need to be conscious of the audience of the publications to which they are sending the release. For example, a trade release, or a release written for business-to-business publications, should not be sent to a lifestyle publication. Prior to drafting the release, the PR practitioner should always research the publications on its media list and the audience. Sometimes the PR practitioner might need to create several versions of one release to make it appropriate for the audiences of different publications that they hope to pitch. Prior to beginning a release, the PR practitioner will also want to decide which news values will be employed in the release.

Spelling or grammar mistakes hinder the readability of the release and can damage the PR professional's credibility. One broadcast news producer we spoke to said that he immediately deletes any releases emailed to him that have spelling mistakes. His rationale is that if the PR practitioner hasn't demonstrated the attention to detail to ensure the release is perfect, he or she might disappoint him on the story lead. With the limited number of cameras he has at his disposal to send to stories, he can't take that risk.

Media releases should not be written like ad copy. This means you should avoid exclamation points or excessive adjectives. If the release sounds more like an advertisement than a newspaper article, it won't lead to media coverage. Be sure to refer to *The Canadian Press Stylebook* so that you follow many of the same conventions that Canadian journalists do. Releases should be written in third person—meaning that "he/she" and "they" should be used instead of "I," "me," "you," or "we."

Above all else, it is imperative that your release be completely accurate. Nothing will damage your reputation among the press faster than having untruths in any of your media materials. Any external facts and figures you use should be sourced. As Andrew Hindes, president of the In-House Writer states, "you never want to put a journalist in the position of having to run a correction because of an inaccuracy in your press material."[16]

Elements of the Media Release In this section we'll examine the various sections of a media release from the headline to the contact information in order to provide general rules.

Headline: The headline of the media release can be either very descriptive or attention grabbing. Typically, for a financial release, the headline will be straightforward and clear, whereas for a new product or event, it will be more attention grabbing.

Body paragraphs: A release should be structured like an inverted pyramid: the most important information is in the first paragraph and the least important information comes at the end. Imagine that the reader is going to read only the first paragraph. What would you want the reader to know? The first paragraph or two should answer the 5 Ws: who, what, where, when, and why. The lower paragraphs include any supplementary information. See Figure 5.1 for more information on the inverted pyramid.

Within the body of the media release, the writer should concentrate on describing the benefits to the audience, not just the features.[17] A feature is a positive element of the product, whereas a benefit helps customers understand how the product or service will make their life better. For example, a feature of a jacket might be that it is waterproof, but the benefit might be that it will allow you to look stylish in any type of Canadian weather. Features are nice-to-haves, whereas as benefits are the reason people act.

Figure 5.1   Effective Press Release Style Formatting

Source: Effective Press Release Style Formatting: Inverted Pyramid. Used by permission from Stacey Miller.

Quotes: Often the body of the media release will contain a quote from a spokesperson. Sometimes you will be asked to draft this quote. Even if you draft the quote, however, you should never distribute a release with a quote that hasn't been officially approved by the person to whom it is attributed. A quote should add new information to the release and be interesting. It should also offer insight into the consumer benefit. For example, instead of saying, "Our company is ecstatic to be launching this new product" you might try, "Customers will love our new product because it will save them time." Another tip for making interesting quotes is to use verbs and action-oriented words.[18]

Boilerplate: A media release should always end with a boilerplate. A **boilerplate** is a short paragraph that describes the organization that is distributing the release. It is similar to a short company history or what would be found on a website's "about us" page. Like the release, it is written in third person.

There are two reasons for including a boilerplate in your release. One reason is to have all the information on your organization in a succinct paragraph so that it is easy for the reporter to find. The second is to avoid detracting from your lead with a lot of background information on your organization.

Contact information: At the top or bottom of a release, the contact information of whoever is designated to handle media calls is provided. This may be someone from inside an organization or a contact from a PR agency, depending on what the client prefers. Whoever is listed as the media contact should be easy to reach and accessible.

```
┌──────────────────────────────────────────────────────┐
│                                                        │
│        FOR IMMEDIATE RELEASE (ALL CAPS, BOLD)          │
│        DATE (BOLD)                                     │
│                    HEADLINE (ALL CAPS, BOLD)           │
│                       SUBHEAD (ITALICS)                │
│        CITY, PROVINCE (BOLD) – BODY COPY               │
│                         BODY COPY                      │
│                         BODY COPY                      │
│                         BODY COPY                      │
│                         BODY COPY                      │
│                        BOILERPLATE                     │
│                  -- XX -- (OR -30-, OR –END-)          │
│        MEDIA INQUIRES (BOLD)                           │
│        NAME                                            │
│        PHONE NUMBER                                    │
│        EMAIL                                           │
│                                                        │
└──────────────────────────────────────────────────────┘
```

Figure 5.2   Components of a Media Release

Once the release goes out, the contact person should make fielding media calls a priority. Journalists find it very frustrating when they receive a release and then can't reach the listed contact.

A media release is typically one page and never more than two. Most media releases are now emailed to journalists or posted through a news wire service such as Canada NewsWire. **News wire** services provide news organizations with content. Some news wire services charge PR practitioners a fee to distribute their releases to media outlets. Others charge news outlets a fee to use the content. Once a release is complete, usually in 12-point standard font such Times New Roman or Arial, and with generous white space and margins, it will be copied and pasted into the body of an email and sent to media contacts. Figure 5.2 provides the **components** of a media release and outlines all the information that needs to be included, in order. Figure 5.3 provides an example of a media release from the Ontario Provincial Police.

Media Advisory

A **media advisory** is sent to reporters to let them know about an upcoming event or announcement. Examples of events for which you might issue a media advisory prior to their occurrence include a press conference, a new store opening, a gala fundraiser, or the launch party of a new restaurant.

Ontario Provincial Police
Police provinciale de l'Ontario

**News Release/
Communiqué**

FROM/DE: WEST PARRY SOUND OPP   **DATE: December 13, 2010**

COUPLE ARRESTED FOR USING COUNTERFEIT MONEY

(Parry Sound, ON) – On December 10, 2010, the West Parry Sound Ontario Provincial Police (OPP) responded to a report of counterfeit money being used at businesses throughout the Town of Parry Sound.

The suspects attempted to spend the counterfeited $100 American bills at two stores before they successfully did so at a local pharmacy.

The continuation of the commission of the offence was thwarted by a united effort of both OPP and local businesses.

As the couple moved from business to business employees were tracking their movements and alerting other businesses in the area as well as updating the OPP officers involved. As many as 8 OPP units were on the lookout and acting upon the updates being provided.

The suspects were located at the Parry Sound Mall and apprehended as they attempted to leave.

OPP officers involved in the investigation included Constables, Detectives, and even the Detachment Commander, Ron Campbell. S/SGT Campbell praised the efforts of all involved. **"It was a perfect example of community policing. Because we all know that many sets of eyes are better than one. Businesses were instrumental in solving the case. It was reported immediately and statements could be taken while details were still fresh in people's minds."**

The accused are scheduled to appear at the Parry Sound House on Thursday January 6, 2011 at 9:00 am to answer to the charges.

- 30 -

Contact: Provincial Constable ▮▮▮▮▮▮▮
          West Parry Sound OPP
Phone: ▮▮▮▮▮▮▮▮▮
Crime Stoppers 1-800-222-TIPS (8477)

www.opp.ca

Follow us on Twitter at: www.twitter.com/OPP_News

Figure 5.3   Ontario Provincial Police Media Release

Source: Couple Arrested for Using Counterfeit Money (News Release) December 13, 2010 © Queen's Printer for Ontario, 2013. Reproduced with permission.

A media advisory is a cross between a media release and an invitation and is formatted much like a media release. Like a release, it should be well written and free of ad-like copy and superfluous adjectives. It should also include contact information and a boilerplate. Media advisories are often sent to **assignment editors**, the individuals at news media who assign stories to other reporters. The media advisory is distributed to the media prior to the event, with the aim of piquing their interest so that they attend and cover it.

A media advisory is typically a one-page document of short, bulleted information. It spells out who will be at the event, where it is, when it is, and what it is. Important location details such as available parking or a map are also included to make it as easy as possible for reporters to attend the event. In the advisory, the specific times that speeches or newsworthy happenings will be occurring should be listed, and reporters should be notified of any interview or photo opportunities.

We Day is a nationwide event that is hosted by Free the Children to unite youth across the country and inspire them to look for ways to get involved in volunteerism, both locally and globally. The events, which take place in various cities across Canada, attract world leaders and celebrities as speakers and performers. The Dalai Lama, Archbishop Desmond Tutu, the Honourable Roméo Dallaire, and Shawn Desman have all been part of the event. The We Day media advisory lists the keynote speakers, states the date and time of the event, provides links to the live webcast, and contains information on how to book an interview. See Figure 5.4 for an example of a media advisory and Chapter 10 for more information on using media advisories in special events management.

Backgrounder/Biography

A **backgrounder** or a biography can be a helpful item to include in a media kit. The purpose of the backgrounder or biography is to provide reporters with in-depth information about a company, product, or person that they might need when writing their stories. A backgrounder also allows the PR practitioner the space to explain a more complicated topic, such as a new technology. A backgrounder provides more contextual information and background than a media release.

Think of a backgrounder as a resource tool that reporters can use as a reference instead of spending a lot of time doing additional research. By providing a backgrounder, the PR practitioner can save journalists time and make it easier for them to write their stories. In a backgrounder, unlike in a media release, the writer is able to expand in longer, more detailed paragraphs. However, even in a backgrounder, it is wise to follow the inverted pyramid, so that the most relevant and important information is presented first. A backgrounder is typically one to two pages.

Fact Sheet

A **fact sheet** provides a bulleted list of short, digestible information for reporters that they can use in their stories. It can be about a product, organization, event, or service. Depending on the subject matter, fact sheets can be fun and creative—for example, a fact

Health Council of Canada
Conseil canadien de la santé

Media Advisory

For Immediate Release

Health Council report points to inadequate health care services for Aboriginal people living in major Canadian cities

What: Current mainstream health care services are not accommodating First Nations, Inuit and Metis people living in urban centres. Mainstream health care services are unwelcoming and in many cases threatening to Aboriginal people. Fear of racial stereotyping and lack of respect for traditional ways of healing, turns many Aboriginal people away from seeking care.

The Health Council of Canada's latest report, *Empathy, dignity, and respect: Creating cultural safety for Aboriginal people in urban health care* highlights the issues and shares examples of practices that are designed with the values and experiences of Aboriginal people in mind.

Find out about the programs that are advancing positive change. Join the Health Council of Canada on December 11, 2012 in Winnipeg to see firsthand how one program - the Aboriginal Patient Navigator Program in Portage la Prairie - is making a real difference in the way Aboriginal people interact with health care services in urban settings.

When: December 11, 2012
               10:00 a.m. – 11:00 a.m. (CT)

               10:00 a.m.   Welcome and introductions by Dr. Catherine Cook
               10:05 a.m.   Opening Prayer
               10:15 a.m.   Remarks by Dr. Catherine Cook and Kathy McPhail
               10:35 a.m.   Premiere screening of *Making health care delivery culturally safe for Aboriginal people in urban centres*
               10:40 a.m.   Thank you and Q&A with John G. Abbott
               11:00 a.m.   Closing Prayer

Where: John Buhler Research Centre Atrium
               Bannatyne Campus, University of Manitoba
               501C-715 McDermot Ave.
               Winnipeg, MB

Who: Kathy McPhail, CEO, Southern Regional Health Authority, MB
               Dr. Catherine Cook, Councillor, Health Council of Canada
               John G. Abbott, CEO, Health Council of Canada

Interview opportunities will be available following the event.

-30-

About the Health Council of Canada
Created by the *2003 First Ministers' Accord on Health Care Renewal*, the Health Council of Canada is an independent national agency that reports on the progress of health care renewal. The Council provides a system-wide perspective on health care reform in Canada, and disseminates information on best practices and innovation across the country. The Councillors are appointed by the participating provincial and territorial governments and the Government of Canada.

To read the report, *Empathy, dignity, and respect: Creating cultural safety for Aboriginal peoples in urban health care*, visit: www.healthcouncilcanada.ca.

For more information or to arrange an interview please contact:
Name of Media Relations Manager, Health Council of Canada, email, office and cell phone contact numbers.

Figure 5.4   Media Advisory Sample

Source: Health Council of Canada. Used by permission.

sheet prepared for a cooking supply store might list the ten kitchen tools that no home chef can live without. A fact sheet can also take a frequently asked questions (FAQ) format to answer some of the questions a reporter might have about a product, or it could be a list of features of a company's product. Community food banks often create fact sheets with statistics about poverty in a community or about the populations that require its services. A fact sheet provides reporters with information beyond that found in the media release and is typically one page. A fact sheet can also be posted online with links to the sources or to more information.

ADVICE TO NEW PRACTITIONERS
PR Writing Tips

In public relations, you are typically writing on behalf of an organization. You are not using our own voice but that of the organization. This means that you must write in a voice that is appropriate to the organization but will also appeal to the target audience.

Choosing the right tone is key. The **tone** is the attitude that the writer projects to the audience about the subject matter. The tone of the organization may be formal and respectful or it may be casual and fun. PR practitioners who work in an agency will often need to adapt their tone continually to meet the needs of their various clients.

Once something is written, it is on the record. Thanks to the cyber world, in particular, every written word lives for eternity. Make sure that none of your written words will embarrass you later.

Irony, humour, and sarcasm are very challenging to transmit in writing. Unless you're talented at this type of writing, save them for face-to-face encounters. And never, never, never send an email that you have written while angry. You will almost certainly come to regret it. Wait a bit and send an email once you're in a calmer state of mind. One trick is to put a two-minute delay on your sent emails. This will allow you to draft an email and hit send but open and revise the email as you calm down.

Check spelling and grammar without exception.

Thinking Like a PR Practitioner

1. Find three examples of recent news articles that contain at least one of the news values.
2. Explain the difference between a media release and a media advisory. When would you use each?
3. Visit a website of a Canadian corporation or nonprofit. From the information that you find there, write a one-page media release on the organization.

Other PR Materials ❹

As mentioned earlier in the chapter, PR practitioners are now expected to be able to expertly write a growing number of pieces. We will cover a few of the key ones here, including speeches, web copy, social media copy, opinion editorials, annual reports, internal communications materials, marketing communications materials, and FAQs. The case of Atlantic PATH demonstrates how many different materials a PR campaign might require. This campaign included media materials, web copy, a newsletter, and marketing communications materials.

SPEECHES

A PR practitioner will often be asked to prepare speeches. A speech may be needed for an employee event, a political event, a trade conference, or any of a number of other events. Speeches differ from other types of writing because they need to be audibly interesting. It is important for the writer to practise saying the speech out loud to understand the time it takes to say it and to catch any words that are hard to pronounce or any sentences that the orator may stumble through.

Prior to starting to write a speech, you will want to research, research, research.[19] Research the event where the speech will be given, the topic you've been asked to draft a speech on, and the person who will be delivering the speech in order to become familiar with their speaking style and tone.[20] When researching the event you will want to find out if it is a formal event or more casual. What is the agenda? Is there anyone speaking after your speaker whom they will need to introduce? Will anyone else be speaking about a similar topic? All of these seemingly small details will influence the content of your speech.

In regards to researching your topic it is extremely important that you know it thoroughly. Lewis Carroll once said, "Take care of the sense and the sounds will take care of themselves."[21] This means if you write something that is well researched and thought out, how it sounds can be sorted out later. Before starting to draft anything you will want to determine how good your speaker is at public speaking. Would a witty speech sound strange coming from them? How do they want to come across? Do they want to change people's perceptions of them? You might also want to interview the speakers you are drafting the speech for about personal stories or anecdotes that they might want to tell.

After research, you are ready to create an outline and start your **first draft**, or first attempt at the written material. When you are writing a speech, you need to consider a couple of language guidelines. In a speech, short words are easier to say and more punchy than long ones. Also, unlike in a media release, you want to use personal language, such as "I" and "you," as it will help create a bond between the speaker and the audience.[22] The speechwriter can use poetic language with adjectives to help paint a picture, as well as tactics such as anaphora, which is the repetition of words or phrases for effect, as used by Dr. Martin Luther King in his famous "I Have a Dream" speech. In this speech, Dr. King used repetition to create momentum and energy.

When prepping the speech for the podium, use large, double-spaced text with lots of white space and number the pages.[23] This will make it easier for the speaker to read and follow the text. Once your speech has been delivered, if appropriate, see if you can repurpose the content into an article or op-ed.[24] You may also want to videotape the speech so you can post it on your company website or on YouTube. To view wonderful speeches and get a sense of different styles and deliveries that work well, watch TED Talks or listen to the Moth podcast. Both are easily downloadable and feature a variety of talented storytellers and presenters.

The IdeaCity Conference in Toronto is an annual event that brings together presenters from all over the world. It features over 50 speakers, ranging from technologists and politicians to artists and entertainers such as Jann Arden. Organized by media mogul Moses

Znaimer, the event has been called a "meeting of the minds." Imagine the hundreds of hours of public relations writing that go into all the speeches. Then there are the introductions for each speaker. Moses Znaimer himself introduces each presenter using written notes. The content of these notes must be carefully written to include information that will make the audience look forward to the presentation as well as sing the praises of the speaker.

PRACTITIONER INTERVIEW

Dave Bourne, Manager for Communications at Scarborough Hospital

Dave Bourne is the manager of corporate communications at the Scarborough Hospital in Ontario. He is the recipient of several PR awards. As part of his work, he writes for a large number of internal and external target audiences that include staff, physicians, and volunteers at the hospital; board members and executives; the provincial Ministry of Health and Long-Term Care; community members and partners; patients and their families; donors; and the media, among others.

Question: What kind of PR writing do you do for your organization?

Answer: On any given day, I might be distilling complex medical jargon into newsletter or website content that can be easily understood by patients or community members. I often have to explain provincial policies and their impact on patients or staff. And to do this, I often take the opportunity to tell stories—the best way to build the reputation of the hospital and to make content meaningful for any audience is to find the human-interest angle. Instead of writing about a policy, for instance, I like to get staff or patients to explain how they are personally impacted. Medical procedures are often written about from the perspective of the patient and how their lives may have been changed for the better.

I also do a lot of strategic communication planning, which, from a writer's perspective, requires a considerable amount of primary research and an understanding of complex issues and communication challenges and opportunities.

And like most corporate communicators, I spend a portion of my time writing speeches, backgrounders, fact sheets, briefing notes, and other documents that support our executives and provide information for key stakeholders.

Question: How big of a part does writing play in your work?

Answer: Strong writing skills and the ability to adapt prose to a wide variety of audiences and communication vehicles are probably the biggest core skills any public relations professional can have. Virtually every tactic I employ as part of a communication strategy involves writing. Whether it's creating content for a corporate newsletter or sharing information using Twitter, I need to be able to incorporate key messages in a way that is understandable and memorable for my intended audience.

Question: How do you tailor your writing to different audiences?

Answer: Often, the key messages that need to be shared are the same, or similar, for each audience. The challenge is choosing the right vehicle to convey the message. In the hospital, electronic communications are not always best, as more than half of the employees do not have dedicated computer access. So we rely heavily on printed communication materials and face-to-face communications at town halls and staff meetings. Externally, we make extensive use of our website and social media to drive traffic to the latest news and information, as well as a number of print and

(Continued)

Dave Bourne, Manager for Communications at Scarborough Hospital

email vehicles that target specific groups. I have come to appreciate that repetition of messaging is key to success, and we often repurpose content for the same audiences using multiple vehicles to enhance message retention.

Question: What is the most challenging aspect of writing PR materials?

Answer: For me, having a significant portion of our external audience read and speak a language other than English presents a challenge. While we have begun translating more of our communications into Chinese and Tamil—the languages most frequently spoken in our community, after English—issues of nuance and cultural interpretation remain difficult hurdles. We rely on the expertise of both internal and external translators who are trained to understand the subtleties of tone, dialect, and culture that can impact the messages we want to convey. It's an ongoing learning process, but I am seeing some positive response in the community as a result of our efforts.

Question: What advice can you give young practitioners on writing?

Answer: My best piece of advice is not to consider writing a tactic, but rather a strategic tool. Public relations is not about churning out newsletter content, media releases, and speeches. Those are just tactics. Public relations is a management function focused on reputation management and helping an organization achieve its business goals and objectives. Writing may be the core skill a young practitioner needs to succeed, but it is closely connected with strategic thinking. You will not succeed with just one or the other.

Note: Dave Bourne accepted a position with another organization after the completion of this interview. For the purposes of this example, we continue to refer to his former position at Scarborough Hospital.

WEB COPY/BLOGS

Writing web copy and blogs is a specialized skill and is often an important PR tactic. We saw in the opening vignette on Atlantic PATH that rewriting the website was part of the overall campaign. It is harder for people to read things on a screen than on a page, so it's important to make the copy quick and easy to read. Short sentences and snappy statements help the reader. Websites, in particular, might have many audiences, and so the writing in different sections may need to be directed toward a variety of groups. For a company website, these audiences might include customers, potential customers, employees, potential employees, suppliers, investors, business analysts, and various media. For example, the PR team at Research in Motion, the Canadian company behind BlackBerry, is continually updating their website, which includes information for several target audiences, including journalists, investors, potential employees, and consumers. A further complication is that the web is available to people all over the world and at all times.[25] Web writers and bloggers should avoid using words that convey a date, such as "today" or "next week," and instead list the date and time.[26] For one reader "today" may be a different date than for another reader in a different time zone.[27]

While writing web copy and blogs, you also need to think about search engines. How will people be searching for your page? Include common search terms in your web copy in the headline or near the top of the page so that search engines can pick them up. Also, use keywords in your links instead of using the generic "click here."[28] Web copy has an advantage over the printed page in that you can incorporate videos, gifs, audio, and links to other content to better communicate your message. Web content also allows for more interactivity as readers can post comments, react to others' posts, and easily share the content through social media. For more information on blogging, see Chapter 7.

SOCIAL MEDIA COPY

Writing for social media is harder than it looks. Though many people think that they are good at social media writing because they have a personal Facebook or Twitter account, writing effectively for an organization on social media is a specialized skill. Social media force a communicator to deliver the message in a concise, snappy, attention-grabbing way. Keeping up with the often overwhelming stream of responses and questions in a pleasant, public-facing way requires diligence. There is little room for error in such a public medium.

Each social media site has its own unique writing requirements. In describing Twitter and Facebook, Susan Orlean, writer for *The New Yorker* and author of *The Orchid Thief*, says, "Twitter is a noisy cocktail party, with lots of chatting and quick interactions, a kind of casual free-for-all. Facebook is a combination high school and college reunion and therapy group."[29] As such, while with Twitter you can tweet a lot without alienating your audience because of all the background chatter, on Facebook if you post more than once or twice a day you will most likely annoy your fans.[30]

The most important element to successful social media writing is personality. Readers don't want to engage with companies online that reverberate corporate-speak.[31] People like to engage with people. In the same vein, it is important to tone down heavy promotion on social media. Companies should use social media as a tool to add value and build loyalty among consumers instead of just sell, sell, sell.[32]

The PR team for Pacific Centre, a shopping centre in downtown Vancouver, conducted a social media campaign that targeted 18- to 25-year-old women who are fashion-forward and buy the latest trends. The copy was written in a fun and edgy style from a fashionista point of view to appeal to this target audience. For more information on social media, see Chapter 7.

OPINION EDITORIALS

Opinion editorials are letters submitted to the editors of newspapers or news magazines. Unlike a media release, an opinion editorial can express personal beliefs. This can be an effective way to get your organization's point of view known. It is also a great way to highlight your organization or CEO as an industry leader or thought

TOWN OF STRATFORD   Memorandum

To: Media Outlets

From: James R. Miron, Mayor

Date: October 19, 2009

RE: Mayor Jim Miron Response Opinion Editorial to Raymark Opinion
           Editorial by Tom Smith of "Save Stratford"

As the Mayor of the Town of Stratford, I am committed to ensuring the safest
and most comprehensive cleanup of Raymark Waste for Stratford's citizens.
Recently, Tom Smith of "Save Stratford" irresponsibly misstated my position and
actions regarding Raymark waste. Frankly, since Mr. Smith and his organization
are vocal supporters of another candidate for Mayor, their motivation and bias
destroys their credibility.

I can simply and affirmatively state that I support the complete and safe removal
of all Raymark waste from Town. I have always advocated for a safe, state of the
art, environmental clean up process that includes real time health monitoring.
My position has been consistent, loud and clear that public health and safety can
never be compromised in the process.

As most of us who have lived in Town for any appreciable period understand,
Raymark waste is an issue that is many decades old and complicated.
Numerous environmental, health, remediation and fiscal issues are interwoven
and must be considered together. Every potential solution carries with it pros and
cons that require (a) citizen input; (b) community consensus; and (c) money from
Congress (a lot of money, in fact, to date, over 220 million dollars was spent as
part of the Raymark cleanup).

The proper cleanup of Raymark Waste has been a priority for my Administration
from day one. One of my first briefings as Mayor was from the Health Director on
Raymark. Years ago I directed the Health Director to lead a team consisting of the
Assistant Health Director; Environmental Conservation Administrator; Town
Planner: Zoning Administrator and members of the Economic Development team
to ensure all Raymark issues were studied and addressed from every
perspective the Town could bring to the process.

Figure 5.5   Example of an Opinion Editorial

Source: Used by permission of Town of Stratford Memorandum.

leader. Usually an opinion editorial is written on a timely topic or a topic that is
slightly controversial. For National Volunteer Week, the director of an organization
that encourages volunteerism might write an opinion editorial about why it is more
important then ever to volunteer.

When writing an opinion editorial, as with a media release, you need to lead with your conclusion.[33] In other words, you must start with you most important information. In the paragraphs that follow you then support your opinion. It is also important to remember that a newspaper's readers will be a diverse and very busy audience. You must capture their attention and speak in clear, direct language, avoiding jargon or acronyms that they might not know.[34]

Action Canada is a leadership and public policy development program. Each year 20 young Canadians are selected to join the 11-month program. Writing opinion editorials is one of the important skills they learn. Action Canada describes it this way:

> Conveying relevant, timely opinions and ideas to the general public is an important skill for leaders interested in making and influencing public policy. That's why Action Canada works closely with Fellows to enhance their skills in writing op-ed and commentary pieces worthy of publication in national newspapers and magazines, both print and electronic, and to familiarize them with the instruments of social media.[35]

See Figure 5.5 for an example of an opinion editorial.

ANNUAL REPORTS

If you work in investor relations or corporate communications, one of your responsibilities may include producing an annual report. An annual report is produced by publicly traded companies once a year to report their fiscal financial results. It typically includes financial highlights, a letter to shareholders from the CEO, and financial statements.

Even though an annual report is a financial reporting tool, it needs to be understood by readers with all levels of financial knowledge. It is not just financial analysts who will be reading the annual report, but also individual shareholders or potential investors. Individual shareholders could include everyone from sophisticated investors to people who know very little about how to read a profit and loss statement. Because of this, the annual report should be easy to read and understand and light on any jargon and technical language.[36] If technical language must be used, it should be clearly defined. You should never take for granted that the reader knows and understands your industry. It is important to provide relevant background information.[37]

It is also useful to understand how annual reports are read. Often they are lengthy, technical documents that only the most avid and interested investor will read cover to cover. For the most part, the document will simply be skimmed. You can make the task of reviewing the report easy on your readers by including bullet points, graphics, call-outs, and short paragraphs.[38]

Finally, be sure to sell a vision in your annual report. Although an annual report is a backward-looking document, as it reports on past financial performance, most investors are looking for clues on how the company will perform in the future. Make sure the report incorporates plans for the future, new innovation, and strategy.[39]

Annual reports share financial results with shareholders and stakeholders.

Source: Alamy

Lionsgate Entertainment's 2011 annual report opens with this paragraph celebrating the organization's successes:

Fiscal 2011 was a year in which we continued to generate strong financial results, achieved record library revenue and filmed entertainment backlog, maintained our growth momentum in our core businesses and made rapid and accelerating progress in the critical transition from traditional to new digital businesses, both domestically and internationally.[40]

For more information on annual reports and investor relations, see Chapter 12.

INTERNAL COMMUNICATIONS MATERIALS

Depending on your role within an organization, you may be asked to draft many of the company's internal communications pieces. These might include employee emails, announcements, presentations, speeches to be delivered to employees, and newsletters, among other materials. Writing internal documents is much like composing any other piece, except in this case the audiences are employees and board members instead of external parties.

While in some ways an internal audience is easier to write for because they already know a lot about your organization (so you don't have to provide them with the same contextual information you would an external party), they have their own distinct culture and needs that have to be taken into account. When writing for this audience, you must consider what motivates them. Employees want to be inspired, and they want to be part of a company that does great things. Employees also want to be valued and have their ideas and suggestions listened to. Make sure you provide both opportunities to deliver communication to employees and forums for them to provide their perspective. For more information on internal communication, see Chapter 9.

The PR team for the Montreal Children's Hospital writes and publishes an employee newsletter called *Chez Nous* in order to inform and motivate their staff. It includes information of interest to employees, such as changes in management, the opening of new clinics, and medical research results.

MARKETING COMMUNICATIONS MATERIALS

PR practitioners are increasingly called upon to perform marketing communications tactics and writing. This can involve everything from **copywriting** (or writing the text for) ads and direct mail pieces to drafting materials such as banners for trade and consumer shows. While these materials need to follow many of the rules of PR writing, they are different in one important aspect: in marketing communications, you pay to have your message communicated. Consequently, you can be a lot more promotional in your writing. In fact, in marketing communications, you can blatantly try to sell or promote your product. The writing style is a lot more simple and direct. The headlines can be attention-grabbing, bold, dynamic, and exciting. You are focusing on what is called the **unique selling proposition** (or key differentiator) of your product or service. As part of the Atlantic PATH campaign, ad copy was written for TV, radio, and newspapers, as well as posters.

Breviro Caviar is a luxury caviar from New Brunswick that is sold around the world. It is a product unique to Canada and is made from the roe of the shortnose sturgeon. For the launch of this new product, the PR team drafted many marketing communications pieces, including the copy on the cans of caviar. They also wrote the brochures, the copy for the website, and the banners to promote the products.

FREQUENTLY ASKED QUESTIONS

PR practitioners are often asked to create frequently asked questions, or FAQs. FAQ documents may need to be developed and distributed for a variety of reasons. If the same questions are often asked of your customer service team, you may create FAQs that are posted on the website or published in a brochure for your customers.

Internally, FAQs might also be created for your sales and customer service representatives for new product launches, new policies and procedures, or issues. This will ensure that they have both a reference document to help them better understand the topic and standard scripting to follow when speaking to customers. FAQs may also be provided to senior managers to use when communicating to employees during times of change or turmoil. For example, an FAQ might be distributed to managers prior to announcing a restructuring. This helps managers feel confident and stay on message when answering difficult questions from employees. FAQs help ensure that stakeholders such as customers, employees, and the media are able to easily find answers to popular questions. When distributed internally, they also ensure that everyone is using the same approved language when answering questions from external parties.

Thinking Like a PR Practitioner

1. When would you use an opinion editorial instead of a media release?
2. A Loving Spoonful is a nonprofit that delivers meals to individuals with AIDS and HIV. Write three tweets for each of the following target audiences:

Volunteers who deliver the meals
Donors who provide donations
Doctors who refer patients to the program

3. How is writing marketing communications materials different from other forms of PR writing?

SASKATCHEWAN RESEARCH COUNCIL'S SMART STORY IDEAS

The Saskatchewan Research Council (SRC) has been active in applied research and technology in the province for 60 years, yet awareness of it among the general public was low. Although it wanted to heighten its profile, the SRC did not have the budget to conduct a large awareness-driving advertising campaign. Instead, the organization turned to PR, which is often more cost effective than mass advertising, with its Smart Story Ideas campaign.

A challenge of conducting public relations for the SRC was that, because it is considered a government agency, media releases and press conferences needed to receive government approval before they could be made public, which could be a lengthy process. The SRC decided to go with an alternative strategy to avoid the delays caused by the approval process.

As part of the Smart Story Ideas campaign, which ran for just under one year, the SRC's communications team, led by Cam Zimmer, pitched stories and prewritten articles to the Saskatchewan media. **Prewritten articles** are articles written in a journalistic style that the media can run without changing. The articles focused on unique SRC services that could be of interest to journalists and the province's residents. They were distributed to coincide with public awareness weeks, to provide an additional incentive for journalists to run them. For instance, an article on a solar heating program was sent to the media to coincide with Earth Day.

The objectives of the campaign were to increase media coverage on the SRC by 10 per cent and to increase visits to the media section of the webpage by 25 per cent. The primary audiences of the campaign were reporters and editors, and the secondary audience was Saskatchewan residents.

One of the challenges of the campaign included convincing internal spokespeople and experts of the benefits of conducting media relations. Internal education was required to bring internal stakeholders on board. Also, because the SRC hadn't conducted media relations for such a long time, some reporters were either surprised to hear from the organization or were only minimally aware of it. Despite these challenges, the results of the campaign were phenomenal and exceeded the defined objectives. Media coverage increased by 45 per cent during the campaign and traffic to the media section of the SRC's website increased by 106 per cent.

To measure effectiveness of the coverage, the SRC used a points system, allocating points based on tone and quality of coverage. Using this points system, the SRC was able to validate that its key messages were being communicated.

Questions

1. Explain the steps needed to write prewritten articles.

2. A Loving Spoonful is a non-profit that delivers meals to individuals with AIDS and HIV. Develop three story ideas for prewritten articles that would appeal to the volunteers who deliver meals for A Loving Spoonful.

Source: Saskatchewan Research Council

AUTHOR'S OWN EXPERIENCE

A Day in the Life of a PR Writer

It is 8 a.m. and you are already hard at work. Your day starts with drafting a report for your manager outlining the success of last night's special event. Then it is on to writing urgent emails. The first one you respond to is from a journalist who is unhappy with the interview she conducted with your spokesperson. You choose your words carefully and answer diplomatically.

At 9 a.m., you are writing the first draft of a media release for the launch of a new Honda dealership. You are new to this **account** (which is how PR practitioners refer to clients) and you conduct some research on the automobile industry before you start writing.

At 11 a.m., the phone rings. It is your client from the credit union. She wants you to make edits to the short speech you wrote for her. She is appearing that afternoon on television to make a large donation on the Show of Hearts telethon.

You drop everything. The speech needs to be rewritten to incorporate her changes immediately.

This is a snapshot of a typical morning when we worked in PR agencies. As you can see, an enormous amount of writing is involved. Rarely does a day go by that does not include writing in some form or another. And a lot of it is done on very tight deadlines. Our ability to write quickly and professionally is one of the greatest strengths we bring to the table. Our writing is strategic and tailored each time to fit the client and the audience. Before committing anything to the screen or paper, we always ask: What do I want to say here? What does the audience need or want to know? What is/are my key message(s)? The majority of practitioners are jacks of all trades—we write and plan and execute a variety of tactics. But some of us become writing specialists and focus our whole careers on this one tactic.

PR Writing

internal communications
- newsletters

media materials
- releases
- advisories
- backgrounders
- biographies
- fact sheets

opinion editorials

- voice
- tone

fundamentals
- key messages
- objectives
- audiences

annual reports

speeches

social media copy

webcopy

marketing communications
- ad copy
- brochures
- posters

Key Terms

assignment editor An individual who selects stories to cover and assigns stories to other reporters.

account A term PR agencies use to refer to their clients, as in "I am working on the Westjet account."

audience The population for which the communication is intended.

backgrounder A media material that provides additional context and information on a person, product, process, or organization.

boilerplate A short paragraph at the end of a release that provides more information on the organization issuing the release.

copywriting A writing style that is used for advertising and other forms of marketing such as direct mail.

email blast An email message sent to a large mailing list at the same time.

fact sheet A bulleted media material that provides facts about a company or product.

first draft The preliminary form of a writing project. It will be rewritten and edited to produce further drafts until a final draft is reached.

ghost writing Writing on someone else's behalf, where it is agreed that he or she will receive the credit.

hometown release A release that targets the local community.

key messages The main ideas the PR practitioner wants to convey to the audience.

media kit A package for the media in which the information they will need is compiled in one place.

media advisory A cross between an invitation and a media release, a media advisory lets journalists know about an important upcoming announcement or event.

media release A document that announces the news about the story at the heart of a campaign. Also called a news release or press release.

news values An angle employed in a release or pitch to make it newsworthy.

news wire A service that delivers content to news organizations.

prewritten article An article that is written by PR practitioners in a journalistic style and can be used as is by the media.

template A model that outlines which information must be included and in which order. It is preformatted and is used as a starting point in creating a document.

tone The attitude that the writer projects toward the audience and the subject matter.

unique selling proposition The qualities that make a product or service stand out from the competition; the reason why a person will choose it over others.

Weblinks

Bad News Releases: 25 Press Release Turkeys
www.theprcoach.com/bad-news-releases-25-press-release-turkeys/

Hans Brinker Budget Hotel Ad
www.youtube.com/watch?v=uv3KqZUY_qc

The Moth
http://themoth.org

Speech Analysis: I Have a Dream—Martin Luther King Jr.
http://sixminutes.dlugan.com/speech-analysis-dream-martin-luther-king/

TED Talks
www.ted.com/talks

TIFF Press Releases
press.tiff.net/press-releases

Under the Influence
www.cbc.ca/undertheinfluence/

We Day Press
www.weday.com/what-is-we-day/press//

WikiHow: How to Write a Press Release
www.wikihow.com/Write-a-Press-Release

Endnotes

1. Richard Cole, Larry Hembroff, and Andrew Corner, "National Assessment of the Perceived Writing Skills of Entry-Level PR Practitioners," *Journalism & Mass Communication Educator* (Spring 2009), 10–26.

2. Ibid.

3. Ibid.

4. "3 Key Messages," *PR Next: Monthly E-zine for PR Professionals*, September 6, 2009. Accessed February 23, 2013, http://prnext.wordpress.com/2009/09/06/3-key-messages/

5. Ibid.

6. "Ask Robert Stephens," *Inc.*, October 1, 2008. Accessed February 23, 2013, http://www.inc.com/magazine/20081001/ask-robert-stephens.html

7. Barbara, K. Mednick, "Tips for Determining a Good News Hook," *Site Booster* blog, October 29, 2010. Accessed February 23, 2013, http://www.site-booster.com/blog/2010/10/tips-4-good-news-hook/

8. Ibid.

9. Ibid.

10. Ibid.

11. Ibid.

12. "10 Greatest Virgin PR Stunts of all Time," *Business Pundit*, August 29, 2011. Accessed February 23, 2013, http://www.businesspundit.com/10-greatest-virgin-pr-stunts-of-all-time

13. Terry O'Reilly, "Handcuffed By Brand Image," *Under the Influence*, CBC Radio, March 24, 2012. Accessed February 23, 2013, http://www.cbc.ca/undertheinfluence/season-1/2012/03/24/handcuffed-by-brand-image/

14. Ibid.

15. Ibid.

16. Amy Jacques, "Honing Their Craft: Insight from 2 Top PR Writers," *Tactics* (February 2012), 8.

17. Andrew Hindes, "PR with Benefits: What 'Mad Men' Can Teach Us About Writing Press Releases," *PR News*, April 5, 2012. Accessed February 23, 2013, http://www.prnewsonline.com/featured/2012/04/03/pr-with-benefits-what-mad-men-can-teach-us-about-writing-press-releases/

18. Marie Overfors, "Writing Better News Releases: 6 Common Mistakes and How to Avoid (Fix) Them," *Tactics* (February 2012), 10.

19. Amy Jacques, "Give Speech a Chance: Crafting a Winning Address," *Tactics*, February 1, 2011. Accessed February 23, 2013, http://www.prsa.org/Intelligence/Tactics/Articles/view/9015/1028/Give_speech_a_chance_Crafting_a_winning_address

20. Ibid.

21. Quoted in Judith Humphrey, "Writing Professional Speeches: Seven Steps for Perfecting your Craft," *Vital Speeches of the Day*, Vol. 54, Issue 11, March 15, 1988, 343–345.

22. Ibid.

23. Ibid.

24. Ibid.

25. "Writing Tips That Clarify Web Copy," *Ideas That Work. Communications Briefings*, Vol. 29, Issue 5, March 1, 2010, 4.

26. Ibid.

27. Ibid.

28. Stephen Spencer, "Search Engine Marketing: Writing Great Web Copy," *Multichannel Merchant*, Vol. 4, Issue 11, November, 1, 2008, 18–19.

29. Matt Petronzio, "10 Pro Tips for Writers Using Social Media," Mashable Social Media, February 2, 2012. Accessed February 23, 2013, http://mashable.com/2012/02/02/social-media-writers/

30. Ibid.

31. "3 Key Messages."

32. Petronzio, "10 Pro Tips for Writers Using Social Media."

33. John McLain, "How to Write an Op-Ed: Perhaps It's PR's Most Underutilized Tool," *All About Public Relations with Steven R. Van Hook*. Accessed February 23, 2013, http://aboutpublicrelations.net/ucmclaina.htm

34. Ibid.

35. "Fellows' Opinion Editorials," Action Canada. Accessed February 23, 2013, http://www.actioncanada.ca/en/fellows/opinion-editorials/

36. Patrick Tuohey, "Ten Things to Keep in Mind When Writing an Annual Report," *IR Update*, September 2002. Accessed February 23, 2013, http://www.marcomresearch.com/pdfs/tenthings.pdf

37. Ibid.

38. Ibid.

39. Ibid.

40. "Financial Reports," Lionsgate Entertainment. Accessed, February 23, 2013, http://investors.lionsgate.com/phoenix.zhtml?c=62796&p=irol-reportsAnnual

What Makes a Successful PR Practitioner?

Students often ask what the key success factors in public relations are and if practitioners share any traits.

While there are many different ways to get to the same destination, top PR practitioners do have some things in common. They all share the most important skills. These can be broken down into two types: competency skills, and personality and attitude skills. Strive to develop your aptitude in these areas.

Competency skills:
Writing and editing
Computer and design layout
Public speaking
Research

Personality and attitude skills:
Risk taking
Creativity
Listening skills
Passion
Perseverance
Thick skin
Self-confidence
Ability to plan and see projects through to the end
Communication and networking skills
Humour (it is not imperative to have this one, but it sure does help!)

Remember that to be successful, you do not have to reinvent the wheel. As inspirational speaker Tony Robbins says, success leaves clues. You can learn a lot from senior practitioners. Ask questions. Pay attention to how they do things. Many will be delighted to share their expertise with you. They were with us.

Chapter 6
Media Relations

Fairway Divorce Solutions was able to leverage media relations to grow its business.

Source: Fairway Divorce Solutions

LEARNING OBJECTIVES

1. Analyze the strengths of media relations and the inherent risks involved compared to other public relations tactics and forms of marketing.

2. Differentiate between the role journalists play in society and the role they play as a conduit to target audiences.

3. Appraise the relationship between practitioners and journalists.

4. Review and select media best able to reach target audiences.

5. Develop a step-by-step media relations action plan.

The Power of Media Relations: Putting an Organization on the Map

Brookline Public Relations (Brookline), a PR agency based in Calgary, was approached by a local organization that was offering a unique alternative to the traditional divorce method. Karen Stewart, the founder and CEO of Fairway Divorce Solutions, had a goal to provide a step-by-step process to dramatically reduce the time, costs, and emotional pain of traditional divorce. By charging a flat rate for services and using a proven approach called The Fairway Process™, Fairway Divorce Solutions created an entirely new category in the divorce industry.

The challenge for Fairway's PR agency was to get the public to understand the new method and view it as a legitimate, superior alternative to the standard legal battles that surround most divorces. Brookline's first priority was designing a media relations campaign that leveraged Stewart's position as a thought leader in alternative divorce solutions. Each month, targeted pitches were sent to key media contacts, and relationships with journalists, assignment editors, and producers were steadily built. Within six months, several interviews with print, radio, and TV outlets had been secured, and Stewart was being featured monthly on a radio show broadcast out of Minneapolis, Minnesota. As the company's profile grew, so did the demand for its services. In 2008, Fairway began offering franchise licences, and the PR team began publicizing this development as well. In addition to profiling Stewart's expertise, Brookline was now targeting franchise publications.

Some of the newsworthy angles that were used to pitch the media included the following:

Valentine's Day: Is there a Valentine's Day after divorce? Brookline pitched Fairway's CEO nationwide to speak on this topic and to share some ways to spend the day if you're separated or divorced.

Back to school: Brookline pitched nationwide media using the angle of the stress of co-parenting during the back-to-school season and tips on creating a successful school rotation schedule that works for both the parents and the kids.

The Calgary Stampede: Brookline pitched Calgary media about the 30 to 40 per cent increase in divorce inquiries that Fairway sees following the Calgary Stampede. Fairway's CEO was positioned as a thought leader on why this trend occurs and what couples can do to avoid it.

In order to maintain a fresh, creative approach when working with clients for a longer period, Brookline keeps up to date on current events and delivers timely pitches to a targeted list of national media from major Canadian cities, such as Toronto, Vancouver, Calgary, Edmonton, Winnipeg, Saskatoon, Victoria, and Kelowna.

The solid success of Brookline's media relations campaign for Fairway led to over 200 media stories, or *media hits*, over a five-year period and more than $1.5 million in PR value. Media coverage included *More* magazine, Business News Network (BNN), *Reader's Digest*, CTV, *Financial Post*, *National Post*, *Alberta Venture* magazine, *Profit* magazine, *Canadian Business*, CBC/Radio-Canada, *The Globe and Mail*, *FranchiseCanada*, and Slice TV. As proof of the success of the media relations campaign, reporters have begun to contact Brookline to coordinate interviews with Stewart as a divorce guru, and interviews are often requested for TV, radio, and print segments. As a result of Brookline's media relations efforts for Fairway, the company has seen explosive growth, with 33 franchises sold in 18 cities across North America to date.

As this opening vignette illustrates, media relations can be a powerful tool in helping an organization meet its public relations and business goals. The media coverage garnered through the campaign raised Fairway's profile with its target audiences, including individuals considering divorce, as well as those interested in becoming franchisees. Ongoing and regular pitches to the media that employed creative story angles contributed to building relationships with journalists and generating excellent media coverage in both national and local media outlets. Brookline's media relations efforts elevated the client's profile and positioned the CEO as the divorce guru. As the organization's profile grew, so did its business success.

Brookline was successful in this campaign because it steadily built relationships with the media. To build these relationships, it is important to know how journalists operate and what topics are of interest to them. Only then is it possible to tailor key messages and media pitches to journalists so that they cover the story. In this chapter we will review these topics and examine the relationship between journalists and PR practitioners. Finally, we will look at the practical information of how to conduct media relations, and we will go over best practices that have generated successful results in the past.

Media Relations Defined ❶

At its most basic level, **media relations** is about creating relationships with the media and journalists. External public relations practitioners need to be able to provide journalists with the information and resources they need in order to write favourable articles about organizations. Media relations can also include pitching journalists at news organizations in the hope that they will be interested in a story and cover it. The goal is to generate coverage in media outlets such as newspapers, radio, television, and digital news channels. Media relations also refers to all the activities conducted with the objective of building a relationship between media and the organization. Media relations is sometimes called *publicity*, and a practitioner is known as a **publicist**.

In a nutshell, this is how media relations works: PR practitioners provide journalists with information and other details needed to cover a story, which might include interviews, photos, or additional information. PR professionals convince journalists to run a story on their organization without paying for it, as opposed to paying for advertising. That is why media coverage is also called *earned* or *unpaid coverage*. The story of Fairway in the opening vignette is a great example of generating earned coverage. Brookline regularly provided journalists with story ideas about Fairway. It also set up interviews with

CEO Karen Stewart for various media outlets. These efforts generated a generous amount of earned media coverage in a host of media outlets, including the *National Post*, CTV, and CBC.

If working with the media sounds stressful and you are hoping to avoid it, think again. Media relations is typically a key tactic in an external public relations campaign. If you work for a public relations agency, media relations will often be a key component of your responsibilities. Media relations can be a powerful external PR tool and has the potential to propel an organization to great success. As Fairway's profile grew and its CEO became known as the divorce guru as a result of all the media coverage, the company's business success also grew.

In regards to how it is executed, media relations can involve a variety of tasks, from writing to travelling with journalists. Here are a few examples:

- Writing a media release to publicize George Stroumboulopoulos's exclusive interview with Oprah on the CBC
- Providing a magazine with clothing from a fashion collection for inclusion in a feature article
- Distributing media materials and product samples to media for a new product launch
- Accompanying travel journalists on a trip overseas to publicize a new hotel
- Organizing a media conference to announce a new government policy
- Pitching story ideas to journalists
- Managing a special event, such as the Toronto International Film Festival, attended by hundreds of journalists
- Coordinating a **media interview** between a reporter and a spokesperson to deal with a breaking issue or crisis

An installation at the Toronto International Film Festival, where special media events are held.
Source: Alex Henry Moore/ Getty Images

BENEFITS AND CHALLENGES OF MEDIA RELATIONS

There are several benefits to using the media as a conduit to reach your target audiences. The first is that if your story makes it into the news, this can have a significant impact. Through media relations, a large audience can be reached in a relatively short time, and media relations can often be more cost-effective than advertising. Also, when a media outlet covers a favourable story, it provides that topic or organization with **third-party endorsement**, or credibility, as if the media have given it a seal of approval. Andy Polansky, Council of Public Relations Firms, describes it this way: "One of the enduring strengths of public relations is its ability to obtain influential third-party testimonials. Having someone else say nice things about your brand has a lot more credibility than saying those things yourself."[1] This is evident in the opening vignette about Fairway. The organization received a host of positive media coverage, which helped build awareness among individuals considering divorce, as well as potential franchisees.

The media are an effective way to reach target audiences, as news mediums are widely consumed by Canadians. In fact, 89 per cent of Canadians follow news and current affairs at least several times a week. Television is the most popular source of news for Canadians, followed by newspapers, radio, and digital outlets.[2]

Some challenges of media relations include a lack of control over if, how, and when the story will ultimately appear and what key messages will be included in the story. Journalists decide how they want to treat information sent to them by PR practitioners. There is no guarantee that a positive story will appear. A good example is what happened to Yves Veggie Cuisine, a maker of veggie foods, during a media relations campaign. The organization was booked on the *Vicki Gabereau Show*, a former national television talk show. This was an exciting opportunity for the company because it meant its veggie foods would be seen by a national audience. Unfortunately, when the host of the TV program tasted one of the veggie products during the show, she compared its taste to that of a hockey puck. You can imagine how disappointed the organization and its PR team were.

Another challenge to overcome is that media coverage is difficult or even impossible to achieve if the story is not **newsworthy** (i.e., containing attributes that make it compelling to news organizations). Even if your story is newsworthy, it is difficult to generate media coverage on busy news days when **breaking news stories** (stories that develop unexpectedly, such as fires or robberies) are competing with yours for the attention of journalists and for space in the publication or broadcast. On top of this, even on slow news days, journalists are bombarded with information, and it can be difficult to get their attention. A typical journalist can receive hundreds of emails a day, making it tricky for PR practitioners to break through the clutter and get their stories noticed.[3] This is why having good relationships with particular journalists can be beneficial when pitching media stories. If a journalist knows and trusts you to provide newsworthy content and resources to support your stories, it is easier to break through the clutter.

Sarah Anderson, Senior Manager, Communications, the Daily Bread Food Bank

Sarah Anderson is senior manager, communications, for the Daily Bread, a nonprofit organization that supports food banks and meal programs. Its mission is to end hunger in the community.

Question: What kind of media relations tactics do you use at Daily Bread?

Answer: We often use media releases, advisories, editorial letters, or opinion pieces, and occasionally traditional media conferences in addition to special events.

Question: Why do you work with the media? What do you hope to achieve?

Answer: Without a huge budget (or any budget) for advertising, the media is very important to Daily Bread, and nonprofits in general. The media can reach a lot more people than I can hope to through our other communication channels, such as print or e-newsletters, social media, and Daily Bread's website. The media broadens our reach to areas of the public that may not know much about us, or the issues we're trying to educate and raise awareness on.

Question: What are some of the challenges in generating media coverage for a nonprofit?

Answer: I think the challenges for nonprofits are the same as those in the corporate world. There is an awful lot of noise out there, and it can be very hard to be heard. Media are often interested in speaking to people coming to food banks about their very personal stories experiencing poverty. In many cases, these are people who don't tell their families or friends that they are struggling and are not interested in sharing their story with the whole world. There's a lot of stigma and stereotypes about people who come to a food bank. While on one hand I need people to speak out and help challenge those stereotypes, I understand that's asking a lot of someone. And there is the additional challenge that some media buy into the stereotypes and that's the story they're looking to exploit.

Question: How do you come up with newsworthy angles?

Answer: I focus on talking with staff and being aware of what's going on in the media, in the nonprofit world, and everywhere in the organization, especially from the program level. I find there are a lot of newsworthy stories that staff know about, but they often think it's not interesting enough. It's my job to look out for those stories and flag them if I think they might work and let staff know what kind of stories I'm interested in and looking for.

It's also about being hyper-aware of what the media is interested in, or what the story of the week is. A story that may have not been interesting three months ago might now be very topical.

Question: What kind of media events have you organized?

Answer: Media events for us are usually activity or event based. We do have an annual high-profile report on hunger that we've successfully used for the past couple of years to launch our fall fundraising campaign. That's probably the most traditional media conference. Other media events are more interesting activities, such as annual public food sorts timed to coincide with Daily Bread's three main fundraising drives. We have six hundred volunteers over the course of two days come to Daily Bread's warehouse to sort food donations. It's very visual and energetic and is all about the community giving back.

Question: Any advice for those who want to specialize in this area of PR?

Answer: To work for a nonprofit, you really have to care about the mission of that organization. If it's not something you can passionately believe in, then it's probably not the right fit for you. You have to be flexible, since at the majority of nonprofits you might be the only communications person there and you sometimes have

(Continued)

to be pretty creative and make the most out of what you have. Working in the nonprofit world is incredibly fulfilling, sometimes exhausting, and always meaningful. But if you don't end up at a nonprofit, don't forget us during your career! We can always use volunteers with your kind of skills.

PROACTIVE AND REACTIVE MEDIA RELATIONS

There are two types of media relations: proactive and reactive. **Proactive media relations** occurs when a PR practitioner approaches a journalist with a story idea, often as part of a communications plan or campaign. **Reactive media relations** takes place when a journalist contacts the PR professional for a story. This tends to occur when there is a breaking story about the organization or when there is an issue or crisis. Needless to say, typically PR practitioners cannot wait for journalists to take the initiative and must take a proactive approach. Proactive and frequent media relations translates into increased media coverage and helps build relationships with journalists. It keeps your organization top of mind. In this way, sometimes proactive media relations can lead to PR practitioners being contacted for stories that they didn't pitch, because they have proven themselves to be reliable and responsive. PR practitioners who are the most successful are those who take strategic action to get their stories included in the news.[4] We saw this exemplified in the opening case study on Fairway. Brookline contacted journalists on an ongoing and regular basis to pitch story ideas, which translated into increased exposure.

The Halifax Regional Police conducts both proactive and reactive media relations. "We strive to be proactive with respect to media relations, but a lot of our work is reactive just based on the fact that policing is a 24/7 operation," says Theresa Rath, public relations manager.[5] The police service proactively releases any significant police incidents to the media at the end of every 12-hour shift, at about 5 a.m. and 5 p.m. daily. The police department also issues at least one proactive weekly news release on crime prevention in order to engage citizens in public safety in their community. The goal of these proactive media releases is to generate positive media coverage with journalists who cover the police beat or who are interested in crime prevention stories. This media relations plan is part of an overall effort by the city's mayor to enhance community safety.

Thinking Like a PR Practitioner

1. Discuss two recent news stories that you believe are examples of reactive media relations. Explain why you believe that they are reactive. How could the organization have been more proactive?

2. Identify two examples of proactive media relations in your community.

3. Compare the benefits of media relations with the challenges. What are some ways to overcome the challenges?

Journalists: Their Role and What They Do ❷

Now that we have looked at the different forms of media relations, it is time to discuss the role of journalists in our society and explain how they function. This information is of relevance to PR practitioners because the more we know about journalists, the better equipped we are to form positive relationships with them and generate media coverage.

It is important to understand that journalists' purpose is not just to cover the stories PR practitioners put forward. They play a much more important societal role. The media have a responsibility, and that is to keep the public informed.[6] Democracies such as Canada need their citizens to be well informed and engaged in order to flourish, and the media play that informative role.[7] News stories help us become aware of and make sense of important events, and allow us to keep tabs on what politicians and industries are up to. Media stories help people make a wide range of decisions, such as which political party to vote for, where to invest money, or which car to buy based on safety records. Alan Daniels, a long-time journalist, describes the role of media in these terms: "Our talent—if we have one—is to report fairly and objectively, representing the interests of our fellow citizens and so protecting all of our rights and freedoms."[8]

The ability to report on timely, significant events and influence decisions is what makes the media one of the most powerful institutions in the world today. The issues that we as a society view as important are filtered through a media that dictates what is newsworthy and what is not. The media may not tell us what to think, but they tell us what to think about. They set the social, cultural, and political agendas of modern society.[9]

Journalists have long played an important role in democratic societies.

Source: Everett Collection/ Shutterstock

The media also determine how organizations and people are perceived by the public. Journalists have the power to control how people who make the news are presented to the public. They are also the ones to decide if a story will be **positioned**, or framed, in a positive or negative way.[10]

One of the goals of journalism is to produce objective stories that enable the public to learn all sides of a story. Although journalists strive to achieve objectivity in their work, they do not always manage to do so because, like the rest of us, they hold their own preconceived ideas and biases. Journalists also pride themselves on getting facts right. The majority are professionals and are not out "to get" or misquote anyone. The last thing journalists want is to make a factual mistake—their professional reputation depends on it. This is why it is imperative that as PR practitioners we never provide journalists with incorrect information. There is no quicker way to damage your relationship.

HOW JOURNALISTS OPERATE

How journalists operate is of interest to PR practitioners because this helps them decide how to best approach the media. To be successful at media relations, it is imperative to understand the journalistic process.

Journalists produce stories of interest to their publications' audiences. They cater their stories to specific **demographics**, which might include the age, gender, and education level of the audience. That is how media build and maintain circulation and viewership numbers. Some media are specialized and target a niche audience, such as the listeners of a radio program on technology. Other media, like national newspapers, have a broader focus and target a more mainstream audience. A national newspaper's readership might encompass a wider spectrum and have less in common than the readership of a parenting magazine. Whatever the audience, journalists will be interested in your story only if they think it will be of interest to their audience.

Some journalists cover a **beat**, or area of specialization, such as business or health, while others cover a variety of topics or general news. Other journalists have the role of assignment editor, where their job is to assign stories to other reporters. To be effective, practitioners must be aware of the types of information or stories likely to be of interest to particular journalists, and this means following their work. If you have a restaurant client, you will want to become familiar with the work of important food editors, reporters, and restaurant reviewers and develop relationships with them. Promoting a food story to a health reporter would waste both your and the reporter's time. It may sound obvious, but it is amazing how many inexperienced PR practitioners make the mistake of pitching to the wrong person. Brookline, the PR agency in the opening vignette, knew to pitch the right story to the right journalist at the right media outlet.

Journalists are busy people who work on tight deadlines. In radio, for example, they can have a story on the air within minutes of interviewing someone. Deadline times vary by media type. Journalists at daily newspapers have a deadline every day, while monthly magazines work with longer **lead times**—the time between when a story is prepared and when it is broadcast or printed. PR practitioners refer to different types of media by their lead time, referring to them as either a long-lead publication or a short-lead publication. An example of a short-lead publication is a newspaper, since you can pitch a story the day before it is printed. An example of a long-lead publication is a monthly magazine. Some magazines work on their issues up to six months before they come out. The Christmas issue of *Chatelaine* magazine, for example, is finished as early as May or June. When working with the media, it is important to know when their deadlines are so that you can take them into account when you are pitching. If you are pitching a Christmas story to *Chatelaine* in September, you will already be too late for that year's issue. When developing a **pitch calendar**, a document where you map out when you will pitch each media outlet based on their lead times, you might decide to pitch your Christmas story to *Chatelaine* in April, to a newspaper in November, and to a radio station in December. See Table 6.1 for examples of lead times.

Table 6.1	Examples of Lead Times	
Type of Media	**Lead Time**	**When to Pitch**
Magazines	Long lead	Three to six months before
Newspapers	Short lead	As the story happens
Newspaper special sections	Long lead	One to two months before
Radio news	Short lead	As the story happens
Radio talk shows	Medium lead	One week before
Television news	Short lead	As the story happens
Television talk shows	Medium lead	One week before
Digital	Short and medium lead	As the story happens to two weeks before

JOURNALISTS' NEED FOR SOURCES

The media routinely rely upon a number of **sources**, or people who provide the information they need to report the news. Think about it this way: news is hardly ever witnessed first-hand by reporters.[11] The media are not typically present to see stories break. They are not standing on the street corner every time a crime occurs; they do not see a company hiring new employees; they are not in the office of the prime minister whenever a decision is made. Therefore, the media rely on sources to provide them with information, and PR practitioners are some of these leading sources. Journalists use the information from PR sources as story ideas and as research. As practitioners, we therefore play a role in determining what information makes its way to the public. Journalists may tell the public what to think about, but they in turn have other individuals helping them decide what deserves attention.[12] This is an important point to remember when contacting a journalist. You are not asking for a favour, but rather are providing a valuable service to journalists and to the public. This is also a responsibility that PR practitioners must take seriously; it exemplifies the importance of being professional, ethical, and truthful (see Chapter 1 for information on ethics). For journalists, Karen Stewart, the CEO of Fairway featured in the opening vignette, became a trusted source of information on divorces because of her professionalism and trustworthiness.

Providing Journalists with What They Need and Building Relationships with Them ❸

Many journalists enjoy working with PR people. They are aware that PR practitioners provide them with valuable information, give them easy access to interviews, supply high-quality photos, and facilitate all other details to get the story written or produced. It is often a win-win relationship. The journalist gets a story idea and valuable information, and the PR practitioner gets his or her story disseminated. Journalists and PR practitioners are aware of the fact that they need each other and that both contribute to each other's professional success.[13]

That said, journalists are fully aware of the self-interests of the PR practitioners who contact them. At times their interests are the same, while at other times they conflict. PR professionals strive to generate positive media coverage for their organizations. Journalists are solely concerned with producing balanced stories, no matter how they portray organizations.

PR practitioners who excel in media relations know how to work with journalists. The PR industry was once dominated by former journalists who deeply understood how the media worked, but this situation has changed with the advent of PR programs. While many former journalists are still attracted to PR, more and more people who choose to enter the field come from other backgrounds. As a result, PR practitioners need to be even more diligent in understanding the reporters to whom they pitch, in order to provide them with what they need and make it easy for them to do stories on their clients or organizations.

PR and journalism are fields of communication that have much in common. Both tell stories catered to specific target audiences, both involve writing, and both work on tight deadlines. There are also major differences. PR practitioners are advocates for organizations, while journalists strive to be objective and balanced in their stories. The more PR practitioners understand about journalists and how they work, the easier it is to present them with stories that meet their needs and with the resources and support they require. And that translates into media coverage.

PROVIDING NEWSWORTHY INFORMATION

To be a good source for journalists, you must provide them with the right kind of information. Generating media coverage depends on not only your knowledge of how journalists work but also your ability to supply them with suitable information.[14] Editors and journalists judge stories based on the newsworthiness of the information, or whether it contains news values. We examined news values in Chapter 5, but the subject is so important to media relations that we will review it again in this chapter. News values are what enable journalists and editors to judge a story's newsworthiness—and decide whether or not a story gets picked up.[15] The more news values a story carries, the better the chances it will make it into the media. PR practitioners must ensure that their story and key messages are tailored to contain news values if they want to generate media coverage.

News values may include the following:

- *Locality:* Relevance to the local community, the city, the province, or the country in which a story takes place. An international story can also have locality if it takes place in a part of the world that is of interest to the public or deals with a topic that affects other nations. Locality is one of the reasons for having community papers. People are interested in events that happen in their community. Something that happens in Vernon, British Columbia, is much more interesting to someone who lives in Vernon than to someone who lives in Quebec City.

- *Immediacy:* A breaking news story. If it happened some time ago, it is already old news. All things being equal, something that takes place today is more newsworthy than something that happened yesterday.

- *Novelty:* Anything that is the first of its kind, a unique new offering, or a new twist on an old story. It could also refer to a stunt.
- *Human interest:* The people behind the story, putting a human face on it. Anything that tugs at your heartstrings, or a feel-good story. The reason why "hometown hero" segments are often on the news.
- *Conflict:* Tension and problems between nations, people, or organizations.
- *Peril:* Fear and stress over the danger of what may happen in the future.
- *Violence:* An act of aggression.
- *Celebrity:* A person, event, or organization that is famous. Things or people that are well known are more newsworthy than those that are not.

Other elements can help make a story newsworthy even without specific news values, simply because the public is highly interested in these topics. A story that contains some of these elements will often generate media coverage:

- Money
- Kids
- Animals
- Crime
- Royalty
- Religion
- Sex

In any media materials and pitches, you will want to make sure that one or more news values are included. If you can't imagine the newspaper headline for a story you are trying to pitch, it is most likely not very newsworthy. A good example of employing news values is the launch of a digital music store by HMV. The organization emphasized the following three news values in a media release that was distributed to media nationally:

- *Locality:* The digital store is Canadian.
- *Immediacy:* It is the launch of a new digital store.
- *Novelty:* The store is Canada's first and only major music download site.

BUILDING RELATIONSHIPS WITH MEDIA

Providing the right kind of information to journalists goes a long way in building the relationship, but it takes more than that. As the name implies, the practice is called *media relations* because it is focused on building mutually beneficial relationships with reporters, editors, and producers. PR practitioners create these relationships with individual outlets and with journalists one-on-one. It is not just the relationship between practitioner and journalist that is forged, but also the relationship between the organization and the journalist. This means that both our professional reputation and that of our organization are on the line in our dealings with the media.

Positive relationships with the media take time to build. They are based on trust and professionalism. Journalists come to know that a certain PR practitioner will provide information that contains all the correct facts, is provided on time, and is of relevance to the target audiences of the media outlet.

Once a positive relationship is established, pitching is easier because journalists are more receptive to a practitioner's story ideas. They may also call PR people proactively to ask if for their assistance for a story. From the opening vignette, the team at Brookline built relationships with journalists for Fairway over time. They regularly contacted journalists with different story ideas until the time came when journalists began contacting them if they needed information about divorce. This shows that they had built strong relationships with journalists who trusted their expertise.

The opposite is also true. If PR practitioners contact the media with stories that are not newsworthy, give journalists information that is false, or fail to give journalists what they need before their deadlines, they reduce their chances of generating coverage. Journalists will be a lot less likely to take your call in the future if you waste their time today and will consider you an unreliable source for stories.

The challenge is that it is getting increasingly difficult to build these relationships. With email and voicemail, opportunities to speak with journalists are not as plentiful as they once were. In addition, journalists' schedules are more hectic than ever, and they spend more time in the newsroom instead of going out to cover stories and attending events.

Jacques Marcoux, publicity manager for the Royal Winnipeg Ballet, works with journalists across Canada to generate media coverage for the organization. Marcoux says

The Royal Winnipeg Ballet believes in developing relationships with the media.
Source: © Terrance Klassen/Alamy

that the "relationship is everything" and that in practice, a public relations professional is a "relationship manager." He offers the following four pieces of advice in building media relationships:

1. *Get face time.* Every opportunity you get to meet with the media, take it. Galas, events, concerts—even if unrelated to your organization, make sure you are always connected.

2. *Be reliable and timely.* No matter how busy my schedule is, if I get a call, request, or inquiry from the media, that automatically becomes my number-one priority until it is completed. I have often received compliments from journalists that I "return email or phone calls quickly" or that they are surprised that I was able to secure an interview "with such short notice." The thing to remember is that reporters are under pressure all the time to meet their deadlines. The easier you make their lives, the more eager they will be to work with you on your next story idea.

3. *Make yourself easily reachable.* If you're out on lunch break, have your cellphone on you and provide media with that number. I have frequently taken calls on my days off. If you can't get the reporter what he needs within the hour, it can often be the difference between great coverage or none at all.

4. *Give appreciation and thank yous.* Once you have received great coverage for an event, follow up with that reporter and thank him or her for the great advance/review. I once sent an arrangement of flowers to a reporter every Mother's Day; I had developed such great rapport with her that we had become friends.[16]

ADVICE TO NEW PRACTITIONERS
Building Media Relationships

- Do what you say you will and always deliver on time. Be trustworthy.

- Understand the needs and deadlines of media and respect them.

- Attend events where there will be media and introduce yourself.

- Always be available to take media calls or return them within the hour.

- If a deadline is approaching and you have not been able to do what you promised you would, call the journalist and explain. Never just let the deadline pass.

- Follow carefully what journalists write about and comment on it. Show them that you know their work.

- Take every opportunity that you can to be helpful to the media. Top practitioners send the media information on topics they know will interest them, even when it has nothing to do with their organizations.

- Always remain professional and courteous and remember that a relationship is a long-term investment.

1. Do a search online for a media release distribution service such as Canada Newswire (www. newswire.ca). You will find a section that includes media releases from different organizations. Identify one that contains three news values or more and another one that is not as newsworthy. Discuss the news values in each media release and the differences between them.

2. Explain two actions you can take to build relationships with journalists in your community.

3. Discuss three things that journalists and PR practitioners have in common. What is meant when we say PR practitioners are not asking for favours when they pitch stories to journalists?

4. Cite two examples of circumstances in which journalists and PR practitioners have had a conflict of interest.

5. Visit the media section of the website of the Canadian Museum of Civilization (www.civilization.ca/cmc/media). Read several media releases. What stories is the museum using to generate media coverage? Generate two story angles that the museum could use in media releases. Identify a second organization that also posts media information on its website and answer the same questions.

The Media Landscape ❹

Having knowledge of the **media landscape**—the scope and the types of media that are available in your organization's market—is essential. The media landscape is constantly changing, whether through the launch and closure of media outlets, the acquisition of outlets by conglomerates or media groups, or job changes by journalists. PR practitioners keep track of these developments in their local markets, as well as nationally. Let us look at the media landscape in Canada. It can be broken down into three major categories—print, broadcast, and digital—and also includes ethnic media and news agencies.

PRINT MEDIA

There are two types of print media: newspapers and magazines. Newspapers cover geographic areas and are of interest to people living in those places. There are three types of newspapers: community (e.g., *WE Vancouver*), local (e.g., the *Ottawa Citizen*), or national (e.g., *The Globe and Mail*). Local and national newspapers are published daily, while community newspapers come out once or twice a week. There are 122 daily newspapers and over 1100 community newspapers in Canada.[17] Keep in mind that these numbers change regularly.

While some magazines also cover geographic areas (e.g., Edmonton's *Avenue* magazine), most focus on specific topics. There is a consumer magazine covering almost every interest and hobby imaginable, from design (*Azure*) and travel (*Outpost*) to business (*Profit*) and entertainment (*Cinema Scope*). There are more than 1200 magazine titles in Canada.[18]

The opportunity: There are numerous opportunities to generate media coverage in print media. Think of all the different sections in newspapers, such as general news, business, and lifestyle. All of these sections have editors and journalists whom you can contact with story ideas. Community newspapers are excellent outlets for stories that have a local angle. Magazines are a good choice to reach an audience that is interested in a specific topic such as fashion.

Consumer and Trade Media

Print media is further divided into two categories: consumer media and trade media. Consumer media are the outlets that are of interest to the general public (*Maclean's* or the *Winnipeg Free Press*), while **trade media** covers specific industries and targets professionals in that industry (e.g., *Canadian Consulting Engineer* or *Canadian Grocer*). There are estimated to be 757 trade publications in Canada.[19]

The opportunity: Trade media are good outlets for stories that target a specific niche or professional audience and where the industry is **business-to-business (B2B)**, meaning it targets other businesses and professionals, rather than consumers. In the Fairway media relations campaign we examined in the opening vignette, we saw that both consumer media such as the *National Post* and trade media such as *FranchiseCanada* were targeted depending on the business objectives.

BROADCAST MEDIA

Broadcast media comprise television and radio. Television features a variety of programming, including news programs, talk shows, and programs on specific topics, such as cooking or travel shows. The broadcast of these programs may be national (e.g., CBC's *The National*), local (e.g., *Breakfast Television Toronto*), or community based (e.g., Shaw TV's *Urban Rush*). Some broadcasters are privately owned (CTV or City TV), while others are public (CBC or Saskatchewan Communications). In total, there are 302 television stations in Canada, including both conventional and specialty (cable and satellite).[20] Conventional channels include stations like Global and CTV, while specialty channels include stations like the Food Network or the sports channel TSN/ADS.

Radio also broadcasts national programs (e.g., CBC's *Radio 2 Morning*), local programs (e.g., Vancouver's *Early Edition* with Rick Cluff), and community programs (e.g., shows on Brandon, Manitoba's CJ-106 radio station). There are over 1200 radio services in Canada.[21]

The opportunity: Media coverage opportunities are abundant in broadcast media. Spokespersons can appear on television and radio talk shows. Feature or lifestyle stories are great for morning shows. More hard-hitting stories can be pitched to news programs.

DIGITAL MEDIA

Digital media are composed of online news organizations. These include traditional media outlets that have an online presence (ottawacitizen.com), as well as those which are exclusively available in a digital format (rabble.ca). In this context, we are talking about professional journalists, not bloggers. (See Chapter 7 for information on bloggers.)

The opportunity: Thanks to digital media, there has been an explosion of media outlets, updated 24/7, providing a massive opportunity for media coverage. Stories will run in the print editions of newspapers and magazines as well as in their digital formats, expanding the audience reach. Some stories might run only in the digital edition of the publication, which will often have a broader reach and higher readership than the print edition. Also, because of the unlimited space in the online format and the need for visuals, it can sometimes be easier to have your story run in the online edition, particularly if you can provide a compelling image.

ETHNIC MEDIA

Ethnic media target a specific ethnicity or language; an example would be the *Ming Pao* newspaper, which is published in Chinese and reaches an audience of Chinese-speaking Canadians. These media also have print, broadcast, and electronic formats. As of this writing, ethnic media in Canada comprise 240 radio stations, 683 newspapers, and 90 television stations.[22] (See Chapter 12 for information on multicultural PR.)

The opportunity: Ethnic media are numerous and very active in several markets across Canada and provide a great opportunity to expand the reach of your message and generate media coverage that targets a specific cultural demographic.

NEWS AGENCIES

News agencies are organizations that employ journalists and sell the stories to other media outlets that subscribe to their service. The main news agencies in Canada are Canadian Press (CP) for print media and Broadcast News for radio. Stories written by CP journalists, for example, can be found in newspapers across the country.

The opportunity: If you successfully pitch a story to a journalist working for a news agency, the story will then be sent to media outlets across the country and could generate media coverage in several newspapers. A good example of targeting a news agency is that undertaken by Yves Veggie Cuisine, a maker of meat-free foods. The company pitched a story about a new product launch to a food journalist working for CP. The journalist wrote a story that was sent out on the wire and resulted in articles published in more than 20 newspapers.

CHOOSING THE TARGET MEDIA

The decision of which media to approach in a campaign is, of course, based on which audience you are trying to reach. The most appropriate media are the ones that reach the most similar audience to the one you are targeting. So depending on your audience, it could be more strategic to generate media coverage in a community newspaper or a trade magazine than in a national newspaper, even if the reach is lower. Pacific Coast Terminals is a sulphur terminal that operates in Port Moody, British Columbia. For this organization, an article in the local Port Moody press was more valuable than an article in the national news because it would reach readers in the community where it operates. To further illustrate this point, imagine an animation studio with a goal to target people working in the industry. Target media would include animation trade publications read by animators, such as *Animation Magazine*. On the other hand, if the objective was to encourage people to watch the studio's animated cartoons on TV, consumer media like

Table 6.2	Types of Media Outlets in Canada
Print	**Outlet Examples**
Daily local newspapers	*Ottawa Citizen, Montreal Gazette*
Daily national newspapers	*National Post, The Globe and Mail*
Community newspapers	*Eye Weekly* (Toronto), *The Coast* (Halifax)
News magazines	*Maclean's*
National magazines	*Fashion, Chatelaine*
Local magazines	*Victoria Magazine, Avenue* magazine (Calgary)
Trade magazines	*Canadian Hairdresser, Canadian Grocer*
Ethnic newspapers	*Canadian Jewish News, India Abroad*
Student newspapers	*The Gazette* (Memorial University of Newfoundland), *The McGill Daily*
Gay and lesbian news	*Xtra!* (Toronto, Vancouver, Ottawa)
Broadcast Media TV	
Local news	*CHEK News* (Victoria), *Global Winnipeg*
National news	CBC's *The National, CTV National News*
Breakfast shows	*Breakfast Television, Canada AM*
National talk shows	*Cityline*
Local talk shows	*Urban Rush* (Vancouver)
Specialty programs	*Ricardo and Friends, Debbie Travis' Facelift*
National news programs	*W5*
Ethnic TV programs	Aboriginal People's Television Network, Fairchild TV
Broadcast Media Radio	
National radio news and talk shows	CBC
Local news	CKWN (Vancouver), 680 News (Toronto)
Local talk shows	*Newsline with Joe Easingwood* (Victoria), *Ottawa Noon*
Ethnic stations	Fairchild Radio, CINA
Student stations	CJSR (University of Alberta)
Digital Media	sgnews.ca
	rabble.ca
	vitamindaily.com

TV Guide would be a better choice. You can see from this example how important it is to understand the different types of media and to correctly choose which to contact based on the goals laid out in your communications plan. And it is not just a matter of being familiar with the media, but also of being familiar with the journalists and editors who work at these outlets. Table 6.2 outlines the types of media outlets available in Canada.

Conducting Media Relations ⑤

Now that you understand some of the key concepts surrounding media relations, we can move on to how it is conducted. Generating successful media coverage involves presenting the media with information and materials that have been packaged in media-friendly ways, in formats that can be used with minimum additional work by media organizations. There are a number of best practices in media relations. Getting the attention of the media can be done in several ways. The first is to conduct simple media relations with a press release or a pitch. The second option is to host an event or stage a media stunt to grab their attention. We will begin by looking at straightforward media relations, which we have broken down into six steps. We will then look at media events as another media relations tactic.

STEP 1: PLANNING

After you have decided in your communications plan that media relations should be one of the tactics employed to achieve your communications objectives, the first step is planning. This includes determining your news values, conducting research, choosing a spokesperson, writing the key messages based on your communications plan, deciding on a course of action, and creating a pitch calendar.

Determining News Values

The PR practitioner needs to determine what news values the story holds. The challenge is to get the key messages across while making sure that these points are newsworthy.

As we have discussed, PR professionals work with the media to get their messages across to the audiences sitting at home reading their morning newspapers or watching the evening news on television. They use the media as a conduit to third-party audiences.

This means that your messages must appeal to your target public. What message can you convey to the public to make them vote for your political candidate? What can you say to a mother to make her buy your organic diapers for her baby? How can you appeal to business executives to make them attend your seminar? It is important to remember that you are not buying an advertisement, so your message must be packaged within a newsworthy story.

Naturalpod.com, a Canadian retailer of natural toys, provides a good example of developing newsworthy media angles. The organization leveraged a breaking news story on a toy recall to generate coverage. It used the following key messages with media: Naturalpod's toys are safe for children, they are made of natural materials, and they are a good option compared to mass-manufactured toys that are often the subject of recalls.

Conducting Research

As we noted in Chapter 4, research can help you uncover information that will strengthen your position and increase your chances of receiving coverage. PR practitioners examine trends, consumer reports, expert opinions, breaking news, and research studies. Brookline, for example, stayed up to date with current events related to separation and divorce to create new story angles to pitch to journalists and generate media coverage for Fairway.

Choosing a Spokesperson

Before media relations can be conducted, a spokesperson must also be chosen. PR practitioners occasionally play this role, but it is more common for someone else within the organization or appointed by the organization to be the spokesperson. Some organizations have one designated spokesperson, while others choose different people for different interview topics. To use the example of Yves Veggie Cuisine once more, the organization has used several spokespersons, including chefs, dieticians, the marketing director, and the company owner. Other organizations hire well-known experts in their fields or celebrities to be spokespersons. For instance, actor William Shatner is the official spokesperson for March of Dimes Canada.

The reason it is important to choose and train (if needed) a spokesperson prior to starting media relations is that you don't want to be left scrambling if the reporter expresses interest in the story and would like to do an interview. After identifying a spokesperson, you'll want to get that person's complete contact information and schedule so that if necessary you are able to book an interview quickly and won't risk missing a potential opportunity.

Constable Brian Montague is one of two spokespersons for the Vancouver Police Department.

Source: Vancouver Police Department/Martin Dee

Constable Brian Montague is the media relations officer of community and public affairs for the Vancouver Police Department. He says of his role as a spokesperson, "I do have regular office hours, but either Randy [his partner] or I are on duty 24 hours a day, seven days a week, 365 days a year. We field hundreds of calls every week from local, national, and international media for information and interviews. I answer about 1700 emails per month."[23] What people often find surprising about his job, he says, is the amount of preparation he must do for each interview. Constable Montague notes,

> Most people think I spend a few minutes talking and answering a few questions on TV about the off event that happened in Vancouver. They would be surprised to know just how much time I spend preparing and researching before going in front of the camera and that the 15 or 20 seconds seen on television is a result of being questioned heavily about one or more topics for 15 or 20 minutes.[24]

See Chapter 8 for more information on spokespersons.

STEP 2: PREPARATION OF MEDIA MATERIALS

The next step is the preparation of information for the media in the form of media materials and the media kit. It is absolutely necessary to have something in writing to provide to journalists prior to contacting them. After you contact journalists, they will often ask if you can send them additional information or photos. PR practitioners sometimes provide journalists with written information packaged in a media kit, which can include a media release, a backgrounder or biography, a fact sheet, and photos. See Chapter 5 for information on media kits and on writing media materials. The following are media relations tools that, in addition to media materials, can help generate media coverage.

Photos

Photos are a great way to illustrate your story and to receive more space in print and digital media. The more interesting and creative the photo, the greater the chances that it will be used. Photos for print media need to be of printable quality. They need to be clear and high resolution, preferably taken by a professional photographer. You will need permission from both the photographer and any individuals who appear in the photo prior to sending it to the media.

Video

A useful PR tool for media is video that illustrates your story, often called *B-roll*. B-roll can include interviews, background images, and footage that would be difficult for the media to obtain on their own. B-roll is used by television and digital media. The video footage must be professionally produced in order to meet broadcast standards. Depending on your budget, B-roll can be very expensive or inexpensive to acquire. Some companies hire film students to shoot footage of their factories or manufacturing process in order to create inexpensive B-roll.

Social Media News Release (SMR)

The **social media news release (SMR)** is an interactive media release that is posted online and includes live links, pull-out quotes, photos, and video footage. Though mostly used by digital media, it is becoming increasingly popular with other media.

Sharon Lassman, director of communications at Score Media, puts it this way:

> As anyone in the PR industry knows, the press release is evolving quickly. Just a few years ago, a traditional release was one of the best ways of communicating a company's message to media, consumers, shareholders, the industry, or anyone interested in an organization's news. Today, people expect something different—and rightfully so. Why shouldn't they get to experience news? Why shouldn't they get to hear about it, see it, touch it, or feel it?[25]

The Pitch Email

Sometimes a story breaks so quickly that the PR practitioner is left scrambling to react. On the other hand, sometimes a story idea isn't big enough to warrant a media release. In those cases, a pitch email may be written, which is a short outline of the story. This is a more informal way to contact journalists, as the message is short and to the point.

Some PR practitioners prefer to conduct pitch calls, as opposed to sending out releases. This way, each pitch is specifically targeted to each media outlet.

STEP 3: THE MEDIA LIST

Once you have organized your media materials, you can turn your attention to the creation of a **media list**. A media list is a compilation of the names, publications, contact information, and deadline notes of the media you are planning to pitch for a particular story. The decision of which media to include on the list is based on the media your target audiences consume. It is important that you have the right contacts in your media database. The media relations campaign has no chance of success unless the right journalists are targeted. Busy journalists will not share information with one another. If you send the news release or pitch to the wrong person, it will most likely be ignored.

The media list needs to contain, at minimum, the journalist's or editor's name, job title or area of specialization, publication (or whether the journalist does freelance work) email address, and telephone number. The mailing address should also be included if you are sending product samples. Some practitioners include helpful information on individual journalists on their media databases, such as deadline times or topics of interest to them. Table 6.3 provides a small sample of a media list for Teletoon, a children's television network. Because of the nature of the business, contacts change regularly.

Journalists change jobs and positions often and so lists must continually be kept up to date. Before the start of a campaign, every media contact needs to be verified, especially if a list has not been used in some time. A good media database is priceless. PR practitioners do not share their media databases outside their organizations because of the value of their contacts.

There are several ways to compile a list. The fastest and simplest way is to subscribe to a media database service. A popular Canadian media database service is offered by Cision

Table 6.3	Sample Media List			
Journalist Name	**Media**	**Title/Position**	**Telephone**	**Email**
Ravin Zahed	*Animation Magazine*	Online editor	1-416-772-9445	ravin@animationmaga-zine.net
Mansha Daswani	*TV Kids Weekly*	Managing editor	1-416-553-2252	mdeswani@worldscreen.com
Cathy Dawson	*The Globe and Mail*	Television writer	1-416-585-5000	cdawson-march@globeandmail.ca
Doug Foley	*The Hamilton Spectator*	Entertainment writer	1-905-526-3333	dfoley@thespec.com
Greg David	*TV Guide*	Assistant editor	1-416-733-7600	gdavid@tvguide.ca

Canada. Subscription services are reliable, but the contacts must be double-checked as there is often a lag time between a journalist moving to another company or role and the database being updated. Other ways to add contacts to a media database are to surf the Internet, search the newsstand, or visit your local library for media directories. Following the news and learning which journalists cover which topics is a great way to find contacts as well. Always think of your list as a work in progress—you will constantly be adding to it and editing it.

STEP 4: DISTRIBUTION

The next step in generating media coverage is to distribute the media information materials to the contacts in your media database. This is done via email in most cases.

The optimum time to distribute a media release is on Tuesday, Wednesday, or Thursday mornings. Traditionally, journalists are busy on Monday catching up after the weekend, and on Friday they are wrapping up their week. Do not include any attachments; journalists are wary of opening them because of the fear of viruses. Let journalists know that you can send photos if they need them. Make sure you have a catchy email subject line to grab their attention.

There are also services that distribute media information materials, such as CNW Group. The PR practitioner hires the service to help create a newsworthy release and distribute it to an expansive media list. The services can also post the releases on their websites, which are well visited by journalists.

In addition to distribution, but not in lieu of it, you can post media information materials and tools in a designated media section on your organization's website. Here you should also include social media site links, as journalists are increasingly turning to social media to find story ideas, leads, and people to interview. It is fast becoming a key way for them to conduct research. Make sure you follow important journalists on Twitter in order to see the types of stories they are researching or looking for information on. The Help a Reporter Out, or HARO, service sends emails to PR practitioners who have signed up when a reporter needs sources, interviews, or information for a story.

STEP 5: FOLLOW-UP: PITCHING THE STORY

After conducting steps 1 through 4, you may hear back from journalists if the story is timely and newsworthy. Your job is to assist them with details and handle requests such as coordinating interviews, sending photos, or providing additional information. After a major announcement, it is possible to receive dozens if not hundreds of media requests.

If your story does not contain many news values, or if it is a busy news day, you may not hear back from journalists. In this case, a call-back, or follow-up call, is an obligatory part of the process. You will need to do a **media pitch**, making direct email or telephone contact with journalists or editors to persuade them to cover your story. Remember that a journalist can receive a hundred media releases a day. You can see how easy it is for a media release to get lost. You must find a way to break through this clutter and capture the attention of the media.

Some journalists prefer to have PR practitioners follow up via telephone, while others prefer email. Some even prefer Twitter. You might need to try all three while working through a media list, depending on your target media's preferences. While it is usually best to start with a follow-up call, if a reporter lets you know that he or she prefers a particular method of communication, you should honour that request.

If you shudder at the thought of a cold call, you are not alone. When you are feeling nervous, it is helpful to remember that you are offering a story that will assist journalists in doing their job. The majority of journalists will work with you when you call them with a good story. The worst that can happen is that they will say they are not interested. Most of your experience with media will be professional and courteous. If you are offering information of value to the journalist, chances are good that you will be well received. That said, a word of warning is in order. Some journalists do not like to receive phone calls. You may encounter a negative reaction from a journalist, especially if you contact them at deadline time. If this happens, apologize and make a note in your media list that this person does not like to be contacted by telephone.

The time you do your pitch also has an impact. Do not call journalists when they are on deadline. They will be less likely to speak to you, since they will be busy trying to finish their stories. For instance, television news producers have more time first thing in the morning, and community newspaper journalists have the most time on the day after the newspaper is published.

Journalists are busy people, so when you call or email you must be quick and get straight to the point. You have only a few seconds to make a good impression and pique their interest. Practise your pitch before you call so that you can deliver it quickly and succinctly.

Follow up with each journalist about one or two days after sending them the media information materials. When you call journalists, do not waste their time by asking if they have received your media release. You will be amazed at how many journalists will not recall seeing your media release. Start pitching the story from scratch and let the reporter know if you can offer product samples, interviews, photos, or B-roll.

Your pitch is also going to be different depending on the type of media you are approaching. For instance, a television story is primarily about the visuals, so you need to sell the visual component of your pitch.

Here is an example of a telephone pitch to a daily newspaper for an educational website, www.canadian-universities.net:

"Hello, I'm calling on behalf of Canadian-universities.net. I have a story that I know will be of interest to your readers. Do you have a few moments? The recession has seen student enrolment at universities and college skyrocket. People are preferring to go to school or stay in school instead of looking for work in this economic climate. I have a great local spokesperson from Canadian-universities.net who can speak on this topic. I can also send you some information. Do you think you might be interested?"

STEP 6: MEDIA MONITORING AND EVALUATION

Once a journalist has agreed to do a story about your organization, you need to keep track of the media coverage by conducting **media monitoring.** In its most basic form, media monitoring can be cutting articles out of publications or downloading news clips and figuring out how much the article or clip is worth by finding out what the news organization charges for a similar-length ad. There are also companies that specialize in tracking and measuring the value of media coverage and analyzing the coverage. Keep all your coverage together and periodically compile a report for your organization, highlighting your media relations successes. In your report, include the publication, the impressions, the length of the segment or article, the tone of the coverage, and the key messages that were delivered. This is how you can measure if your media relations campaign has been successful. Brookline kept track of the success of its campaign through media monitoring and determined that the agency generated 200 media stories and $1.5 million in PR value. See Chapter 1 for more information about evaluation. Make sure you celebrate your success after a well-executed media relations campaign. For big coverage wins, you might want to frame the article and send it to your client or hang it in your office.

ADVICE TO NEW PRACTITIONERS
Conducting Media Relations

- Be a news junkie. Consuming news and analyzing it will help you determine what is newsworthy and what are hot topics or issues. Follow different types of media, from newspapers to magazines to blogs.

- Never take no for an answer. If you keep getting rejected, refine your pitch, redefine your story, and try other media. Don't give up. People who are good at media relations are the ones who are persistent. You need only a few people to say yes in order to deliver great coverage.

- Keep in mind that luck also plays a factor. You can't control what other stories break on the same day as yours.

- Do your homework and know what you are talking about.

- Listen to your instincts when pitching a story to media.

- Practise your pitch out loud many times until you are comfortable with it.

- If they are not on deadline, call journalists first thing in the morning when your energy is high. Pitching media can be stressful and exhausting, so try to do it while you are still fresh.

MEDIA EVENTS

Events are a good way to make a story timely and attract the attention of the media. There are two ways to go about holding an event. First, you can invite the media to an event where there are other audiences in attendance. For example, when Toronto Blue Jays pitcher Kyle Drabek visited an elementary school to speak to students about fitness, journalists were invited as well. Second, you can organize an event exclusively for the media, as when the Canadian Toy Association invited media to a beach event to see—and play with—the hot new toys of that season. With an exclusive media event, you must be sure that your event or announcement is newsworthy enough for the media to take time out of their busy schedules to attend. If you are unsure, it might be better to issue a media release, as media events can be costly. However, some stories are always told with a corresponding media event, such as the unveiling of fashion collections or the announcement of quarterly results for public companies. A good example of a media event is that of VisionMed, a laser eye clinic that introduced a new eye surgery technology in its clinics. Broadcast and print media were invited to witness a live surgery on a patient. Immediately following the procedure, the patient read from a newspaper without glasses to illustrate how well the technology worked.

Media may also be interested in an event if it is fun and creative enough to pique their interest. For instance, Celestial Seasonings hosted a media event in Victoria to launch a new line of teas. The company selected a popular local restaurant and worked with the chef to develop appetizers and cocktails made with their teas. The media were given recipes and product samples at the event.

Keep in mind that journalists work in a deadline-driven environment and are busy people. Getting them to a media event is no easy task. Journalists are not easily persuaded to leave the newsroom to get the story. The event must be in an accessible location and the story must contain several news values to be attractive to the media. It also helps to have an element to the story that journalists will have access to only if they attend the event.

The media are typically invited to an event with a media advisory one week before the event and again a few days before. The final step is a follow-up call to gauge interest and to encourage attendance. See Chapter 10 for information on organizing media events, and Chapter 5 for information on media advisories. Examples of media events include news conferences, deskside briefings, photo opportunities, stunts, and specialized media events.

News Conference

A **news conference,** or media conference, is a media event where a spokesperson makes a statement in front of journalists, followed by a question-and-answer (Q&A) period. News conferences are held for stories that are extremely newsworthy, are quick breaking, or have enough buzz or anticipation surrounding them to warrant the event. An example of such an announcement is the one held for the launch of the Apple iPad in Canada.

The biggest mistake PR people make when it comes to news conferences is to organize one when the story does not warrant it. As one practitioner says, "There must be a real reason for a press conference. Otherwise, the next time one is scheduled, the media might not show up."[26]

When inviting journalists to attend a media conference, the key is to give them enough information to entice them, but not so much that they will have all they need to cover the story without attending.

The City of Toronto uses both media releases and news conferences to communicate complex issues and events to the city's residents through the media. Kevin Sack, Strategic Communications for Toronto, believes that preparation is key in terms of understanding news values, knowing who the key media are, and planning answers to the reporters' possible questions.[27]

Constable Brian Montague of the Vancouver Police Department also hosts regular press conferences. Of these media events he says,

> My colleague, Sergeant Randy Fincham, and I hold regular press conferences for our local media to discuss what has happened in the city overnight as well as give updates on ongoing investigations. We also announce any public advisories or suspect descriptions, asking for the public's assistance. In the event of a major or particularly newsworthy event such as a homicide or hostage-taking, I will scrum the media at the location to provide the public with accurate and current information.[28]

In another example, the Telecommunications Workers Union organized a media conference in Ottawa in front of Parliament to bring attention to the number of jobs that are being lost in Canada. To illustrate their point, they unveiled a truck that had a clock on it showing how a job was lost approximately every 40 seconds. This event proved successful because it provided an interesting photo opportunity for media, and it was held in a location where many journalists work. See Chapter 10 more information on media conferences.

Deskside Briefings

In a **media deskside briefing**, a spokesperson visits a journalist to present information face to face. This is an effective tactic to use when a story is better told one-on-one, such as when you're demonstrating a new technology or discussing complex issues. It also takes advantage of the fact that journalists are busy and can find it hard to leave their offices. If they can't come to you, offer to go to them! Again, success will depend on the newsworthiness of the information you will share with the media during these meetings, as well as the appeal of the spokesperson. A draw for journalists might be when the spokesperson is visiting from out of town and this will be a rare opportunity to meet him or her. Deskside briefings should be kept brief, about 20 minutes at most.

Charlie Baden, blendmaster for Celestial Seasonings, conducted a deskside briefing tour in Montreal and Toronto, travelling from the organization's headquarters in Colorado. He demonstrated how to brew the perfect cup of tea, talked about the creation of new tea flavours, and discussed the health benefits of tea. He also provided journalists with a sneak preview of tea flavours that were not yet on the market.

Photo Opportunities

Photo opportunities, or photo ops as they are commonly called, can be held as stand-alone events or as part of larger events such as media conferences. A photo opportunity is a compellingly staged visual that the media can take pictures of and then print. It might be a ribbon cutting, a cheque presentation, or a celebrity walk down a red carpet. The key is to make the photo opportunity interesting for journalists, with newsworthy elements to photograph.

Spring Media's Boink for Good stunt has received national press coverage, while raising money for a great cause.
Source: Spring Advertising

A good example is the photo opportunity held by the RCMP to generate media coverage for its Christmas toy drive. The event was held at the airport just as an RCMP plane filled with toys was about to depart for the North Pole before Christmas. Santa Claus and reindeer were also present to make the story even more interesting for the media to photograph. When pitching photo ops, you will usually direct your pitch to photo editors, who are in charge of assigning photographers to various stories.

Stunts

Stunts are often a hybrid of a PR and marketing tactic and employ the novelty news value. Stunts are designed to be unusual and buzz-worthy. They get people talking and generate media interest. Stunts raise awareness and are particularly helpful if an organization is having trouble gaining coverage through other news values. Some stunts break world records, while others do something unexpected or funny. Spring Advertising raises money for the Greater Vancouver Food Bank each year by donating money for every bounce passersbys are able to do on a pogo stick at their Boink event. Seeing adults on a pogo stick is a funny visual that gets much attention. The event also has an edgy title, since Spring Media provocatively refers to it as Boink Day. This stunt has garnered national media coverage.

On October 14, 2012, Red Bull sponsored the stunt Red Bull Stratos: Mission to the Edge of Space, in which an Austrian skydiver broke three world records by skydiving from

By sponsoring extreme sports and stunts, Red Bull is able to raise awareness through media impressions.
Source: © John Green/Alamy

the stratosphere.[29] This was a dangerous stunt for Red Bull to associate its brand with, as much could have gone wrong, including loss of life. Thankfully, the stunt was a success, reinforcing Red Bull's slogan that it "gives you wings." The stunt garnered 8 million views on YouTube and was shown on 40 TV stations and 130 digital sites.[30] In social media, 61 million impressions were attributed to the stunt.[31]

ADVICE TO NEW PRACTITIONERS

Media Events

Media conferences:

- Organize a media conference only if the information is time sensitive and is better shared in a media conference setting.

- Make sure your story is newsworthy enough to attract the media. Reporters are very busy. It has to be a big story to draw the media to it.

- Make sure you have a spokesperson who is well known in the field or famous enough to attract the media. If that person is not usually available or is from out of town, even better.

- Remember that you are going for coverage as opposed to attendance. Consider whether your story could be better told in the form of a media release and a good pitch.

Media briefings:

- Make sure you reconfirm all appointments right before the meetings. The media's schedule often changes without notice.

- Sell the newsworthiness of the visitor and the story to the media.

- Make the meeting brief. Promise to be finished within 15 to 20 minutes.

- Never be late and do whatever it takes to get there on time. Get a car and driver for the day to ensure smooth transportation from one location to another.

Specialized Media Events

Some industries have their own media relations customs, which includes specialized media events. A good example is the travel and hospitality industry. PR practitioners in this field will accompany a group of travel journalists to a destination. This is called a *familiarization tour*, or *FAM tour*. Airlines, hotels, and tourism boards often team up to create these tours. A small group of journalists are flown business class to the destination, put up in one of the best hotels, and brought to some of the best sites and restaurants in the destination. In addition to FAM tours, individual journalists are provided with complimentary or discounted tickets and rooms. Although complimentary travel can lead to positive media coverage, there is no guarantee of it. Journalists always remain free to cover the story as they wish. To avoid conflicts of interests, many organizations do not allow their journalists to accept such perks.

Another media tactic exclusive to the travel industry is the Media Marketplace, a yearly event organized in New York by the Canadian Tourism Commission. There, PR practitioners meet with a different journalist every 15 minutes to pitch story ideas.

Catherine Adams, former media manager for Whistler, says such an event provides great opportunities to raise awareness and forge media relationships. She can meet with 20 different media in one day, ranging from *InStyle* magazine to Condé Nast publications. According to Adams, "It comes down to being prepared. You need to do your homework and be familiar with a publication and their stories and the reporter. I custom-tailor my stories to the reporter. If I'm talking to *Shape* magazine, I may pitch a story of a mountain biking camp for women," she says.[32]

Thinking Like a PR Practitioner

1. Hundreds of journalists from all over the world descend on the Toronto International Film Festival every year. The festival hosts a myriad of events for the media, including the red carpet, media conferences, film viewings, one-on-one interviews with filmmakers, and receptions. Consider all the details that need organizing and list ten that you believe are the most vital to the success of the media relations for the festival.

2. You must organize a photo opportunity for the opening of a new luxury boutique hotel. Assess what you can do to make the event newsworthy and of interest to the media. Which news hooks would you employ? Write the media advisory for this photo opportunity. Examine examples of media advisories at Canada Newswire (www.canadanewswire.ca) to assist you, or refer to Chapter 5.

3. Create a social media release for the boutique hotel. Describe in detail three elements that you will include. Keep in mind that you must attract media attention with the release. Visit Canada Newswire's section dedicated to social media news releases (smr.newswire.ca) and describe five recent examples. Do you believe they generated coverage? Why or why not?

4. It is common for new PR practitioners to feel anxious about conducting follow-up with journalists, especially by telephone. Do you believe you will feel this way? Why or why not? Cite three steps you can take to successfully conduct telephone pitches to media.

CASE STUDY TARGETING ETHNIC MEDIA OUTLETS: HAMAZAKI WONG

A good example of a targeted ethnic media campaign is the one Hamazaki Wong, a full-service multicultural communications agency, conducted for Air Canada in the lead-up to the Vancouver Winter Olympics.

To raise awareness of Air Canada's role as the official airline of the Olympics and Paralympics Winter Games and its support of athletes, the in-house communications team organized a special event for journalists on the tarmac at the Vancouver airport. The event centred around the unveiling of an airplane decorated with colourful images of winter Olympic sports. The event also featured the company CEO as a spokesperson and several Olympic athletes who were sponsored by Air Canada. All of these features provided journalists with a selection of different photo opportunities.

The event targeted many types of media, including Chinese media. Canada's Asian residents are an important target audience for Air Canada, as it offers services to many destinations in Asia. The task of making the event of interest to Chinese journalists and generating media coverage in Chinese publications fell to Iris Chen, a Chinese-speaking publicist at Hamazaki Wong. Chen has worked with Chinese media for several years and has strong relationships with them.

"Calling each journalist personally to pitch the story in advance of the event is key to getting them to attend," she says. "Chinese media are usually very understaffed. It is always a challenge to compete for the attention of assignment editors with other 'hard news' stories."

Tailoring the pitch to Chinese journalists was worth the effort, as the event was attended by several major Chinese media outlets.

Onsite, Chen greeted each journalist, distributed Chinese media information materials, and assisted with translation and interviews. In addition, a time was designated exclusively for Chinese media to interview the CEO of Air Canada.

"This enables journalists to ask questions that are more relevant and interesting to the Chinese community," Chen explains.

The campaign resulted in media coverage in key Chinese media, including newspapers such as *Sing Tao*, *Ming Pao*, and *World*

Hamazaki Wong conducted media relations with ethnic media for Air Canada in the lead-up to the Vancouver Olympics.

Source: McNair Flight Collection/Newscom

Journal; television such as Fairchild TV, Talentvision, and Omni; radio such as AM1470 and FM96; and electronic media such as westca.com.

Following the event, an event summary with photos written in Chinese was sent to journalists who had not attended. This tactic generated additional media coverage in publications including creaders.net, a popular Chinese digital news portal in North America.

Questions

1. Appraise the work that was done to tailor the event for Chinese media. Break down the steps that were taken to generate the media coverage.

2. Assess whether you need to belong to an ethnic group and/or speak the language to successfully target this media audience.

AUTHOR'S OWN EXPERIENCE

Media Relations for Law Firms and Lawyers

One of our clients was a leading law firm that hired us to conduct media relations in order to announce the results of court cases that it had won. The objective was to raise awareness of the law firm and help it attract new clients. As this was a new category for us and we did not know much about the topic, we spoke with a few journalists to ask them how they liked interviewing and working with lawyers. We discovered that journalists found it challenging to work with lawyers, as they often would use legal speak that did not make sense to the general public. In addition, when verdicts came down in the court, the documents did not always make clear what the decision was or how much money had been awarded. Journalists depended on the lawyers to explain the information to them and the lawyers typically did not make it easy. Based on this information, we decided that we could be of assistance. The first thing that we did was organize a media-training session where we trained the lawyers from the firm on how to use everyday vernacular during interviews and make the court decisions easy to understand.

We then compiled a media database of all the journalists and editors who covered legal matters and breaking news.

Whenever the law firm received a positive verdict, the media relations work had to be done very quickly and we had to contact journalists immediately. We wrote short email pitches and also got on the telephone to call journalists. A pitch email could look like this:

"A decision has just come down in the court of appeal that I think will be of interest to your listeners. It is about a man who was gravely injured by hospital staff. We can send you the decision and I can also set up an interview with the lawyer, if you are interested."

The information tended to be interesting to journalists, as most court cases contained a large number of news values including locality, immediacy, conflict, human interest, and perhaps even peril and novelty. We set up interviews with the lawyers and distributed the court verdict to the media.

Sometimes, the news broke so quickly that a story would appear on the radio within ten minutes of the interview. Often, several of the TV outlets carried the story on their evening news and local newspapers published the story the next day. It was exciting to conduct media relations for the law firm because the media were so eager to run the stories and the story appeared so quickly following the pitch. The secret to us moving so quickly was preparation. We kept our media database up to date and were ready to move within minutes of receiving a telephone call from our client announcing yet another victory.

Media Relations

writing
- materials
- key messages
- pitches

events
- briefings
- advisories
- photo ops
- conferences

journalists
- conduit audiences
- serving society role
- objectivity
- deadlines

- coverage
monitoring
endorsement

pitching
- follow-up
- stories
news values

relationships
- sources
useful
newsworthy
information
- credibility
building
trust

broadcast
TV
radio

landscape
- ethnic
- print
newspapers
magazines
trade
consumer

Key Terms

beat A journalist's area of specialization or the topics and subjects he or she covers. Beat examples include police, health, transportation, business, and lifestyle.

breaking news stories Events and stories that are currently developing and are receiving coverage in the news media; often refers to unexpected stories such as natural disasters, corporate crises, or scandals.

business-to-business (B2B) An organization that targets other businesses and professionals, rather than general consumers. An example would be a maker of cardboard packaging that sells its products to appliance manufacturers.

demographics Information that can be deduced and researched about a target audience, such as income, education, age, or interests.

editorial All written articles and other features, except for advertising, that are found in newspapers and magazines; also refers to an opinion piece written by the editor.

lead times The lapse of time between when a story is prepared and produced and when it is printed or broadcast and presented to the public. Lead times vary enormously and can be as short as an hour or as long as six to eight months.

media deskside briefing An event consisting of a spokesperson visiting a journalist in the newsroom or office to present information in person.

media interview A meeting either in person or by telephone during which a journalist asks questions of an individual. The answers are recorded or written down and used by the journalist in a story.

media landscape The scope of media and the types available in a specific market or location, including all the print, broadcast, and digital media available there.

media list A database of carefully researched and selected journalists and media outlets, with their contact information, who will be targeted in a media relations campaign.

media monitoring Keeping track of stories and other media content produced by print, broadcast, and digital media on a certain topic, industry, or organization. Copies of all the stories are collected and presented in media-monitoring reports.

media pitch Direct contact with journalists or editors via email or telephone in an effort to persuade them to cover your story. Pitches are usually brief and customized to the media outlet.

media relations Activities that build or maintain an organization's relationships with media. Also refers to PR practitioners providing information to journalists at news organizations in the hope that they will be interested in the story and cover it. The goal is to generate coverage in media outlets such as newspapers, radio, television, and digital news channels.

news agencies Organizations that employ journalists and sell the stories they produce to other media outlets that subscribe to their service.

news conference An organized media event at which a spokesperson makes a scripted statement in front of journalists, followed by a question-and-answer (Q&A) period.

newsworthy Deemed by the media to have the qualities needed to make it into the news. Newsworthy stories contain several news values.

photo opportunities An event, or a period during an event, at which media take photos that have been staged and arranged for them. Also describes the people, setting, and objects that the media will be able to photograph at the event.

pitch calendar A calendar that maps out when you will pitch your story to which publications, depending on their lead time.

positioning Telling a story from a particular angle or perspective to make it appear in a certain light or to emphasize certain parts of the story. Positioning of a story is done by both PR practitioners and journalists.

proactive media relations A publicist's taking the initiative to contact a journalist with a story idea. The action is part of a plan or campaign with the goal of generating media coverage for organization.

publicist The person in a PR agency or in-house communications department who focuses on generating media coverage through media relations.

reactive media relations An organization's responding to media inquiries that it did not initially contact the journalist about. This tends to occur when there is a breaking story about an organization or during issues or crises.

social media news release (SMR) An interactive media release that is posted online and includes such elements as live links, pull-out quotes, photos, and video footage.

sources People who provide information to journalists which is used as research or to generate stories. PR practitioners account for a large percentage of sources.

trade media Media outlets that cover specific industries and cater to professionals in that industry, rather than the general public.

third-party endorsement A positive story about an organization appearing in the media and bestowing credibility upon it.

Weblinks

Brookline Public Relations
www.brooklinepr.com

Canada Newswire
www.newswire.ca

Canadian Association of Journalists
www.caj.ca

Canadian Journalism Foundation
www.cjf-fjc.ca

Canadian Press
www.thecanadianpress.com

Cision
ca.cision.com

Council of Public Relations Firms
www.prfirms.org

Halifax Regional Municipality Media Room
www.halifax.ca/mediaroom/index.html

Hamazaki Wong
www.hamazakiwong.com

Magazines Canada
www.magazinescanada.ca/

MediaSmarts
http://mediasmarts.ca

Newspapers Canada
www.newspaperscanada.ca

Reuters Canada
ca.reuters.com

Score Media
www.scoremedia.com/

Spring Media
http://springadvertising.com/boink-day-2012/

Under the Influence: Marketing Stunts
www.cbc.ca/undertheinfluence/season-2/2013/03/02/marketing-stunts-2/

Endnotes

1. A. Polansky, "PR in the Age of Social Media," *Advertising Age*, November 29, 2010, S3.

2. Leslie-Anne Keown, "Keeping Up with the Times: Canadians and Their News Media Diet," *Canadian Social Trends*. Accessed March 6, 2013, http://www.statcan.gc.ca/pub/11-008-x/2006008/pdf/9610-eng.pdf

3. Amy McCarthy, "Journalist Explains When and How to Follow Up a Pitch," *Ragan's PR Daily*, August 23, 2011. Accessed March 6, 2013, http://www.prdaily.com/Main/Articles/Journalist_explains_when_and_how_to_follow_up_a_pi_9290.aspx#

4. P. Schlesinger, "Rethinking the Sociology of Journalism: Source Strategies and the Limits of Media Centrism." In M. Ferguson (ed.), *Public Communications: The New Imperatives* (pp. 61–83). London: Sage, 1990.

5. Theresa Rath, interview with the author.

6. D. McQuail, "Media Regulation," Unit 11 of the M.A. in Mass Communications (by distance learning), Centre for Mass Communication Research, University of Leicester, United Kingdom, 2005.

7. D. McQuail, *McQuail's Mass Communication Theory*. London: Sage, 1983.

8. Alan Daniels, interview with the author.

9. A. Sreberny-Mohammadi, "Forms of Media as Ways of Knowing." In J. Downing, A. Mohammadi, and A. Sreberny-Mohammadi (eds.), *Questioning the Media: A Critical Introduction* (2nd ed.; pp. 23–38). London: Sage, 1995.

10. E. Bird and R.W. Dardenne, "Myth, Chronicle and Story: Exploring the Narrative Quality of News." In J. Carey (ed.). *Media, Myths and Narratives: Television and the Press* (pp. 67–86). Thousand Oaks and London: Sage, 1988.

11. A. Anderson, "Environmental Pressure Groups, Ecological Activism and the Media," Unit 77 of the M.A. in Mass Communications (by distance learning), Centre for Mass Communication Research, University of Leicester, United Kingdom, 2001.

12. D. Morgan, "Mass Media, Bias, Power," *Parliamentary Affairs*, vol. 40, no. 1. Accessed March 6, 2013, http://pa.oxfordjournals.org/content/40/1/136.extract

13. J. Ginneken, *Understanding Global News: A Critical Introduction*. London and Thousand Oaks, CA: Sage, 1998.

14. H. Gans, *Deciding What's News*. New York: Pantheon, 1979.

15. S.L. Caruthers, "Media, Globalisation and 'Other People's Wars,'" Journalism Reader of the M.A. in Mass Communications (by distance learning), Centre for Mass Communication Research, University of Leicester, United Kingdom, 2000.

16. Jacques Marcoux, interview with the author.

17. "FAQ," Canadian Newspapers Association. Accessed March 3, 2013, http://www.newspaperscanada.ca/about-newspapers/faq-about-newspapers

18. "Put Magazines to Work," Magazines Canada. Accessed March 3, 2013, http://www.magazinescanada.ca/uploads/File/Ad%20Services/PutMagazinesToWork2010.pdf

19. "Industry Statistics," Canadian Business Press. Accessed March 6, 2013, http://cbp.ca/history/#/stats/overview/

20. "TV Basics 2007–2008," Television Bureau of Canada. Accessed March 6, 2013, http://www.tvb.ca/page_files/pdf/TVBasics2007-2008.pdf

21. Canadian Radio-television and Telecommunications Commission, *Communications Monitoring Report 2008*. Accessed March 3, 2013, http://www.crtc.gc.ca/eng/publications/reports/policymonitoring/2008/cmr2008.htm

22. "Visible Minority Media in Canada," Medi Smarts. Accessed March 6, 2013, http://mediasmarts.ca/diversity-media/visible-minorities/visible-minority-media-canada

23. "An Interview with Constable Brian Montague," Canadian Public Relations Society Vancouver, February 22, 2013. Accessed March 6, 2013, http://cprsvancouver.com/interview-constable-brian-montague

24. Ibid.

25. Dave Forde, "Is the Social Media Release Here to Stay?" *PR in Canada*, October 21, 2010. Accessed March 6, 2013, http://www.princanada.com/industry-opinion-is-the-social-media-press-release-here-to-stay

26. S. Fields, *Career Opportunities in the Sports Industry*. New York: Ferguson, 2010, p. 90.

27. C. Smith, "Media Relations Demands Custom Approach," *newperspective*, vol. 9, no. 4 (Spring 2010). Accessed March 6, 2013, http://www.cprstoronto.com/site/newsletter/pdf/CPRS_%20Spr10FINAL.pdf

28. "An Interview with Constable Brian Montague."

29. Terry O'Reilly, "Marketing Stunts," *Under the Influence*, CBC Radio, March 2, 2013. Accessed March 6, 2013, http://www.cbc.ca/undertheinfluence/season-2/2013/03/02/marketing-stunts-2/

30. Ibid.

31. Ibid.

32. Catherine Adams, interview with this author.

When Problems Show Up, So Does the PR Practitioner

If there is one thing you can be sure of in PR, it is that problems will arise. Despite the best-laid plans, things derail. Campaigns are filled with fires that need putting out. It is your job to solve problems and generate results in the face of adversity. This task comes with the job description.

Problem solving takes on many forms. Your organization is dealing with a product recall and the phone is ringing off the hook with calls from journalists. The keynote speaker has not shown up minutes before the scheduled speech. A blogger has written a negative story about your new product launch. The projector conks out just before a big presentation. A rumour is spreading among employees that there will be layoffs. You have to deal with an irate community leader.

The trick is to stay calm and think strategically about possible solutions. You also need to develop a thick skin in this industry, as sometimes people will take their stress out on you. And, most importantly, you should not take it personally. Senior practitioner Charlotte Wardell says that was the biggest lesson she learned on the road to success.

Charlotte conducted media relations for an airline that received negative media coverage no matter how she pitched the story. "Dealing with constant negative media coverage is the most challenging and most frustrating part of PR. In periods like that, it's important not to take it personally, and I know how difficult it is not to do that. You need to keep the larger issues in mind and keep focused on the big picture," she says.

The same goes for when you are the cause of the problem. We all make mistakes. The key is to fix them and be accountable for your work. Skip the self-criticism, and instead look at what needs to be done. What lessons you can you learn to ensure you don't make the same mistake twice?

As former corporate communications manager at the Vancouver Playhouse, Meredith Elliott attributes some of her success on her willingness to fix mistakes. "When you are accountable, people start trusting you. It's not that you won't make any mistakes. That will happen for sure. It's that people will trust that you will fix them."

Chapter 7
Social Media

Rogers' company blog, RedBoard, helped build its relationship with its customers and improve its online reputation.

Source: © Sam Dao/Alamy

LEARNING OBJECTIVES

1. Explain why social media has not changed the fundamentals of public relations and why the technologies of social media are tools to be used in a PR campaign.

2. Define the guiding principles of social media.

3. Explain how individuals become trusted sources of information in the digital age.

4. Describe some of the challenges and opportunities that social media creates for public relations practitioners.

5. Identify the different types of social media tools available.

Rogers Communications and the Launch of *REDBOARD*

Rogers Communications, Canada's largest wireless voice and data communications provider, recognized that it needed to amp up its efforts to develop meaningful relationships with its customers and improve its online reputation. This insight led to the launch of a company blog called *RedBoard* (redboard.rogers.com), which was created as the online persona of the Rogers brand.

RedBoard was launched a year after Rogers formed its social media team, which was dedicated to participating in online conversations that were already taking place about the brand. However, the company quickly realized that many of the online conversations around the brand were negative. Because of this, Rogers recognized that it needed an online space where it could share its news and have a dialogue with consumers. It also wanted to drive customers to its e-commerce site.

When launching the blog, Rogers had several key decisions to make. The company did not want to attempt to be everything to everyone and end up being nothing to anyone. The company decided to focus on the "early to middle adopters" of technology as its audience. These customers tend to be Millennial and Gen Y demographics and are often smartphone users. Since this segment tends to be interested in the latest gadgets and intolerant of "corporate speak," Rogers believed they would be the most responsive to open, transparent online dialogues.

Recognizing that, for *RedBoard* to be a success, other online stakeholders would need to validate it, Rogers actively sought the support of journalists, bloggers, and employees. The company encouraged both its external and internal communications teams to engage these secondary audiences. It was more important to Rogers to have engaged readers than to have a large number of followers. Knowing that other company blogs average 16 comments per post, the goal for *RedBoard*, a brand-new site, was 10 in the first year.

Based on the objectives of deepening customer relationships and improving its online reputation, *RedBoard* was a great success for Rogers. Following its launch, the negative online comments about Rogers fell by half and the positive comments almost doubled. The company had also projected 880 published comments in 44 weeks. Instead, the site achieved 10,423 comments. Today, the blog is a dynamic, interactive space, which houses video content and streams Twitter comments live.

Social media is changing the practice of public relations. This is especially true in Canada, which has the most social network users per capita in the world. In 2011, 47.4 per cent of Canadians were active on social media, with 45 per cent of the population on Facebook.[1] This number is expected to increase by 800,000 users a year, representing too many opportunities to reach your target audiences to ignore.[2]

While many of the communications principles remain the same with social media, PR practitioners need to be participating in the online conversation 24/7. No longer can communicators provide information to consumers only when it's convenient to them.

Gone is the standard news cycle—the dialogue never stops. As we have just seen in the opening vignette, conversations about Rogers were already ongoing online before the organization joined in. With *RedBoard*, Rogers began participating in the dialogue and engaging readers with great success, almost doubling positive comments and improving its online reputation.

Social media offers the PR practitioner more tools to create content and share information with the audiences they are trying to reach and engage. It also provides a listening and research tool to find out audiences' opinions or thoughts on various issues and topics.

In the digital age, public relations is no longer simply a matter of transmitting messages to key audiences. These audiences now communicate back to you and talk to one another about your organization, and they are doing so in increasing numbers. This presents new opportunities for PR practitioners, as well as some challenges.

Many new public relations positions are being created because of social media. Newly created titles include social media manager and digital expert, to name a few. Sometimes people outside of the industry think they would be good at social media because they use Facebook or Twitter personally. This assumption is typically false. Social media, like public relations in general, requires communication skills, education, and experience. The complexities of handling social media as part of an organization's communications strategy are very different from having a personal online presence.

There is one point above all to remember about social media from a PR perspective: social media is about people first. The technologies and tools used to reach these people are secondary, as is exemplified by the *RedBoard* blog. Rogers determined exactly who its target audiences were—in this case young, early to middle adopters of technology—and then created the blog and its content specifically for them.

In this chapter we will begin by examining PR in the social media age by looking first at the principles that have not changed and then studying how PR has evolved. We will also learn about the new opportunities that social media offers PR practitioners, as well as the challenges it presents. Finally, we will examine some of the most popular social media tools that are presently being used by PR practitioners. The technologies of social media, which are ever changing, include such applications as Facebook, Twitter, and wikis.

PR in the Social Media Age ❶

Social media can be defined as digital media that is both created and consumed by users. Its advent has created a very exciting time for public relations and has opened up a score of opportunities to reach target audiences in ways that were previously unimaginable. PR practitioners now create their own media content and share this information with local communities and niche audience segments. The Rogers *RedBoard* blog is a perfect example of this. Rogers was able to communicate directly with a targeted audience of Millennial and Gen Y technology users. Digital media, with its borderless, ownerless diversity of opinions and voices, is bringing profound changes to the way we communicate.

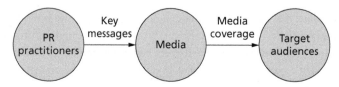

Figure 7.1 Traditional Model of Public Relations

Traditionally, public relations practitioners communicated with their target audiences in the way shown in Figure 7.1.

PR practitioners drafted the message and communicated it to their target audiences, using the media as a conduit. They often depended on the media, such as newspaper reporters, to pick up the message and transmit it to key audiences. In most cases, the public provided very little feedback, with the exception of limited traditional channels of communication, such as customer service lines or letters to the editor.

As social media's popularity has increased, the public are no longer quiet consumers of media and messages. Audiences are now full participants in the transmission of information and producers of media. They respond to organizations and share information with one another. They create **user-generated content**, which they share peer to peer.

An interesting example of this development is what is referred to as "mommy bloggers." Popular mommy blogs include yoyomama.ca and urbanmommies.com. Mothers are an active and powerful force in digital media, as they share information with one another on everything from baby product reviews to the best medical care. They influence one another's decisions because one mother will tend to trust the words of another. Effectively outreaching to mommy bloggers is now highlighted in PR events such as the ShesConnected conference in Canada.

The clothing retailer H&M learned just how quickly and effectively mothers share peer to peer, setting **viral campaigns**—campaigns that are shared quickly and widely through social media—into motion. After one mother was asked to stop breastfeeding in the company's Vancouver store and was ushered into a dressing room against her will, a large group of women showed up at the store to publicly breastfeed in what was called a "nurse in." The event attracted national media coverage, featuring the retailer in an unfavourable light.

Mommy blogs, such as the popular *yoyomama*, are an effective way to reach mothers in Canada.
Source: Stuart Monk/Shutterstock

WHAT HAS NOT CHANGED IN PR: THE FUNDAMENTALS

As exciting as this digital revolution is, the fundamentals of public relations remain unchanged. The practice of public relations still centres around defining objectives and identifying target audiences and influencers. Social media, like all other types of communications, is about putting people first. This principle of public relations has not changed in the digital age. One of the first steps in any campaign is to consider your target audiences: the people you are trying to reach, to engage, and to communicate with. It is essential to know your audiences well so that you can decide how best to reach them and which tactics to use, whether that be YouTube, newspapers, or a combination of both, for example.

In making this decision, as in formulating all PR plans, you need to ask, Who is the audience that you are trying to reach? Once the target audiences are identified and researched, the decisions about key messages need to be made. What messaging will be most appealing to the audience, and what information could you provide that will be of interest or of value to them?

At this point, decisions about the best social media tools and technologies to use come into play. Where will you find your target audiences—i.e., what social media tools do they use? Facebook, Twitter, blogs, and wikis are simply tools that public relations practitioners can use to communicate with their target audiences. These technologies come and go; they rise and fall in popularity. However, the foundation of solid communication will never change. Remember that the tools of social media are technologies that can be learned. The crucial skills to develop are the principles of good communication and the expertise to apply them. Public relations remains about the ability to think strategically and to communicate effectively with your target audiences. Social media should be viewed as one tactic in a public relations strategy, never as the strategy in and of itself. See Chapter 4 for more information about strategy and the fundamentals of a PR campaign.

THE ADVANTAGE OF A PR PERSPECTIVE IN THE DIGITAL AGE

Social media experts come from many sectors, including information technology (IT), advertising, and customer service. The difference is that PR professionals approach social media based on the principles of public relations. PR practitioners possess an advantage in the field of social media because they understand strategy and how to target key audiences with their message. Though many people understand technology and how to use social media tools, they do not necessarily understand how to effectively share information with others, what to talk about, what messages to communicate to further the interests of the organization, or how to handle an issue or crisis.

This reality reinforces the fact that social media is about people and communication. Tools and media forms may come and go, but public relations is always about listening, dialogue, relationships, and communication. Social media as a public relations tactic is first and foremost about the audience, not about technologies and tools.

Technological developments burst onto the scene quickly in this new digital world. Take, for example, the exploding popularity of Twitter. It grew 82 per cent in just nine months in 2011, reaching 100 million active users.[3] Similarly, popular social networks, such as Myspace, might quickly fall out of fashion once new ones launch.

The future is sure to hold many more changes for social media tools. What may work effectively at one time may not work at another. It is important that PR practitioners stay up to date with these new developments so they know where they will find their target audiences next.

SOCIAL MEDIA: ONE PR TACTIC IN AN OVERALL CAMPAIGN

Though it is currently very trendy, from a PR perspective, social media is often just one component of an overall campaign or one of the many tactics available to meet your objectives. Just as event planning is but one tactic a PR practitioner may employ in a campaign (as opposed to professional event planners, who focus exclusively on this specialty), social media is one tactic in the PR practitioner's large array of tactics that can be employed to reach communication objectives.

This means that traditional media, including newspapers, magazines, radio, and television, still has a strong role to play in public relations campaigns, but it is no longer the only option. The **media mix**, or combination of media, used by PR professionals now includes traditional and social media.

If history is any guide, social media will not bring about the disappearance of other forms of mass media. It may push them to evolve and change their content or mode of delivery, but it will not drive media, such as TV or newspapers, to extinction.[4] Digital media provides an alternative and a complement to traditional media.

Some PR practitioners and communications agencies specialize exclusively in social media campaigns. These agencies assist organizations in finding their online communities, reaching out to them, and then measuring the impact that a campaign is having online. More commonly, though, PR agencies provide overall PR services including social media relations but do not concentrate exclusively on it.

Thinking Like a PR Practitioner

1. Describe two advantages that PR professionals have over other social media experts.
2. Explain why we say that the foundations of PR have remained the same in the digital age.
3. In the case of H&M, what would you have done if you were the public relations practitioner for the retailer?

The Evolution of PR with Social Media ❷

Although the fundamentals of PR have remained the same, social media has changed the ways we engage our target audiences in the digital world. The best practices of public relations have always been concerned with listening to target audiences, but in the past PR practitioners often distributed their key messages through one-way communication. Today, two-way communication, which involves listening and interacting, is no longer just a best practice but a mandatory one to achieve success in the digital age.

Communication is not a monologue of information delivered to your audiences. Communication is an open dialogue, in which you listen, respond, and share. That is the definition of two-way communication. Social media brings this concept to an exciting new level of implementation. It is the most engaging of all PR tactics in terms of two-way communication and relationship building. As Figure 7.2 illustrates, PR practitioners used to mostly practise one-to-many communications; with the help of the media, they talked to many people at once with very little opportunity for feedback from the audience. Social media facilitates many-to-many communication. With social media, many people talk to large groups of people at once, with a lot of opportunity for feedback. Audiences are not only communicating back to the organization, but communicating with each other. While this provides an opportunity for rich dialogue, it also means that PR practitioners need to work more than ever. Gone are 9-to-5 working hours. As for taking a break during statutory holidays, Krisleigh Hoermann says, "Crises tend to occur the Friday night before a holiday, so no [you can't take a break], but you can scale back a little and ensure you have fun."[5] The PR practitioner must be constantly listening and engaging with the audience when the conversation is happening.

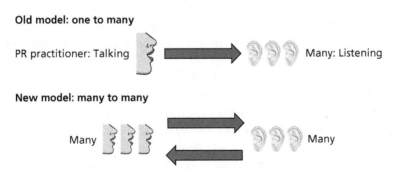

Old model: one to many

PR practitioner: Talking ➡ Many: Listening

New model: many to many

Many ⬌ Many

PR practitioner: Listening, participating, responding, engaging

Figure 7.2 Social Media and the Opportunity for Many-to-Many Conversations

THE NEW RULES OF ENGAGEMENT OF SOCIAL MEDIA

Social media has introduced more than just two-way communication to PR. It has also introduced a host of other guiding principles that PR practitioners must embrace and follow to successfully participate in this new medium. These guiding principles are known as the **rules of engagement**. The most pertinent ones for PR practitioners include those dealing with information sharing, engagement, permission, trust, and transparency. Social media experts also talk about honesty and generosity. More than ever, the actions of the PR practitioner are guided by these principles.

Let us look first at information sharing. This involves creating relationships by thinking of people first, offering them information that will be of value to them, and being generous about it. The content of the Rogers blog is custom-written for its target audiences and provides information that will be relevant to young, early to middle adopters of technology. Adding value, either through interesting, exciting, entertaining content or through improved customer service, needs to be at the centre of any social media campaign. PR practitioners need to ask themselves, "Why would anyone want to engage with our brand online? What can we offer them?" In order to provide value to consumers, Johnson & Johnson launched a website called Healthy Essentials, which offers coupons and articles with topics such as tips on how to nurse a sick child.[6] Shelley Kohut, director of communications and public relations for Johnson & Johnson Canada, says, "We're going to communicate with our consumers and nurture and build that relationship with them beyond the transaction. That's our goal."[7]

Social media principles also include listening to your audiences and responding proactively and appropriately to their thoughts, comments, and inquiries. It is important to develop real conversations as opposed to merely delivering sales pitches. That is exactly how the social media team at Rogers manages *RedBoard*. They show their readers that they are focused on delivering value by engaging and responding to them.

One of the guiding principles of *RedBoard* was also to be as open and transparent as possible with target audiences. This helps build trust between the organization and the audiences. As we saw in the opening vignette, their target audiences are intolerant of "corporate speak" and want to have a real conversation with Rogers online.

Asking permission is another key principle of social media. As we have noted, a PR campaign may include a media mix composed of traditional journalists and digital media producers. Each should be approached with a different strategy. For a new cosmetic product launch, for example, you would send a product sample to journalists at key media outlets such as *Chatelaine* magazine, the *National Post*, and *Fashion TV*. In the new age of media, permission is key in keeping with the principle of putting people first. You must ask bloggers if they would like to receive a product sample and make it clear that there are no strings attached before sending it. You should never send it without first seeking permission.

While some bloggers are journalists, many are not, so the rules of engagement are different. Many have professions outside of their blog and run the blog from their home, so their privacy and space must be respected. They do not have an office you can call or deliver packages to, and so you must correspond with them on their terms. They also usually don't respond well to mass pitches and press releases. Customized, individualized messages work much better. Most people do not like a hard sell on social media. If they feel marketed to, they will simply not follow you and will block you from their social media. This is why it is important to provide value and enhance your audience's social media experience, not detract from it.

Just as you need to ask permission from bloggers before sending samples, you also must ask permission before posting others' photos or quoting them on social media. Whether it is an employee, a volunteer, or a customer, make sure you get the subject's permission before posting anything online. If the subject is a minor, make sure his or her parents also agree to the posting.

TARGETING VERY SPECIFIC AUDIENCES: HYPERNICHE AND HYPERLOCAL

Before the digital age, it was difficult for PR practitioners to identify, find, and target audiences for topics that were not mainstream. The strategy involved tactics such as identifying trade publications, newsletters, or specialized mailing lists. Now practitioners can find communities online for any topic, ranging from corkscrew collectors to health care advocates. There are many more opportunities for content placement, but the audience is more fragmented. Instead of being able to reach all audiences at once, we must now speak to them individually. While this takes more time, the payoff can be larger because you are delivering the right information to the right audience. In turn, our efforts become much more focused on targeted, or **hyperniche**, audiences. We also have more opportunities to talk to local communities, or **hyperlocal** audiences. It takes time to conduct research and find these communities, but the effort is rewarded once you have found them and started engaging with them. It is worth re-emphasizing that this task can be accomplished only by knowing your target audiences well and putting the relationship with them first.

Nature's Path, North America's leading manufacturer of organic cereals, provides a great example of an organization using social media to reach its target audiences, some of which are very specialized. Nature's Path engages its audiences and establishes two-way communication, using a variety of technologies and tools to meet its PR objectives. The company is successful in the new media age because it always keeps its audiences top of mind, identifies where the audiences are interacting, and selects the best tools to reach them.

The PR team at Nature's Path employs a large portion of their overall initiatives on social media, and they expect that to grow. They have a Twitter account, a Facebook fan page, a blog, an interactive website, and a YouTube channel where they post videos they produce. They also do extensive blogger outreach, aiming to talk to about 50 bloggers a month.

"It's really amazing because we can be very specific in the communities we target," said a PR manager at Nature's Path. "When we are launching a new gluten-free cereal for children, for example, we can talk directly to the mothers and parents that are interested in this subject. Social media is about talking to less people but having a more personal connection. It's about forgetting talking points and having real conversations with people."[8]

Nature's Path uses social media to target niche audiences.
Source: © Carolyn Jenkins/Alamy

Thinking Like a PR Practitioner

1. Define two-way communication.
2. Explain the rules of engagement of social media.
3. Cite two reasons why social media producers such as bloggers are approached differently than journalists.

The New Media Influencers [3]

In Chapter 2, we studied how PR practitioners identify and work with influencers to reach and influence their target audiences. The digital age has created a great number of **new media influencers**—social media users who influence others and gain followers—and given them the power to reach their peers widely and immediately.

"I'm sorry, but you did not get the job. Yes, you did handle the Tylenol scare and developed best practices for Sarbanes Oxley, but the other candidate, well ... he knows how to blog."

Source: Cartoonresource/Shutterstock

Jeff Hamada's blog, *Booooooom*, is viewed as an authoritative Canadian art blog.
Source: Booooooom Design Inc.

Online influencers can include key bloggers with either large audiences or smaller but important audiences, or individuals on Twitter, Facebook, or Pinterest who have a large following. Often bloggers will have a large Facebook and Twitter following, which provides more opportunities for audiences to be exposed to information. Jeff Hamada's art blog, *Booooooom*, is seen as an authoritative figure in Canada's art scene. Because of the popularity of his blog, his Twitter and Facebook profiles also have large audiences. On the other hand, Debbie Shing, who works for Mark Anthony, a wine distributor, does not have a blog but has a large Twitter following as a result of her knowledge of the alcohol industry and important wine events. Because of her large following, she is often contacted by companies that are interested in reaching her followers.

Some new media influencers have become more trusted and respected than corporations and even traditional news organizations. The public is now more inclined to trust the individual providing them with information than the outlet where they obtained the news, especially as people now consume their news and information from so many different **touch points**—communication channels where audiences interact with brands or information. For example, we may first see a story on Twitter or on Facebook and then read something else about it in a blog. We may even follow Twitter comments about a news story that we are also simultaneously watching on the news. When evaluating these sources, we look at the trustworthiness or social capital of the content provider and not the medium or technology where it appears.

David Armano, a social media expert and communicator, calls this phenomenon the development of the "brand individual," where trust is put in individuals as opposed to corporate brands. This means that everyday people become trusted sources of information, as they create content and publish their opinions and ideas. These new media users can have great influence on their peers and on one another.

Becoming a Trusted Brand Individual

Becoming a trusted brand individual as a PR practitioner depends upon your ability to follow social media's rules of engagement. It is about generosity: provide your audiences with information that they care about and need, as opposed to making a pitch for your organization. Two-way communication is key in creating a trusting relationship with your audiences.

Listening and responding honestly to your audience's concerns goes a long way toward becoming a trusted brand individual. It is key that both you and the organization demonstrate these values and that they are applied systematically over the long term. A public relations career is built over many years, and your reputation is essential to the success of you and your organization.

Canada has many trusted brand individuals on many different topics. Some of the most influential include Adele McAlear, who has become a trusted source for information on marketing; Kate Trgovac, on social media; Rebecca Bollwitt, on events and happenings in Vancouver; Michael Geist, on politics; and Terry Fallis, on public relations.

The impact for PR practitioners is twofold. First, they want to identify the brand individuals who can make a difference for their organizations and foster relationships with them. By providing these brand individuals with a positive experience with their product or service, they can influence their network. These influencers have the power to help PR practitioners meet their public relations objectives by talking to others about their organization. Chris Abraham, director of the online social media PR firm Abraham & Harrison and the author of a blog called *Marketing Conversation*, estimates that influencers and opinion leaders using social media each influence between 100 and 1000 people, and they can reach up to 1 million people in the case of a celebrity.[9] Second, PR practitioners themselves can become brand individuals as they communicate on behalf on their organizations. In order to do this, they must be transparent and authentic, and provide interesting information.

Thinking Like a PR Practitioner

1. Discuss the blogs that you read regularly.
2. What makes you trust some online brand individuals and not others? Describe what differentiates them.
3. Describe how a PR practitioner can become a brand individual.

Opportunities and Challenges for PR Practitioners in the Digital Age ❹

Social media presents many new opportunities for PR practitioners, as well as new challenges. Opportunities include reaching niche communities, communicating directly with an audience, having campaigns go viral, and being able to learn more about an organization's competitors. Some of the new challenges social media presents include losing control of the message, dealing with a fragmented audience that is time-consuming to reach, and managing issues and crises.

OPPORTUNITY: REACHING NICHE COMMUNITIES

The first opportunity results from the explosion of new media, which enables PR practitioners to reach niche communities that had never before been targeted or received regular coverage in the mainstream media. There are online communities built around almost any topic imaginable, and legions of blogs cover every subject under the sun. Stories or topics that were once considered too niche for mainstream media can be pitched and covered at length in blogs dedicated to that topic.

OPPORTUNITY: COMMUNICATING DIRECTLY WITH AUDIENCES

Another opportunity for PR practitioners is that they no longer have to depend on traditional media to pick up their stories to reach their target audiences. The middleman or gatekeeper has been removed. PR practitioners can distribute the content themselves directly to the right audiences and the right influencers through their own blogs, Facebook pages, or Twitter streams. They can then hear their audiences' feedback in order to adapt their messaging. This is exactly what Rogers did with its *RedBoard* blog. Rogers communicates directly with its target audiences of Millennial and Gen Y early to middle adopters of technology, listening and responding to them.

OPPORTUNITY: GOING GLOBAL

Another benefit of the digital age is the possibility of campaigns making a global impact on a small budget. Social media has broken through geographical boundaries. Korean pop sensation Psy demonstrated the global reach of social media with his hit song "Gangnam Style." A song that might never have become popular outside of South Korea under the old media model became a viral international hit thanks to YouTube. At the end of 2012, the video had over 1 billion views from around the world.

Psy become a worldwide celebrity after his "Gangnam Style" music video went viral.
Source: © Pictorial Press Ltd/Alamy

Similarly, a campaign implemented in Canada can be discussed all over the world by bloggers and users of other social media tools. An example of a Canadian viral video sensation is the video of an eagle picking up a toddler in a Montreal park. This Internet hoax was created by four Montreal students for a simulation workshop class. Their assignment was to create a video that garnered over 100,000 YouTube hits. The four students did better than that by creating a 3-D animation of an eagle picking up a toddler in a park and then dropping the toddler nearby.[10] The animation looks lifelike and soon went viral. While the students quickly declared that it was a hoax, the video received tens of millions of YouTube views.

OPPORTUNITY: GAINING MARKET INTELLIGENCE

Social media also provides an abundant source of information about an organization's competitors. Social media content is an excellent source of market intelligence that PR practitioners previously did not have access to or had to pay large sums of money to obtain. Social media is a bit like a focus group that happens in real time. So much can be gained from looking at the competition's messaging, target audiences, and digital media tactics. PR practitioners can also hear what target audiences are saying about their own company or their competitors and find out how engaged their customers are. A warning, though, if you participate in any online discussions, always identify which company you are representing. It is highly unethical and almost always counterproductive to pretend to be someone you are not online. Do not pretend you are a passive consumer and bash your competitors or praise your own products on Facebook, on Twitter, or in the comment sections of blogs. Chances are someone will identify who you really are, causing you and your organization embarrassment.

CHALLENGE: LOSING CONTROL OF THE MESSAGE

A challenge facing public relations practitioners with the rise of social media is that they no longer have exclusive control over their organization's messaging. They are now but one voice out there talking about an organization, a product, or a good cause. With so many users talking about any given topic, or posting user-generated comments on brands, it is important that organizations participate in social media. They need to take part in the conversation that is already occurring about them. They should not try to have exclusive control over the message, as social media makes this impossible. Deleting negative comments from your site's comments section or from Facebook will seem inauthentic and not transparent. It is better to address the criticism and provide answers to people's concerns.

McDonald's Canada addresses consumers' questions and criticisms head-on with the launch of its social media campaign "Our Food. Your Questions." This started as a Canadian and digital-only campaign in which McDonald's promised to answer any questions consumers had about its products through online videos and posts. The campaign was so successful that it grew to include traditional media and gained international PR coverage.[11] Judy John, CEO of Leo Burnett Canada, says, "McDonald's had a business problem: People wondered about the food. The idea gets at the heart of the problem and solves it. And this idea is big, it goes beyond a program or promotional idea. It's a platform. It's authentic. It's social, it's getting buzz."[12] Like McDonald's Canada, PR practitioners should try to learn from and react from the conversations happening around their organizations.

CHALLENGE: DEALING WITH FRAGMENTED AUDIENCES

A further challenge is that audiences are much more fragmented than in the past and will become increasingly so over time. When there were fewer media, each outlet had a larger readership or audience. One message to one outlet went a long way toward helping to meet PR objectives. Now the campaign must be tailored to smaller, more focused audiences. This process can be more time-consuming and expensive but ultimately more rewarding, as there is more opportunity to tailor each message and deliver more value to each audience.

CHALLENGE: CONFRONTING ISSUES AND CRISES

Many organizations are wary of joining the digital age because they feel that they must let go of the reins—they will not be able to control the conversation as they once did. However, the conversation has already begun and is ongoing, whether an organization decides to participate or not. PR professionals and their organizations need to weigh the costs of not being involved in this conversation.

Not everything discussed online about your organization will be positive, no matter what organization you work for. Regular, ongoing monitoring of what is said on the Internet about your organization and assessment of your online reputation are essential. This monitoring enables PR practitioners to know if an issue or crisis is brewing and if action is needed. Free services like Google Alerts or the search functions in Twitter or HootSuite, a social media–monitoring dashboard, can help you monitor the conversations for potential issues.

It is beneficial to be part of the conversation even when what is being said about your organization is negative. In terms of social media, the key actions to consider are collaborating, engaging, and participating. These objectives can generally be achieved even during an issue or crisis. Just by having a presence online, and by listening to and participating in the conversation, you can raise the **social capital** of your organization—the worth of your social network in terms of influence and sharing. In some cases, these actions may bring a favourable resolution to the issue and turn the situation around. By being part of the conversation, you can also manage issues that might become larger without intervention. For example, as we saw with McDonald's Canada's "Our Food. Your Questions." campaign, the company was able to address concerns about its food publicly, potentially stopping misinformation about its products. For more information on issues and crisis communications, see Chapter 11.

Campaigns like McDonald's Our Food. Your Questions is a good example of transparency on social media.
Source: © Caro/Alamy

Thinking Like a PR Practitioner

1. After reviewing all the opportunities and challenges, judge whether practising PR has become easier or harder in the digital age.
2. What kinds of information can you gather about your competitors through social media? Why might this be beneficial?
3. What does it mean to have a more fragmented audience?

The Tools and Technologies of Social Media ⑤

The last subject we will cover in this chapter is the tools and technologies of social media that practitioners use to communicate with target audiences. As we explored earlier, the decision regarding which tools to use is based on whom we are trying to reach and how we can engage them.

In an interview on fastcompany.com, Charlene Li, the author of the book *Groundswell* and a social media consultant, advises that the first step in a social media campaign is to think about the relationship an organization wants to create with its target audiences.

> Companies will come to us and say, "We need a blog." Ok, great. Why do you want a blog? They go, "Well, our competition has a blog. Or my CEO wants a blog." It's rarely with a good understanding of what kind of relationship they want to build with the people they're trying to reach. Focus on the relationship first.[13]

Keep in mind, once again, that these technologies change and evolve quickly, with new developments bursting onto the scene regularly.

Going back to the example of Nature's Path, the decision about which technologies to employ was based on researching where people who are interested in gluten-free products talk to one another and share information. There is no point in being on Pinterest if gluten-free conversations are not happening there. For a new gluten-free cereal launch, product giveaways were conducted on Twitter and Facebook, and information and products were sent to gluten-free bloggers, including *The Celiac Maniac*, *Gluten Free Expedition*, and *Gluten Free Betsy*.

BLOGS

A blog is a contraction of the term *Web log*. A blog is similar to an opinion column in the sense that a person writes his or her own personal commentary or curates content from other places. There are individual blogs and corporate or organizational blogs, such as Rogers Communications' *RedBoard*.

Blogs can be approached in two basic ways, and your PR strategy can include one or both. The first is to create a blog for your organization, and the second is to have a blogger outreach program, one similar to media relations, in which you contact bloggers instead of or in addition to journalists.

Blogger Outreach

Blogs are one of the most exciting developments in public relations. The advent of blogs created countless new avenues through which to disseminate information and reach target audiences. There are blogs for every topic under the sun, many of which have a dedicated community following them. The audience may be more fragmented than ever

Writing Blogs

- Remember that a blog is only the technology. You should never start one just because it is trendy. You must decide on and commit to the editorial content of your blog.

- Make sure you have the time and resources to support a blog. Blogs can be time-consuming, as they must be updated regularly to be effective—at least once a week. If you go too long between updates, you risk having your audience lose interest.

- If you are doing the writing on behalf of someone else, acknowledge it. Ghost writing should be disclosed.

- Be aware that a blog on a specific topic can be short term. For example, a three-week blog on the rebranding taking place at your organization can work well.

- Ask yourself this question first: What information can I offer in terms of contributing to the communities I am trying to engage with my blog?

as a result, but it also can be targeted in a way never seen before. Traditional media outlets may still have a larger audience, but a blog's audience of 1000 fervent followers can be as or even more powerful in helping you meet your PR objectives than a national newspaper with a wider readership.

Example of How to Approach a Blogger Outreach Campaign

The first step in a blogger outreach campaign is to conduct research to find out which bloggers are talking about your topic or organization. If you have not been participating, you will probably find that there is a whole conversation already taking place without you. Some of it may be positive and some may be negative. You want to be engaged and part of the conversation. The more engaged you are, the higher your social capital will rise.

To find blogs, start with a Google search or a site like Technorati, which is a blog aggregate site that carries the most popular blogs by subject. Another great research tool is to look at **blog rolls**—the lists of all the blogs that other bloggers follow. A good blog roll is a precious commodity.

As with traditional publications, you must get to know these blogs. Read many current and archived entries to get a good sense of editorial content and what will be of interest to a blogger. Next, compile a database of appropriate bloggers and start engaging them and building a relationship with them.

Unlike your relationship with traditional media, you will need to introduce yourself and seek permission before you start pitching to bloggers or sending them product samples. Your pitches must all be custom-written for each blogger. You can use the same key messages but tailor the message for each blog. You should aim to engage and build a relationship with 12 to 20 bloggers per topic. It is difficult to maintain a relationship with more than that, especially at the beginning. A good way to begin a relationship with bloggers is to offer them a product or service to give away to their readers. Many bloggers build their followers through giveaways, and so they appreciate the opportunity to provide something of value to their community.

Negative Blogs

There will likely be times when your organization will be negatively discussed online by a blogger. As in issues and crisis management, further discussed in Chapter 11, the way you handle the situation will make all the difference. Some of the worst cases turn into positive relationship building when an organization listens, interacts, and takes action to remedy what went wrong. You may want to contact the blogger directly to see what you can do to fix things, as it is quicker and more personal. A best practice for public relations professionals is always to stay calm and listen, as in all issues and crisis situations, no matter what the other party says or does.

In his blog, PR practitioner Tom Lyons recommends the following to turn a negative situation into positive outcome:

> When handing a negative blog, what not to do is just as important as what to do. Unless you are clearly dealing with someone less than honest, do not:

- Ignore the post and hope it just goes away. Even if it does not go viral, it will live on the Internet indefinitely, waiting for someone to discover it.
- Be defensive or challenge her version of what occurred. Again, think about how you'd like to be treated if you had a legitimate complaint.
- Expect that what you say is just between you two. Everything you say or imply is likely to end up posted. Speak accordingly.[14]

Source: Negative Blogs: How to make lemonade from lemons December 1, 2009. Used by permission by Tom Lyons.

Organizational Blogs

Another tactic you can employ is to create a blog for your organization, as Rogers Communications did with *RedBoard*. This can be an efficient tool to communicate directly with your target audiences and make sure that you are part of the conversation.

Blogs can be written from many different perspectives. For instance, an organization can have a blog from its CEO, one from a top researcher, and one from someone working in customer relations. A blog can also have one author or multiple authors.

The telecommunications company Rogers uses its company blog, Redboard, to provide useful content to its target audiences.

Source: © Mark Blinch/Reuters/Corbis

Pitching Bloggers

- Customize your pitch for each blogger. Read what they wrote as far back as you can and position your story in a way that will be of interest to them.

- Make sure they cover the topic you are pitching on and explain clearly why you think this story will interest them.

- Engage them before you pitch. Introduce yourself and let them know which organization you represent. It is imperative that you be transparent and honest. All information is public in the media age.

- Offer your assistance. Many bloggers are single-person operations. Maybe they'll take you up on your offer.

- Never mass email.

- It takes more time to build a blogger database than a media database, but it is worth the effort. A great way to find bloggers on a certain topic is look at a blogger's blog roll. It can be a very valuable source of information.

During a speaking engagement on best practices in the digital world, Kate Trgovac, owner of the social media consultancy LintBucket Media and a well-known blogger, recommended having a team of corporate bloggers so if one individual leaves, the campaign will not collapse.

From a PR perspective, it is important to know what the editorial content of your blog will be and what direction it will take. To be effective, blogs need to appeal to and engage your target audiences, so you must consider what topics will be of interest to them. One recommendation is to write out a list of all topics you want to cover over a period of time and have several entries written before going live. Sites such as WordPress and Blogger are easy tools for creating organizational and corporate blogs. Also, remember that building readership takes time. Make sure you set realistic goals for how many people you want reading your blog, and communicate those goals internally, both to avoid getting discouraged and to make sure everyone has realistic expectations.

OTHER TOOLS AND TECHNOLOGIES OF SOCIAL MEDIA

Blogs are just one tool that can be used in a social media campaign. In public relations, rarely is only one tactic used to reach your communication objectives. It should also be noted that not every tool is right for every campaign or every organization. A Pinterest page might not be right for an organization that does not operate in a highly visual space but might be the perfect platform for an interior design firm. The following are other tools that can be effective.

Your Own Website

One of the first elements to consider in social media is the website of your organization. After all, it remains one of the most powerful tools for sharing information with consumers and the media. Also, many of the initiatives that you will be undertaking with social media will result, if you are successful, in driving traffic to your organization's website, where your audience can learn more information, purchase your product, or donate to your organization.

Whereas before, a website was a vehicle to share company information and messaging, it is now an interactive tool for a two-way conversation with your target audiences. The key is to make the website interactive, with opportunities for feedback and posting, and to include multimedia aspects such as videos, blogs, and links to your accounts such as Facebook, Digg, and Twitter.

A well-thought-out, up-to-date media section on your website can also be a great resource for journalists and bloggers. Key contacts, past media releases, bios, fact sheets, backgrounders, and easily downloadable images can be housed there to make it easy for the media to find the information they need to create their story.

Wikis

A wiki is a collaborative website containing pages that are written and edited by groups of people. The most well known wiki is Wikipedia, although there are many more wikis, some of which are highly specialized, like wikicars.org for automobile enthusiasts. Wikis can be an effective tool to reach specialized and influential audiences. The key is to be open, to be completely transparent, and to contribute and share information. Wikis are not the forum to talk about your brand or organization, but rather to provide information and educate and engage your audience.

Miniblogs

There are also miniblog technologies such as Twitter. The shortness of the texts (140 characters or less for Twitter) allows messages to transmit quickly from user to user. Users reply to and forward one another's messages in a public manner.

Twitter can be a valuable listening and customer service tool. Through Twitter, companies that have customers who benefit from regular updates, such as transit companies or airlines, can provide up-to-the minute information on topics such as flight delays or route detours. If you hear of individuals on Twitter experiencing a problem with your product, you can help them through Twitter. This public exercise might also assist others who are having the same problem.

The Salt Spring Coffee Company ran a campaign called "#needalift?" that aimed to help customers having a lousy day. The first phase involved searching for local Tweets where individuals wrote that they were having a bad day. These people were then sent a bag of coffee and a tumbler, which generated a lot of positive tweets and retweets about the organization.[15]

Many individuals are now receiving their news from sites such as Twitter. Thirty-three per cent of adults under 30 report that they receive their news from a social networking site—almost as many as those who receive their news from television (34 per cent) and more than those who receive their news from print (13 per cent).[16] Also, because news on Twitter can travel so fast, a negative or incorrect news story can gain traction quickly. This is why it is important that even if an organization doesn't have a Twitter account, its communications team is still monitoring what is being said.

PRACTITIONER INTERVIEW

Michael Gleboff, Social Media Specialist

Michael Gleboff is a social media PR specialist who has worked in-house conducting campaigns in the animation, video game, and mobile industries, as well as in a PR agency.

Question: What kind of social media tactics have you used?

Answer: Research and planning are the most important aspects of a successful social media campaign. Once you know what you want to achieve and who you want to reach, you utilize tactics that best fit those goals. Most importantly, you want to be proactive and not reactive. Social media is about outreach and engagement, so you want to always be aware of what people are saying about your brand and working to influence it. To do that, you need to be reaching others through as many platforms as you can—Twitter, Facebook, LinkedIn, Pinterest, etc. Always be creating content that's compelling and can incentivize action, and craft it to best fit the channel you're distributing on (i.e., you shouldn't be broadcasting long-form content as multiple posts on Twitter).

Search engine optimization is another a key tactic in getting your work noticed. Using key words and planning ensures you're receiving the broadest reach with your content and pulling in unique views from search engines like Google and Bing. Finally, enable and encourage your community to share your content. Web tools like a "Share button" will provide greater ease for users to aid in distribution and gaining solid word-of-mouth traction. You're working to make yourself more visible and available, so any help is always effective and appreciated.

Question: What kind of results can you achieve with social media?

Answer: There's a lot you can achieve with social media so long as you've established goals and the means with which you'd like to reach them. Whether that's improved customer service, a wider reach of brand awareness, or even just more views on your blog posts, it's an incredibly versatile tool that can get you where you want to go in terms of digital representation. Ultimately, though, your results will focus on finding new ways to engage your customers and keep them coming back.

Question: What aspects motivate you?

Answer: I love the immediacy of social media. To be able to make an effort in engaging someone or a group of people and see the direct result is an incredibly thrilling opportunity, especially matched with social media's creative and two-way nature. You're putting yourself out there, like you would in real life, and connecting with others in a much more visceral way than standard marketing that aims more toward numbered results. And I'm in social media because I thrive in working with others, so the social aspect is definitely an incentive for me. It's a job where you try and make others excited about what you're excited about, and I find that pretty great.

(Continued)

Michael Gleboff, Social Media Specialist

Question: What is a typical day like?

Answer: A typical day usually involves a large range of tasks and contributions from different teams. Often social media specialists will spend a good portion of their day doing research and gathering data that can be applied across the organization. As well, a strategist's job includes creating solid content to be published across multiple online platforms in many different formats. This could be anything from scheduling and posting a series of blog entries to filming a video for the company's website. You'll also be constantly checking and managing social media accounts, ensuring that customer questions are being answered and discussion is being generated. Aside from that, you'll be on top of current trends and always looking for new ways to reach out to your public effectively.

Question: What are the challenges in working in social media?

Answer: Personally, I think the biggest challenge is understanding how to use it properly. Being a relatively new tool with a large capacity for unique application, it's easy to lose sight of your objectives and how social media platforms can best achieve them. Figuring out what works for your organization, your strategy, and your public is key to running successful campaigns and it's not an easy thing to do. Obstacles that can clutter your vision and as act as challenges in themselves include a lack of time and preparation, creating a realistic strategy, and figuring out your core targets—these things that are meant to build toward your goals, and if not properly considered, can be what turns a great idea into an unsuccessful campaign.

Question: What advice would you give anyone who wants to work in this field?

Answer: You have to be loud. Social media is a field that's easy to quantify, so all it takes for someone to see your passion is a quick Google search and a look at your online profiles. You want to stand out and show that you're comfortable saying something. Don't be afraid to show personality, but know when to use discretion. Reach out to everyone you can and find online communities that you can be involved in—networking goes a long way in social media and all it takes is a simple "hello." And know your stuff when it comes to the online environment. Things like basic programming and web design can make a huge difference in your appeal to potential employers. Finally, have fun with it. Personality is the key to success and there's no better way to get noticed than by being genuine and enjoying what you do.

Question: What has been a favourite campaign?

Answer: While working at a video game studio, our marketing team was tasked with launching a social media campaign around an upcoming title being released. It was an online game targeted at kids between the ages of 12 to 15, a demographic not likely to be on something like Twitter. Our goal was to encourage players to create accounts and support our social media efforts for the launch, and as well have them engaging each other outside of the game. To do this we started by looking to our established customer base and those of similar products and organizations. We learned that we needed to incentivize: give users a reason to follow you, and a reason to keep coming back.

Knowing that our fans and the general gaming community were passionate about the development process, we worked with the art team to create a contest that would allow three creative fans the chance to have a design they created implemented in the game. Users were encouraged

(Continued)

to share entries and accumulate support for their piece through coordinated social media and at the same time spreading word about our upcoming launch. They would then vote and curate on our official forums and begin to establish a base for the community. In the end, we had successfully launched our social media accounts as platforms for community managers to continue to engage the community and support it through new content and similar events.

Social Networking Sites

Facebook, Myspace, and LinkedIn are some of the most popular examples of social networking sites. Organizations, brands, and causes participate and become users by creating a page. Pages include videos, photos, and links, as well as discussion groups that can be used to engage with your audience and respond to individual inquiries and concerns. Keys to maintaining your page include updating it regularly, responding in a timely manner to comments and inquiries, and keeping it current. Google is highly responsive to Facebook, and your pages can be indexed in the same way as web pages.

Podcasts and Vodcasts

Podcasts (audio) and vodcasts (video) are recordings edited to be in the same format as radio or television programs on certain topics or commentaries. These tools enable you to produce your own radio or TV shows and disseminate them via the Internet directly to

Facebook is an example of a highly popular social networking site.

Source: MCT/Newscom

Jian Ghomeshi's *Q* on CBC Radio is also a popular podcast.

Source: From the Twitter service @jianghomeshi

your target audiences. People either listen to them online or download them directly to their players or computers. You can also pitch story ideas and suggest names of potential guests to be interviewed by the hosts. This can provide excellent coverage for spokespersons from your organization. Many radio shows are also run as podcasts, including *Under the Influence*, *Q*, and *WireTap*, all from CBC Radio.

Video-Sharing Sites

Video-sharing sites such as YouTube are a popular tool to share and view video clips. On YouTube, companies can create their own channel to share videos on, such as corporate videos, commercials, video news releases, and vodcasts. Videos are a great way to share useful information, entertaining videos, or how-to videos with an audience. In its "Our Food. Your Questions." campaign, McDonald's used online videos to answer consumers' questions about its food, such as, "Why does your food look different in ads than in your restaurants?"[17] The clothing retailer Mexx also used English and French YouTube videos to raise awareness of its brand. These how-to videos offered useful fashion lessons, such as the "how to tie a tie" video.[18]

As discussed in Chapter 11, Maple Leaf Foods effectively used YouTube when listeria was found in its foods, resulting in illness and the death of several customers. The crisis strategy the company employed included video messages from president and CEO Michael McCain expressing how sorry he was and explaining what Maple Leaf Foods was doing to remedy the situation.

Forums

Forums are online discussion groups and communities where people who share the same interests get together to share information and socialize. They generally form around specific topics, such as pregnancy, fitness, or hobbies. They can be an effective way to reach a very targeted, niche, or local community. You can either join a forum or start your own. Sites such as Yahoo! host a number of forums.

Bookmarking

Bookmarking on sites such as Delicious.com and Digg.com allows members to submit stories and information on their favourite sites, which can then be shared with all members. These bookmarking sites can do wonders to drive traffic to your website if a story about your organization appears on one of them. On some, such as Digg.com, people vote on their favourite stories, providing additional endorsement. In terms of influence, the homepage of Digg.com receives substantially more visitors than that of the websites of Canada's top media such as *The Globe and Mail*.

Photo Sharing

Flicker and Instagram are examples of photo-sharing sites where users can upload their photos and share them with others. Many of the photos on these sites can be used by others free of charge as long as credit is given to the photo provider. Sites like Instagram allow you to easily post your photo to social media sites, such as Facebook and Twitter. An example of a company doing interesting things on Instagram is Sharpie, the maker of markers. The company posts photos of images hand-drawn with its markers to its account.[19]

Thinking Like a PR Practitioner

1. You have been assigned to create a blog for your organization and need to compile the subject of the first five entries. Brainstorm what they can be for:

- The Royal Canadian Air Force (target audience: new recruits): *www.rcaf-arc. forces.gc.ca*

- Canadian Blood Services (target audience: blood donors): *www.blood.ca*

2. Discuss how you would decide which social media tools to use in a campaign.

3. Explain how to approach a blogger.

Sites like Pinterest are similar to Flicker or Instagram, but instead of sharing their own images, users share images collected from online sources. Users share photos, videos, and other content on their boards for others to see. Organizations can use Pinterest to provide content to their customers. For example, *Flare Magazine* pins fashion- and beauty-related photos that readers would enjoy.

CASE STUDY SAVING THE GREAT BEAR RAINFOREST

A social media campaign was devised to save the Great Bear Rainforest.
Source: © Steven J. Kazlowski/Alamy

The following case study illustrates how a campaign can reach and engage its target audiences by using multiple social media platforms. The campaign messages were all actionable, easily enabling the public to support the cause.

A consortium of environmental groups retained Capulet Communications, a digital communication agency, to pressure the B.C. government to ratify an agreement to create a nature conservancy. Capulet's role was to raise online awareness of the campaign and get signatures for a petition to be sent to the B.C. government. The campaign was titled "Keep the Promise: Save the Great Bear Rainforest."

British Columbia's Great Bear Rainforest is the world's largest intact coastal temperate rainforest. It is a precious piece of land since it is home to a large number of animals and plants, such as migratory birds, salmon, and the unique white spirit bear.

Capulet employed several online tactics to meet its objectives. The agency created a Facebook group, which recruited 4000 members. The page encouraged members to sign an online petition. It also asked them to donate their own Facebook status message to the campaign for one day. Capulet organized a photo contest in which 200 Flickr users submitted photos related to the reasons why the government needed to keep its promise to conserve this ecologically significant rainforest. The agency also pitched the story to bloggers who cover environmental issues, resulting in positive social media coverage. Other PR tactics included a Twitter feed and the online promotion of a YouTube video.

Success for the campaign was measured in the number of emails that were sent to the government through the official campaign website (100 a day at its height) and the number of people who signed the petition (16,000). As a result of the campaign, the B.C. government kept its promise and ratified the agreement.

Questions

1. Discuss how social media tools were used in this campaign. What other platforms would work?

2. Explain what is meant by "the campaign messages were all actionable."

AUTHOR'S OWN EXPERIENCE

Habitat JAM

My public relations agency was retained by Habitat JAM for a 72-hour online event and conversation on urban sustainability issues sponsored by the Canadian Government, UN-HABITAT, and IBM. The objective was to provide a forum where people all over the world could share best practices on different urban topics, such as affordable housing, safety, and sustainable development. The goal was to create a global problem-solving session in which practical solutions successfully tested in some cities, such as ways to improve the living conditions of slum dwellers or cost-effective water filtration systems, could then be shared and implemented by others. We decided to employ a strategy using a media mix that included traditional media and social media.

A media conference was organized to reach international journalists at Canada House in London, England. We also targeted digital media, bloggers, and online communities by distributing information to them in many different languages. Results included coverage that was global and that appeared in print, broadcast, and online media in a variety of languages and countries, resulting in tens of thousands of people around the globe signing up for Habitat JAM.

Social Media

tools
- photo & video sharing
- forums
- bookmarking
- podcasts & vodcasts
- social networking
- blogs
  outreach
  organizational

opportunities
- global
- market intelligence
  competition
- direct
  target audiences

- niche
  hyperniche
  hyperlocal

fundamentals
- key messages
- objectives
- target audiences
- strategy
- media mix

new media
- influencers
- brand individuals
  trusted

challenges
- many voices
- fragmented audiences
- issues & crises

rules of engagement
- two-way communication
- transparency
- trust
- permission
- sharing

Key Terms

blog roll A list of all the blogs another blogger follows.

media mix A combination of different media.

new media influencers Social media users whom others follow and who influence others.

hyperlocal Extremely local communities.

hyperniche Extremely targeted audiences.

rules of engagement Practices and behaviours expected of social media participants.

social capital The worth of a social network with regards to influence and sharing.

social media Digital media that are both created and consumed by users.

touch points Communication channels where audiences interact with brands or information.

user-generated content Information that is created by social media users.

viral campaign A popular campaign that is quickly and widely shared among viewers through social media.

Weblinks

Booooooom
www.boooooooom.com

Capulet Communications
www.capulet.com

Charlene Li interview in *Fastcompany.com*
www.fastcompany.com/articles/2008/06/interview-charlene-li.html

David Armano
darmano.typepad.com/

Directions4Success
directions4success.wordpress.com

"Gangnam Style"
http://www.youtube.com/watch?v=9bZkp7q19f0

"Golden Eagle Snatches Kid" Internet Hoax Video
http://www.youtube.com/watch?v=CE0Q904gtMI

Groundswell book
www.forrester.com/Groundswell

Habitat JAM
http://en.wikipedia.org/wiki/Habitat_Jam

LintBucket Media
www.lintbucket.com

Maple Leaf Foods Listeria Recall video
http://www.youtube.com/watch?v=zlsN5AkJ1AI

Marketing Conversation
www.marketingconversation.com

Nature's Path
www.naturespath.com

Endnotes

1. Michael Oliveira, "Canada's 'Most Socially Networked' Title Slipping Away," *The Globe and Mail*, February 29, 2012. Accessed February 5, 2013, http://www.theglobeandmail.com/technology/digital-culture/social-web/canadas-most-socially-networked-title-slipping-away/article550205/

2. Ibid.

3. Mark Hachman, "Twitter Continues to Soar in Popularity, Site's Numbers Reveal," *Pcmag.com*, September 8, 2011. Accessed February 5, 2013, http://www.pcmag.com/article2/0,2817,2392658,00.asp

4. A. Sreberny-Mohammadi, "Forms of Media as Ways of Knowing." In J. Downing, A. Mohammadi, and A. Sreberny-Mohammadi (eds.), *Questioning the Media: A Critical Introduction* (2nd ed.; pp. 23–38). London: Sage, 1995.

5. Quoted in Steve Goldsten, "Happy Holidays! Now Get Back to Monitoring Your Social Channels," *PR News*, December 21, 2012. Accessed February 5, 2013, http://www.prnewsonline.com/free/Happy-Holidays!-Now-Get-Back-to-Monitoring-Your-Social-Channels_17637.html

6. Susan Krashinsky, "For Advertisers, There's a Virtue to Being Useful," *The Globe and Mail*, January 3, 2013. Accessed February 5, 2013, http://www.theglobeandmail.com/report-on-business/industry-news/marketing/for-advertisers-theres-a-virtue-to-being-useful/article6928296/

7. Ibid.

8. Interview with author.

9. Chris Abraham, *Marketing Conversation* blog. Accessed January 10, 2010, http://marketing-conversation.com/

10. Michael Posner, "Behind the Eagle Internet Hoax: Four Montreal Students Create Video for Class Assignment," *The Globe and Mail*, December 19, 2012. Accessed February 5, 2013, http://www.theglobeandmail.com/arts/behind-the-eagle-internet-hoax-four-montreal-students-create-video-for-class-assignment/article6578890/

11. Susan Krashinsky, "The Best Ads of 2012 (Picked by Those in the Know)," *The Globe and Mail*, December 13, 2012. Accessed February 5, 2013, http://www.theglobeandmail.com/report-on-business/industry-news/marketing/the-best-ads-of-2012-picked-by-those-in-the-know/article6338360/?page=all

12. Ibid.

13. Kermit Pattison, "Charlene Li on Flaming Laptops, Sleeping Technicians, and the Streisand Effect," *Fastcompany.com*, June 30, 2008. Accessed, February 5, 2013, http://www.fastcompany.com/articles/2008/06/interview-charlene-li.html

14. Tom Lyons, "Negative Blogs: How to Make Lemonade from Lemons," *Directions4Success* blog, December 1, 2009, accessed February 5, 2013, http://directions4success.wordpress.com/2009/12/01/negative-blogs-how-to-make-lemonade-from-lemons/

15. Eve Lazarus, "Salt Spring Coffee Gives Customers a Lift Through Social Media," *Marketing*, August 4, 2011. Accessed February 5, 2013, http://www.marketingmag.ca/news/marketer-news/salt-spring-coffee-gives-customers-a-lift-through-social-media-33341

16. Debbie Wetherhead, "Back to Basics: Media Training Never Goes out of Fashion," *Public Relations Tactics*, November 2012. Accessed February 5, 2013, http://www.prsa.org/Intelligence/Tactics/Articles/view/9972/1057/Back_to_basics_Media_training_never_goes_out_of_fa

17. Krashinsky, "The Best Ads of 2012."

18. Ibid.

19. Saya Weissman, "5 Brands Doing Cool Things on Instagram," Digiday.com, December 7, 2012. Accessed February 5, 2013, http://www.digiday.com/brands/5-brands-doing-cool-things-on-instagram/

Entry-Level Positions

In our agency, new recruits were responsible for creating and updating media databases, organizing media coverage, sourcing materials such as creative content for media information kits, conducting market research, and identifying industry trends, in addition to some administrative duties such as photocopying, coordinating couriers, and running errands.

The most common job title for entry-level positions in public relations is coordinator or assistant. It generally means that the job involves working with a more senior person and assisting him or her with projects and campaigns. Coordinators and assistants are expected to be organized, detail oriented, deadline driven, and to provide general assistance even for tasks that do not fall under their job description. The tasks you will perform upon first being hired in a public relations capacity will vary depending on the size of the organization that you join.

It is important to remember that public relations is a fast-moving field and that opportunities for promotions are numerous for a hard-working, fast learner. Managers are quick to reward new practitioners who show many of the personality skills described in this book.

The following are examples of entry-level tasks and responsibilities:

- Attending industry functions
- Performing administrative duties
- Sourcing materials for a variety of applications
- Obtaining quotes
- Taking on any task that senior practitioners do not have time for
- Responding to requests for information from the public
- Researching and writing media materials
- Updating social media tools
- Updating websites
- Pitching story ideas to the media
- Media monitoring
- Competition monitoring and market intelligence gathering
- Assisting senior practitioners with campaigns
- Creating and maintaining media lists and other contact databases
- Assisting with or planning events
- Providing on-site assistance at events
- Sourcing all kinds of materials
- Conducting research
- Performing administrative tasks such as filing, photocopying, and assembling media information kits

Chapter 8
Media Training

*Mt. Kilimanjaro was climbed by Warren Macdonald, who is an internationally acclaimed
environmentalist, motivational speaker, and author, who gives many media interview.*

Source: © E.R. Degginger/Alamy

LEARNING OBJECTIVES

❶ Explain the role that media training plays in preparing spokespersons to work with
the media.

❷ Analyze a story and identify newsworthy interview content in it.

❸ Summarize the skills needed to successfully deliver key messages to the media.

❹ Develop a custom-tailored media-training session.

❺ Critique a spokesperson's media interview.

Warren Macdonald: Getting the Message Out with Media Training

Warren Macdonald is an internationally acclaimed environmentalist, motivational speaker, and author. He gives speeches at corporate and inspirational events where he talks about triumphing over adversity. He should know. While Macdonald was hiking on a remote Australian island, a rockfall caused a one-ton boulder to fall on and crush his legs. It was two days before help came, and the accident cost him his legs—both were amputated at the mid-thigh.

Macdonald's story was featured on a television series titled *I Shouldn't Be Alive*. A media relations campaign was organized to raise awareness of the series, and Macdonald was selected as a spokesperson. He conducted media interviews to publicize the episode he was featured on. The **media tour**—the line-up of interviews organized for a spokesperson as part of a campaign—included appearances on *Oprah* and the *Larry King Show*. Faced with the prospect of appearing on some of the most popular television talk shows ever, Macdonald signed up for media training.

Macdonald realized that journalists were enthralled with the story of the accident and would spend the whole interview discussing the subject. While that was interesting, he wished to talk about his life after the accident. His goal for sharing his story was to let people know that triumph is possible after tragedy. The accident was not the end of his life, but a new beginning. Since then, he's hiked Kilimanjaro, written books, and travelled the world speaking to people. Macdonald wanted to ensure that he had an opportunity to speak about those topics in the interviews.

During two media-training sessions, Macdonald learned how to manage an interview and control his message. He learned he didn't have to depend on a journalist's questions and could use techniques to steer the conversation. He also learned to speak succinctly about his accident and to fine-tune his story so that there would be time to speak about the other topics.

Macdonald aced his appearance on *Oprah*, where he told his story and delivered all the key messages he had hoped to share. Afterwards, *Oprah* told him his message would be an inspiration to anyone who heard it.

Media training provides spokespersons with the skills they need to manage media interviews and to tell their story. It does this by helping them gain a better understanding of how the media work and how they, as spokespersons, can get their messages out. Individuals who work with the media and receive media training come from a wide variety of backgrounds, including

- CEOs and heads of corporations
- Politicians
- Curators at a prominent art gallery expecting a backlash because of a controversial exhibit

- Rookie professional athletes
- Kate Middleton before her marriage to Prince William
- Pop stars
- Actors doing a media tour to promote a new movie

Media training helps spokespersons develop content or define what they are going to say. As we saw in the opening vignette, media training helped Warren Macdonald manage the way he would tell his story and focus on what he wanted to share with target audiences: his life after the accident. Media training also assists spokespersons with delivery, or learning how to articulate their key messages. Macdonald learned valuable tricks and tools during the training session to do just that.

Conducting media-training sessions is one of the responsibilities of the PR practitioner, and we need to know how to provide this counsel to our spokespersons. When we pitch a story to the media, they likely will ask for an interview. Or sometimes the media will phone the PR practitioner, hoping someone in the organization can provide comments on a certain topic. We need to have spokespersons ready and trained for when this happens.

In this chapter, we will look at three different aspects of media training. The first is content, or what to say during interviews. The second aspect we will study is delivery, or how to say it. And the third aspect we will examine is how a PR practitioner conducts a media-training session and prepares the spokesperson for media interviews. It is the PR practitioner's job to ensure that spokespersons are successful when working with journalists. But we will start by looking at the fundamentals and introductory concepts of media training.

Media-Training Fundamentals ❶

In Chapter 6, we saw how the preparation of a spokesperson to conduct interviews is a standard element of a media relations campaign. **Media training** is the process by which a spokesperson is taught how to work with journalists and how to manage media interviews. It is said that media training began in the 1970s after the CEO of a large corporation turned to his advertising agency for help when he was asked to give an important television interview. The ad agency reviewed both good and bad interviews and then set up a mock interview and training session. The CEO aced his interview, and media training gained momentum.[1] The benefits of media training are numerous. Media training instructs spokespersons on what to say and teaches them how to say it. It permits spokespersons to learn how to manage media interviews and how to get their key messages across. It also empowers them to become more comfortable and confident in dealing with the media. By learning these skills, Warren Macdonald was able to conduct successful interviews with Oprah and Larry King. Before media training, the interviews would focus on the accident and Macdonald dutifully answered all the interviewer's questions until the time ran out, but he often felt

Media training is important for everyone from celebrities like Kristin Davis to politicians, police chiefs, business owners, or anyone who gives media interviews.

Source: KBA/ZOJ WENN Photos/Newscom

that these were missed opportunities. After media training, he was able to maintain control over the topics that were covered, which allowed him to focus on the messages that he knew would help others going through difficult times in their own lives. As media trainer Virgil Scudder states, "Winners come in with a story to tell and know how to tell it . . . . Answering questions is like paying a toll on the toll road. You have to do it, but you're there to take a trip."[2] Because of media training, Macdonald was able to bring his audience on the trip he wanted to take.

Media training is done for good-news stories, such as Macdonald's interviews, as well as in times of issues and crisis. As part of the media-training session, the practitioner pretends to be a journalist and conducts mock interviews, grilling the spokesperson with difficult questions to help him or her practise the answers. These interviews are caught on video and replayed and critiqued. We will examine this in more detail later in the chapter.

The Halifax Regional Police holds a media-training session for approximately 15 officers annually. The officers are put through various role-play exercises, including one-on-one interviews with journalists, media scrums, and news conferences. They also tour the newsrooms of a newspaper, radio station, and TV station. Theresa Rath, public relations manager, explains,

> This is a four-day course where they learn about why we invest so much time and effort in media relations, and how we do it. It provides insight into the world of the journalist and what is expected of them, and demonstrates why we must have a strong relationship with local media. After all, if we don't tell our story, someone else will tell it for us but they will not have the police perspective and may not necessarily have the facts straight.[3]

THE IMPORTANCE OF MEDIA TRAINING

No one wants to be caught unprepared by the media. A little training goes a long way in helping a person feel confident in front of journalists. Media interviews can occur without warning, as in the case of reactive media relations or during times of crisis. For example, a reporter may call you out of the blue and start asking questions about an issue that was

Media training involves conducting mock interviews in front of a camera and then reviewing the footage.

Source: IvicaNS/Shutterstock

not even on your radar. Even in proactive, planned campaigns, a spokesperson cannot be asked to conduct interviews and represent his or her organization without **counselling**, or guidance and advice, and rehearsal. It would be a gross mistake to send your spokesperson out in front of the media without preparation. As one media trainer puts it, "It may seem as if speaking the truth should be enough to build credibility and trust, but that's rarely the case. Exposing oneself to media scrutiny requires more than simple candor. It requires knowledge, training, and a keen understanding of how reporters write the news."[4] Think of it from this perspective. Reporters devote a lot of time to conducting research and carefully preparing questions before going into an interview. Why wouldn't the interviewee or spokesperson do the same?

Spokespersons are not born, they are made. Conducting an interview is not a natural way to speak. It is a skill that is developed. Some individuals are naturally better at it than others, but everyone can learn how to talk to journalists. With preparation, a media interview need not be stressful or scary. Instead, each meeting with the media can be a positive experience that provides an opportunity to get your messages across and tell your story.

If you watch the television news or listen to a radio news program and find that the interviewees speak really well, you can be sure that they have been media trained. The more practice people have, the better at it they become. Diligent organizations do not only train their spokespersons once, when they appoint new people to the role, but regularly conduct **refresher sessions**, or media training designed to maintain trained spokespersons' skills. Experienced spokespersons get regular media training to keep their skills in top-notch shape and to go over new key messages. Figure 8.1 illustrates the media-training cycle in which a spokesperson is prepared for an interview and gets practice either through role-plays or real-life interviews. The interview is then reviewed and critiqued to see what could be improved upon, and then the cycle starts again. Continuous improvement is the objective of the media-training cycle.

Figure 8.1   The Media-Training Cycle

In addition to preparing spokespersons for media interviews, media training teaches them to be better overall communicators. With media training and practice, spokespersons learn how to customize their messaging for target audiences, including consumers, stakeholders, and employees. They also learn about **streamlining messages**—the process of simplifying messages and removing superfluous words—and learn how to apply them throughout various communication tactics.

As we have discussed, PR practitioners work behind the scenes to organize media relations campaigns, but in some organizations, they also play the role of the spokesperson. In this case, the PR practitioners themselves will receive the media training. But most often the spokesperson will be a CEO or senior leader within an organization. Some organizations have different spokespersons trained to handle different types of interviews. For example, the CEO of a large restaurant chain might handle interviews by business journalists that focus on the finances and expansion plans for the organization, while the head chef focuses on menu-related interviews by food and beverage editors.

Fear of Speaking with Media

It is not uncommon for individuals to be nervous about speaking to journalists. This is especially true if they have had a negative experience in dealing with the press or gave an interview that went badly. Some people worry that they will make a mistake or that what they say will be taken out of context. They regard the media as manipulative and untrustworthy. They also worry that journalists might be aggressive and ask difficult questions that they cannot answer. They may fear that they will embarrass their organizations and, even worse, lose their jobs if the story is unfavourable.

This reluctance to work with the media is common and includes spokespersons from different backgrounds, from business executives to government leaders. Media training addresses all these fears and helps spokespersons feel more comfortable about the uncertainties of media interviews. It helps them build their confidence, so they know that no matter what happens, they will be able to remain calm and collected and provide a clear, succinct sound bite. Media training also assists in calming anxiety by providing a safe space to practise and learn from mistakes before conducting a genuine interview.

Overconfidence in Interviews

Not everyone believes in the value of media training. PR practitioners occasionally encounter resistance by spokespersons who believe that their skills are adequate without training or that working with the media is easy. These individuals can be challenging to media train because they don't see the value in improving their interview skills and prefer to "wing" interviews.

When working with this kind of trainee, the media trainer needs to use examples of interviews that have not gone well to try to convince the client that practice is important. Some media trainers will surprise the client with a mock phone interview after a media-training session and then write a fake news story based on the answers to show how the client might be portrayed in print. Unfortunately, however, it is often not until the overconfident client experiences a poor interview first-hand that he or she truly appreciates the value of media training.

JOURNALISTS' OPINION OF MEDIA TRAINING

Sometimes journalists and the public view media training with suspicion. They assume that trained spokespersons will give a less honest interview or apply techniques to avoid giving answers to questions they do not like. However, media training is not conducted to manipulate journalists in any way. Instead, its purpose is to enable spokespersons to tell their story in a media-friendly way. Just as written information is organized in ways to make it easy for journalists to work with, media training does the same for the spoken word. As we learned in Chapter 6, journalists decide what information will be included in their stories and how organizations will be positioned. Media training increases the chances that PR professionals will get their key messages out. Spokespersons become less dependent on journalists' questions and are able to make sure they are delivering their messaging. The case of Warren Macdonald perfectly illustrates this. His goal was to learn ways to get important information out to his target audiences. Media training helped him do that.

So why do journalists have mixed feelings about media training? On the one hand, spokespersons who are trained know exactly how to assist journalists by providing the content they need for their stories. They also provide newsworthy information during interviews and great sound bites. They are professional and reliable sources of information. On the other hand, some journalists believe that spokespersons deliver rehearsed information and do not really answer their questions. They may also believe that the spokesperson is controlled by a PR practitioner who will swoop in and stop interviews that are not going well. They are weary of spokespersons who appear to be too smooth or polished.[5] This sentiment is evident in Trudy Lieberman's article for the *Columbia Journalism Review*, "Answer the &$%#* Question." In it she notes, "Media training teaches people all the fancy steps they need to answer the questions they want to answer, not those of an inquisitive reporter. The result: In too many cases interviews become excuses to practice public relations, and instead of shedding light, they cloud public discourse."[6] Unfortunately, this opinion is held by many journalists. However, proper media training should be about helping spokespersons deliver their story or key messages in an authentic, truthful, and professional way, not about "spinning" or "dodging questions."

Because of journalists' love-hate relationship with it, media training is sometimes treated like an open secret with journalists. They know about it but do not want it brought to their attention. For this reason, it is not advisable to hover over a spokesperson during an interview. It is a better strategy to be discreet in most situations and trust that the media training has armed your spokesperson appropriately. It never looks good when a PR practitioner intervenes during an interview, and this should be done only in extreme circumstances, such as when your spokesperson is being harassed.

As part of a story on whether video programming for babies was detrimental to their development, a CBC television journalist interviewed a spokesperson with Baby Einstein, a maker of educational videos for babies. During the interview, the spokesperson was asked challenging questions and fumbled, seeming unprepared for this type of questioning. Suddenly, the PR practitioner intervened, putting an end to the interview. This was all caught on camera and broadcast during the evening news segment. The impression left with the audience was that the organization had something to hide, when in fact the PR practitioner was simply being overprotective.

Now that we have examined the fundamentals and the importance of media training, we will look at interview content, or what to say during interviews.

Content of Interviews: What to Say ❷

The first principle of media training—similar to that of public relations in general—is to have clarity around what you want to say. It is important to know what messages you want to convey to your target audiences. The interview is conducted with a journalist, but the messages are intended for the people who will read the story, see it on television, or listen to it on the radio. The media are a conduit to our target audiences. In the opening vignette, Warren Macdonald went on the media tour to get the word out about the television series but also about himself as a speaker. He worked with the media to communicate to his target audiences. He wanted to send a message that it was possible to triumph over very difficult circumstances. The media training helped him decide exactly what he was going to say to make his message appealing to both journalists and their audiences at home.

Key messages such as Warren Macdonald's are developed or fine-tuned during media-training sessions. All the information shared during interviews must be based on news values to make it of interest to journalists. If the information is not newsworthy, it will most likely be edited out. You need to create interesting angles and ask yourself why the target audiences should care about your topic. The best sound bites are short, to the point, and interesting. (See Chapters 5 and 6 for more information on news values.)

Spokespersons rehearse their key messages and tweak them during the sessions until they are completely comfortable with them. They also learn and rehearse the answers to the difficult questions that may be asked of them. It is important that they leave the media-training session feeling confident in the messaging they want to deliver and their ability to convey it.

Rolling Stone magazine was criticized by several other media for its treatment of Justin Bieber during an interview. The young pop star was asked questions on abortion, a difficult subject that could stump even older, more experienced spokespersons. Some journalists claimed that he was too young to be asked such questions. Another journalist asserted that Justin Bieber was fair game in light of all the media training he had received.[8]

THE SPOKESPERSON AS EXPERT

Spokespersons are considered experts in their field or topic. That is why journalists are interested in interviewing them. It is unlikely that the journalist will know more about a particular topic than the interviewee does. That said, spokespersons must still do their homework and prepare talking points on the subject matter. They must become familiar with every aspect of the industry and topic. That means doing research when necessary.

Of course, spokespersons are not expected to know everything or have answers for every question that a journalist might ask. When they do not know an answer, they can simply say so and tell the journalist that they will get back to them. There is nothing wrong with spokespersons admitting they do not know an answer to a question. The important thing is that they never, under any circumstances, make up or exaggerate information. Sometimes our instinct to fill a silence or to please an interviewer will cause us to give an answer to a question even if we are not confident about the information. We need to resist this urge at all costs. Telling the truth and providing reliable information to the public is the cornerstone of being a good spokesperson. The guiding principles of all interactions with journalists are honesty and integrity. We cannot misrepresent information or outright lie. Nothing will ruin your reputation with journalists and the public faster than being caught providing untrue information. In the digital world, stories do not disappear and lies will follow you forever, tarnishing your personal reputation as well as your organization's.

PRACTITIONER INTERVIEW

Shawn Hall, Public Relations, Telus

Shawn Hall works in public relations at Telus. He also acts as one of the corporation's spokespersons and has received media training. It is not uncommon for him to conduct dozens of interviews on many different topics each week.

Question: What are some of the challenges of being the spokesperson?

Answer: It's a high-pressure role, no matter how long you've been in it. While a spokesperson often speaks to the positive stuff to some extent, you'll often find yourself setting up someone else for the positive interviews but handling the crisis or long-term issue yourself—that's what they hired you for.

The challenge is often in research—how do you get the information from your organization that you need to effectively craft an answer in time to meet the deadline? Some departments—legal or security in particular—may not want to share information with you, as they are afraid you'll share sensitive information with media. It's critically important that you have the same focus on internal relationships that you do with media if you're going to be able to gather the information you need to meet deadlines, and meet them with something meaningful to say. Focus on getting all the key details together and some examples, quotable quotes, and facts to back

them up. If you can't get the information you need before the interview starts, it'll be a tough one, and you won't come off as knowledgeable.

Question: Are you ever nervous before an interview and how do you deal with that?

Answer: Sure. I deal with it by reminding myself, it's not personal, and taking the time I need to relax and feed my soul. Whether it's spending time on the beach or in the woods, with your kids or out with friends, do what you need to maintain balance and keep your focus on the stuff that matters. Don't let it keep you up at night, or you're no good to anyone the next day.

What really makes me nervous is going into an interview feeling unprepared. Take the time you need to prepare properly—for me, that means making sure I've spoken to the right people inside our organization and really understand the subject matter, that I have a deep understanding as a storyteller rather than just enough to craft three basic messages. We often stop at three generic messages and figure we're ready—go deeper, and you'll come off as credible rather than a stuffed shirt, and media will appreciate your expertise. Nothing makes for a worse interview than not knowing what you're talking about. If that means going out for ride-alongs

(Continued)

with frontline staff every week for your first six months, then do it.

Question: How do you prepare for an interview?

Answer: Research is the big thing. As I wrote above, don't stop at the first three messages that come to mind or you'll end up with hollow messages full of jargon and platitudes without any substance. Think it through, ask a lot of questions, gather stats.

Media want emotion, they want visuals. Think about what you can give them that's emotional as well as in the best interest of your organization. What can you give them that's more visually interesting than filming a talking head?

Question: Do you custom-tailor your answers depending on the media format?

Answer: Yes. Radio stations like short clips, and often run three or four versions of a story on a rotation; I try to give radio stations 15- or 20-second clips, three or four different ways, so they can use different quotes in variations. TV is going to run just one story with a slightly longer clip. It's a visual medium, so always think about what you can offer them that visually tells your story. With print, you're a storyteller. They want the whole story, and they want it to resonate emotionally with their readers, so find the emotional appeal, and tell a story that keeps the reporter engaged.

CONTROL OVER CONTENT

Journalists come into an interview with a completely different objective than the spokesperson. Reporters desire to create an objective story and are not concerned with how your organization is positioned. The spokesperson's goal for the interview is to put the organization in the best light possible and to meet their public relations objectives. Despite these seemingly conflicting purposes, both parties can leave an interview getting exactly what they need. That is what good media training can deliver. In the case of Warren Macdonald, journalists were typically interested in asking questions about the accident and focusing on the gory details of it. Macdonald's goal was to talk about how he triumphed following the accident. With media training, he was able to both answer the journalists' questions and deliver his key messages of rebuilding a good life following a tragedy. His ability to do that earned him high praise from Oprah.

Journalists come to the interview with a set of questions and strategies to get the spokesperson to deliver what they need from the exchange, but spokespersons are not at the mercy of journalists. Far from it. Journalists may control the questions, but spokespersons control the answers. Therein lies their power. Ultimately, they direct how the interview will go by choosing their answers, no matter what the journalists ask or how they ask it. "Remember it's not the reporter's job to make you look good; that's your job."[9]

Spokespersons decide what they will share with the media and, ultimately, with the public. Some topics are to be kept confidential or private. It may not be advisable, for

"But how could me speaking
at the Secret New Products Seminar
break our Confidentiality Agreement?"

Source: Cartoonresource/Shutterstock

instance, to share information such as annual sales figures in a competitive marketplace. Topics that will be off-limits during interviews are covered in the media-training sessions, and spokespersons are shown how to handle questions they do not want to answer. Journalists know that there are topics that spokespersons do not wish to discuss, but that does not mean they will not try to get them to comment on them anyway. A senior journalist reports being surprised at the information people share with him: "I ask questions where I know I am pushing my luck. And I'm always amazed that people answer them. I am not God. People do not have to tell me anything they don't want to, but often they do."[10] While saying "No comment" can make it look as though you have something to hide, there are ways to redirect the conversation to information you are able to share. As Richard Weiner, a New York public relations practitioner, attests, "There are twenty-seven different ways to avoid the question and twenty-seven ways to say no comment."[11] We will examine these in the following section on delivery.

KEEPING KEY MESSAGES UP TO DATE

All the interview content and key messages should be regularly reviewed and kept up to date. While there are many standard key messages that will be used for numerous interviews and communications pieces, new key messages are also developed for specific events or groundbreaking news. For example, a bank CEO who appeared on a live telethon to give a donation was provided with key messages developed specifically for the event.

Spokespersons are urged to review the standard or newly prepared key messages before each interview. They are taught to never to do interviews on the fly and to always take a few moments to review messaging and to compose themselves before speaking to journalists. For example, if a journalist calls them, they do not need to respond on the initial call. Instead, they should ask for the journalist's contact information and **deadline** for story submission and tell the journalist that they will get back to him or her shortly. This will give them time to review their key messages in preparation for the interview. PR practitioners often provide counselling and rehearsal opportunities right before interviews either in person or via telephone.

Jami Symons is an award-winning stylist and one of the spokespersons for AG Hair Cosmetics, a maker of hair-care products. He conducts print and television interviews regularly and has received numerous media-training sessions where his key messages are updated to include new product launches, fashion and lifestyle trends, and any issues the organization faces. The media-training sessions have also taught him how to be comfortable in front of the camera and given him numerous camera-ready skills, such as answering questions while styling someone's hair on television talk shows. We will look at the development of some of the skills in the next section on interview delivery.

Thinking Like a PR Practitioner

1. How much control do spokespersons have over the answers they give in an interview?
2. Read your local newspaper and find a story where a spokesperson is quoted. Determine the key messages that the spokesperson got across—if any.

Interview Delivery ❸

Once the content of interviews is decided, it is time to think about delivery, or how to say it. This step also involves learning how the media work, building good relationships with them, and avoiding pitfalls such as missing deadlines. (See Chapter 6 for more information on how the media work.)

As we examined in the opening vignette, Warren Macdonald knew what he wanted to say. He simply needed assistance with how to say it. In media training, he learned how to return to his key messages of courage and hope, while still answering the questions about the accident and ordeal. Warren learned to manage the interview. As one media trainer says, "The reporter has 100 per cent control over the questions and the topics, but we interviewees have 100 per cent control over our answers."[12]

This section goes over techniques that are taught to spokespersons about how to deliver their key messages.

QUOTES AND SOUND BITES

During interviews, spokespersons must speak and deliver key messages in quotes. A **quote** is a brief statement or extract from an interview that is used in a story because it is newsworthy. Being quotable means delivering your answers in a short, interesting, media-friendly way. Not everything a spokesperson says will make it into the story. Only what the journalist considers the most interesting and newsworthy parts of the interview will be included. Sometimes nothing a spokesperson says will make it into the story, depending on how many other people the journalist interviewed and the quotes they were able to provide.

A **sound bite** is a quote delivered specifically for radio or television. Some sound bites are so catchy that they are often repeated and have become sayings that the public remembers. An historical example of this is Pierre Trudeau's answer "Just watch me," after he was asked by a CBC reporter about his plans to revoke civil liberties in 1970, when government officials were kidnapped by the Front de Libération du Québec (FLQ) in Quebec.[13] This phrase remains part of the public's memory of Trudeau.

An effective sound bite is neither too long nor too short. Typically, sound bites for radio and television are 15 to 30 seconds long. Important points should be made at the beginning of the sound bite to make sure they are not edited out. Any supporting information is provided after the main point is made.

Spokespersons have to take a pause between sentences to enable television and radio editors to use the quote. If sentences are too close together and cannot be edited into shorter sound bites, the media might not be able to use them. It is a great shame

Pierre Trudeau provided the media with many powerful sound bites during his time in office, including the infamous "Just watch me."
Source: Boris Spremo/Newscom

when an interview cannot be used because the sentences are too long and close together.

While practice makes perfect when it comes to sound bites, they must sound spontaneous and not too rehearsed. Instead of memorizing stock answers, spokespersons should remember the ideas that they want to convey. It is also best to use simple language that can be understood by the public. Journalists may not use a quote because it is incomprehensible and filled with **jargon**—language that is used within a certain industry that might not be understood by others outside the profession. Every industry has its jargon and professional expressions, but unless a spokesperson is speaking with a trade publication, it is best to leave it out.

Bridges

Bridges are a common technique at a spokesperson's disposal to manage a media interview. They are a way to bring a wandering interview or a negative question back to the subject area the spokesperson wants to discuss. After the question is asked, the spokesperson provides a brief answer and then uses a bridge statement, such as, "it's also important to mention," which allows the spokesperson to proceed to his or her key message. This is a technique that requires a lot of practice to master and to use confidently. Warren Macdonald successfully learned to use bridges during media training. They enabled him to get back to his post-accident story when journalists wanted to focus solely on the accident. However, when inexpertly used, a bridge can give the impression that you are just avoiding the subject. Some examples of bridge phrases include

- A question I am often asked …
- Let's talk about the bigger picture …
- What is important to remember is …
- There is more to the story, specifically …
- Have you considered …
- An interesting example of this is …

Hooking

A hook is an interview technique designed to get a journalist to ask you a question that will allow you to discuss a key message. In **hooking**, you answer a question with an interesting ending that piques the journalist's interest so that he or she asks you a follow-up question about it. For example, a jewellery company might end a question with a comment about the new trend of fair-trade diamonds. The journalist would then ask the spokesperson to elaborate on this new trend. This would allow the spokesperson the opportunity to discuss the company's commitment to fair-trade diamonds. An effective hook will create a situation in which the interview would seem incomplete if the journalist did not ask a follow-up question to allow you to explain something you mentioned in the previous answer.

Flagging

Flagging is a media technique that needs to be used sparingly or it loses its impact. It is also a technique spokespersons often feel the most comfortable using because it feels natural. In **flagging**, the spokesperson draws attention to a salient point by using words that notify the journalist or the audience that what the spokesperson is saying is important and they should pay attention. Examples of flagging terms are "The most important thing to remember," "It is critical that you know," "I can't stress enough," or "More importantly." For example, a spokesperson with a health authority who has a key message around the importance of handwashing during cold and flu season might end an interview with this flag: "While we've discussed many things today, the most important point to remember is that washing your hands regularly throughout the day will help prevent the spread of colds."

Going Global

Going global is an interview technique that is particularly useful in a negative interview. This is when spokespersons deflect ownership of a particular issue by stressing that the problem is larger than their company. When using this technique, they would start an answer by saying how the issue affects others in addition to their organization and finish by saying how their company is addressing it. For example, a mining company spokesperson who is asked about the environmental impacts of his or her business might answer, "All resource-based companies struggle with the issue of … but here's what we're doing to address it." This technique reminds the audience that the negative aspect of the story cannot be owned only by the organization and that it affects all organizations in the industry.

Going global could also work for an individual. For example, a musician who is asked about his heavy partying might answer, "A musician's lifestyle encompasses a lot of late nights and a lot of temptations to party. It's something that I believe most musicians struggle with. However, based on recent events, I now realize that I need to …"

Body Language

Spokespersons are taught about body language and all the messages that we convey through nonverbal communication. **Body language** includes everything from the way spokespersons stand, to what they do with their hands, their facial expressions, and where they look. For instance, crossing your arms is considered aggressive, whereas leaning toward the interviewer indicates engagement.

NHL commissioner Gary Bettman makes his opinion clear through his body language and facial expression at a news conference.
Source: WARREN TODA/Newscom

Distracting mannerisms or nervous habits are also brought to the attention of the spokespersons, such as swaying while they talk or excessive gesturing. You want your spokesperson to look calm, at ease, trustworthy, and confident. These are all impressions that spokespersons can make with the right body language. For instance, smiling during good-news stories will go a long way toward sending a positive message but could look smug during a crisis.

Being Nervous

The media-training sessions also help spokespersons learn how to manage feelings of nervousness before an interview. Some spokespersons may be quite anxious prior to meeting with journalists, and the last thing you want is your spokesperson to appear like a nervous wreck. It is quite normal to have an adrenaline rush before such a performance, but there are techniques that can help you use this to your advantage and stay focused and present. Spokespersons are taught to take a few moments before each interview to centre and calm themselves and to practise breathing techniques. Spokespersons are also advised to stay away from caffeine before an interview as it can amplify their anxiety.

The Myth of Off the Record

Spokespersons learn to be on guard while they are in the presence of the media. As one practitioner puts it, "Reporters are not your friends." Remember, it is the journalist's job to uncover information and share it with the public. The most important rule is not to share anything you do not want to see in the media. Do not say something to a journalist and then claim that it is off the record. There are never any guarantees that the information will not be used. Keep what is confidential confidential. Wait until you are safely away from reporters before saying anything you would not want the public to hear or know, no matter how discreet you think you are being. In the presence of journalists, always remain professional.

Many a spokesperson has been publicly embarrassed by making an aside that was overheard and made public. Some have lost their jobs over it. A case in point is the spokesperson for then prime minister Jean Chrétien who made an offhand and obviously off the record remark, calling U.S. president George W. Bush a moron in front of two journalists at an international meeting. The comment made headlines throughout the world, and she lost her job.[14] Spokespersons also need to be wary of their microphones still being on after an interview and having their conversation or offhand remarks recorded.

TIPS FOR DIFFERENT TYPES OF MEDIA

While most of the interview techniques discussed are applicable to any type of interview, different mediums call for different interview styles. This is because each type of communications vehicle has its own way of delivering the information. For example, television is a very visual medium, whereas radio is oratory focused. For a TV interview, PR practitioners will want to consider the visual elements, whereas for radio they will want to give some thought to the soundscape in the background of the audio recording. For a radio interview about the importance of public transit, it may be effective to have the interview take place in front of a bus stop, where the listener can hear buses coming and going, as long as the soundscape is not too loud.

Television

The first tip for television interviews is to never look at the camera. Spokespersons should look at the person interviewing them and ignore the camera entirely. The only time that spokespersons would look straight at the camera is when they are in one location and are being interviewed live from another. You often see this type of interview on television news.

Television is a visual medium, so your appearance is important. That includes how you look, what you wear, and where you stand. Eyes win over ears every time in getting your message across on television. In fact, research conducted by Albert Mehrabian at the University of California, Los Angeles, shows that audiences base only 7 per cent of their impression on the words that are spoken. The majority of the impression, 93 per cent, is based on tone of voice and body language.[15]

Body language speaks loudly on television. Viewers will be asking themselves if they can trust the spokesperson. This is why the interviewee must appear calm, collected, and confident. After all, the spokesperson is the expert on the topic. If the interview is a good-news story, smiling lets viewers know that everything is positive.

Physical appearance counts for a lot as well. Spokespersons need to look the part. Their clothes and props need to reflect their role and industry. For example, a doctor might want to wear a lab coat and a stethoscope. Simple clothing in medium tones like blue, without patterns such as polka dots, looks the best on television. The clothing must also be comfortable so that the spokesperson does not fidget, adjusting straps or pulling down skirts.

A female spokesperson might consider wearing more makeup than usual, as it must be heavy to show up on television. You do not want your spokesperson to look pale. Some television programs such as talk shows will have a makeup artist on hand to do the makeup prior to the interview.

Again, because television is a visual medium, where your spokesperson stands, or what is known as the *visual backdrop*, is also important. The spokesperson should be positioned somewhere interesting that tells the story or raises awareness of the organization. Television producers want to see more than just **talking heads**—people positioned on camera so that all the audience can see is their head and upper body. As the PR practitioner, you might want to suggest that the interview take place in front of company signage, a logo, or an identifiable product. This will help leverage the branding opportunity, if the story has a positive angle.

If asked a negative question in a TV interview, the spokesperson should never repeat it. This is because the journalist's questions will often be edited out of the interview when it is aired on television. If the spokesperson does not repeat the negative question and simply bridges into his or her messaging, most likely the viewers will never know the question was asked.

Radio

Radio is fast-paced, and there is little time to get comfortable or establish a rapport with the interviewer. The message is limited to what can be heard, and short, simple sentences work best. Hand gestures or facial expressions cannot be seen to help convey the message, and so interviewees must be clear and expressive with their words and tone of voice.

Some interviews are conducted by telephone, and they can either be live or prerecorded. It helps to stand up so that the voice sounds stronger and smile for good-news stories. People may not be able to see the smile, but they will hear it in a spokesperson's voice.

When interviewing for radio, short, simple sentences combined with an expressive tone of voice works best.
Source: © Blend Images/Alamy

Other interviews are conducted in the studio and include open-line programs where listeners call in. This can present challenges, as you cannot predict what people will say and some callers might have negative comments. The best way to handle negative calls is to remain professional and stick to key messages. This is definitely not the time to become defensive and get into an argument with a caller.

Print

Print interviews tend to be longer and more in-depth than television or radio interviews. Newspaper journalists attempt to tell both sides of a story and have more space for details and quotes. They may interview the competition or get opinions that conflict with yours. A further challenge is that, in print, the audience does not hear the words of your spokesperson directly, so there is an opportunity for the spokesperson to be misquoted or for quotes to be taken out of context. Their words are either quoted or interpreted and then paraphrased by the journalist.[16]

A photographer may be sent to take photos for the story. PR practitioners must come up with interesting photo ideas that will put their spokespersons in the best light and help meet their objectives. If a photo runs, it means more space in the newspaper for your organization.

Digital

All rules for the other formats apply to digital media. One word of caution: do not treat digital journalists more casually than other types of media. If anything, traditional media often get story ideas from their digital counterparts, who are increasingly first to report the story. As Paul Nixey of the PR agency Nixey Communications says, "A blogger should be treated just as well as the editor of *The Globe and Mail*."[17]

TRICKS JOURNALISTS USE TO GET PEOPLE TO TALK

A good journalist has learned techniques to get people to talk and to open up. Journalists conduct interviews with all kinds of people, some of whom may be very nervous or completely unquotable, answering questions with only a yes or a no. Journalists use different tricks to make their interviewees comfortable or to get them to open up to them. Sometimes journalists act in a friendly way, thinking that interviewees will relax and trust them. Or they can be aggressive and use their authority to get the information they want. The point is that no matter how the journalist acts, the spokesperson must remain the same: professional, exuding calm and confidence, and answering questions by incorporating key messages. Here are a few journalistic techniques to be aware of.

The Silent Treatment

Some journalists ask a question and after the spokespersons have answered it, stare at them and remain silent. They use this tactic to encourage people to talk more. Many of us are uncomfortable with silence and rush to fill it. The problem is that the more you talk, the greater the chances that you will sway away from your key messages and perhaps divulge something you should not.

How to deal with it: It is not the spokesperson's job to keep the interview going—it is the journalist's. Answer the question and then remain silent yourself. Wait for the journalist to ask the next question. The less you talk, the lower the chances that you will say something risky or off-message.

Leading Questions

Some journalists ask questions that they hope will make you answer in a certain way. The question prompts the answer. For example, a question like, "Does your organization still make defective products?" may prompt an answer such as, "We do not still make defective products." The problem with this answer is that the journalist has encouraged you to speak of defective products, which is not the way you want the organization described, and put you on the defensive.

How to deal with it: Do not let journalists put words in your mouth or lead you in a certain way. Take your time to answer the questions and use your own language. With a question like the one above, try an answer such as, "We have always made top-quality products."

The Columbo Question

The name of this type of questioning comes from the 1970s television series *Columbo*, where a police lieutenant got people talking and relaxed and then slipped in the real question. It takes advantage of the principle that the best information comes at the end of a conversation. The journalist may ask a last question on the way out, or call back a few days later to ask one last question when your guard is down.

A Columbo question is a journalistic technique that is based on the interview style of the police lieutenant from the 1970s TV series *Columbo*.
Source: © Pictorial Press Ltd/Alamy

How to deal with it: Stay on your toes until the interview is 100 per cent over and you are no longer working with the journalist on the story.

The Machine Gunner

In this technique the journalist fires so many questions at once that you do not know which one to handle. The goal here is to confuse you so that you discuss topics that you had not planned to address.

How to deal with it: Pick out the question that you would like to answer, and ignore the rest. Journalists will repeat themselves if they are really interested. Always ask for clarification if you do not understand a question.

Hostile Interviews or Friendly Interviews

Overly hostile or friendly interviews can be used as ruses to elicit answers. The journalist is neither your friend nor your enemy. Do not be fooled by either tactic. Negative stories have come from very friendly journalists, and positive stories have come from cranky ones.

How to deal with it: Treat both types of interviews the same way by remaining calm and professional. There is an old adage that you should never pick a fight with someone who buys ink by the barrel. By staying polite and not taking a hostile interview personally, you increase your chances of garnering positive coverage.

WHAT NOT TO DO IN AN INTERVIEW

While every interview situation is unique, there are answers and tactics that are never good practice and are to be avoided at all times. Here are some of those don'ts:

- Never say, "No comment." "No comment" is a comment. It makes it seem as though the organization is hostile to the media or has something to hide. It is preferable to say something along these lines: "We are investigating the situation to determine the best course of action."

- Never lie, speculate, or even guess. If you do not know an answer, admit it and offer to get the information and get back to the journalist.

- Never use jargon unless you are being interviewed by a trade publication.

- Do not be late or cause a journalist to miss a deadline. Always get back to journalists when you say you will.

- Do not walk out in the middle of an interview.

- Do not put your hand on the camera lens to stop an interview.

- Do not treat journalists as adversaries but as people who have a job to do. As Sally Stewart writes in *Media Training 101*, "What reporters want is usually pretty simple: they want their calls returned, they want a quote for their story, and they want to do their job and go home. Don't make your relationship with reporters complicated."[18]

SPECIAL CIRCUMSTANCES

There are certain circumstances when the normal rules of an interview do not necessarily apply. These include media conferences, media scrums, and negative news stories.

The Media Conference

During a media or press conference, the spokesperson makes a presentation and answers questions from journalists. Media conferences are typically for important announcements when many journalists will want to receive the information at the same time. The media conference provides access to the media and is more efficient than meeting with the media individually.

Media conferences provide spokespersons with an opportunity to conduct interviews with many journalists at once.
Source: George Pimentel/Getty Images

For example, when a British Columbia hospital delivered conjoined twins, several media conferences were hosted at the hospital because of the enormous media interest in the story. Press conferences are especially popular when the spokespersons are athletes or politicians.

The media conference is a special circumstance that demands management of the media. Journalists may all put up their hands at the same time or even speak simultaneously, and the spokesperson must decide which questions to answer first or even which questions to answer at all. Media will be notified of the media conference in advance and it will have a specific start and end time. (See Chapter 6 for more information on media conferences.)

The Media Scrum

The **media scrum** is one of the most intense media situations to find oneself in. It is a spontaneous media conference in which journalists surround a person to ask questions. It generally takes place right after an important meeting, such as a court case or government session. It also happens around celebrities when the journalists are not kept at arm's length.

Media scrums can be friendly or extremely aggressive, depending on the nature of the story. The challenge is to hold your ground as journalists vie for your attention and stick their microphones close to your face while throwing questions at you. The trick here is to remain calm, turn to one journalist at a time, and answer the question that you wish. When you are finished, thank the reporters and gently make your way out. Try not to show hostility, anger, or panic. Generally, the crowd of journalists will part to let you leave, though they may pursue you with additional questions.

When the Story Is Negative

Toronto mayor Rob Ford in a media scrum.
Source: Vince Talotta/ZUMA Press/Newscom

Generally, PR practitioners conduct media interviews even if the topic is negative because it is their opportunity to get their side of the story out. If they do not, no one is going to do it for them. However, in some circumstances it is best to not respond to a journalist's questions. For instance, if the story is extremely negative and you have no offsetting evidence to offer, it may be best not to participate. You would first assess the interview request and then politely decline. PR practitioners very rarely take this position. Written media statements are provided in some cases when it is very important that the message be controlled or if a spokesperson isn't available. For example, a grieving family might issue a media statement after an accident when they want to issue a message to the public but are too distraught to provide interviews. (See Chapter 11 for more information on dealing with challenging media situations.)

How to Conduct Media-Training Sessions ❹

Now that we have examined the two principles of media interview preparation (content and delivery), we will learn how to conduct media-training sessions. PR practitioners are the ones who organize and conduct these sessions for their spokespersons. They tend to be half a day to one day long, though sometimes longer programs are held, as we saw in the example of the Halifax Regional Police.

Each media-training session is custom-tailored to the spokesperson's experience level and to the current specific circumstances between the organization and the media. For example, the media-training sessions conducted during an issue or crisis are different than those in preparation for the launch of a new product. The training can be organized one-on-one for an individual spokesperson or for several individuals at the same time. For example, the Liberal Party organizes media training for all rookie MPs to prepare them to work with journalists in Ottawa. One MP puts it this way: "We're doing our preparation for the House so that the media don't misquote us."[19]

The sessions are a combination of theory, so that spokespersons can learn how the media work, and hands-on practice of techniques. The objective of the media-training session is to enable the trainees to conduct media interviews with skill and confidence. Media training also enables spokespersons to feel empowered and not at mercy of journalists' agendas.

Spokespersons are taught how to manage interviews, keep control, and stay calm in even the toughest circumstances. They learn about scrums, media conferences, and the different types of media. Media training also covers how to build media relationships. Participants receive handouts and written materials with useful information so that they can review concepts. They are also provided with a copy of their mock interviews, which we will examine in the next section.

The sessions are fast-paced and are not meant to be easy. They are extremely challenging and attendees will most likely be exhausted at the end of the day. After all, this is the opportunity to prepare the spokesperson as thoroughly as possible.

BUILDING SPOKESPERSON CONFIDENCE

As difficult as the media-training sessions can be—especially for rookies—they are also the forum where spokespersons are nurtured and their confidence is built up. Remember that it is common for spokespersons to be nervous, if not downright fearful, about working with journalists. Spokespersons' morale can be quite low, especially after they have begun to learn some concepts but have not yet mastered them. They may feel that they will not be able to improve. The PR practitioner plays the role of teacher, cheerleader, and motivator in encouraging spokespersons to believe that they can do it. Thus, PR practitioners must walk a fine line, being tough and preparing their spokespersons well, and crushing their confidence.

By the end of the session, the spokesperson needs to have developed the skills necessary to conduct an interview, as well as the confidence to believe they can do it well. Sometimes, if the spokesperson is not improving as quickly as the media trainer would like, the trainer may recommend that the spokesperson receive more training or suggest to the company that a different spokesperson should be identified until the individual has mastered the techniques. It is best to never put anyone in an interview situation until he or she is confident and ready.

ADVICE TO NEW PRACTITIONERS
What You Need for a Media-Training Session

- A safe space such as a boardroom where confidential matters can be discussed freely
- A whiteboard or flip chart on which to write key messages as they are tweaked
- An agenda
- Handouts with tips and tricks
- A camera with a tripod for steadiness
- A microphone
- A television or computer screen on which to watch the interviews
- Additional lighting if required

Remember to make sure all the equipment is tested and works prior to the session.

Mock Interviews ⑤

During media-training sessions, mock interviews are conducted and videotaped with someone playing the role of the journalist and asking the spokesperson questions. This is often the PR practitioner, but at times a trained journalist is brought in to do the interviewing, such as when the PR practitioner prefers to not be the one to ask difficult questions of the spokesperson, who might be a superior in the organization or a client.

During the simulated interviews, the spokespersons must be challenged and questioned thoroughly. If there are any embarrassing topics, they must be addressed, and better by you than by a real journalist. You do not want your spokespersons to be caught off guard by a question and lose their poise live on camera.

The interviews are reviewed immediately and critiqued, enabling spokespersons to view themselves on camera and learn from their mistakes. Although many find it uncomfortable, this review acts as a powerful learning tool. The PR practitioner and spokesperson watch the interviews together and discuss what the spokesperson did wrong but also, more importantly, what he or she did right. As we have mentioned, although the questions can be tough, it is important to remember that the sessions should also aim to build the confidence of the spokesperson. Critiques must be handled carefully and diplomatically, and include reinforcing positive feedback.

The PR practitioner must provide information that will enable spokespersons to improve their performance in the next round of interviews. PR professionals will also want to help boost spokespersons' confidence if the mock interview went poorly, and calm their fears if they are anxious.

The critiques of the interviews include every aspect of message content and delivery that we have examined in this chapter, including the following steps:

- The key messages are analyzed and tweaked.

- Answers to difficult questions are reviewed.

- The interviewees are taught how to speak in sound bites and quotes, and to keep answers short and to the point. Interviewees are assessed for whether they speak too quickly or too slowly or if they pause between sentences.

- The interviewees practise the use of bridges to come back to their key messages.
- Body language and posture are reviewed, as is whether they are fidgeting, smiling, or looking stressed.
- What to wear during interviews is also discussed.

PR practitioners must be able to assess whether spokespersons are ready to meet with journalists and if they have the necessary skills to conduct an interview. These assessments include the following questions:

- Do they appear calm and confident when they answer questions?
- Do they remain professional when asked difficult or aggressive questions?
- Do they have answers to the difficult questions, and can they deliver their key messages?
- Can they speak in sound bites?
- Can they successfully employ bridges and other techniques to manage the interview?
- Are they smiling if it is a good-news story?
- Do they understand how to dress for media interviews?
- Do they understand how to adapt their interview style to the various types of media?
- Do they know how to treat journalists and how to work with them?

If based on your answers to the questions above you do not believe your spokesperson is ready, you may need to recommend more training or try finding a different spokesperson. A poor or unprepared spokesperson can do a lot of damage, so you must feel confident that your spokespersons will represent the organization well before you allow them to meet with the media. That said, in most circumstances, spokespersons can be trained to become effective at working with journalists. Some even become media stars and are often requested for interviews about a particular topic. For example, in an article he wrote for *The Globe and Mail*, Ryan Caligiuri, the founder of Ryan Caligiuri International, tells of a client of his who became a successful media expert by **newsjacking**, or using news headlines to gain publicity for the organization:

> A lawyer client of mine specializing in privacy has been having some newsjacking success. When stories about Google keeping consumer information came out this year, for instance, he reached out to the media to offer his opinion, and has now become recognized as a privacy expert to whom media turned multiple times in 2012 on privacy-related matters. This has done much to raise his profile.[20]

By leveraging a well-prepared, articulate spokesperson whom the media trust for regular commentary, you can receive much positive exposure for your organization.

1. Do you think you are capable of asking your spokesperson challenging questions? Why or why not?

2. Watch the evening news or a news program such as *W5* or *60 Minutes* that contains interviews with spokespersons. Select one and judge how well the spokesperson did overall. Give two reasons for your opinion.

CASE STUDY THE COOKIE INCIDENT: A CAUTIONARY TALE

One of the goals of media training is to improve a spokesperson's media relations skills and allow him or her to be prepared to deal with journalists in all kinds of situations, even ambushes. One of the most interesting cases of a media interview gone wrong is that of Stephen Duckett, the former CEO of Alberta Health Services. Duckett essentially lost his position because of poor media skills and, as strange as it seems, a cookie.

This is what happened. Following an important meeting on an ER crisis the province was experiencing, Duckett was approached by several journalists asking questions. Walking quickly as journalists followed him with their mics and cameras, he repeatedly refused to answer their questions, instead brandishing a cookie and repeating: "I'm eating my cookie."

Undeterred, the journalists kept following, making comments such as, "Was it not ridiculous that he was concerned with his cookie while the people of Alberta were concerned with the state of their health care?" Duckett became increasingly displeased as the journalists pursued him. This mobile media scrum lasted several minutes as he made his way from one building to the next.

Needless to say, the story was aired on television networks and picked up by print, radio, and digital media. Instead of being about the ER crisis, the story became about Duckett and his cookie, and was named the "cookie incident." The story was described in one media outlet as "He refused to talk to reporters about a meeting on the province's ER crisis because he was too busy eating a cookie."[21]

The video of Duckett and his cookie was posted on YouTube and got over 100,000 hits in just a few days. The public was outraged that he refused to speak to the media about this important issue. Duckett lost his job within a week of the story first appearing online.[22]

While it is challenging to find yourself surrounded and followed by journalists, it is possible to manage the situation successfully. In this case, things deteriorated so quickly because Duckett broke all the rules of media training by refusing to speak to the media.

Had he taken a few moments to address journalists politely, no matter how busy he was, the story would have played out much differently.

In most situations where media interviews go terribly wrong, the outcome could have been avoided with adequate preparation and coaching.

Questions

1. Go to YouTube and look at the video of the cookie incident (key words: Duckett cookie). Analyze what happened and how Duckett handled the media inquiries. What steps could he have taken to work with the journalists in this case?

2. Write three key messages that Duckett could have used in this situation.

3. Was Alberta Health Services justified in terminating Duckett for his poor performance with the media? Why or why not?

AUTHOR'S OWN EXPERIENCE

When You Are the Spokesperson

While I stayed in the background the majority of the time, there were some instances when I played the role of spokesperson for clients. Sometimes it was because the spokesperson was unavailable that day and, as the PR practitioner, I was the only other person who was media trained and familiar with the key messages. In other cases, I conducted French media interviews on behalf of my English-speaking clients.

I did print, radio, and television interviews and spoke about topics ranging from home repairs to children's toys. To prepare for each interview, I had one of my colleagues grill me with questions. I was well prepared in terms of content because I had developed it for my clients. I practised my delivery, my sound bites, and my key messages.

I also made sure that I dressed the part when arriving for an interview. I wore a conservative business suit for an interview on a new online bank and a more casual outfit for speaking about teas. I also took to the stage more than once at various trade shows my clients attended.

In addition to being a spokesperson for clients, I have acted as spokesperson for my own public relations agency, conducting media interviews to garner publicity for our firm or to speak about breaking industry news topics, such as how a media strike was affecting the PR industry.

There is an adrenaline high that comes with media interviews that some people love and others hate. Whether you love giving interviews or hate them, the same rules apply to the PR practitioner as they do to the people they train: always remain professional, tell the truth, and do your homework!

Key Terms

body language Nonverbal communication and all the ways people express themselves without using words, including eye contact and facial expressions.

bridge A phrase or words that enable you to smoothly jump from one topic to another. Bridges are used in interviews to go from the subject a journalist introduces in a question to the topic the spokesperson wishes to address.

counselling The expertise and advice PR practitioners provide and the way they guide and direct their organizations and their spokespersons.

deadline The time by which a journalist must have a story submitted.

flagging A media technique by which the spokesperson verbally draws attention to an important key message.

hooking A media technique by which the spokesperson entices the journalist to ask a follow-up question about a topic the spokesperson would like to discuss.

jargon Industry-specific language that is not used by the general population.

media scrum A spontaneous media conference during which journalists surround the spokesperson with their mics and ask questions. It generally takes place following an important meeting.

media tour The media outlets and journalists a spokesperson meets during a campaign. This can involve travelling to different markets.

media training The process in which the spokesperson is taught how to work with journalists and how to manage media interviews.

newsjacking Using news headlines to gain publicity for your organization.

quote A brief statement or extract from an interview that is used in a story because it is newsworthy.

refresher session A media-training session that is conducted with someone who has already been trained. The goal is to remind the spokesperson of the principles of media relations, provide an additional opportunity for practice, and introduce new key messages.

sound bite A quote delivered specifically for radio or television.

streamlining messages The process of honing and simplifying key messages to get rid of superfluous words and ideas.

talking head A person talking on camera with only his or her head and upper body visible. It is one of the most common shots for television news segments.

Weblinks

CBC archival clip of Pierre Trudeau's "just watch me" clip
http://www.youtube.com/watch?NR=1&feature=fvwp&v=DeTsQQ22Uwc

IABC media training guide
iabcstore.com/prmediarelations/mediatraining.htm

Mr. Media Training blog
www.mrmediatraining.com

PR agencies
www.presentwithease.com/mediatraining.html
http://www.elevenpr.com

PR News
http://www.prnewsonline.com/news/6167.html

PRWatch
www.prwatch.org/spin/2008/11/7990/journalists-sale

Warren Macdonald
www.warren-macdonald.com

Endnotes

1. Virgil Scudder, "Don't Wing It: Media Training Is Necessary for Today's Leaders," *Public Relations Tactics*, vol. 19, no. 11 (November 2012), 14.

2. Trudy Lieberman, "Answer the &%$#* Question: Ever Wonder Why They Won't? They've Been Media-Trained. And the Public Loses." *Columbia Journalism Review* (January/February 2004), 5.

3. Theresa Rath, interview with the author.

4. J. Ansell, *When the Headline Is You: An Insider's Guide to Handling the Media*. San Francisco: Jossey Bass, 2010, p. xi.

5. Ibid.

6. Eric Bergman, "The Ethics of Not Answering," *Communication World* (2005, September/ October).

7. M. Blanchfield and J. Bronskill, "Harper's Message Control Is Unprecedented, Critics Say," *The Globe and Mail*, September 20, 2011. Accessed February 19, 2013, http://www .theglobeandmail.com/news/politics/harpers-message-control-is-unprecedented-critics-say/ article1375533/?page=all

8. "Did Rolling Stone Take Advantage of Justin?" *OK USA*, March 7, 2011, 36.

9. T.J. Walker, *Media Training A–Z: A Complete Guide to Controlling Your Image, Message and Sound Bites*. New York: Media Training Worldwide, 2004, p. 5.

10. Alan Daniels, interview with the author.

11. Lieberman, "Answer the &%$#* Question," 4.

12. Walker, *Media Training A–Z*, p. 4.

13. "Trudeau, Just Watch Me," *The Globe and Mail*, October 5, 2010. Accessed February 5, 2013, http://www.theglobeandmail.com/news/national/trudeau-just-watch-me/article4327998/

14. "Canadian Official Called Bush 'a Moron,'" *CBC News*, November 26, 2002. Accessed March 11, 2013, http://www.cbc.ca/news/story/2002/11/21/moron021121.html

15. Albert Mehrabian, *Silent Messages*. Belmont, CA: Wadsworth, 1971.

16. L. Gidluck, *Media Training Guide*. Regina, SK: Benchmark Press, 2006, p. 19.

17. Paul Nixey, interview with the author.

18. S. Stewart, *Media Training 101: A Guide to Meeting the Press*. Hoboken, NJ: John Wiley & Sons, 2004, p. 16.

19. Abas Rana, "Rookie Liberals Signing Up for Media Training Workshops," *The Hill Times*, August 11, 2004. Accessed February 19, 2013, http://www.hilltimes.com/news/2004/11/08/ rookie-liberals-signing-up-for-media-training-workshops/14293

20. Ryan Caligiuri, "Seven Top Marketing Trends for 2013," *The Globe and Mail*, December 14, 2012. Accessed February 19, 2013, http://www.theglobeandmail.com/report-on-business/ small-business/sb-marketing/advertising/seven-top-marketing-trends-for-2013/article6311967/

21. "Alberta Health Board Replaces Controversial CEO," *CBC News*, September 20, 2011. Accessed February 19, 2013, http://www.cbc.ca/news/canada/edmonton/story/2010/11/24/edmonton-duckett-future.html

22. Ibid.

Money Talk

While you are entering the field of public relations because you have a passion for communicating, it is good to know that you can also make a decent—and even an excellent—living in this profession.

Public relations salaries vary widely depending on experience, the type of industry, and whether you are working in-house or in an agency.

On the lower end of the spectrum, an entry-level professional can expect a salary of $28,000 to $32,000.[1] This figure can be as high as $40,000 for some positions.

The good news is that with just a few years' experience, time invested in professional development, a lot of hard work, and two or three promotions, a young professional's salary quickly increases to the $60,000 range.[2]

The city that you live in also dictates how much money you can expect to earn. For example, salaries are typically higher in Ottawa and Calgary than they are in Vancouver and Fredericton.[3]

The following median salaries provide a reference point for the various positions in Canada:

- PR coordinator: $43,000
- PR manager: $57,000
- Vice president or director: $70,000
- President or CEO: $108,000[4]

Salaries tend to be higher for entry-level positions in-house compared to those in agencies. This does not hold true the higher you climb. Salaries in-house and in agencies become more consistent at the more senior level. Not surprisingly, corporate positions typically pay more than nonprofit ones.

And, of course, if you open your own successful PR agency, there is no limit to your earning potential. The top agencies in Canada are multi-million-dollar operations.

Notes:

1. "FAQs," Canadian Public Relations Society Vancouver. Accessed February 19, 2013, http://www.cprsvancouver.com/faqs#How%20much%20does%20PR%20pay

2. B. Morton, "Bright-Eyed Public Faces for Corporations a Hot Commodity," *The Vancouver Sun*, March 10, 2007. Accessed February 19, 2013, http://www.canada.com/vancouversun/news/archives/story.html?id=d8c64257-a84a-4eb5-b6bc-4b5f77af8ce0

3. "Public Relations Communications Media Salary Canada," Living in Canada. Accessed February 19, 2013, http://www.livingin-canada.com/salaries-for-occupations-in-public-relations.html

4. "PR Salaries and Labour Trends in Canada," prclass. Accessed February 19, 2013, http://prclass.wordpress.com/2006/11/06/pr-salaries-and-labour-trends-in-canada/

Chapter 9
Internal Communications

Best Buy Canada implemented an internal communications plan specifically to address the challenges and opportunities posed by the Vancouver Olympics.

Source: © Michael Neelon/Alamy

LEARNING OBJECTIVES

❶ Define internal communications and outline its importance to an organization's success.

❷ Explain how organizational culture can affect internal communications and vice versa.

❸ Outline the various tools at an internal communicator's disposal and explain when they might be used.

❹ Explain the function and components of an internal communications plan.

Best Buy Canada's Medal-Worthy Olympic Preparation Plan

On July 2, 2003, it was announced that Vancouver, British Columbia, would host the 2010 Winter Olympics. Both the nation and Best Buy Canada were ecstatic. At the same time, Best Buy's internal communications team knew that this event would pose a serious challenge for the company's internal communications team.

Canada's largest retailer and e-tailer of consumer electronics, Best Buy Canada operates two brands—Future Shop and Best Buy—with over 200 stores and 20,000 employees across the country. As a major retailer located near several Olympic venues with the highest traffic, where over 130,000 additional visitors were expected daily, Best Buy realized it would be presented with numerous opportunities and challenges during the 17 days of the Olympic Games. The internal communications team understood that it would take a coordinated effort with support from the City of Vancouver and the Vancouver Organizing Committee (VANOC) to adequately communicate to employees during this hectic time and to ensure that all employees, from head office to the retail sales staff, were equipped with the information they needed.

The challenges included the potential for riots, acts of vandalism, longer commute times for employees, and delayed service assistance or deliveries because of congestion. The opportunities included the potential for increased sales and for higher team engagement. To help mitigate the challenges and capitalize on the opportunities, the internal communications team came up with the objective of developing and implementing a communications strategy and plan that would embrace the spirit of the Games, inform the many stakeholders of their roles, and ensure seamless operations.

The audiences for the internal communications plan included head office employees and the retail operations teams for Future Shop and Best Buy, including the 500 Vancouver store employees who would be directly affected by the Games. These diverse audiences required different communications channels in order to effectively communicate the key messages. At the store level, communication was mainly face to face. Opening managers read out news bulletins in the morning meetings, and employees logged on to the intranet for updates and additional information. At head office, face-to-face communication in the form of **town halls** (internal company meetings), intranet, and email blasts were used.

Prior to developing the communication materials, a great deal of research was required, mostly to secure an understanding of the physical challenges presented by the Games, such as traffic changes, road closures, and other obstacles that would affect shipping, scheduling, or sales. Best Buy engaged key contacts from VANOC and the local transit authority, including them in presentations to company leadership. The company also benchmarked its U.S. counterparts who had hosted the Olympic Games in Atlanta, Georgia, and Salt Lake City, Utah. The Best Buy Canada team was dismayed to find that best practices had not been documented and vowed to create an internal document that could be shared with other cities in the future.

After months of preparation and weekly team meetings, Best Buy's internal communications team developed an internal communications plan. The team also worked with human resources (HR) to develop alternative work arrangements to make commuting easier for employees during the Games. To implement the plan, the team developed communications tools, including an Olympic intranet site, PowerPoint presentations for the leadership team, email blasts, internal TV messages, and town hall meetings. Finally, a crisis plan and a decision tree (a diagram that facilitates decision making by showing the appropriate course of action of various scenarios) were circulated among the leadership team as a precaution leading up to the Games. By developing and executing a solid communications plan and preparing for the unexpected, Best Buy was able to take advantage of the opportunities presented by the Olympic Games, while making sure that employees felt armed with the right information. This ensured the organization was able to navigate the Games with ease.

In public relations, much of the discourse is focused on external communications, yet one of the most important stakeholder groups for any organization is its employees. For Best Buy, meeting the needs of this audience meant devising an entire communications plan solely for its employees during the Olympics. The plan ensured that Best Buy employees had the information they needed to do their best work during the Olympics, so that the organization could take full advantage of the opportunities the Games offered.

Many of the same techniques outlined throughout this textbook for external public relations, such as timely, candid communication and communications planning, can also be applied to internal communications. Internal communications teams apply the same thinking and strategies behind communications to external stakeholders and turn them inward, so that the messaging is consistent between both audiences.

However, public relations practitioners must remember the unique set of concerns of their target audiences, in this case employees, which may include job security, protection of culture, fear of change, opportunities for growth and development, fairness, and so on. Also, as we saw in the Best Buy case study, because internal communications has some crossover into the HR function as it pertains to employee satisfaction and morale, internal communicators need to be familiar with best practices for both communications and human resources.

In today's competitive business environment, organizations want to attract and retain talented employees. Some of the benefits of effective internal communications are higher employee morale, retention, and, as we saw in the case of Best Buy, performance. Many studies have linked higher job satisfaction and performance to well-executed internal communications.[1] Companies that ignore this important function often neglect the opportunity to help shape and form a strong, productive organizational culture. Effective internal communications can also assist a company to achieve its external public relations goals. Employees may be either a company's greatest ambassadors or the greatest sources of negative outward communication. Disgruntled employees may spread their discontent to their friends and families or leak negative information to the media, especially during a crisis.

In this chapter, we will concentrate on how communicators can deliver effective communications internally and avoid some of the common pitfalls of the practice. We will also examine the internal communications function, specifically concentrating on the pros and cons of various communications vehicles. We will then examine organizational culture and how it affects internal communications. We will also look at all the different ways in which internal audiences communicate informally, and wrap up the chapter with the development of an internal communications plan.

Internal Communications Defined ❶

Imagine you are working for a large organization with hundreds of employees. After working there for several months, you receive an email from HR letting you know that your company has merged with another and that, while no actions have been taken yet, the company is hoping to increase the efficiencies of the two organizations by eliminating redundant positions. As an employee, how would this news make you feel? How would it make you feel if you received the information via email instead of in person, or by an HR representative instead of the CEO? Most employees would start sending out their resumés and looking for a new position after receiving such important news in this insensitive manner. Communicating vague or incomplete information, especially through a vehicle that does not provide an easy forum to ask questions, can start the rumour mill humming.

As we can see from this example, while an internal communications team has many different tools and communications vehicles at its disposal, not all of them are appropriate in certain situations. Just as it would be a waste of time for most CEOs to call an in-person meeting to let employees know that the shared kitchen will undergo renovations, it could seem cold and unfeeling to deliver important news, such as layoffs, through email, especially from someone other than the CEO.

Before we elaborate on the tools and vehicles available to an internal communications practitioner, it is useful to define internal communications. **Internal communications** involves communications with an internal audience, such as employees, franchisees, stockholders, or board members. Internal communications may be done through the public relations team or through a designated internal communications team. In some organizations, the human resources department assumes this role. Internal communications can be top-down, from senior management to the employees, or bottom-up, from employees to senior management, but it should always be a two-way dialogue. Communicating with employees is a specialized function that is important for two reasons: first, effective employee communications builds morale and improves employee retention and performance, and second, it enhances an organization's external communications program.[2]

An important function of strategic internal communications is to help increase employee buy-in for an organization's goals, purpose, and vision.[3] In this section, while we will lay out best practices for some of the communications vehicles internal communicators might use, it is important to note that each organization's employees and culture are different, and it is up to the communicators to judge whether the guidelines apply to their organization or situation. For example, if a company spans multiple continents and has employees who speak various languages, a CEO might not be able to have face-to-face meetings regarding the same issues as a CEO of a 100-person, localized company might. Furthermore, there might be competing cultures within one organization that the internal communicator will need to take into consideration. For example, in a hospital, the doctors might have their own culture and like to receive information one way, whereas the nurses may have a different culture that requires a distinct communications strategy.

When Toronto Hydro wanted to educate its employees on work safety and decrease work injuries, it created a communications plan custom-tailored to its employees. The majority of Toronto Hydro's employees are men who are interested in sports. Toronto Hydro developed a creative way to increase employee buy-in for its safety plan. The organization created the Toronto Hydro Safety Olympics to help attract employees' attention. The campaign used humour and turned employees' jobs into mock-Olympic events. The campaign used emails, newsletters, posters, flyers, and face-to-face "safety cafés." It also ran radio commercials to reach employees in the field who were not able to attend meetings.[4]

THE KEY COMPONENTS OF INTERNAL COMMUNICATIONS

Internal communications can sometimes be treated like the ugly stepsister to external communications. This is because external communications can deliver the glory and big wins. It can seem glamorous to get a story on the six o'clock news or to plan a

While internal communications doesn't typically receive the same exposure as external communications—sometimes treated as the ugly stepsister to Cinderella—it is a vital component of any organization's communications strategy.
Source: WALT DISNEY PRODUCTIONS/Album/Newscom

launch event. Thus, internal communications is sometimes overlooked or executed as an afterthought; however, it is vitally important to the goals of an organization. The Olympic Games presented a huge opportunity for Best Buy as its retail stores were located near several Olympic venues and large numbers of visitors were expected. The only way that the organization could take advantage of the additional traffic was if its employees were prepared and had the information they needed in order to be effective. Their job performance depended on the information communicated to them by internal communications tactics.

Internal communications becomes especially important in times of change and crisis. As people become more anxious, internal communications teams need to stop any misinformation from circulating. They also need to be transparent and receptive to questions in order to keep employees engaged and productive.

Galen Weston, the executive chairman of Loblaw Companies, was honoured with the Canadian Public Relations Society Toronto CEO Award of Excellence in Public Relations in large part because of his emphasis on communicating with his employees through newsletters and by answering employee questions. On the importance of internal communications, Weston says, "The CEO's vision has got to be imparted to the employees and they need to communicate it to their various customers and stakeholders."[5]

Galen Weston received the CEO Award of Excellence in Public Relations because of his organization's focus on internal communications.
Source: John Kennedy/Newscom

Internal communications is a fine balance between providing too little information and too much. Employees become suspicious and concerned when there isn't enough communication.[6] However, too much information can be overwhelming, leading to much of the information being ignored and therefore rendered ineffective.[7] It can also make employees less productive because they waste time sifting through information that is irrelevant to their tasks. Having said this, if you are unsure of how much to communicate, Robert Waterman Jr., co-author of *In Search of Excellence*, advises, "When in doubt, tell people too much."[8] As a general rule, employees would rather be overcommunicated with than undercommunicated with.

In order to better understand what communications practices helped organizations reach their long-term goals and objectives, Deloitte and Touche studied ten international companies and identified four key components of effective internal communications:[9]

1. *Clear, consistent messaging:* Organizations need to be consistent by delivering a couple of key messages that are disseminated regularly throughout the organization.

2. *Open, candid communication:* Employees need to trust that they will receive truthful, helpful information when they ask for it.

3. *Sharing of information:* Employees need access to the right information to do their jobs effectively. They also require opportunities to share best practices so that they can learn from their peers.

4. *Practising what is preached:* The behaviour and communications of senior management must be consistent. Employees will look to the leadership team for behavioural cues.

Thinking Like a PR Practitioner

1. Choose one of the four key components to effective internal communications and describe some potential problems that a company might encounter if it does not have this component.

2. Describe the internal communications practices of a company you have worked for. Was the internal communication effective? What did the organization do well? What areas could it improve on?

Organizational Culture ❷

Understanding an organization's culture is important to the discipline of internal communications because each influences and affects the other. While internal communications can influence an organization's culture by strengthening or shaping it, organizational culture dictates the internal communications pieces that are created and the messages that are delivered. It should be noted that an organization's culture can take a long time to shift, even with an effective communications team, because it often takes a long time to develop and become ingrained. Thus, an internal communications team should not expect that an organization's culture will change overnight. It takes strong, consistent messaging and leadership over time to alter a culture in a significant way.

Organizational culture has many definitions, but for our purposes we will define it as the shared values, beliefs, and "learned responses" of an organization's employees.[10] Some of the factors thought to strengthen an organizational culture include a long corporate history and low employee turnover.[11] This is because longevity helps facilitate the sharing of company myths, symbols, and rituals.[12] An organization's culture can be influenced by many factors, including the external culture the organization operates within, senior management, and strong employee cliques.

Developing a solid, positive organizational culture is beneficial to a company because it leads to more efficient communication between employees, as well as higher levels of participation and commitment.[13] As Marty Parker, managing director of Waterstone Human Capital, explains, "Corporate culture drives employee values. Employee values drive behaviour. And behaviour is critical to delivering business plans and goals."[14] However, organizational culture is not always positive. It can be negative if it starts hindering productivity or the goals of the organization.[15] An example of a negative organizational culture is provided by Enron, where a culture of the "ends justifying the means" and lavish spending at the highest levels of the organization may have contributed to the company's ultimate destruction.[16] Since culture is both a product of and an influence on communications, the internal communications team needs to assess which aspects of the organization's culture it would like to reinforce and which it would like to change through internal communications strategies and tactics. The internal communications team also needs to be conscious of how informal communications, which is much harder to influence, may affect the organization's culture.

A culture of lavish spending and risky behaviour contributed to Enron's demise.

Source: EZIO PETERSEN/Newscom

INFORMAL INTERNAL COMMUNICATIONS

While formal communications is important for shaping an organization's culture and increasing employee morale, informal internal communications also plays a large role. **Informal communications** is communication among employees that does not come from the internal communications team or management, such as discussions at company events, lunchroom conversation, and water-cooler chatter.[17] While it is easy to think of casual conversation as unimportant gossiping, internal communicators need to be aware of any potentially detrimental gossip that is circulating. Even though gossip is informal, it can have serious implications for an organization's culture. Rumours provide insight into the fears and anxieties of employees. When internal communicators hear of rumours that are circulating, they should try to provide timely, truthful information to stop the gossip and provide Q&As and talking points for managers so that they will be armed to address the concerns.[18]

Rumours often circulate when employees feel information is being kept from them. Employees can generally sense when change is about to take place.[19] By failing to be candid and transparent, a communicator can actually stimulate more rumours because, in a communications vacuum, employees will speculate about what is about to happen, which leads to more gossip and anxiety. In the next section we will explore some of the communications tools that internal communicators can use to assist them in communicating effectively in order to promote a productive workplace environment.

COMMUNICATION WITH GEN Y EMPLOYEES

Many employers are concerned with how to communicate with their younger employees as they are very active in shaping organizational culture. These employees tend to be young, ambitious, and social media savvy. Thus, there is a fear that traditional communications vehicles might not get their attention. In order to connect with and engage these employees, internal communications specialists are looking for creative ways to deliver their messages. Instead of face-to-face meetings, they are distributing YouTube

Communicating effectively with employees from Gen Y, also called Millennials, provides unique challenges for employers.
Source: Luis Alvarez/Getty Images

videos of executives' speeches or instructional videos. They are also looking for social and environmental causes to partner with in order to motivate this often idealistic group. An active community relations strategy, which we discuss further in Chapter 12, can help companies attract and retain top talent and increase **employee engagement**—employees' attachment and feelings of satisfaction regarding their organization or job.

As Gen Y employees, also called Millennials, tend to be highly engaged online, it is important for a company to ensure that its social media policy is distributed and understood throughout the organization. A social media policy is essential for every organization. Employees are going to post and tweet about your organization, so it is best to have a clear, concise code of conduct. Furthermore, bad employee conduct that is subsequently posted online could tarnish a company's brand. Some companies quickly fired employees who were seen, in photos posted on social media, looting and vandalizing shops during the 2011 Vancouver Stanley Cup riots.[20]

A good example of social media guidelines is Canada Post's "Social Media Employee Policy."[21] Canada Post has its social media policy posted on its website for both its employees and the public to see. Guidelines for employees for both personal and work-related social media activity include

As photos from the 2011 Vancouver Stanley Cup riots circulated online, some employers fired identifiable employees.

Source: imago sportfotodienst/Newscom

- Avoiding posting defamatory or obscene content
- Identifying themselves as employees of Canada Post if they post material or topics related to their work
- Keeping Canada Post information confidential
- Publishing only accurate information about the company[22]

These guidelines help ensure that all employees understand the company's position on social media while not trying to ban it completely. They also provide the company with recourse if an employee doesn't comply with its rules regarding social media.

Internal Communications Tools ❸

Communicators have many tools at their disposal for communicating with their organization's employees. However, each tool has its own set of pros and cons. Furthermore, each may be appropriate only in certain situations. Some of the tools available are information-pull technologies and some are information-push technologies.[23] **Information-pull technologies** are tools that allow employees to access information they need and "pull" it as desired. An example of this type of communication is a company intranet or internal social media site that provides updates and announcements.[24] **Information-push technologies** are tools that "push" information onto employees by providing it when employees have not necessarily asked for it, such as email announcements.[25] Employees also have preferences for how they would like to be communicated with, even if they are not the most efficient communication methods. For example, while most employees prefer face-to-face meetings to most other forms of communication, this is not a very efficient form of communication. Sometimes practicality needs to be weighed against employee preferences.

Prior to deciding which tool to use to communicate with employees, it is useful to examine the content of the message. Internal communicators should consider the complexity of the message. Is it simple and straightforward or convoluted and confusing? Also, what type of emotional reaction will it spark? Does the message consist of neutral information, or is it highly charged, controversial news? Internal communicators will also want to consider how important the information is. Will this information cause changes in people's jobs, or will it have very little impact? Finally, they should consider how routine the information is. Is this message something that is communicated regularly, such as a quarterly update, or is this the first and only time this news will be delivered? While every organization is different, the more convoluted, emotionally charged, impactful, or nonroutine a message is, the more it will warrant a higher degree of interpersonal communication, such as a meeting. The more simple, neutral, nonimpactful, and routine the messaging is, the more likely a less personal mode of communication, such as a company newsletter or an email, will be appropriate.

Internal communicators also need to consider the delivery method and speed with which a message needs to be delivered. Is this a message that should come from senior management or from HR? How quickly does it need to be communicated? Employees should receive important information before other stakeholders and before it appears in the media. Employees do not like hearing news about their organization from external sources.

Ultimately, internal communicators need to consider all the factors highlighted above in combination with their organization's internal culture and use their good judgment about how to distill the information. As we saw in the Best Buy opening vignette, some internal communication campaigns involve several tools. Best Buy created an Olympic intranet site and used email blasts, PowerPoint presentations, and internal TV messages to ensure its employees were well informed during this important time. Here we will consider some positives and negatives about some of the most frequently used communications tools (see Table 9.1).

EMAIL

Communicating through email has many benefits for organizations. It is fast, easy, and free. It is also convenient for both the sender and the receiver.[26] Employees can read emails when it is most convenient in their schedule. Email also helps flatten an organization, as CEOs and senior management can communicate to the entire organization at the same time.[27] Visuals or video links can be included in emails, as well, to help communicate a message.

Despite its many benefits, email has some cons. Email can feel cold and impersonal. It can be hard to explain complicated or confusing information in an email, and email does not provide an opportunity to read people's body language to ensure that they have understood the message. The high volume of emails that people receive is also a drawback. Many emails are scanned instead of read for comprehension. Emails can get accidently deleted or buried and forgotten. Thus, the sender cannot know for sure if the receiver has actually received and understood the message. Arts Umbrella, a nonprofit organization that organizes arts programs for children, uses email regularly to communicate with its employees. Susan Smith, director of programming and marketing at Arts Umbrella, explains, "For us, the reason that email has been such an important tool is we have such a varied staff with varied schedules. We have people that only come in on a Saturday, and most of our administration staff works only Monday through Friday, so for us it's been really crucial."[28]

Table 9.1	Pros and Cons of Various Communications Tools	
Tool	**Pros**	**Cons**
Email	Efficient and cost-effective; can flatten the organization; employees can read on their own time	Can seem impersonal; not a good forum for questions and answers; too many emails can feel overwhelming for employees; if employees have a large volume of emails, the message may get lost or be left unread
Intranet, internal social media site, or company website	Serves as an archive; employees can read on their own time	Management cannot assume that employees are frequently checking the website or intranet
Company newsletter/blog	Allows for more in-depth information on subjects to be provided; helps to create and sustain a strong company culture	Not a good vehicle for delivering timely information; may not be read by everyone
Face-to-face meetings	Employees' preferred method of communication; provides an opportunity for two-way dialogue	Time-consuming; can be hard to organize; can lead to lower efficiency if there are too many meetings
Video conferencing or Skype	Adds a personal element to the communication; good for companies where employees are geographically separated	Not as personal as a face-to-face meetings; less opportunity to read employees' body language, reactions
Bulletins or posters	Good for breaking through the clutter; effective for non-office environments like a warehouse	Would not work for organizations with employees who are geographically dispersed; if there are too many postings they will be ignored
Phone messages	Signals that the message is important but still lets employees listen and absorb it on their schedule; good for sales teams who are geographically dispersed	May not be appropriate for every organization; does not provide an opportunity for questions and answers
Social media	Cheap and great for sharing videos and pictures; appeals to younger or more tech-savvy employees	May be intimidating for some employees; might not work in organizations where many employees do not have access to a computer or smartphone

"What if, and I know this sounds kooky,
we communicated with the employees."

Source: Cartoonresource/Shutterstock

INTRANETS, INTERNAL SOCIAL MEDIA SITES, AND COMPANY WEBSITES

A company intranet, internal social media site, or website is a great place to post news announcements and updates and to archive documents so that employees can retrieve them later. As with email, photos and videos can be posted to these sites to help communicate important or complicated messages. However, most employees do not have time to search or check the intranet or website regularly for new information.[29] As with email, it is difficult to confirm receipt or understanding of the information.

COMPANY NEWSLETTERS OR BLOGS

Often the internal communications team will work closely with the human resources department to create an employee newsletter or blog. Employee newsletters and blogs are designed to enhance a sense of community and to reinforce company messaging and goals. However, company newsletters are often not the best option for time-sensitive or critical information, as they often come out only monthly or quarterly. They are also often not the place for communicating sensitive information for the first time. A blog offers the advantage that communicators can post information whenever it is needed instead of having to wait for the next regular issue of the newsletter.

FACE-TO-FACE MEETINGS

A face-to-face meeting can take different forms. It can be a town hall meeting where everyone in the organization gathers, or a meeting where department heads or managers provide information to their teams. A face-to-face meeting could even take place through video conferencing. Some companies have a 24-hour rule, meaning that once the department heads or managers are told an important piece of information, they have 24 hours to disseminate it to their reports.

Employees like to receive information directly from upper management; often they perceive information that flows down through the levels of management as filtered and no longer the true message. Employees also like face-to-face meetings because the communication loop can be closed. The manager submits the information, the employee receives it, and the manager has an opportunity for instant feedback on whether or not the employee has received and understood the message and whether he or she accepts it.[30] Having said this, face-to-face communication with upper management, especially within large organizations, can be time-consuming and impractical. Having to plan around so many different work schedules can also be difficult.

VIDEO CONFERENCING OR SKYPE

Video conferencing or Skype can add a personal touch to a message while overcoming the barrier of distance. However, not being in the same room as employees can provide a disadvantage for some announcements as it is harder to read body language. Also, technical issues may arise that can detract from the meeting.

BULLETINS AND POSTERS

Bulletins and posters are a way to grab attention. Emails and the intranet may get lost or be left unread, but bulletins and posters can interrupt employees' routines and stand out, especially if they are placed in a high-traffic area such as a lunchroom. Bulletins are also effective in nonoffice environments like warehouses and factories, where employees do not have much access to a computer during the workday.

PHONE MESSAGES

Some organizations, particularly ones with employees who are geographically dispersed, such as a sales force, have the capability to leave voicemail messages for everyone in the organization at once. This method provides the opportunity to provide a personal message while communicating efficiently with a large, geographically separated audience. Again, a drawback of this communication tool is the inability to ensure that employees received the message and to answer questions at the time the message is disseminated.

SOCIAL MEDIA

Companies are looking for new ways to reach employees through social media. Some companies create YouTube training videos for employees to watch or use LinkedIn to help employees connect with each other.[31] However, although using social media might appeal to younger or more tech-savvy employees, it could be intimidating to others. It might be appropriate to host a social media–training session to ensure all employees are comfortable receiving information this way before launching these tools.

MTS Allstream used a social media program to engage its employees. On the company intranet, it created an "Idea Factory" where employees can enter suggestions. Other employees can view these ideas and vote on their favourites, which are then reviewed by management.[32]

ADVICE TO NEW PRACTITIONERS

Creating a Readable Employee Newsletter

While employee newsletters can be a great way to reinforce the company's values and strengthen the organizational culture, internal communications practitioners need to make sure they are not spending a lot of time creating a document that nobody reads.

Here are some tips for developing an engaging company newsletter:

Serve it how people want it. Do not email it if most of the company is not at a computer all day. In a warehouse environment you may need to have printed copies passed out or posted in the lunchroom.

Highlight people. Employees want to feel appreciated and be treated like individuals.[33] The company newsletter provides a great opportunity to recognize individuals for their accomplishments both inside and outside of work.

Be transparent. Be honest about how the company is doing.[34] Everyone in the company should be on the same page about the organization's financial picture. A newsletter is a great place to highlight how the organization is performing against its goals.

Use the newsletter to reduce the overall number of emails. Instead of sending one-off emails with updates and information, try to accumulate any nonurgent messages in the newsletter.[35]

Make the newsletter visually appealing and easy to scan.

Avoid including pointless filler. Everyone is busy. Do not worry about making the newsletter long. Keep it short, prioritizing relevancy over length.

Thinking Like a PR Practitioner

1. Identify two communications tools and describe a situation or scenario where they would be appropriate communication methods.

2. Think of a company you have worked for. Create an editorial outline for its employee newsletter. What are the different types of articles you could include?

The Internal Communications Plan ❹

As we saw in the Best Buy example, developing an internal communications plan is important in order to identify any problem areas, put a strategic plan in place, and measure the results after implementation. By having a plan in place with concrete objectives and a roadmap on how to accomplish them, Best Buy was able to successfully navigate the 2010 Vancouver Olympic Games. With so many stakeholders and potential disruptions, imagine how disorganized this time might have been if the company had not had this important guide to refer to.

A communications plan can be developed for a specific project or campaign, as in the Best Buy example, or for a specific time period. Internal communications plans are not static documents. They should be reviewed and revised as needed. The best communications plans have widespread buy-in throughout the organization and have the internal communications team's performance evaluations or bonuses tied to the goals outlined in the documents.

WHAT EMPLOYEES WANT FROM INTERNAL COMMUNICATIONS

It may seem obvious what employees want from a communications program; however, in the day-to-day routine it can be easy to forget the basic principles of communicating to employees. Employees feel valued by their organization when they are the first to be told news, when they are listened to and given the opportunity to ask questions, and when their suggestions are taken seriously.[36] Employees also desire more information than merely what they need to perform their functions.[37] They want to feel that they understand what is going on in their organization. Having this inside knowledge helps them deepen their sense of community.[38]

Employee communication needs to be two-way. Senior management should not be seen as unapproachable or as communicating to the organization without providing a forum or capacity for employees to respond or ask questions. Employees feel well communicated with when a wide variety of communications tools are employed, such as those listed in the previous section.[39]

PRACTITIONER INTERVIEW

Richard Williams, Manager Communications, BC Principals' and Vice-Principals' Association (BCPVPA)

As manager of communications, Richard Williams is responsible for communicating with the association's external audiences and internal audiences, including members.

Question: What are some of the tactics you use to communicate with members?

Answer: We distribute a weekly electronic newsletter to members during the school year, publish a magazine five times per year, have a website and a Twitter account, and use Facebook on an as-needs basis. We conduct online surveys as required as well as hold annual elections for the board of directors via online ballot, which has tremendously increased voter participation.

Question: Please give me details of one example.

Answer: In July 2011 we filmed approximately 20 principals for individual two-minute unscripted

(Continued)

Richard Williams, Manager Communications, BC Principals' and Vice-Principals' Association (BCPVPA)

videos. Principals spoke about their passion for education, their roles and responsibilities. The videos were released between September and December 2011 and posted to a Facebook page. Videos were promoted with members and they were encouraged to share them with their local school communities. Some of those videos, and soon all of them, will be available on the BCPVPA YouTube channel.

Question: Do you have any other audiences that you consider internal and that you communicate with?

Answer: Internal audiences are our members, although they are sometimes divided into interest groups—elementary, middle, secondary, urban, rural, Professional Learning reps, etc.

Question: What are some challenges in communicating with and engaging members?

Answer: Our members are extremely busy. They work in a fast-paced school environment and have overall responsibility for the staff, students, and culture of the school. With so many respon-

sibilities and demands on their time it is difficult to get their attention. Communications from the association have to be concise and informative.

Question: Do you use different tactics to communicate with external audiences?

Answer: We have many external audiences and, depending on the group, may send them either our magazine or our weekly newsletter. We also have to find new ways to engage them and others, which is why we have adopted social media such as Twitter and, on an as-needs basis, Facebook. The association president has, in the past, spoken to community and service groups on the role of the principal and vice-principal while touring the province and visiting with our members in their schools. The president also writes op ed pieces for distribution to community newspapers on occasion. The association advocates to government on behalf of its members and public education and, as such, maintains contact with MLAs and appropriate ministry departments.

DEVELOPMENT OF AN INTERNAL COMMUNICATIONS PLAN

A solid internal communications plan should be the guiding document for an organization's employee communications. It becomes the document that the internal communications team checks its strategies and tactics against to see if they meet the goals of the organization. Depending on the size of the organization, the internal communications plan may be a component of a larger communications plan, or, as we saw in the Best Buy example, it may be its own document.

Before you develop your communications plan, it is important to know your audience. You need to understand their average age, seniority, education, and expectations. You may want to conduct a communications audit or review any past employee engagement surveys. As part of the communications audit, you will review current and past communications pieces to see if the mission and values of your company are reflected in all the messaging or identify where there may be weaknesses. Another benefit of having a documented plan is that it may be shared with other teams in order to better the entire organization. See Chapter 4 for more information on communications audits and PR plans.

The following are some of the components that are included in an internal communications plan:

Objectives: Clear, measurable objectives are identified and listed.

Target audiences: Each target audience is outlined.

Key messages: The top messages that you want each target audience to know and understand are detailed.

Strategies and tactics: A list of key strategies and the tactics that support them is provided.

Budget: The budget is outlined, as well as the resources available to implement the plan.

Evaluation:[40] Metrics are decided on and put in place to evaluate whether the internal communications plan has delivered on the objectives outlined in the document.

Once the internal communications plan is drafted, it should be shared with all key stakeholders. Once it is implemented, it should be regularly reviewed and updated.

EVALUATION

It is important to note that internal communications never ends. It is constant and evolving.[41] As an organization changes, becomes larger, enters new markets, or goes through tough times, its internal communications strategy, like its external communication strategy, will need to change and adapt. In order to know what is working and what is not, and when to change strategy, it is important to do engagement surveys.

Annual employee surveys are a great way to check in and see what strategies, tactics, and messages are working and which are not. It may also be useful to do surveys after significant campaigns or events. Some of the aspects you may want to measure include engagement, behaviour, and contentment. When doing surveys you need to have a benchmark to compare your results against. Results have little meaning without a point of reference. Is an 80 per cent job satisfaction rating good or bad? It depends on how your organization did in the past or how other industries are doing. A score of 80 per cent might be good in some industries and bad in others. If the job satisfaction at your company used to be 90 per cent, 80 per cent would be viewed as negative; however, if it used to be 40 per cent, 80 per cent would be seen as a great success. A **benchmark** is a marker that you measure your survey results against. The benchmark could be a previous year's survey results or it could be the average employee engagement results in the sector or among other companies of similar size.

Another way to receive feedback on how your internal communications team is performing is to form a staff panel.[42] This staff panel would include a diverse range of employees from various departments who agree to meet occasionally to answer questions, conduct surveys, or participate in focus groups on the organization's internal communications.[43] From this group of employees, you will be able to gauge how others are receiving the message. Once you effectively measure the performance of your plan, you will be able to adapt and improve your internal communications. See Chapters 1 and 4 for more information on evaluation.

See Chapters 1 and 4 for more information on evaluation.

Thinking Like a PR Practitioner

1. Name three components of internal communications that employees require.
2. You have been brought into an organization to improve its internal communications. What are the first steps you would take?

CASE STUDY MAPLE ORGANICS

Maple Organics is a Canadian manufacturer of organic skin-care products. As part of this relatively young, fast-growing company, founder Rosy Atwal and the communications team understood that they would have some internal communications challenges ahead.

The company, which launched the first line of organic baby skin care products in Canada to be certified by the U.S. Department of Agriculture (USDA), offers its customers around the globe organic baby and adult skin care solutions. With a small head office team and a number of sales reps across the country, it can be difficult to motivate and engage the entire organization. While the head office employees are close to the day-to-day decisions and direction of the organization, the fear is that, because of physical distance, the sales team will feel removed from and uninvolved in the organization, leading to a lack of motivation. A lack of motivation could mean lower sales, so implementing successful internal communications is vital to the organization's growth.

While it was exciting to be part of new company, the communications team knew that, because of its young organizational culture, every decision could have a large impact on its development. Also, as the company grew and hired more staff, the culture would need to adapt. Atwal and her team wanted to be strategic about what type of culture Maple Organics would develop. In order to achieve this goal, they knew they needed a solid internal communications plan to get them through this first critical stage in the company's history.

Questions

1. If you were a member of the Maple Organics communications team, how would you start developing a plan? What are some key elements you would want to measure?

2. Name three internal communications tools that you would implement to communicate to the internal stakeholders and explain why.

3. What are some of the challenges related to the culture of a new, fast-growing company?

Xantrex

Fast-growing companies often find that their internal culture is developing and changing quickly. They may also find it hard to foster a sense of community interdepartmentally. Often departments work in silos and do not socialize regularly or know employees in other departments very well.

To try to foster a strong company culture throughout all departments at Xantrex, a company that develops and manufactures mobile power products, we implemented an employee newsletter, where we could celebrate the employee accomplishments both within the work environment and outside it. For example, one of the accomplishments we celebrated was an eco-friendly house that an employee built himself.

We also celebrated the organization's successes and charitable giving. These types of internal newsletters can go a long way toward helping employees get to know their colleagues better and fostering a sense of community.

Internal Communications

tools
- face-to-face meetings
- company newsletter
- company website
- intranets
- bulletins
- posters
- email

informal internal communications

organizational culture influenced by
- management
- industry
- employees
- external environment

internal communications plan
- continuous evaluation

practise candid communication
- clear consistent messaging
- trust employees
- lead by example

Key Terms

benchmark A marker that you choose to measure other results against and that provides context to the results.

employee engagement A measurement of employees' attachment and feelings of satisfaction regarding their organization and their job.

informal communications Communication among employees that is not disseminated from the internal communications team or management, such as water-cooler chatter.

information-pull technology Tools that allow employees to access information as they need it—e.g., the company intranet.

information-push technology Tools that deliver information to employees that they have not asked for—e.g., company emails.

internal communications Communication that occurs within a company or organization where the main audience is the employees and board members.

organizational culture The shared values, beliefs, and learned behaviour of an organization's employees.

town hall An internal meeting where employees are able to ask questions and share ideas with senior leaders.

Weblinks

Canada Post Social Media Employee Policy
www.infopost.ca/en/social-media-employee-policy/

Internal Communications: It's Not Rocket Science
http://novascotia.ca/cns/pubs/ItsNotRocketScience.pdf

The PR Coach
www.theprcoach.com/internal-communications/

Strategic Communications: An 8-Step Process for Creating Effective Internal Communications Plans
www.stratcommunications.com/media/cushycms/Resources_83_2776689510.pdf

What Do People do All Day? Employee Engagement
www.youtube.com/watch?v=m2GUI5r09g0&feature=youtu.be

Endnotes

1. Candace White, Antoaneta Vanc, and Gena Stafford, "Internal Communication, Information Satisfaction, and Sense of Community: The Effect of Personal Influence," *Journal of Public Relations Research*, 2010, 65–84.

2. Ibid.

3. Ibid.

4. International Association of Business Communicators, *Toronto Hydro Winter Safety Olympics*, 2007. Accessed February 22, 2013, http://discovery.iabc.com/view.php?pid=1354

5. Kristin Laird, "Weston Wins PR Award," *Marketing*, January 4, 2009. Accessed February 22, 2013, http://www.marketingmag.ca/news/pr-news/weston-wins-pr-award-6509

6. White et al., "Internal Communication, Information Satisfaction, and Sense of Community."

7. Ibid.

8. K. Finch, C. Hansen, and R. Alexander, *Internal Communications: It's Not Rocket Science*. The Province of Nova Scotia, 2010. Accessed February 21, 2013, http://novascotia.ca/cns/pubs/ItsNotRocketScience.pdf

9. Ibid.

10. K. Sriramesh, James E. Grunig, and David M. Duzier, "Observation and Measurement of Two Dimensions of Organizational Culture and Their Relationship to Public Relations," *Journal of Public Relations Research*, vol. 8, no. 4 (1996), 229–261.

11. Ibid.

12. Ibid.

13. Ibid.

14. "WestJet Tops Canada's 10 Most Admired Corporate Cultures," Melcrum Internal Comms Hub, January 18, 2008. Accessed February 21, 2013, http://www.internalcommshub.com/open/news/corpcult2008.ca.shtml (site discontinued).

15. Sriramesh et al., "Observation and Measurement of Two Dimensions of Organizational Culture and Their Relationship to Public Relations."

16. Neela Banerjee, David Barboza, and Audrey Warren, "Enron's Many Strands: Corporate Culture; At Enron, Lavish Excess Often Came Before Success," *New York Times*, February 26, 2002. Accessed February 22, 2013, http://www.nytimes.com/2002/02/26/business/enron-s-many-strands-corporate-culture-enron-lavish-excess-often-came-before.html?pagewanted=all&src=pm

17. Michael Bush, "Internal Communication Is Key to Repairing Toyota Reputation," *Advertising Age*, March 1, 2010, 1–20.

18. Karyn Arkell, "Better Internal Communications," *New Zealand Management*, November 2010, 58.

19. Ibid.

20. Tony Wilson, "Social Media Conduct Could Get You Fired," *The Globe and Mail*, June 19, 2012. Accessed February 22, 2013, http://m.theglobeandmail.com/report-on-business/small-business/sb-managing/human-resources/social-media-conduct-could-get-you-fired/article4346982/?service=mobile

21 "Social Media Employee Policy," Canada Post, October 25, 2010. Accessed February 22, 2013, http://www.infopost.ca/en/social-media-employee-policy/

22. Ibid.

23. White et al., "Internal Communication, Information Satisfaction, and Sense of Community."

24. Daniel Markovitz, "How to Break Free from Email Jail," *HBR Blog Network*, August 27, 2012. Accessed February 22, 2013, http://blogs.hbr.org/cs/2012/08/how_to_break_free_from_email_j.html

25. White et al., "Internal Communication, Information Satisfaction, and Sense of Community."

26. Ibid.

27. Ibid.

28. Sondi Bruner, "Five Ways to Improve Internal Communications at Your Nonprofit," Charityvillage.com, July 4, 2011. Accessed February 22, 2013, https://charityvillage.com/Content.aspx?topic=five_ways_to_improve_internal_communications_at_your_nonprofit

29. White et al., "Internal Communication, Information Satisfaction, and Sense of Community."

30. Finch et al., *Internal Communications: It's Not Rocket Science*.

31. Steve Nicholls, "Improve Internal Communication with These 10 Tips," *The Globe and Mail*, July 13, 2012. Accessed February 22, 2013, http://www.theglobeandmail.com/report-on-business/small-business/sb-tools/top-tens/improve-internal-communication-with-these-10-tips/article4256432/

32. Jeremy Lloyd, "MTS Allstream Uses Social Media Tools for Internal Communication," *Marketing*, July 22, 2010. Accessed February 22, 2013, http://www.marketingmag.ca/news/marketer-news/mts-allstream-uses-social-media-tools-for-internal-communication-4073

33. Elizabeth Castro and Marsha Burton, "Ensuring Your Corporate Employee Newsletter Is Relevant by Turning Business Concepts into Tangible Stories of Success," *The PR Coach* blog, March 26, 2011. Accessed February 22, 2013, http://www.theprcoach.com/internal-communications/

34. Ibid.

35. "Internal Newsletter Ideas, SnapComms.com. Accessed February 22, 2013, http://www.snapcomms.com/solutions/internal-newsletter-ideas.aspx

36. Finch et al., *Internal Communications: It's Not Rocket Science*.

37. White et al., "Internal Communication, Information Satisfaction, and Sense of Community."

38. Ibid.

39. Ibid.

40. Linda Pophal, "An 8-Step Process for Creating Effective Internal Communications Plans," *Strategic Communications*, 2009. Accessed February 22, 2013, http://www.stratcommunications.com/media/cushycms/Resources_83_2776689510.pdf

41. Finch et al., *Internal Communications: It's Not Rocket Science*.

42. Arkell, "Better Internal Communications."

43. Ibid.

How Do I Find a Job in Public Relations?

Finishing your public relations program can be bittersweet. On the one hand, you have completed all your projects and exams and are armed with wonderful, new knowledge. On the other hand, you now have to start the sometimes daunting task of finding a job. Many students find looking for work frightening, but it doesn't have to be as scary as you think.

Here are some tips that can help you make sure you are well situated to find a job at graduation:

Network. I know, you have heard it before, but it is true: a strong network is an enormous asset when you're trying to find a job. Many jobs never get posted and come about from knowing the right person at the right time. Go to industry events, student events, career fairs—anywhere that you might meet a person who is looking for someone like you.

Volunteer. Volunteering your newfound public relations skills for a worthy organization is a great way to meet people, develop your skills, build your resumé, and generate references. Reach out to causes that you are passionate about and see if you can help them with their outreach, social media, or messaging. A word of caution, though: do not offer to help if you do not have the time to do a good job. You want to make a good impression.

Start with an internship. Internships are a wonderful way for students or recent graduates to gain some practical experience in public relations. Even though unpaid internships have lately been heavily criticized, they are often the stepping stones that new graduates need between their education and their first job in the industry.

Put the word out. Tell everyone you know about your career goals and that you are looking for a job. You want to be top of mind if they come across opportunities through their networks.

Develop an elevator pitch. An elevator pitch is a short speech about yourself that you can give in less than 30 seconds (or the time you would have with someone in an elevator). It should be quick and engaging but also sound natural.

Set up information interviews. Approach people in organizations or jobs that you find interesting and set up interviews to ask them questions about their company and their career path or how they got to their position. These are great opportunities to learn about an industry and how successful people have progressed into their roles. Information interviews also help strengthen your interview, networking, and presentation skills.

Do not worry. There are lots of great jobs for talented young PR professionals like you. Stay positive and sooner or later you will find the perfect opportunity.

Here is a true story you might find inspiring:

It is never too early as a PR student to start gaining experience that will make you more employable and provide you with the opportunity to make industry contacts. Erin Raimondo was a full-time student in Kwantlen Polytechnic University's public relations diploma program when she began using the power of social media to network, meet industry contacts, and secure both paid and unpaid internships. In one case, Erin attended a speaking engagement by a leading Canadian social media expert and consultant. Before attending the speaking engagement, Erin began following the speaker on Twitter and on her blog and started developing a relationship with her.

Many conversations later, Erin was offered a summer internship in the speaker's consultancy. Erin secured a second internship by tweeting questions asking if anyone knew of a PR agency looking for an intern. She was able to generate a lead, which led to an internship in a top Canadian PR agency. Social media has also made networking a lot easier for Erin. At PR industry functions, she regularly meets in person the contacts whom she previously knew only in the digital world. Erin is now well established in her career—and all her jobs were generated through the power of networking.

Chapter 10
Special Events Management

Drake at the 40th annual Juno Awards.
Source: © ZUMA Press, Inc./Alamy

LEARNING OBJECTIVES

❶ Outline why PR practitioners need to understand event planning and the various types of events they may be involved in.

❷ Identify the main components of an event plan and explain why they are important to the success of the event.

❸ Outline how an event is executed.

❹ Summarize how an event is evaluated.

❺ Explain special event PR.

Public Relations for the Junos: Supporting the Canadian Music Industry and Capturing the Attention of the World

Public relations has been vital in building the Juno Awards into the prestigious awards ceremony it is today. For over a decade, the PR agency Holmes Creative Communications (HCC) has been managing the public relations initiatives for the awards, in partnership with the Canadian Academy of Recording Arts and Sciences (CARAS). The goal of their efforts has been to put the Junos on the map and to raise awareness of Canadian artists.

Since its beginning, the awards have grown in both scale and substance. When the Juno Awards were first launched, the celebration itself consisted of only two events—an industry gala awards evening where 30 awards were presented, and a concert and awards show that was broadcast on television. In contrast, the 2011 Junos, the 40th anniversary of the awards, consisted of seven Juno-sanctioned events and 10 partnered events managed by a CARAS full-time staff of over 20 employees and 8 PR practitioners from HCC, who worked 12- to 14-hour days. The team also recruited more than 60 PR volunteers to assist with the event.

Part of the fun and challenge of the Junos is that the show travels to a new host city every year, criss-crossing the country from coast to coast. This means that each year the team needs to source new local suppliers and familiarize themselves with a new venue. The number of Juno Week events is also continually expanding.

For HCC, the Junos represent an opportunity to build on a known brand and promote the Canadian music industry nationally and internationally. HCC's objectives for the event are fourfold:

1. To make the JUNO Awards broadcast the most watched entertainment event in Canada
2. To generate excitement and awareness in each host city while also promoting the location
3. To drive awareness and build the celebrity status of nominees and winners
4. To foster Canadian pride for this national and cultural tradition

In order to meet these objectives and gain media coverage, HCC launches an ambitious media relations plan each year. Over 200 Juno nominees are announced at a press conference that draws more than 100 media outlets. After the press conference, HCC sends out "hometown hero" releases to the hometowns of each nominee announcing the nominations. HCC also works with each record label and artist to pitch stories to fashion and lifestyle editors leading up to the awards. In addition to attracting the interest of the media, HCC works to engage the community where the Junos are hosted by reaching out to key organizations such as the board of trade and local universities.

For the awards event, HCC creates two backstage media centres for reporters to enable live coverage. A Q&A stage is also constructed so that winners can answer questions from reporters after receiving their awards. Needless to say, the on-site media logistics for the Junos requires months of planning. This preshow planning includes designing the photo pits, planning crisis communications, training volunteers, and writing and distributing press releases.

All these efforts pay dividends for the Canadian music industry by increasing national and international media coverage and sales. The Junos have such a powerful effect on awareness and sales for Canadian artists that in 2010, after winning New Artist of the Year, Drake saw his album sales almost double. The Junos also help drive tourism and spending in the host cities. Finally, and perhaps most importantly, the public relations efforts around the Junos help foster a sense of pride among Canadians for our nation and our homegrown talent.

Well-planned and expertly executed special events can be a powerful PR tactic to meet an organization's communications and business objectives. The Junos are an excellent example of this. They have been instrumental in putting Canadian music on the map and driving sales. Events can provide great exposure for organizations, and PR practitioners who specialize in events can make it look easy, but do not be fooled—event planning is hard work that can involve long hours and a high amount of risk. The opening vignette illustrates the enormous amount of work that is involved in managing events and the media relations surrounding them. Imagine what it takes to put on the series of events that the Junos encompass. Putting on an event of this scale requires a large team and a sizable budget. These types of events can also be risky. What happens if there is a snowstorm and the performers are unable to get to the venue? What happens if there is a power outage? When putting on a special event, organizers need to consider every small detail and prepare contingency plans.

Not every event a PR practitioner plans is as massive or as prominent as the Junos. Other examples of the kinds of special events that a PR practitioner may be involved in organizing and managing include the following:

- The launch of a seasonal clothing collection for a major retailer such as Winners
- A booth at a business-to-business electronics trade show such as EPTECH to target industry professionals like engineers
- A dinner and wine-tasting fundraiser for the nonprofit organization the Children's Wish Foundation
- A media conference during an issue or crisis, or to announce a new product launch
- Media relations for a community festival such as the Winnipeg International Children's Festival
- A Christmas gala for employees
- A President's Choice travelling barbecue sampling truck

A special event is one of PR's most attention-grabbing tactics and a great way for companies to interact with their stakeholders. However, no event should be rushed into. PR practitioners always need to assess whether an event will meet their PR objectives. As we mentioned previously, events are a big investment of time and money, and PR practitioners must make sure that an event is the right tactic for their organization.

In some cases, PR practitioners are in charge of all the details of organizing the event, in addition to conducting the media relations to publicize the event. In other cases, practitioners focus on the event promotions and media relations, while event planners do the rest. When the rock band Nickelback conducted their world tour, a PR agency handled all media relations, including the distribution of a media release in Canada to announce the tour, the concert locations, and the date that tickets would go on sale.[1] Teams of PR practitioners also work in-house conducting media relations and social media relations at film festivals such as the Toronto International Film Festival and the Vancouver International Film Festival.

In this chapter we will begin by examining why an understanding of event planning is imperative for public relations practitioners and the various types of events they may be called upon to plan. We will then look at special event management in three sections: pre-event (the plan), event day (execution), and post-event (evaluation and debriefings). Finally, we will look at promoting special events through media relations and social media relations.

Types of Special Events ❶

While almost everyone has planned an event during their lives, whether a birthday party, a baby shower, or a wedding, it takes experience and a special skill set to plan an event professionally. PR practitioners who plan events are organized, detail-oriented problem-solvers. Consider all the details that went into organizing the Junos media events. The HCC team is passionate about making sure hundreds of small details add up to an outstanding event.

It is not uncommon for students to decide to enter the field of PR because of their interest in planning events. While some professionals focus exclusively on special event planning, almost all public relations practitioners will have to plan an event at some point during their careers. This event might be a stunt, a press conference, a community event, or an awards ceremony. However, there is a difference between a PR person and a professional event planner; for the PR practitioner, a special event is only one tactic among many options. The PR practitioner must use his or her judgment to decide if the tactic is the right one to deliver on the goals of the organization. The PR practitioner brings strategic planning skills to the task.

A good example of the strategic thinking that PR practitioners can provide for events is illustrated by the team in charge of raising awareness of Purolator's status as an Olympic sponsor. The public relations team organized an official announcement at an event for more than 100 employees that was hosted by the Purolator president and featured Olympic athletes and the Olympic mascots.[2]

It cannot be overstated how important it is for all PR practitioners to be familiar with the fundamentals of organizing events. Even those practitioners who do not want to be event planners will invariably be asked to take part in some form of event planning and execution at some point in their careers. Special events help organizations meet their objectives. In the opening vignette, we noted that the Junos were created to help the Canadian Academy of Recording Arts and Sciences meet its objectives of promoting Canadian music and raising awareness of Canadian artists, and to help drive sales of their music.

While the term *special event* may bring to mind such things as media conferences and galas, in reality many events are low-key and even corporate in nature. These include trade shows, presentations, and annual general meetings. The type and size of event is chosen based on an organization's specific objectives and budget.

Melany Chretien is the communications officer for the municipal government of Russell, near Ottawa. As part of an ongoing community relations program, she plans and executes a variety of events, including new building launches, fundraisers for community groups, and civic events.[3] Like Melany, PR practitioners may be asked to work on or organize a plethora of events varying in size and formality. These events range from modest corporate functions, such as employee-training sessions, to glitzy hospital galas. To help illustrate this point, we will devote the first part of this section to defining the various types of important events PR practitioners may be involved in. The scope of this chapter is not large enough to encompass all PR events; therefore, we will provide an overview of the key ones: media events, conventions and trade shows, product launches, awards programs, political events, civic or community events, tournaments, fundraisers, street teams, internal events, and other events.

MEDIA EVENTS

Some events are organized exclusively for journalists to generate media coverage, and to network and build relationships with reporters and editors. These events can include media conferences, such as the one described in the opening vignette, which is organized every year to announce the Junos nominees and is attended by over 100 media outlets. A news conference is typically held when an organization has an important announcement that it wants all interested media to hear at once and when the organization believes there will be questions the media will want answered. When planning a news conference, think of how it will appear in the different types of media. Could you have a backdrop with your logo that would appear in broadcast media? Does the venue provide optimal sound for radio? What will photographers take photos of that would identify your brand?

Another type of media event is one that provides journalists exclusive access to a new product launch before it goes public. An example of this type of event is organized by Future Shop. The electronics retailer sometimes invites journalists and bloggers to receive advance previews of new product launches. Future Shop called one of these events "Future Shop Media Mobile Speed Dating." At this event, journalists were introduced to several of the retailer's new mobile devices.[4] For more information on media events, see Chapter 6.

CONVENTIONS AND TRADE SHOWS

Conventions are industry events where organizations host booths to help educate attendees. PR practitioners may organize conventions for their organizations or participate in industry ones. They may also attempt to secure speaking engagements at conventions for key spokespersons or company CEOs.

Like conventions, trade shows are a great place for public relations professionals to make connections with customers, suppliers, and trade media. **Trade shows** are mostly business-to-business events where companies display their products or services, meaning that the end customer usually does not attend. For example, at the Canadian Health and Food Association (CHFA) trade show that is held every year in three cities (Toronto, Vancouver, and Montreal), companies that produce food or health products create booths that retailers such as Safeway and Loblaws can visit to learn more about the products. Other examples of popular trade shows include Toronto's Property Management Exhibition and the Franchise Show in Montreal. **Consumer-facing** shows, or shows that the end consumer attends, include Winnipeg's Wellness Show and Victoria's Total Health Show.

The role of a PR professional at a trade show could include planning and managing the booth, liaising with the show's organizers, setting up media interviews, and stocking the media room with media materials. A trade show is a great opportunity to meet with new and existing clients, as well as to make a good impression with the media. Since many industry-specific media attend trade shows, PR practitioners will want to ensure their booth stands out from the others. Often PR practitioners will contact reporters on the trade show's media list prior to the show to let them know their booth number and to arrange interviews with their spokespersons.

PRODUCT LAUNCHES

A new product launch can be an exciting reason to throw an event that will attract the attention of the media and of key target audiences. As we noted in Chapter 5, immediacy, or when something is considered new, is an important news value that PR practitioners should use as best they can. When deciding whether or not to throw an event for a product launch, the PR practitioner must evaluate how newsworthy the launch is. Is the product revolutionary, or is it just a simple line extension? Also, some products tend to be naturally more exciting than others. Apple has no problem getting media coverage of each new iPhone launch, whereas it may be difficult to get coverage for the launch of a new flavour of granola bar or a new type of soap. Often fashion designers will host a fashion show for the media and clients to attend when they launch a new collection.

Fashion collections are launched with special events attended by the media and important customers.
Source: © LAN/Corbis

When Obakki, a popular Canadian clothing designer, launched a fall/winter collection, it organized a fashion show in a beautiful church lit by candlelight.[5]

AWARDS PROGRAMS

As we saw in the opening vignette on the Junos, an awards program can involve managing a series of events, such as a media conference, a red carpet, and exclusive galas. Some associations throw awards events to recognize their members and to gain media coverage. The East Coast Music Awards and Conference, held in different locations in the eastern provinces every year, not only aims to raise awareness of regional musicians but also offers professional workshops.[6] Some popular public relations awards programs include CPRS National Awards of Excellence and IABC's Gold Quill Awards.

POLITICAL EVENTS

Political events can include rallies, fundraisers, press conferences, and debates. Political events may have different objectives, such as raising money, increasing a candidate's profile, or generating media coverage. An example of a political event is municipal party Vision Vancouver's booth at Car-Free Day Vancouver, an event during which streets in

Quebec City's Winter Carnival draws media and tourists to the city each year.
Source: CARNAVAL DE QUEBEC/ Newscom

Carnaval de Québec, Xavier Dachez

Vancouver are closed to traffic and mini street festivals are held in various neighbourhoods. Having a booth allowed Vision Vancouver's elected officials to meet their constituents and demonstrate the party's commitment to the environment.[7]

CIVIC OR COMMUNITY EVENTS

Civic or community events such as parades and festivals can become signature events for a city, attracting tourists and benefiting local businesses. Examples of large community events are Winterlude in Ottawa, Winter Carnival in Quebec City, and the annual Pride Parade in Toronto. Toronto's Pride Parade is the largest of its kind in North America. Every year a large number of tourists arrive in Toronto to take part in the parade, raising the city's international profile. A team of PR practitioners ensures that the festival receives the maximum amount of media coverage.[8]

TOURNAMENTS

Tournaments are important PR events for the sports community and often involve corporate sponsorship by companies hoping to raise their profile through a halo effect from that sport. For example, the RBC Canadian Open, a golf tournament, is sponsored by RBC. Golf Canada employs a dedicated PR practitioner who helps raise the sport's profile at events such as this.[9]

FUNDRAISERS

Fundraising events can be a great way to raise funds for and promote deserving charities. A fundraiser can also raise the profile of and build goodwill for the organization throwing the event. Each year firefighters host the Bright Nights lights display in Vancouver's Stanley Park to raise money for burn victims. The PR team hired by the firefighters organizes a launch party the night before the festival is open to the public and coordinates media relations.

Another good example is the fundraising campaign that the communications team at the Alberta Legislative Assembly conducted for the United Way. The team planned a series of events and other tactics that included a bagel breakfast and a Thanksgiving bake sale. They also developed a cookbook, *What's Cooking in the House*, with recipes provided by MLAs, caucus staff, and employees, that was sold to raise additional funds.

Street teams take to the streets to promote a product or cause.
Source: Michael Loccisano/Getty Images

STREET TEAMS

Street Teams are groups of employees or volunteers who go out into busy or popular streets to help promote a product or cause. You often see street teams on busy streets, such as Queen Street West in Toronto, Robson Street in Vancouver, or Government Street in Victoria, handing out products such as gum or sodas for companies. Mini Canada used street teams for its 2011 holiday campaign, sending out eight elves and three gift-wrapped Minis onto Toronto's streets. A Facebook contest was also launched where consumers could virtually see how many people they could fit into a Mini.[10]

INTERNAL EVENTS

Some events are conducted to meet an organization's objectives for internal target audiences such as employees or shareholders. These objectives might include rewarding employees for a successful year, team building, increasing morale, enhancing employee skills, and so on. Christmas parties and training sessions are examples of internal events. The communications coordinator for the OpenRoad Auto Group organized a Christmas gala for employees that featured an American Idol–type contest. Employees auditioned in the months before the event, and a video of the auditions was shown during the dinner. The finalists then performed live and a winner was selected. This event proved popular with employees, as everyone cheered for their favourite "Idol." See Chapter 9 for more information on internal communications.

Staying on Top of Event Trends

- By their very nature, trends are always changing, and it is important to stay on top of them when organizing events. Get to know what is hot, new, and exiting so that you can organize standout events incorporating these trends.

- Consider trends in all aspects of planning your event, from the venue to the decorations, entertainment, cocktails, and food. Southeast Asian ingredients and ethically produced food are hot right now in the culinary world, while trendy colour palettes include metallics and neons.

- Apply the trends that you see around you in various fields, such as fashion and music, to special event planning. One event planner says, "We follow trends and forecasts from the fashion, automotive, paint, and furniture industries, to name a few."[11]

- Incorporate trends in technology to transform special events. As they become better, cheaper, and easier to use, new technologies are increasingly being used in planning and executing events—e.g., online registration or ticketing tools, mobile apps for meetings, iPads and tablets, and HD video for speakers presenting remotely via Skype.[12]

- Go with the greening trend in planning your event. Environment Canada, for example, has a green meeting guide. A green meeting ensures that all aspects of an event, including its location, food services, transportation, and the provision of materials, are approached with pollution prevention in mind in order to reduce its environmental impact.[13]

ANNUAL GENERAL MEETINGS

PR practitioners involved in investor relations are often responsible for events organized for shareholders, such as the annual general meeting (AGM) and quarterly conference calls. Public companies host an AGM once a year to review the organization's financial performance with shareholders and to elect the board of directors. Business media are often invited to AGMs. See Chapter 12 for more information on investor relations.

OTHER EVENTS

In addition to the types of events described in this section, a PR team might be involved with a variety of other events. Some special events fall under several event categories—for example, the Politics and the Pen annual gala in Ottawa, an

Ottawa's annual Politics and the Pen gala is an annual award ceremony and fundraiser.

Source: The Writer's Trust of Canada

award ceremony and fundraiser for the Writers' Trust of Canada. This event is sold out months in advance and is a must-attend for politicians, writers, and leaders in the arts and business communities. It features high-profile political or artistic hosts—one year it was co-hosted by the American ambassador to Canada and the Canadian ambassador to the United States. At the gala, a prize is given out for Canada's best political writing. The event has a host of sponsors, such as Bell and CIBC, as well as media sponsors such as *The Globe and Mail*.[14]

Pre-event: Creating an Event Plan ❷

Now that we have examined the types of events that a PR practitioner may be called upon to organize, we will focus our attention on how to organize the events. We have broken down this process into three sections: the pre-event, when the event plan is drafted; the execution of the event on the day of; and the post-event, when evaluation and debriefings take place. Let us look first at pre-event plans.

While it can be tempting to dive right into the details of an event, the most important stage is planning. By committing your thoughts to paper in the form of an event plan, you will ensure that you do not waste time or money going in a direction that does not match your overall vision. Taking the time to create an event plan will ensure that you think through your audience, budget, and resources to avoid wasting time and energy. It will also allow you to get buy-in from your clients or managers. It is important that they understand and are aligned with your thinking with regards to the size, scope, and budget of the event.

An event plan includes many of the components of a PR plan but is tailored to a special event. (For more information on a PR plan, see Chapter 4.) Like a PR plan, an event plan needs to be strategic and include some key components. Once these elements are planned, you get to have fun, be creative, and see how you can bring magic to your event to make it memorable. The key components of an event plan include:

- Target audiences
- Objectives
- Event outline
- Event logistics
- Budget
- Measurement
- Issues management

Figure 10.1 The Flow from Objectives to Tasks in the Event Plan

The target audience and objectives of an event drive the strategy of the event, which makes up the event outline. The strategy of the event then drives the tactics and tasks of the event, which determine the event logistics. Figure 10.1 shows the flow from objectives to tasks. Let us now look at each component of the event plan in turn.

TARGET AUDIENCES

When Birks wanted to attract the Italian community to its stores and increase jewellery sales to this target audience, it organized a special Italian Night. All the evening's elements were customized for the Italian community, including catering by a leading Italian chef and a fundraiser for the local opera company. Additionally, Birks conducted research to find a key influencer within the Italian community, choosing a high-profile philanthropist to emcee the event. Birks' efforts to attract this potential consumer audience is a great example of audience targeting.

Defining your target audiences ensures that the events you are planning will be of interest to the specific groups you are hoping to attract. It this case, target audiences will be your potential guests. The number of guests can range from just a handful of people at an internal event to hundreds of delegates and journalists at a conference. A target audience might be broad, for example, Canadian moms, or very specific or niche, such as Calgary Shar-Pei dog owners.

Once you decide on your target audience, you will be catering the special event to them. That includes all details such as the type of event, the location, and the timing to accommodate their schedules. An evening event might work for office-working professionals but not for people in the service or restaurant industry. If your event is targeting families, you might have a lower response if you host it over spring break, when many families travel out of town. In the opening vignette on the Junos, the target audiences of several of the events were journalists, so these events were tailored to accommodate their needs and schedules, including setting up media centres and the media conference.

OBJECTIVES

The reasons to host an event are varied. However, in the event plan you want to be specific about the goals of the event and how they will be measured. If the goal is to raise money for charity, how much would you like to raise? If the goal is to increase customer loyalty, what does that look like? Will you measure goal achievement through a survey or by increased sales? Some other reasons you might have to host an event are to:

- Motivate employees
- Increase your network
- Attract new customers
- Attract members, volunteers, or visitors
- Mark a milestone
- Educate
- Obtain media coverage
- Show appreciation to employees, volunteers, or customers

As discussed in Chapter 4, your objectives should follow the SMART principles of being specific, measurable, achievable, relevant, and time bound.[15] This means that they should be detailed and clear, have a measurable component, be relevant, and have a specific deadline. For example, an objective might be "To host a media conference on January 5 at 2 p.m. that is attended by ten editors and five bloggers. The media conference will also generate three media mentions following the event."

In the opening vignette on the Junos, we saw that the objectives of the media relations campaign surrounding the awards ceremony was fourfold: to make the Juno Awards concert broadcast the most highly watched entertainment event in Canada; to create excitement, awareness, and profile for each host city visited and the Juno events taking place there; to drive awareness and build celebrity status for Juno nominees and winners; and to engender Canadian pride for this national cultural tradition.

EVENT OUTLINE

The event outline is where you get to be creative and come up with the magic—it is where you get to decide what happens at your event. The most important concept in event planning is to create an unforgettable experience for your guests. Ideas are limited only by the imagination of the event planner. First and foremost, you want your guests to enjoy themselves. Remember that you should not base your decision on the kind of event you would like to attend, but on the preferences of your guests. The entire event is tailored to them.

The sky is the limit when it comes to the kinds of events you can execute—literally. You can have your guests dine up in the sky on a platform that is hoisted by crane 50 metres above the ground. American Express Canada organized such an event in Toronto for both card members and the public, called "American Express Presents Dinner in the Sky."

A series of 22 lifts were planned, with some featuring gourmet cuisine and celebrity chefs. In one lift, VIP members dined with the president and CEO of American Express Canada. Other lifts were reserved for traditional media and bloggers. The event resulted in substantial media coverage in many outlets such as *The Globe and Mail*, the *National Post*, Global TV, and *Marketing* magazine. There was even a **live feed** (a live on-location broadcast) from *Breakfast Television*, which broadcast a segment from the top. The event created awareness of American Express and boosted new card member applications.[16]

The event outline includes all the details of your event, including:

Venue: Where will your event be held? Will it be outdoors in a spectacular setting, in a hotel ballroom, at a convention centre, or in an intimate restaurant for just a few guests?

Theme: Will there be a special theme to your event?

Decor: How will the venue be decorated? What kind of look, tone, and atmosphere will you create?

Food: Will there be food? If so, what kind of food will be served? Hors d'oeuvres or a formal five-course menu? What equipment and accessories will be needed? Napkins? Plates? Forks? Extra garbage bins?

Drinks: What alcoholic and/or non-alcoholic beverages will be offered? For the launch of her Toronto boutique, Montreal-based designer Stacey Zhang organized a cocktail party for media, bloggers, and some key influencers such as stylists and models. The event created buzz and generated substantial media coverage in publications such as *Toronto Life* magazine, *Fashion* magazine, and the *Toronto Star* newspaper.[17]

Gifts: Will guests receive anything to take away with them, such as promotional items? Will there be gift bags? Can you find partner companies to donate items to the gift bags?

Speakers: Will anyone make an address, opening remarks, or a **keynote speech** (a speech from a presenter who is the main draw)? If you do not have a speaker for your event but would like one, a **speakers bureau** can assist. This is a roster of speakers who can be hired to give presentations or speeches and emcee events. At the International Conference on War-Affected Children held in Winnipeg, individuals representing several organizations and government bodies made speeches and addresses, including a UNICEF representative.

Entertainment: Will there be music or other kinds of entertainment?

Dress code: How will your guests dress? Is the event black tie, semi-formal, business, or business casual? You may need to inform your guests of the dress code on the invitation. For example, at Cadillac Fairview's annual corporate retreat, employees are asked to wear business casual clothing to their meetings and semi-formal clothing for the evening dinners and parties. Being unclear about dress code expectations can cause an embarrassing situation for your guests. Justin Bieber made headlines and received much criticism when he met with Prime Minister Harper to receive a Diamond Jubilee Medal wearing overalls with one of the straps unbuttoned. Prime Minister Harper later joked on Twitter: "In fairness to @justinbieber, I told him I would be wearing my overalls too."[18]

Charity element: Will there be a charity element to your event? This is a great way to provide an extra incentive for guests to attend and to create goodwill in the community. For example, Birks organized a gala fundraiser to raise funds for Plan Canada's Because I Am a Girl initiative, a program that aims to educate girls throughout the world. The event, held in Birks' flagship store in Montreal, was called A Night for Girls to Shine and was hosted by *e-Talk*'s Sophie Gregoire-Trudeau. Olympian Jenn Heil, an ambassador for the program, gave a speech at the event, which raised $95,000.[19]

Dignitaries: Having a dignitary attend your event is wonderful, as it emphasizes the significance of the event to guests and the media; however, it can add a layer of complexity to planning. Special rules govern how dignitaries should be invited to and addressed and presented at events. For example, a Lieutenant-Governor is always supposed to follow a procession into a room last and attendees should rise for his or her entrance.[20] A Lieutenant-Governor should be addressed as "Your Honour." A mayor of a municipality should be addressed as "Your Worship." Make sure you conduct research to ensure you are following proper protocol. When in doubt, consult the dignitary's aide or assistant. Also, ensure you invite dignitaries at least six months in advance, as they often have very busy schedules.[21]

EVENT LOGISTICS

The next part of the event plan, event logistics, sets out all the important details of the logistics. This includes vendors, venues, staffing, and paperwork.

Vendors

Many event planners use vendors that they know and trust. This is because so much money and time can go into an event that they want to ensure everything is perfect. If the band doesn't show up or the food is subpar, the entire event can be ruined. If you are not going with a vendor you have used in the past, be sure to obtain a minimum of three quotes and ask for references. Look at blogs that describe other events the vendor has supplied to get a sense of how the event turned out.

When you decide to hire a vendor, make sure you are clear in your expectations and on the deliverables. Get everything you agree upon in writing. Also, ask how the vendor would like to be paid. Does the vendor need a deposit? Will you need to have cheques at the event? Does the vendor take cash only?

After the event, remember to thank all your vendors and suppliers by phone or email. If they have done a good job, make sure they know how much you appreciated their hard

Table 10.1	Vendors for Special Events
Vendor	**Services Provided**
Music	Hires DJs, bands, orchestras, singers
Caterer	Provides food and drinks
Talent agency	Books everything from magicians to musicians
Rentals	Supplies equipment such as glasses, cutlery, tables, stages, chairs
Florist	Creates flower arrangements
Decorator	Takes care of the overall look and details of the decor
Bartender	Prepares and serves drinks
Photographer	Takes professional photos of event
Videographer	Takes videos of the event
Valet	Parks cars of attendees
Speakers bureau	Provides a roster of guest speakers available for hire
Audiovisual	Provides equipment such as sound systems and lighting, technical expertise
Gift and favours	Specializes in creating custom items for events
Printer	Creates invitations, banners, or other printed items

work. This will help you build a positive reputation with vendors you might use in the future. Table 10.1 lists the vendors you may need to hire.

Venue

Choosing a venue is an important part of event planning because it will often inform many of your other decisions, such as how many people can attend and what type of entertainment you can accommodate. The type of venue you choose will also play a large role in your guests' experience. Special events can be held everywhere: on beaches, on mountaintops, onboard boats, in restaurants, and at convention centres. Many famous city landmarks and buildings offer rental space, including the CN Tower in Toronto, the Vancouver Aquarium, the Moncton Press Club, and the Winnipeg Art Gallery.

Some of the things to take into consideration are how big a space you need and whether the location is convenient for your guests. Parking is another important consideration. You will want to make sure that your location is close to public transit or that there is ample parking if most guests will need to drive. Noise restrictions are also a consideration. If you are planning to hire a band or a DJ, particularly in a residential area, you should check with the municipality about any noise restrictions in the area.

Some venues, such as hotels and golf courses, are one-stop shops in the sense that they can assist you with a large number of your needs such as catering, staffing, and decor. Others are more like empty shells where you need to independently hire all the vendors that you will need. Usually, these venues offer more unique experiences because you can tailor everything to your client's vision, whereas hotels and golf courses often have set event packages. Going with a location where you hire the vendors yourself can appear cheaper than going with a package, but once you factor everything in that you need to obtain yourself, including licenses and permits, you may find the cost savings are not as significant as you expected.

Staffing

Staffing includes the list of staff, paid and unpaid, that will be needed in order to successfully host the event. Staff can include hosts and hostesses, valet parking attendants, runners, greeters, a set-up and tear-down crew, security, media relations staff, caterers and servers, bartenders, and musicians or other talent.

Sometimes event staffing involves recruiting and managing volunteers. Each year *Vancouver Magazine* hosts its city-wide restaurant awards, for which numerous volunteers are recruited. The RBC Canadian Open golf tournament is another event that requires the recruitment and coordination of hundreds of volunteers every year. Since it is held in a different city each year, the recruitment always begins from scratch.

Contracts, Permits and Other Paperwork

Most people do not realize how much paperwork is involved in an event. In addition to the contracts that you will need to sign with each vendor, you will often need permits if you are going to make a lot of noise, want to have a street team in a public place, or need to block street parking for your valet service. There are also many licences you will need to either acquire yourself or make sure your vendors have, such as Serving It Right and Foodsafe certificates in British Columbia. Depending on how large your event is and the budget, you may want to consider purchasing event insurance, so that you can recoup the costs if the event gets cancelled and so that you are covered if any sort of accident happens at the event. Note that some paperwork will take up to two months for processing, so you must allow yourself plenty of time to get everything done and build this time into your event timelines.

There can be a lot of liaising with the municipal government to find out what you need to do in terms of paperwork. The City of Toronto organizes 30 special events every year, including Winterlicious, a culinary event, in addition to helping hundreds of other organizations put on their events within the city's limits. To make the process smoother, it has created a planning guide for event planners that outlines all the procedures, forms, and applications needed. The guide also answers a host of questions, from "Can I close a city road for my event?" to "Can I serve alcohol?"[22]

BUDGET

It is essential to have a clear understanding of the potential costs associated with the event you are planning to execute. As the event planner, you are responsible for researching and tallying every expense, from the price of bottles of wine to the cost of nametags. Every detail, no matter how minuscule, has a cost attached.

Sticking to a budget when planning an event can be hard. Just like guest lists, budgets tend to balloon before you realize what is happening. One or two things may cost a bit more than you planned, or you may need to purchase a couple of items that you did not anticipate. All these small extra expenses start to add up quickly.

You need to get estimates from all the vendors. When coming up with a realistic budget, it helps to start by asking some of your larger vendors for quotes. If you work for a PR agency, you will also need to include a fees estimate for the agency's time. Once you have tallied all expenses and created a budget, you need to examine it to see whether it is reasonable and doable for your organization or client. It might be a fabulous idea to have a celebrity perform at the event, but can you afford it? You may need to go back to the drawing board and find ways to cut costs. For instance, can you find a cheaper supplier or do something in-house instead of contracting out? The total costs should be compared to the potential payback of what will make this a meaningful business investment for your organization or client. Table 10.2 provides a budget example for a special event with 100

Table 10.2	Budget Example: Fresh Tracks Launch
Item	**Cost**
Printing invitations (travel postcards)	$850
Invitation design	$360
Postage of invitations	$542
Liquor licence	$10
Rentals (linens, glasses, napkins)	$625
Catering (appetizer platters)	$1500
Wine	$1040
Beer	$140
Juice	$60
Servers	$500
Entertainment (band)	$450
Flowers	$275
Decorations	$175
TOTAL:	$6527

Estimate Gathering

Once you have written your event plan, it should be clear whom you need to gather estimates from when planning the budget.

First, check with your venue to see what they provide and related costs—there is a lot to be said for one-stop shopping. Selecting a venue that offers many related services such as audiovisuals and catering may keep your costs down.

Next, gather two or three estimates from competitive suppliers. If you have trusted suppliers already, you may be able to negotiate better prices once you have received a few other quotes.

If you are new, make it clear you are looking to create a long-term relationship with a vendor. You also may be able to negotiate a discount. Some vendors have nonprofit rates if your organization or client is a charity. If your event is a fundraiser, you may even be able to get some services donated.

Be sure to be very clear on what it is you want from suppliers, put it in writing, trust their expertise, and sign contracts that are clear in responsibilities and costs—the last thing you want is a supplier who is not clear on what you expect or who charges you extra for items you thought were included.

Remember that sometimes the cheapest supplier is not always the best one. As the old adage says, you get what you pay for. It is very important to have suppliers you can rely on should any crises arise. A good supplier understands the nature of the events industry and the need to sometimes act immediately and ask questions later.

guests for the launch of the travel agency Fresh Tracks. The event had an international travel theme with world music and food from different countries.

MEASUREMENT

The last decade has seen increasing sophistication in the events industry. It is vital in today's business environment that events be meaningful. This means that there should be measureable objectives tied to the events. Key metrics might include the number of attendees, the money raised for a charity, or ratings on satisfaction surveys. While it is important to measure the success of an event, PR practitioners also need to manage the expectations of their clients or organization. It is sometimes necessary to bring them back to earth with regards to their expectations. No matter how amazing the organizer, one event cannot be relied upon to meet the year's sales quota, change public opinion in one go, increase awareness by 100 per cent, motivate each and every employee, and provide scores of new business contacts. However, a successful event can help set an organization on the right path to achieving these objectives.

An event plan must also include information on how you will judge your event after it has been held. This decision must be agreed upon by the PR practitioner and the manager or client. We will go over some of the specific ways in which events are measured later in this chapter.

ISSUES MANAGEMENT

Your plan must also address any eventualities that may occur during the event. Though many crises can be prevented through careful planning, a savvy event planner knows there is always the possibility that something could go wrong. In 2010, during the Queen's visit to Canada, a massive power outage struck Toronto two hours before a state dinner was to be hosted at the Royal York hotel for the Queen and Prince Philip by the prime minister, leaving the event planners scrambling.[23] While pre-planning can help ensure that an event proceeds smoothly, a PR practitioner must always be prepared for the worst-case scenario. What if the keynote speaker doesn't show up? What if a guest injures herself? What if there is a power outage or a fire? Always think through what might happen and have a contingency plan. In the case of the Queen's dinner, it was decided that the event would proceed using the hotel's backup power to light the room as much as possible and cook the food.[24]

Even practitioners who have seen it all cannot always predict what will take place. At a 2011 Grey Cup luncheon in Vancouver, a fistfight broke out between two Canadian Football League legends and former rivals, Angelo Mosca and Joe Knapp. Both men were in their early 70s; one of them was in a wheelchair and the other used a cane.[25] Shocked organizers rushed to break up the fight. At least no one can say event planning is boring!

Thinking Like a PR Practitioner

1. Explain why creating an event plan helps deliver a successful event.
2. You have been hired to organize an exclusive gala for important dignitaries. List three ways you can help avoid a crisis at the event.

The Day of the Event: Execution ❸

You have spent countless hours planning the event, and then suddenly the big day arrives. This is when you go from planning to execution. Now is the time for action. As the event planner, you must provide guidance and leadership, and be prepared to deal with any eventuality. You are the first to arrive and the last to leave. It is your responsibility to make sure that everything goes smoothly, and to do that, you must be on-site. You will also have to take care of a myriad of last-minute details.

Some details to consider the day of the event include the following:

■ Bring a change of clothes. If you are setting up all day your clothes may get dirty.

■ Make sure you are reachable at all times via phone, text, and, if it is a large venue, a two-way radio. Bring a cellphone charger just in case.

- Show professionalism. You are working the event—you are not a guest. Remember that you are being paid and must remain professional; some planners will never drink alcohol at an event until everything is completely wrapped up. Also, do not get in the event pictures, especially ones being taken by the media. Let your client or your CEO be in the spotlight. It is your job to make him or her look good.

- Provide leadership. Ensure that all players fulfill their contracts. You are the leader on the day of the event, and it is your job to provide clear expectations and leadership to all vendors, staff members, and volunteers.

- Remember that a smile will reassure both yourself and those who are helping you. Never look like you are panicking, no matter what happens. You must look confident and in control at all times. Things will go wrong behind the scenes—they almost always do—but if you stay calm and professional, you will be able to solve any problem that arises without your guests noticing.

- Try to have delegated to the point that you are free to hand-hold or direct others during a crisis—you cannot be stuck at the coat check or in the kitchen helping with the catering.

- Do a walk-through with all the players beforehand at a team meeting. You must rehearse to make sure that everyone is on the same page. Just as there is a sound check before a concert, a dry run of any technical aspects of the event (lighting changes, sound checks, computer shows, presentations, entertainment, etc.) is essential.

- Be prepared to hold your client's or manager's hand. The nicest people can become stressed once on-site at an event, mostly because they may have a bigger stake in this than you.

- Allow time for your spokesperson or speaker to go over his or her speaking notes with you. Always have an extra set with you just in case.

- Be approachable. It is important that you be available for everyone to communicate with. Once you have identified a problem, find someone else to deal with it so that you can talk to the next concerned client or guest. You can rectify errors only if you know about them. In his book *Special Events*, Dr. Joe Goldblatt describes walking the room and talking to guests to find out how the event is going: "If you were to attend any banquet where I am responsible for the event, you might be surprised to see me wandering from table to table and asking guests how they are enjoying dinner. In doing this, I am able to uncover any gaps in execution of the plan."[26]

- When you book your suppliers, ensure they will provide you with qualified personnel on-site to operate the equipment. If your supplier is hired for set-up of only one small component, do not let the staff leave until you are 110 per cent certain that you do not need them anymore—better to pay them extra than end up trying to operate the machinery yourself.

The day of the event will fly by and before you know it, you will be cleaning up. Try to take a moment during the event to take a deep breath, look around the room, and take in how wonderful it is. You have worked hard and should take a small, private moment to celebrate before it is all over.

Fawn Mulcahy is a PR practitioner with expertise gained working both in-house and in PR agencies. She has a wealth of experience organizing events across Canada, from Halifax to Victoria, and in Los Angeles, Las Vegas, London, Davos, and Moscow. She recommends the following when it comes to event execution:

> Be as organized as possible with timelines, supplier lists, speaking notes, etc. If you are as organized as possible, and have everything planned down to the last minute, then you will have capacity for the one thing that will invariably go wrong. If you are organized, then the thing that goes wrong won't overwhelm you.
>
> Something will always go wrong on the day of the event, but it's up to you to be the "calm in the face of the storm" and handle the challenges with grace. Never, ever freak out!
>
> The best thing that you can do to avoid the pitfalls of events is to work with trusted suppliers as partners and let them do their job as they know best. Pay them fair market value for their expertise, keep them apprised of any changes or special needs, and then step back and let them do their magic. Let your audiovisual partner worry about the sound system; it can give you the capacity to focus on the areas of importance, like the guest experience.[27]

ADVICE TO NEW PRACTITIONERS

Event Itinerary and Vendor List

On the day of the event you need to have all necessary information at your fingertips. It must be printed out for easy access and distribution. The first must-have document is a vendor list that includes all of the contact information of every vendor that is participating in the event. This document will also include all other important contacts such as clients or emergency contacts.

Part of your planning will include a very detailed event itinerary. This will outline not only what happens at the event, but also what needs to happen prior to and following the event in order for it to be executed properly. The itinerary should be given to all vendors to ensure everyone understands the day's timeline and so there is no confusion.

Here is an example:
8:30 a.m.: PR practitioner arrives
9:00 a.m.: Staff arrives
9:45 a.m.: Audiovisuals arrive and set up
10:00 a.m.: Caterers arrive and set up
    Rentals arrive and set up
10:30 a.m.: Sound check
11:00 a.m.: Florist arrives
12:00 p.m.: Guests arrive
    Drinks are served
    Guests mingle
12:30 p.m.: Speech begins
12:45 p.m.: Speech ends
    Lunch starts
1:45 p.m.: Lunch ends
2:00 p.m.: Guests depart
    Tear down
4:00 p.m.: PR practitioner leaves

Post-event: Evaluation and Debriefings ④

Following any event, no matter how big or small, it is time to both evaluate the event and debrief with your event team. As we saw in Chapter 1, evaluation and measurement are instrumental in PR today. Special events take time and money to stage, and organizations want to know whether the event was worth the resources. PR practitioners must take the time to evaluate whether it was a success and if it met objectives. It is important to look at the event using the measurement criteria you and your client or manager have set for the event and included in your special events plan. Some of the ways that special events are measured include the following.

GUEST ENJOYMENT FACTOR

Most often, the main goal of any event is for guests to enjoy the experience, making this is an important point of evaluation. This is where you analyze the comments and anecdotes that you collected from guests during the event. Surveys are also used following the event as a more formal evaluation method to assess the satisfaction level of guests. The surveys can be given immediately after the event, or as a follow-up via telephone, email, or mail.[28] A great free tool that you can use for a fast and easy survey is SurveyMonkey. If you are going to follow up after an event, you should not wait more than a couple of days to execute the survey as guests will begin to forget important details.

ATTENDANCE

Attendance measurement is an assessment of the number of people who attended the event, and whether they were the right target audience. While everyone likes to see a large turnout for their event, often the right audience is more important than the number of attendees.

SALES

Sales at the event and following the event can also be metrics for special events. The Birks Italian Night that we examined earlier in this chapter was measured in part by attendance and in part by sales. The cash registers were open for business that night. If sales are a measurement of success, then targets should be set prior to the event. In the case of the Junos that we examined in the opening vignette, one of the measurement tools is sales of Canadian music following the event.

FUNDRAISING RESULTS

The amount of money raised by ticket sales and other fundraising activities at the event, such as a silent auction, is the main objective of a fundraiser event. The Birks event also had a fundraising element for the local opera. Guests were encouraged to buy keys that could open a vault to win a piece of jewellery. All those funds went to the opera and success was measured by the donations raised.

VOLUNTEER RECRUITMENT AND RETENTION

The number and expertise of volunteers recruited at an event can also be a measurement tool. Other events look to keep their volunteers happy and are organized as volunteer appreciation events. Metrics for volunteer retention would be assessed in the months or year following the event.

PRACTITIONER INTERVIEW

Debra Goldblatt-Sadowski, on SPiN Toronto

Debra Goldblatt-Sadowski is the president of publicity and promotions at rock-it promotions, a public relations agency that specializes in special event management and celebrity outreach. rock-it was hired to organize SPiN Toronto's launch event. SPiN Toronto is a Ping-Pong social club that is co-owned by the Academy Award–winning actor Susan Sarandon. The event was a media relations success and was attended by CTV, CBC, *ET Canada*, the *National Post*, and *The Globe and Mail*.

Question: Did you organize the event or focus on the PR?

Answer: We had a hand in planning the event, but our main initiative was the PR. We were also responsible for sending out the invite, managing all guest lists, RSVPs, and more.

Question: What challenges did you face?

Answer: Coordinating flight and hotel logistics for some of the guests that we brought in from Los Angeles and New York proved challenging, as there were several last-minute changes. However, every event and client has challenges. The key is to stay organized and calm and to roll with the punches.

Question: Who were the guests?

Answer: This was a combination of media, actors, athletes, and influencers. Everyone from members of the Toronto Argonauts to Judd Nelson [actor, *The Breakfast Club*] and actors from *Degrassi: The Next Generation* were in attendance, along with major national newspaper, online, and broadcast outlets.

Question: What kind of invitations did you issue?

Answer: We use an online program called MailChimp to format and distribute invitations. We create a custom invite list for each client. We distribute the invitation approximately two weeks prior to an event. We allow people to receive the invite and then we follow up personally via email and phone.

Question: How long of a lead time did you have?

Answer: We've worked with SPiN Toronto since their inception. We hosted a pre-party at an outside venue to gain some buzz and give people a sense of what to expect. The soft opening followed with the official launch party.

(Continued)

Debra Goldblatt-Sadowski, on SPiN Toronto

Question: What did the event feature?

Answer: Four special guests were flown in for the event including table tennis champion Soo Yeon Lee and Ping-Pong pros Wally Green and Kazuyuki Yokoyama. The New York founders were all in attendance, as well as partner Susan Sarandon. There were featured drinks including a signature rum punch, and selected items from the menu were served including mini grilled cheeses, BBQ popcorn, devilled eggs, mini tacos, and oven-baked pretzels.

Question: Was Susan Sarandon a big draw for journalists?

Answer: Inevitably an Academy Award–winning actor is going to be a lure for both media and partygoers. We also offered interviews to select media outlets—a combination of print, online, and broadcast—with Susan prior to the party at the venue.

Question: What were the results? What did you consider success?

Answer: Our efforts produced over 50 million impressions with over 100 pieces of media coverage in print, online, and broadcast. Definitely a success and we continue to build on results on a weekly basis.

Susan Sarandon at SPiN Toronto.
Source: BFA/SIPA/Newscom

MEDIA COVERAGE

While we saw in the interview on SPiN Toronto that the PR agency measured the event's success in media impressions, generally media coverage is a secondary goal for an event. It is definitely a nice added benefit but is usually not the primary goal, unless the occasion is a media event. If media coverage is an important objective you will need to think about accommodating reporters' schedules. For example, because many TV news stations reduce their camera numbers on the weekend, it can be hard to get TV coverage unless you shoot B-roll and send it to the stations following the event (we will discuss B-roll at the end of the chapter).

DEBRIEFINGS AND SHOWING APPRECIATION

It is important to hold a **debriefing session** with your team as close to the end of the event as possible—within a couple of days to allow the experience to settle in yet not enough time for important details to be forgotten. Small issues that may have been frustrating on the day of the event but are insignificant when looking at the larger picture can be put into perspective—this way they may be mentioned but with a calm head. While in the debriefing session, it is important to remember that during an event everyone is under stress and so should be shown some understanding. The debrief should not be used to blame others or to complain about the client or vendors. Instead, the debrief should focus on celebrating success and learning from any mistakes. During the debrief it is important to emphasize that you are holding the meeting in order to improve the next event, not to place blame.[29]

To learn from each event, keep detailed records of what took place. Ask the vendors on-site how it went, if there were any problems and how they could have been avoided, and what could be done better in the future.

ADVICE TO NEW PRACTITIONERS

Event Kits

- As the event planner, you must be prepared for all eventualities. Consider creating an event kit. An event kit is a box filled with all the items that may come in handy. An event kit may help you out of more than one bind.

- Event planners each have their own can't-do-without items, but some common ones include:

Band-Aids, duct tape, masking tape, crazy glue, scissors, a stapler, staples, pens (include thick felts, coloured felts, highlighters, regular ball points), string, twine, monster clips, paper clips, bottled water, power bars, nylons, Tylenol, throat lozenges, first-aid kit, flashlight, screwdriver, set/multiple head screwdriver, small hammer, flats, smartphone recharger, USB key

PR practitioners often go through an evaluation form at the post-event meeting. The form is customized for the event but generally covers the topics of how well the venue suited the event and whether guests enjoyed themselves.

The final step in any event is to show appreciation for everyone who was involved. Never forget to recognize your staff, volunteers, and suppliers with thank-you notes. Not only is it just the right thing to do, but it strategically ensures that your team feels appreciated and will make an extra effort the next time around.

Special Event PR ⑤

Planning and executing an event are only part of the battle. The special event also needs PR to get the word out to target audiences that it is happening, to secure attendance, and to meet other objectives such as raising awareness of your organization or product. No matter how great the event, if audiences do not know about it, they won't attend.

PR practitioners have a real advantage over other event planners because they know how to organize the special event and are also able conduct the event PR. There are many tactics that can be employed in event PR. We will go over some of the most commonly used ones in this section.

MEDIA RELATIONS

Think again of the Junos and the media conference that is organized to announce nominees. It is attended by over 100 media outlets. This conference is organized to raise awareness of the upcoming Junos and to promote the nominees. In cases such as this, the PR team wants to secure results prior to the event itself. The goal can be to sell tickets or encourage others to attend or watch the event on TV. This is the case with event listings (see below). In other cases, the objective is to get the media to attend the event itself in order to cover the event or announcement. The Junos PR aimed to do this as well.

Media Advisories

The first key to getting media to attend your event it to let them know it is happening. One of the best ways to do this is through a media advisory. A **media advisory** is a combination of a media release and an invitation. It is formatted much like a release, as outlined in Chapter 5, but explicitly lists the details of the event, including time, date, location, address, directions, parking information, any guest speakers, and any interview opportunities, and it notes whether the media need to RSVP to receive a press pass or to be put on the media list (see Figure 10.2). The purpose of the media advisory is to persuade the media that an event is worth covering and to give them all the information they require to make attending the event easy and stress free.

Health Council of Canada
Conseil canadien de la santé

Media Advisory

For Immediate Release

Health Council of Canada to release progress report on health care renewal in Canada

What: Federal, provincial and territorial governments continue to make efforts to reform our health system. The Health Council of Canada reports on the progress they have made. Council Chair, Dr. Jack Kitts, will reveal Canada's current status on home and community care, health human resources, telehealth, access to care in the North, and health indicators.

Progress Report 2012: Health care renewal in Canada, the Health Council of Canada's newest report coming June 4, 2012 will inform Canadians of what governments are doing to fulfill the commitments made, and what results have been achieved to date.

Interview opportunities are available following the presentation.

When: June 4, 2012 at 1:00 p.m. ET

Where: Li Ka Shing Knowledge Institute at St. Michael's Hospital
30 Bond Street, Toronto, ON, M5B 1W8

Who: Dr. Jack Kitts, Chair, Health Council of Canada
John G. Abbott, CEO, Health Council of Canada

-30-

About the Health Council of Canada
Created by the *2003 First Ministers' Accord on Health Care Renewal*, the Health Council of Canada is an independent national agency that reports on the progress of health care renewal. The Council provides a system-wide perspective on health care reform in Canada, and disseminates information on best practices and innovation across the country. The Councillors are appointed by the participating provincial and territorial governments and the Government of Canada.

To read comments from guest bloggers and other health industry leaders, or to download the full report (on June 4) visit: healthcouncilcanada.ca.

For more information or to arrange an interview, please contact:
Media relations manager, Health Council of Canada, email, office and cell phone contact numbers

---

Figure 10.2   Media Advisory from the Health Council of Canada

Source: Health Council of Canada. Used by permission.

Once the media advisory is drafted, the PR practitioner sends it out prior to the event and then again on the day of the event as a reminder.

Photo Advisories and Releases

If an event has a highly visual component, such as people in costumes or a parade, you can try to secure coverage through a photo advisory. A **photo advisory** is usually sent to photo editors and is similar to a media advisory, except it is very detailed in the types of photo opportunities there will be and what time they will occur. Photo advisories are well worth the effort. A great picture can land on the front page of the newspaper, which will inevitably please your client or manager and help you achieve your communications objectives.

A **photo release** is typically sent to the media following an event. Photo releases are sent to media outlets who expressed interest in the event but were not able to attend with a photographer. It is a good investment to hire your own photographer to document the event and to have professional quality images to send to the media. In the photo release, you include a great photo and a paragraph describing the event. You also include a photo caption below the picture that identifies any people in the photo. Prior to sending a photo to the media it is important to ensure that the photographer and any subjects in the photo have provided their consent. In addition to the photo release, you will send a high-resolution version of the photo.

B-Roll

Broadcast newsrooms are incredibly busy places with a limited number of cameras. Even if a producer agrees to send a camera to your event, if a larger news story breaks, such as a fire or a protest, the TV station might not have a camera available. One way to attempt to secure coverage of your event is to hire a cinematographer to take B-roll footage. **B-roll** is film coverage of the event, and maybe an interview or two with a VIP, that you can provide to the media so that they can air it with their own commentary. Filming B-roll can be expensive, so it is important to ensure that the event is interesting enough for the media to broadcast. Also, make sure the footage can be put to other uses, such as posting on your company website or sending out to your customers, in case the media decide not to use it. Though sometimes expensive, for the right event, B-roll can result in broadcast coverage that you would not have generated otherwise.

Reebok Canada provided B-roll to media throughout Canada following an event at Young and Dundas Square in Toronto where a flash mob of 250 people performed a fitness routine. This was part of a global PR campaign that took part in New York, Paris, and Tokyo.[30]

EVENT LISTINGS

A fantastic, free, and easy way to let the general public know about an upcoming event is through an **event listing**. Most community papers, community blogs, radio stations, and TV stations have an event listings section where they list upcoming community events for free. Each publication has its own format requirements, but they generally need a short blurb that lists the event, time and place, cost, and information on where to find further details. Event listings editors are bombarded with requests, so the trick to seeing your event in print or on air is to submit the event information as far in advance as possible, preferably no less than six weeks prior to the event. You will also want to make your event sound as exciting as possible in the space allowed. Local blogs, like Ottawa's apt613.ca, will also alert their readers to upcoming events.

SOCIAL MEDIA

Another way to let the public know about your event is to put it on your organization's website, write about it in your own blog, tweet about it, and put it on your Facebook page. You might also consider hosting a contest to give away a pair or two of free tickets to reward your followers for their loyalty and to generate some buzz.

The City of Toronto has a PR practitioner who handles all public relations for its many civic events. One of the events it hosts is the Scotiabank Nuit Blanche, an all-night contemporary art event. Nuit Blanche is a 12-hour event with a mandate to make contem-

PR for Scotiabank's Nuit Blanche includes social media.
Source: Steve Russell/ZUMA Press/Newscom

porary art accessible to large audiences. It is an international event that began in Paris and is now held in cities all over the world, including New York, Tokyo, and Rome.[31] PR for the event includes a dedicated website, an electronic newsletter, Facebook, and media relations.

INVITATIONS

We consider invitations a form of public relations because they may be the first way that your guests hear of an event and inform their first impression of it. Increasingly, invitations are sent via email, through an e-vite. You can position your event in a certain way by the type of invitation you decide to send. Think of the difference between the impression made by a high-end sleek invite printed on thick stock and that made by an e-vite. You can be as creative with your invitation as you are with your event. For the launch party of the Beauty Bar, a fashionable boutique of cosmetics and hair care products, the invitations consisted of beautiful, neon-pink hat boxes each containing a printed invitation, information about the boutique, and product samples.

MEDIA SPONSORS

A great way to bring attention to an event that is open to the general public is to secure a media sponsor. Print, broadcast, and digital media all sponsor events, meaning that they agree to give you a certain amount of free coverage in return for your promotion of their news outlet at the event. For print, this can mean free ads or guaranteed media coverage; for radio, it might be a broadcast interview or a mention in a segment on community events. Each deal is negotiated on its own terms.

To make the deal of interest to a media outlet, you must offer advantages in return and convince the sales team that the people attending your event are their target audience. An example of a media sponsorship is *Chatelaine* magazine's annual sponsorship of the Walk for ALS, a fundraiser that takes place in over 80 communities across Canada. As part of the sponsorship deal, *Chatelaine* provides the ALS Society of Canada with editorial mentions in its print and online versions, in addition to sending its own team to participate in the walk.[32]

Thinking Like a PR Practitioner

1. Look through your local newspaper and describe a news article where you believe the coverage was secured through a photo advisory. Explain why you believe this.
2. Find an ad or a poster for an upcoming event, such as an art exhibit or a concert, that has a media sponsor. Discuss how the sponsorship was obtained.
3. Who are the bloggers or journalists in your community who attend events and publish information and photos about them? What types of events do they typically cover? How could you make them interested in your event?

CASE STUDY NANUK RELAUNCH

Nanuk is the polar bear mascot of the College of the North Atlantic (CNA), Newfoundland and Labrador's public college and one of the largest postsecondary educational and skills-training centres in Canada. After the mascot had not been used for years, the college decided to relaunch it. The communications team was charged with creating a buzz around Nanuk's comeback. Their campaign had three main objectives:

1. Use Nanuk to show prospective students that CNA is a fun place to get an education
2. Generate school spirit and an emotional attachment to the mascot
3. Emphasize key messaging during the event to create awareness of college programming

The primary audience was potential students and people who influence student decisions, such as parents and guardians.

It was strategically decided that to reach a large number of people, the best way to proceed was to team up with one of the province's most popular events, the Herder finals hockey game at Mile One Stadium in St. John's. The official unveiling of the mascot would take place there in front of a crowd of sports fans, many of whom were the target audience.

The communications team arranged for the college to have as big a presence as possible at the game. They ordered a large number of promotional items to distribute and for people to wear. They also purchased 100 tickets to the Herder game for staff and students to attend.

Each person was given a Nanuk T-shirt, and an entire section in the stadium was devoted to staff and students wearing Nanuk shirts and other college merchandise. The mascot was very visible throughout the event and interacted with the crowd while the game was in session. Key messaging about CNA was announced during the event, and a CNA booth was set up at the stadium's main entrance to distribute information and promo items to the target audience. In addition, Nanuk and a number of his helpers—each dressed in Nanuk hockey jerseys—were permitted on the ice during intermissions, where they distributed promotional items for the college to the audience.

The relaunch was considered a success based on the number of people in attendance, the messages conveyed to the crowd, and the overall crowd reaction to Nanuk. Since the relaunch, CNA continues to build upon the fantastic foundation that was laid at the Herder game, creating four additional mascot suits to keep up with the province-wide demand for appearances of Nanuk at campus and community events.

Questions

1. Describe five elements that went into the unveiling of the mascot at Mile One Stadium.

2. How would you have handled the relaunch? Create an event plan for the relaunch of Nanuk.

Fun Media Events

Getting journalists to events can be tricky. They are very busy and invited to so many events that it is hard to make yours stand out. One way to ensure attendance is to make your event fun and feature a one-of-a-kind opportunity. For the launch of a new inflight menu for Cathay Pacific Airways, we organized a special media event. The menu featured the food of a prestigious Hong Kong restaurant. We decided to fly the chef to Canada and put on a cooking class for journalists in both Vancouver and Toronto, the Canadian cities from which Cathay flies. This event was an exclusive opportunity to learn how to make Chinese food from a master.

Once the event was planned, it was then a question of executing it twice. Invitations consisted of beautifully designed Asian scrolls on which all the information for the event was written. Food, travel, business, and ethnic media were invited.

The chef proved to be a big draw and the event was filled to capacity.

The cooking class was held in the morning to accommodate media schedules and took place in a professional kitchen near the airport. Journalists were able to savour the foods they had prepared at a sit-down lunch following the class, where a short speech was delivered by Cathay Pacific's vice president for Canada. The event enabled the airline to enhance its relationship with key journalists and generated substantial media coverage.

Another fun event that we organized was to celebrate the anniversary of Teletoon. A birthday party was thrown for the cartoon network, which featured playful cartoon decorations and gourmet versions of kids' foods like burgers. There was also a huge birthday cake with cartoons on it. Guests included business, entertainment, television, and trade journalists, and industry insiders such as animation studio executives.

special event management

pre-event
- issues management
- plan
- event outline
- objectives
- audiences
- event logistics
- budget

types
- conventions & trade shows
- fundraisers
- civic or community
- tournaments
- street teams
- internal events
- media
- political
- awards

evevt PR
- invitations
- sponsors
- media
- social media

day of event
- management

post-event
- showing appreciation
- debriefings
- evaluation

Key Terms

B-roll Rough footage PR practitioners provide to news stations to try to secure coverage.

consumer-facing Any communications, marketing piece, or event that the end consumer will see.

debriefing session A meeting where team members review how an event went and discuss any key learnings.

event listing Free listing of events offered by local media.

keynote speech A speech given by a presenter who is the main draw.

live feed Live broadcast of a television or radio segment from a location outside the studio.

media advisory A cross between an invitation and a media release, a media advisory lets journalists know about an important upcoming announcement or event.

photo advisory A media advisory that lets photo editors know about a photo opportunity.

photo release A media release in which a photo is sent to the media for publication.

speakers bureau A roster of speakers who are available for hire.

trade show A business event where many companies in the same industry display their products or services.

Weblinks

Car Free Day Vancouver
www.carfreevancouver.org

Environment Canada's Green Meeting Guide
asi.abelearn.ca/UserFiles/Servers/Server_118790/File/ASI_DataStick_2008/Green_Meeting_Guide_07.pdf

Event Protocol
www.govrelations.ualberta.ca/en/Protocol.aspx

CanadianSpecialEvents.com
canadianspecialevents.com

Invitations and Function Guidelines for the Lieutenant Governor of Nova Scotia
http://lt.gov.ns.ca/protocols-request-forms/invitations-function-guidelines/

RBC Canadian Open
www.rbccanadianopen.com/innerpage.aspx?x=QBrd%2FZIfUNnjmITJJxfG3MmimJ%2Bvg%2BOSP1Fbh5t
riehjCa45m2xoXfxRvi9uV5jw

Speakers Bureau
www.speakers.ca
www.nsb.com

Special Event Professional Associations
canspep.ca
isescanada.ca/

Special Event Trade Shows
canadianspecialevents.com/cseme_toronto/
www.incentiveworksshow.com/

Toronto Pride
www.pridetoronto.com

Toronto Special Events Planning Guide
www.toronto.ca/special_events/event-support/

Endnotes

1. "Nickelback Roars Back to the Live Stage with Their 2012 North American Tour Beginning April 10th," Canada Newswire, January 11, 2012. Accessed February 20, 2013, http://www.newswire.ca/en/story/904155/nickelback-roars-back-to-the-live-stage-with-their-2012-north-american-tour-beginning-april-10th

2. D. Forbes, "Purolator Delivers the Goods for the Vancouver 2010 Olympic and Paralympic Winter Games," PR in Canada, March 7, 2008. Accessed February 20, 2013, http://www.princanada.com/purolator-delivers-the-goods-for-the-vancouver-2010-olympic-and-paralympic-winter-games

3. Melany Chretien, interview with the author.

4. D. Forde, "Optimum PR Texts Up Some Speed Dating with Future Shop," PR in Canada, August 24, 2011. Accessed February 20, 2013, http://www.princanada.com/optimum-pr-texts-up-some-speed-dating-with-future-shop/

5. "A Service for Obakki," blogs.theprovince.com, May 4, 2011. Accessed February 20, 2013, http://blogs.theprovince.com/2011/05/04/a-service-for-obakki/

6. "Mission and History," East Coast Music Association. Accessed February 20, 2013, http://www.ecma.com/about

7. "About," Car Free Day Vancouver. Accessed February 20, 2013, http://www.carfreevancouver.org/about/; "Meet the Vision Team at Car Free Day Events," Vision Vancouver, June 17, 2011. Accessed February 20, 2013, http://votevision.ca/events/110617/meet-vision-team-car-free-day-events

8. "2011–2012 Media Releases," Pride Toronto. Accessed May 27, 2013, http://www.pridetoronto.com/about/media/media-releases

9. RBC Canadian Open. Accessed February 20, 2013, http://www.rbccanadianopen.com/innerpage.aspx?x=QBrd%2FZIfUNnjmlTJJxfG3MmimJ%2Bvg%2BOSP1Fbh5triehjCa45m2xoXfxRvi9uV5jw

10. D. Forde, "Mini Elves Invade the Streets of Downtown Toronto," *PR in Canada*, December 14, 2010. Accessed February 20, 2013, http://www.princanada.com/mini-elves-invade-the-streets-of-downtown-toronto

11. L. Hurley, "Special Event Pros Forecast Color Trends for 2011–2012," *SpecialEvents.com*, October 5, 2011. Accessed February 20, 2013, http://specialevents.com/decor/special-event-pros-forecast-color-trends-for-2011-2012

12. C. Ball, "Meeting Technology Trends to Watch for 2011," *Canadianspecialevents.com*, no. 11 (2011). Accessed February 20, 2013, http://issuu.com/canadianspecialevents.com/docs/cep22issuu?mode=window&pageNumber=4

13. Environment Canada Environmental Affairs Division, *Environment Canada's Green Meeting Guide*, August 2007. Accessed February 20, 2013, http://asi.abelearn.ca/UserFiles/Servers/Server_118790/File/ASI_DataStick_2008/Green_Meeting_Guide_07.pdf

14. "Politics and the Pen," Writers' Trust of Canada. Accessed February 20, 2013, http://www.writerstrust.com/News/Events-(1)/Politics-and-the-Pen.aspx

15. "Setting SMART Objectives," Government of Saskatchewan. Accessed February 20, 2013, http://www.psc.gov.sk.ca/ISWP/smartobjectives?Anc=97fdb7a3-656c-475e-ac4f-0eb54d5e3338&Pa=cca90bef-7f6e-44e4-92ce-2323e0889c45

16. "Best Event or Experiential Marketing Campaign," PMAA Awards. Accessed February 20, 2013, http://www.pmaa-awards.net/documents/Cat%209%20Best%20Event%20or%20Experiential%20Mkt.pdf

17. B. Borzyrowski, "Is a Launch Party Still a Smart Way to Build a Buzz?" *The Globe and Mail*, February 8, 2012. Accessed February 20, 2013, http://www.theglobeandmail.com/report-on-business/small-business/sb-growth/the-challenge/is-a-launch-party-still-a-smart-way-to-build-buzz/article2329580/

18. "Justin Bieber Explains Why He Wore Overalls to Meet Stephen Harper," *The National Post*, November 26, 2012. Accessed February 20, 2013, http://arts.nationalpost.com/2012/11/26/justin-bieber-explains-why-he-wore-overalls-to-meet-stephen-harper/

19. "A Golden Night for Birks, Canadian Olympians & Girls in Burkina Faso," Plan Canada. Accessed February 20, 2013, http://plancanada.ca/Page.aspx?pid=2927

20. "Invitations and Function Guidelines," Lieutenant Governor of Nova Scotia. Accessed February 20, 2013, http://lt.gov.ns.ca/protocols-request-forms/invitations-function-guidelines/

21. "Protocol," University of Alberta, Office of University Relations. Accessed March 25, 2013, http://www.govrelations.ualberta.ca/en/Protocol.aspx

22. *Toronto Special Events Planning Guide*, City of Toronto. Accessed February 20, 2013, http://www.toronto.ca/special_events/event-support/

23. "Queen Unfazed by Toronto Blackout," *CBC News Toronto*, July 5, 2010. Accessed February 20, 2013, http://www.cbc.ca/news/canada/toronto/story/2010/07/05/queen-toornto.html

24. Ibid.

25. Dogan News Agency, "Canadian Football Icons Get into a Fistfight," *Hurriyet Daily News*, November 29, 2011. Accessed February 20, 2013, http://www.hurriyetdailynews.com/default.aspx?pageid=438&n=canadas-sports-icons-get-into-a-fistfight-2011-11-29

26. J. Goldblatt, *Special Events*. New York: John Wiley & Sons, 2002, p. 56.

27. Fawn Mulcahy, interview with the author.

28. Goldblatt, *Special Events*.

29. H. Freedman and K. Smith, *Black Tie Optional: The Ultimate Guide to Planning and Producing Special Events*. Hoboken, NJ: John Wiley & Sons, 2007.

30. "Reebok Launches The Sport of Fitness with 250 Person Flash Mob," Canada Newswire, February 21, 2012. Accessed February 20, 2013, http://www.newswire.ca/en/story/925515/-r-e-p-e-a-t-video-b-roll-available-via-cnw-reebok-launches-the-sport-of-fitness-with-250-person-flash-mob-15-000-pound-shipping-container-and-demonst

31. "Scotiabank Nuit Blanche Toronto," Scotiabank. Accessed February 20, 2013, http://www.scotiabanknuitblanche.ca/

32. M. Kwong, "Top 10 Charity Walks," *Chatelaine*, May 3, 2011. Accessed February 20, 2013, http://www.chatelaine.com/health/fitness/top-10-charity-walks/

Maintaining Composure and Being Thick-Skinned

There is no denying it—PR can be stressful. You deal with new situations, such as breaking issues and crises, all the time; you interact with media who are on short deadlines, and with clients and spokespersons who are stressed out themselves. Whatever the circumstances, you must remain professional, calm, and diplomatic. Stress comes with the territory and if you lose your cool, you will also lose the confidence that others have in your ability to manage the situation. You need to keep focused to deal with the challenges of this profession.

"You must keep a poker face on at all times. You can never be the one to look like you are freaking out. It's often about maintaining composure," says one senior PR practitioner.

Be your calm and collected self. If you need to remove yourself from a situation to get grounded again, do so as quickly and diplomatically as you can. Go take some deep breaths, get centred, and then come back to deal with the situation.

Once the task is done and the day is over, it is important to find healthy ways to manage your stress. Some talented PR practitioners do not stay in the industry for long because they cannot deal with the pressure. Others find stress management techniques only after suffering physical and emotional symptoms such as ulcers, weight loss or gain, bad backs, or insomnia. This is why it is important to take care of yourself and incorporate stress management techniques right from the get-go.

There are many ways to manage stress. Some practitioners enjoy exercise like lifting weights, swimming, or running. Yoga, meditation, dancing and singing to favourite songs, walks, and laughing with friends are also effective. Getting enough sleep, eating well, taking regular vacations, and nurturing a positive attitude will also help you keep in good shape and feeling as though you can react to any situation. Think of public relations as a marathon instead of a race and you will be less likely to burn out. Pace yourself. And, as important as your work is, also remember that it is just PR, not brain surgery. Lives are usually not at stake in the PR profession.

Chapter 11
Issues Management and Crisis Communications

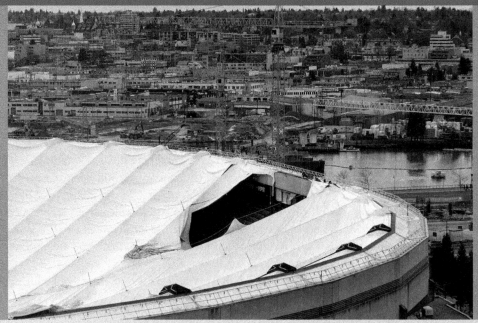

When BC Place's roof collapsed in 2007, Reputations managed the crisis response. Source: NICK DIDLICK/EPA/Newscom

LEARNING OBJECTIVES

❶ Define issues management and crisis communications and summarize the scenarios that a crisis can encompass.

❷ Identify the components of a useful crisis plan and explain why they are an essential tool during a crisis.

❸ Summarize what is involved in crisis prevention.

❹ Outline how the response theory is used in current crisis events.

❺ Explain how social media is changing crisis communications management and describe how PR practitioners must change to adapt to the shift.

The Sky Is Falling: Communicating BC Place's Roof Collapse

BC Place stadium is a downtown Vancouver landmark, seating over 60,000 spectators. Its roof is one of the world's largest air-supported, Teflon-coated, fibreglass domes, and on the afternoon of January 5, 2007, it suddenly collapsed. Luckily, no one was injured, but the deflating dome sounded like an explosion, shocking Vancouver residents who, within minutes, were sharing YouTube videos of the event in offices and homes across the city.

Linda Bilben is no stranger to crisis. As a partner in Vancouver's Reputations PR agency, Linda has worked with clients on high-profile incidents: an accidental employee death at Canada Place and the proposed closure of Vancouver's safe injection site, Insite.

With a robust crisis plan in place at BC Place, Linda's team was able to respond to the media within two hours of the roof collapse. According to Linda, one of the most important components of crisis response is giving reporters access to information. After the roof collapse, Linda's team logged over 1500 calls, giving journalists 24/7 access to information on what was happening. Even when there was no new information to report, Linda would let reporters know when they could expect the next update.

Social media also played a role in this crisis. News of the roof's collapse spread quickly on YouTube. In the social media age, Linda argues that monitoring and responding in a crisis needs to be done in real time. Organizations also need to be active on social media, because that is where many reporters are now getting their news. If company spokespersons are not communicating in this space and directing reporters and the public back to the official website, other sources will be sought out.

The BC Place crisis demonstrates how problem solving and flexibility are important traits for a crisis communicator. Some of the challenges that Linda faced during the crisis response included operational hiccups; for instance, the response team thought the roof would be up within a week, but it ended up taking much longer because of various timing delays, such as the hold-up of building materials at the U.S.–Canada border. Another challenge Linda faced was a reporter who was receiving inaccurate information daily from a BC Place employee. Eventually, Linda decided to deny this reporter access to information updates, as she felt he was not printing the truth anyway.

Of crisis response, Linda says that the most important advice for new communicators is to stay calm and to be the third-party voice of reason no matter what the situation. Times of crisis are highly charged emotional situations within organizations. It is the PR practitioner's job to provide clear-headed expertise.

Following a crisis, in order to restore an organization's reputation, the conversation needs to be steered to a more positive story. One of the ways Linda did this for BC Place was to introduce the media to the technology that was being used to fix the roof. She even invited reporters to go up in harnesses to inspect it. Within a month, the BC Place story had changed from a roof collapse to the innovative technology that went into fixing the roof, giving the organization the chance to repair its reputation.[1]

Crisis communications and issues management are some of the most challenging and rewarding aspects of the public relations profession. When a crisis hits an organization, it can be incredibly stressful. Imagine being in the BC Place scenario yourself. The roof has collapsed and you are suddenly thrown into action, providing access to information for the media 24/7. It is also the PR practitioner's responsibility to ensure that after the initial crisis has passed, a new, more positive story is introduced, as was done with the introduction of the technology angle to the media. This is a great example of how a crisis can turn into a positive news story. In some cases, a crisis can also force an organization to deal with its challenges and become a better and stronger business. For public relations departments, a crisis can mean new recognition for the value of communications and an increased budget allocated toward future crisis plans.

In crisis communications and issues management, the PR practitioner plays a lead role in three important and interrelated areas: (1) prevention, (2) preparation, and (3) response. Each of these functions is important in its own right, but these three crisis components are also intertwined. Although the response component tends to receive all of the glory because it is the most public facing, prevention and preparation are no less important, even if they are usually conducted privately within an organization. It is almost impossible to generate a good response without having diligently prepared for a crisis. Linda was able to move so quickly after the collapse of the BC Place roof because the organization had a solid issues and crisis plan in place. Furthermore, prevention leads to the best outcome of all. No one will ever lament the crisis they did not have to respond to. After examining what defines a crisis, we will look at each of these three roles in depth. Figure 11.1 outlines the circular nature of prevention, preparation, and response in issues and crisis management.

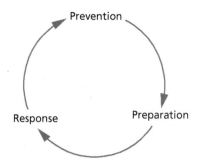

Figure 11.1 The Circular Nature of Prevention, Preparation, and Response in Issues and Crisis Management

Defining Crisis and Issues Management ❶

First, it may be helpful to define **crisis**. In an organizational context, a crisis is "a specific, unexpected and non-routine event or series of events that create high levels of uncertainty and threaten, or are perceived to threaten, an organization's high priority goals."[2] The collapse of the BC Place stadium roof examined in the opening vignette certainly fits this definition.

Crises and issues can affect a company's profitability, reputation, and consumer trust; however, crises are a reality of any business environment and something that companies must diligently prepare for.[3] This reality has hit home for companies such as Nike, which in the past has come under fire for allegations that its factories use child labour; and Nestlé, which has suffered consumers' wrath around the globe for the destruction of rainforests to produce palm oil, which is an ingredient in some of its products, and the company's defensive attempts to control the conversation on social media. Despite events such as these, not all organizations have an issues and crisis plan in place. This speaks volumes to how unprepared many organizations are when a crisis does hit.[3] It doesn't have to be this way. The sections below will outline how to prevent, prepare, and respond to a crisis situation.

Generally, when we discuss **issues management**, we are referring to a negative media event that does not involve life or limb or a serious crime and that has not yet seriously damaged an organization's reputation. However, issues need to be monitored because without a proper communications strategy, they can quickly spiral into a full-blown crisis. Few environmental developments happen with little or no warning. They usually start as a murmur and get louder and louder until they can no longer be ignored.[4] For example, many food companies, like Kraft Foods, responded quickly to initial reports that trans fats were unhealthy. Kraft Foods even got ahead of the crisis by reformulating its recipes in 2005, well before the first U.S. state banned trans fats in 2010.[5] Issues are like smoke, telling of an upcoming fire. The examples given throughout this chapter will consist of both crises and issues.

The various responses that communications teams deploy depend on whether crises or issues are the result of internal decisions, such as illegal activities or a recall, or external factors, such as product tampering or an earthquake. In either case, communications must be swift, transparent, and authentic. In the case of internal decisions causing an issue or crisis, the organization will need to provide the public with apologies and work to rebuild trust following the event. In the case of external factors affecting an organization, if the organization can provide effective communications during the adverse event, the public will often be understanding or even sympathetic

Table 11.1	Examples of Crises and Issues That May Affect an Organization	
Natural Disasters	**Workplace Accidents**	**Nonaccidental Happenings**
Earthquake	Employee injury or death	Crime
Tornado	Nuclear accident	Sexual harassment
Flood	Explosion	Terrorism
Extreme weather patterns that affect supply/services	Oil spill	Reputational damage
Lighting strike	Product deficiencies	Child labour accusations
Fire	Machinery malfunction/ accident	False advertising/claims
Hurricane	Environmental disaster	Hostile takeover
Tsunami	Product recall	Bankruptcy
Power outage that affects the normal course of business		Negative industry event
		Shifting consumer opinion/new study on an issue that negatively affects your industry
		Political decision that negatively affects your industry
		Litigation
		Labour disputes/strikes

Source: M.W. Seeger, "Best Practices in Crisis Communication: An Expert Panel Process," *Journal of Applied Communication Research*, vol. 34, no. 3 (August 2006), 232–244.

to their plight. Table 11.1 provides examples of crises and issues that can affect an organization.

Thinking Like a PR Practitioner

1. Outline one example of a scenario from each of the three categories in Table 11.1 that might affect an organization and explain how the specific scenario and category might change the nature of the crisis response.

2. Identify three organizations that have been affected by different scenarios in Table 11.1.

The Crisis That Wasn't: Prevention [2]

No one likes to think about worst-case scenarios. However, it is a PR practitioner's job to prepare an organization for both good and bad media coverage. It can be hard to convince management to devote resources to preventing something "that may never happen." PR practitioners must make the case internally for putting crisis prevention resources in place. It may have seemed unlikely to the team preparing the issues and crisis plan for BC Place that the roof would collapse, but that is exactly what happened. With a well-thought-out plan in place, the PR practitioner was able to act quickly when the crisis broke.

Sometimes it takes a crisis or a powerful description of the worst-case scenario to make crisis preparation and prevention a priority. As secretary of state, Hillary Clinton said while speaking to European Parliament after the 2009 financial crisis, "Never waste a good crisis."[6] She saw the economic turmoil as an opportunity for countries to rebuild their economies with more consideration for the environment and climate change.[7] Similarly, following a crisis, organizations can rebuild themselves to be stronger and more resilient.

Crisis management can be thought of as having two components: preventing a crisis from happening and managing a crisis once it has occurred.[8] In this section we will examine how to prevent a crisis from erupting and how to prepare an organization.

ADVICE TO NEW PRACTITIONERS
Preparing Your Organization for a Crisis

Make sure your organization's crisis plan is kept up to date. Regularly check that the right people are on the call/email chain list and that their phone numbers are current.

Your organization's next crisis exists within your organization today. Work to identify it and then fix it or prepare for it.

Make several copies of the crisis plan and give a hard copy and an electronic copy to all key stakeholders. Also, be sure to keep an up-to-date hard copy off-site, in case the organization's head office and servers are affected by a fire, flood, or earthquake.

Do not expect to get much sleep during a crisis.

Avoid speculating when talking to reporters. It will only cause you more grief if it turns out your speculation was wrong. Tell reporters that you will get back to them when you know the answer.

Be aware that "No comment" is a comment.

CONDUCTING ENVIRONMENTAL SCANNING

It is important for PR practitioners to conduct daily environmental scans. This is where you scan and monitor various media, including newspapers, blogs, Twitter, and so forth, for topics and trends that may affect your organization. It is important to distinguish between scanning, which involves attempting to detect emerging problems, and monitoring, which is keeping track of identified issues to make sure they do not escalate.[9]

Some issues, like BC Place's roof collapse, happen all of sudden and become a crisis instantly. With others, there may be clues in the media for weeks, months, or even years before the issue becomes a major crisis. For example, prior to 2000 villagers in Mehdiganj, India, marching to demand Coca-Cola close its bottling plant because of how much water the company was using in the drought-threatened region, there had been complaints for years from other similar towns with Coca-Cola bottling plants.[10]

It is important to remember that especially with social media, a crisis can flare up even on the weekend, and an organization cannot afford to wait until Monday to begin its response. Someone on the communications team should be scanning for issues online, even on Saturdays and Sundays. Google Alerts and Twitter Search are practical, free ways to conduct environmental scans and monitor the topics or trends that might become problematic for the organization. For example, if your organization makes soy-based products, you will want to keep a close eye on articles or studies that discuss any negative side effects of eating soy. While a single article may quickly disappear and never cause your organization any trouble, if you start to see momentum in the coverage, you will need to start getting prepared. See Chapter 4 for more information on environmental scanning.

GETTING A SEAT AT THE TABLE

Good communicators ensure they have a seat at the management table. The public relations department should insist on being involved in every major company decision. This is so that they can bring a communicator's point of view to the decision-making process and raise concerns over stakeholders' possible perceptions of those decisions.[11] Communicators often play the role of providing common sense in their organizations, as they are often tuned in to key audiences and their viewpoints and will better understand how they will interpret important decisions.

Communicators should be ready and willing to raise concerns about potential problems within the organization. Actions they may take include lobbying internally to bring more sustainable practices to the organization or recognizing and communicating the risks of certain policies or practices that might be viewed negatively by an external audience. What would you do if you found out the cosmetic company you worked for tested on animals? Or that something that was regularly claimed in promotional materials was false? How would you convince senior management that these unsavoury practices need to be halted? These are the types of issues that PR practitioners need to look out for and provide counsel on. PR Practitioners need to help management better understand how the public would react if they found out about these types of practices.

BUILDING RELATIONSHIPS

To illustrate the importance of building strong relationships as part of a crisis prevention strategy, here is a stark example of company executives failing to conduct due diligence when choosing and maintaining a supplier. In late 2008, the Peanut Corporation of America (PCA), a peanut supplier for many U.S. and Canadian food manufacturers, was linked to approximately 700 cases of salmonella and 8 deaths, leading to panic among consumers.[12] PCA's refusal to comment, provide information, or an explain the largest recall in U.S. history only heightened consumers' anxiety. With so much uncertainty, many consumers stopped buying peanut products altogether. This led peanut butter sales to drop by 25 per cent.[13] As a result of the lack of information, many manufacturers of products that contained peanuts, including those who did not use PCA as a supplier, were forced to respond to consumers and the media. These proxy responders were at a disadvantage because they were not privy to the entire story.[14] They had to try to rebuild consumer confidence in their products with the information they had.

As part of their crisis prevention initiatives, communications teams should make a concentrated effort to build relationships with suppliers, community partners, the public, and first responders, or anyone whose support an organization might need during a crisis situation.[15] Having good relationships with suppliers and first responders can help you react to a crisis in a timely manner. Building these key relationships will provide an opportunity to coordinate with suppliers and first responders prior to any issues, so that your procedures are aligned. Having the support of your suppliers is especially important in recall situations, where you may need them to provide critical information on the raw materials of the product or to produce important documents.

Building strong relationships and trust with community partners and the public is also important. Studies have shown that having a reservoir of goodwill built up with the public is vital to successful crisis management.[16] This is because response messages will be seen as more credible and trustworthy if an organization has built credibility and loyalty before an issue breaks. If they fail to build this public goodwill prior to a crisis, organizations will have a more difficult time communicating with the community during a stressful period, as well as some trouble rebuilding any lost social capital once the crisis is over. In 2010, the Toronto Transit Commission suffered from a series of issues that damaged its reputation, including a fare hike, a sex scandal involving the then TTC Chair, and a photo of a TTC worker sleeping on the job that was tweeted on Twitter.[17] GCI Group's president, Marion MacKenzie, suggests that the TTC has an opportunity to build higher levels of trust with consumers prior to issues breaking. She says, "If [riders] think you're great, they will probably give you a bit more latitude."[18] MacKenzie believes that the TTC can earn this trust by better communicating about the TTC's focus on innovation and convenience and building relationships with riders well before another crisis breaks.

While continuously working to prevent crisis situations from happening, the savvy organization is also preparing for the possibility of a crisis. This is because a crisis can blindside an organization and may involve issues that have not even been flagged as potentially problematic even with diligent preparation.

Thinking Like a PR Practitioner

1. Name five stakeholders with whom it is important to develop good relationships prior to a crisis. How might an organization go about doing this?

2. You discover an unethical practice at your organization and are worried it could result in a crisis situation. How would you respond? Name a challenge you might face.

Hoping for the Best, Preparing for the Worst: Preparation ❸

Like prevention, crisis preparation needs to be a coordinated effort that involves many departments and requires buy-in from the top levels of management. Unfortunately, sometimes it takes a crisis to convince management how important it is to have a well-thought-out crisis prevention plan in place.

A crisis plan has been described as "a critical, short-term component of long-term legitimacy management."[19] **Legitimacy** refers to the right for a company to exist in the public's opinion because it shares their values. Dealing with crises effectively is an essential part of managing an organization's right to exist in the eyes of consumers and the public.[20]

THE CRISIS TEAM AND PLAN

The most important first step for an organization in preparing for a crisis is putting together a strong crisis team. A crisis plan will be useless if the team behind it is not equipped to implement it or is not flexible enough to deviate from the plan when necessary.[21] The crisis team should be robust enough to make important decisions and to move quickly. Once the crisis team is in place, its members should work toward developing a **crisis plan,** or a detailed manual on how to respond in a crisis situation.

The right time to make a crisis plan is today.
Source: Aquir/Shutterstock

Some elements that should be incorporated into a crisis plan include:

- A designated crisis management team
- Clear, defined responsibilities for each crisis team member
- Media contact lists
- Emergency contact information
- Spokespersons
- Key messages
- Audiences
- Processes for disseminating information
- Templates for response materials (e.g., media release, web statement, letter to customers, letter to suppliers, letter to retailers, internal email, Facebook statement, customer service script, etc.)
- Media lists
- Processes for engaging social media
- Policies and procedures for internal and external communications
- Potential threats ranked by probability and potential severity[22]

Recall that by following the organization's crisis communications plan, Reputations was able to rapidly respond to the BC Place roof collapse. Within two hours, the PR agency issued a statement to the press, launched a webpage for updates, organized a press conference, answered and documented incoming press calls, and formed a command centre.[23]

Note that one crisis plan may not be enough. Depending on the organization, the crisis team may want to have one for each of the scenarios that most threaten their organization. For example, a mining company may have one plan that addresses workplace accidents, one that addresses labour disputes and strikes, and one that addresses environmental boycotts. Furthermore, as we saw in the PCA example, it might be wise to consider creating a joint plan with your main suppliers or creating a plan for the event that one of your suppliers or a major industry player is involved in a crisis and is unresponsive.[24]

Once a crisis plan is in place, it is important to do a major update at least annually and tweaks every couple of months. It cannot be stressed enough how important it is for any crisis plan or manual to be continuously updated and revised. Nothing is worse than responding to an emergency only to find that many of the people listed in the plan are no longer with the organization or that the majority of the phone numbers are outdated. This can delay the response immensely. And in a crisis, minutes count.

Let us look at an example of issues management preparation in action. In 2004, Brewers Distributor Ltd. (BDL) suffered a major labour strike. BDL, a Calgary-based beer distributor, is owned by Molson Breweries and Labatt Breweries of Canada. The company provides the wholesale distribution of beer for these two companies across Western Canada.

The labour dispute resulted in beer shortages throughout British Columbia and Alberta during the May long weekend. At the time, Molson and Labatt made up 90 per cent of beer sold in British Columbia, and the strike lasted from May 1 until May 15.[25] This meant that many liquor stores, pubs, and restaurants had to scramble to find small breweries to stock their shelves. BDL took a beating in the media during the strike for failing to quickly resolve the labour dispute and failing to communicate with customers and the media.

When its union's contract came up for renewal again several years later, BDL hired a PR firm to prepare the company from a communications perspective in the event of another long strike. With the help of the PR agency, BDL was able to prepare for and try to prevent another crisis. Luckily a new contract was negotiated and no strike took place. Though many of the communications tools that had been developed were never needed, it was nonetheless important to have devoted the time and resources to issues management preparation so that the organization would not be caught unprepared as in the past.

PRACTITIONER INTERVIEW

Heath Applebaum, National Director of Communications, Canadian Diabetes Association

Heath Applebaum is an international award–winning communications professional with over 15 years of crisis and reputation management experience. He is currently the national director of communications for the Canadian Diabetes Association and has held leadership roles for multinational corporations such as MasterCard, Pepsi, Cadillac Fairview, Deloitte, and RBC Financial Group.

Question: What kind of issues and crises have you worked on?

Answer: Over my illustrious corporate, agency, and consulting career I have dealt with dozens of high-profile crises across many industries, from financial services and health care to high tech, real estate, consumer packaged goods, and professional service companies. This has meant engineering complex crisis communications strategies with executives to prepare business continuity and guide enterprise risk management plans to just about every conceivable scenario—from high-profile product recalls to the G20, H1N1 pandemic, floods, fires, fatal workplace accidents, suicides, CEO resignations, technology failures, explosions, strikes, lockouts, terrorism, child abductions, active shooter scenarios, environmental protests, significant ethical leadership breaches, and much, much more.

Question: What is the most challenging aspect of this work?

Answer: Perhaps the greatest challenge associated with crisis management is its unpredictability. While certain patterns emerge over time, each crisis is unique, so remaining calm and composed is important when the stakes are high, executives are sweating, your adrenaline is rushing, and a scrum of TV cameras are camped outside your headquarters demanding CEO interviews. The key is to make sure when a crisis strikes or escalates that you've completed 95 per cent of the preparation, leaving only 5 per cent for perspiration. By developing and testing your plans in advance and earning the buy-in of the leadership team and the trust of your employees, you will be far better positioned to respond quickly and decisively. As the dynamics of the situation evolve, having flexible

(Continued)

Heath Applebaum, National Director of Communications, Canadian Diabetes Association

contingency plans is important, but ultimately trusting your professional instincts and knowing your stakeholders may save your job and the stock price.

Question: Can an issue or crisis always be resolved positively?

Answer: I am a firm believer that a crisis is the greatest opportunity for a communicator to truly demonstrate leadership and integrity by protecting their organization's most valuable asset—its reputation. Especially for publicly traded companies, how quickly, authentically, and ethically a company responds will play a crucial role in how resilient they are and impact their likelihood to recover. Having said that, some contentious situations are unlikely to earn you any accolades or fan mail. If your company fires 2000 employees after it is discovered your CFO had an ethical lapse in judgment, then you may only expect to neutralize the negative exposure.

Crises certainly test your resolve and your principles because the temptation of most legal departments and your boss is often to revert to damage control mode. The problem is that this fear-induced silence merely sparks greater media and regulatory scrutiny. Silence is assumed to be an admission of guilt in the unforgiving court of public opinion.

Question: What attitude must you bring to the table during a crisis or issue?

Answer: Confidence, collaboration, and perseverance. Do what you say and say what you do—that will go far in earning the respect and support of your colleagues and leadership team. Based on my experience, a crisis always appears magnified in the heat of the moment. Therefore, the advice I give to executives is to take decisive action, apologize, and outline what concrete steps are being taken to reduce

the risk of these circumstances repeating. But following that, avoid making rash, knee-jerk decisions that you may regret in time. Reputations are built one day at time and one decision at a time, so keep that in mind and you will look at your job and protecting your organization's reputation in an entirely new way.

Question: What advice can you give young practitioners when it comes to being ready for an issue or crisis?

Answer: The five Ps for successful crisis management—proper preparation prevents poor performance. Given the blinding speed of change in our digital world, companies' reputations can be tarnished quickly and irreparably with the click of a mouse. The days of "no comment" and bridging media questions by repeating vague key messages are long gone. To build and maintain public trust, we must strive to nurture a meaningful two-way dialogue with the stakeholders that impact their organization during the good times to build a reservoir of goodwill. Those are the relationships that will largely determine whether you thrive or merely survive a crisis. By failing to prepare, monitor, and anticipate business risks, you are ultimately preparing to fail.

Question: Do you need many years' experience or can young practitioners handle crisis management themselves?

Answer: Having learned crisis management through many years in the demanding trenches of corporate boardrooms and through two PR graduate schools, I incorporate the latest research findings to inform my practical experience and intuition. I believe learning is indeed a lifelong process and so young communicators should find a mentor whom they can learn from in order to avoid making career-limiting moves.

DR. COVELLO AND THE APP TEMPLATE

One of the most renowned crisis response experts is Dr. Vincent Covello, the director of the Center for Risk Communication in New York. To help organizations prepare for crisis situations, Covello developed the APP template for crisis response, which says communicators should:

1. Anticipate
2. Prepare
3. Practise[26]

Enbridge had to go into crisis mode when a pipeline spill occurred in Michigan.
Source: Jim West/Getty Images

Anticipate

The act of anticipating involves trying to predict what crises might occur and what actions will need to be taken if they do. Though you might not be able to predict exactly what type of incident might befall the organization, knowing your industry can help you anticipate and prepare for specific probable scenarios.[27] For example, a food company should anticipate a food recall, and a theme park should anticipate an injury on one of its rollercoasters.

Prepare

Once a communications team has anticipated several potential scenarios, they can start to prepare by putting together the materials mentioned above, such as crisis manuals and key messages. Covello believes that 95 per cent of questions that will be asked in a crisis can be predicted and prepared for in advance.[28]

Practise

At the very least, spokespersons should be media trained and coached on the key messages. **Mock drills**—simulating crisis scenarios in order to practise crisis response—are a popular way to prepare an organization for a crisis. Practising various crisis scenarios is one of the best ways to prepare for a real crisis. It is also useful for helping to identify any holes or weaknesses in the plan and revise it. However, as Enbridge's CEO Patrick Daniel learned after the company's pipeline spill in Michigan, it is important to do your practice sessions in realistic situations. The Calgary company's CEO told *Report on Business Magazine*,

> No exercise [in emergency preparedness] under controlled circumstances can ever really prepare you. If you do exercises, don't do them in fair weather. There we were, with the Kalamazoo River in floods after three 50-year record rains. We don't do our spill exercises in pouring rain and with the rivers in flood. So do your disaster planning when things are at their worst, because that is most likely when Murphy is going to hit you.[29]

Having a solid plan in the event of a crisis and practising some of the policies and procedures can help a communications team respond in a more efficient and timely way during a real crisis situation. It will also help strengthen the response delivery and increase the probability of a successful resolution.

Thinking Like a PR Practitioner

1. How do you think Reputations applied the APP template to the BC Place roof collapse? What challenges do you think they faced getting buy-in?

2. What do you think some of the hurdles in developing a robust crisis plan might be? Name two.

3. What type of activities might BDL's PR firm have undertaken to prepare the company for another potential strike?

4. Name five components that a crisis plan for BDL might include.

5. What type of activities might BDL's PR firm have undertaken to prevent the strike from escalating?

Response ④

While some industries are more prone to crisis situations than others, it is only a lucky few companies who escape any kind of crisis, no matter how much prevention they engage in. Mistakes, disasters, and unforeseen events can befall any organization. This is why, in addition to prevention and preparation, a communicator must understand the mechanics of crisis response. The PR team for BC Place responded swiftly to the roof collapse. Within the span of two hours, they were able to distribute a media statement to journalists, launch a webpage to provide ongoing information, organize a media conference, and answer media calls. They also provided information to journalists 24/7 throughout the crisis, letting them know when the next updates would be available, even when there was no news to share.

In 2008, the much-respected, Toronto-based Maple Leaf Foods shocked Canadians with its listeria crisis. The company's contaminated meat products resulted in 20 deaths.[30] Owing to the crisis, 234 Maple Leaf products were recalled, costing the company $30 million in lost sales.[31] Though this was a challenging time for the organization, its crisis management of the situation won Maple Leaf Foods accolades from the Canadian PR community and won them consumers' regained trust and confidence. In fact, by January 2009, approximately 75 per cent of Maple Leaf Foods' sales had been brought back to pre-crisis levels.[32] In this section, we will examine what a good response looks like in a crisis situation and why the Maple Leaf Foods response is heralded as the gold standard.

So what did Maple Leaf Foods do that worked so well? For one, the company accepted responsibility immediately. The company also made it clear that it was willing to rectify the situation, no matter what it cost the organization.[33] CEO Michael McCain's immediate, emotional, and public apology was commended as a courageous and compassionate response, especially since many companies respond to a crisis with denial and blame.[34]

Another part of Maple Leaf's response that was effective was the speed with which the company acted and its efforts to keep the media informed with daily press conferences and email communications. During a crisis that affects public health or well-being, the public has certain rights. These include being told factual and timely information about what is occurring and the risks.[35] Thus, effective crisis communication is timely, transparent, and candid. Furthermore, as we will see in the section on social media and crisis communication, with social media, timely crisis response has taken on a whole new meaning. With Twitter, Facebook, and YouTube, a crisis can gain steam before an organization even realizes it is happening. For example, Domino's Pizza was caught off guard when its employees posted a YouTube video of themselves doing inappropriate things with a pizza. By the time Dominos had a chance to respond 24 hours later, the video had gone viral and the company had lost complete control of any messaging it might have been able to execute.[36]

Part of providing timely information is being accessible to the

Maple Leaf Foods' handling of the listeria crisis is seen as one of the top examples of crisis management in Canada.

Source: Ryan Remiorz/Canadian Press Images

media and consumers. During crisis response, spokespersons should carry their cellphones at all times and there should be regular press updates, whether by email communication or media conference. As we saw in the BC Place example, Reputations logged 1500 media calls and were accessible 24 hours a day, 7 days a week for duration of the crisis.

THE CCO TEMPLATE

As we noted above, Dr. Vincent Covello is regarded as one of the top crisis experts in North America. One of his most famous templates for crisis response is the CCO template, an acronym for compassion, conviction, and optimism.[37] Under this template, when making a statement in a crisis, whether in a press conference, interview, or apology ad, spokespersons should show that they care about the stakeholders by expressing compassion or empathy for the victims; demonstrate conviction that the organization is taking the right steps to resolve the crisis; and display optimism about the future and how the organization will improve. Covello also notes that when delivering this message of compassion, conviction, and optimism, spokespersons need to provide nonverbal communication that matches the verbal communication. According to Covello, these nonverbal signals make up 75 per cent of a communicated message.[38] Michael McCain of Maple Leaf Foods did both these things in his TV and YouTube apologies. In the videos, he showed compassion by apologizing to the victims and the public, conviction by outlining Maple Leaf's steps to contain the outbreak, and optimism by promising a better future. In regards to nonverbal communication, his actions and expressions matched his words perfectly. His face was a mask of concern and regret. At times he looked as though he might cry. Watching the video, the audience received the impression that Michael McCain truly meant what he was saying. Three Canadian surveys found that audiences who had viewed the apology videos had a much higher opinion of the company than those who had not.[39] This response helped Maple Leaf Foods begin to repair its battered reputation and rebuild consumer trust.

REBUILDING A REPUTATION

Following a crisis, an organization must focus on rebuilding its reputation and regaining consumers' trust. This step could include providing media updates on new processes and equipment or becoming more involved in charitable organizations and corporate social responsibility activities. At Maple Leaf Foods, Michael McCain personally led reporters through the company's facilities to highlight the improved safety procedures.[40] As Linda Bilben pointed out in the opening case study, it is important that, once a crisis is under control, an organization start changing the conversation to a good-news story. The PR team for BC Place did this by working with reporters to develop science and technology and human interest stories.[41] The crisis recovery phase takes time and should not be expected to be completed in a matter of weeks or even months. Trust is a hard item to regain. And especially in the new era of social media, it can quickly be lost.

SOCIAL MEDIA AND CRISIS RESPONSE ⑤

In September 2008, McNeil Consumer Healthcare felt the swift repercussions of a social media issue. After the company launched a series of magazine and online ads for the pain reliever Motrin that mommy bloggers found snarky, Twitter and other social media sites erupted with disapproval. The negative reactions led McNeil's director of marketing to issue an apology and pull the ads.[42]

Motrin caused a social media backlash with ads that linked the baby carrier to a fashion accessory.
Source: © Johner Images/Alamy

The vice president of marketing for McNeil, Kathy Widmer, issued an apology to bloggers who had posted about the ad. She said that she was also a mother of three girls and that Motrin had nothing but appreciation for parents. She apologized for disappointing mothers and promised to remove the ads as quickly as possible.[43]

Social media is changing the landscape of crisis communications and issues management. Though the principles of crisis communications and issues management have not changed, the speed and agility with which you need to react and the difficulty in controlling your message have changed. Companies now have to react not only with press conferences and news releases but also with up-to-the-minute Twitter and Facebook responses. People are no longer content to wait until the next day's paper to find out what is going on. The online world is alert and active 24 hours a day, 7 days a week, and the public expects you to be as well during a severe crisis situation.

Communicators need to monitor all forms of social media and be ready to disseminate information through them. For example, when the BC Place roof collapsed, footage was quickly shared on YouTube by the public. When responding to issues on social media, communicators need to follow the principles of transparent and authentic communication. Earlier in this chapter we described how Nestlé, after coming under fire on its Facebook page for using palm oil from suppliers that were destroying rainforests, did little to win back consumers' trust with its social media responses. Nestlé threatened to delete negative comments from its Facebook page and came off as defensive in its comments.[44] Of Nestlé's response, Ken Evans, senior vice president of Apex Public Relations, says, "Brands have to be able to defend themselves in the social media [sphere], but in a constructive way that clarifies the situation. Not once in those early responses did we hear anything about the issue."[45] Nestlé needed to better acknowledge the public's concerns, explain its position, and allow for an open dialogue.

Social media policies and procedures—including who is responsible for what, who can and cannot respond on social media, templates for social media videos, and updates—should be part of the crisis plan or manual. The crisis manual should also include plans for what to do if social media sites are down.

Though it may seem overwhelming, social media sites can be a great tool for disseminating information without the media filter that constrained communicators in the past. In fact, social media tools, such as Facebook and especially Twitter, have become critical communications vehicles for disaster organizations like the Red Cross in order to communicate essential information to the public about their services and programs in crisis situations.[46] Instead of waiting for the news cycle to publish or broadcast important updates, communicators can go directly to the public with status updates. Maple Leaf Foods was able to disseminate its apology message to a wider audience by posting it on YouTube, in addition to running it through traditional television advertising. Through Twitter, airlines are able to give up-to-the-minute information to delayed passengers.

Though social media can help PR practitioners monitor issues and respond to crises, as we saw in the Domino's Pizza example it can also cause or aggravate a crisis situation. This is because organizations can lose control of their messaging quickly. The Domino's Pizza example underlines the importance of having social media policies and guidelines for employees and having recourse if these policies are breached, in addition to including social media scanning and response within an overall crisis strategy.

POST-CRISIS EVALUATION

Following a crisis it is important to conduct a post-crisis analysis of what was done well and what was not. This step is sometimes missed by even the most seasoned practitioners. This is because the period during a crisis can be so intense and exhausting that once it is over, all those involved want to do is put it behind them and get back to "business as usual." This is a mistake. Critiquing the crisis response will help the practitioner build a stronger crisis communications plan and respond more effectively and efficiently in future.

One area that is especially useful to analyze performance is timeliness. Some of Canada's most seasoned crisis responders work with organizations to improve the speed at which they can disseminate information. As the Greyhound case study at the end of the chapter shows, through continuous practice and improvement, Greyhound was able to respond to the public and the media with a statement within an hour of the crisis breaking. One way to improve the speed of response is to identify the **bottlenecks**, or constraints in the system, that restricted timeliness in the past. For example, was it difficult to receive the proper approvals needed to send out the required information? Were too many people allowed to provide input and changes to the key communications pieces, thus slowing down the process? Were some members of the crisis team difficult to reach, making it hard to gather important, accurate information? Did spokespersons lack the necessary training to feel confident relaying information to the media? Whatever the various bottlenecks may be, it is vital to identify and find remedies to streamline the process for the next issue.

It is also worth reviewing the crisis to determine whether the decisions made exacerbated or prolonged the crisis and then evaluating how things might be done differently in the future. Labatt Breweries found itself in a crisis situation when *The Montreal Gazette* printed a photo from accused murderer Luka Rocco Magnotta's Facebook page that showed him drinking Labatt Blue; such a connection would be damaging to any brand. Labatt was accused of making a bad situation worse by threatening to sue *The Gazette*, prompting a slew of Twitter jokes, with the hashtag #newlabattcampaign trending in Canada.[47] In less than 24 hours, Labatt issued a statement saying that the company would no longer be pursuing the lawsuit. Of the response, Ken Wong, a marketing professor at Queen's University, states, "I can understand their motivation for doing this but they clearly didn't think things through. At this point, they'd be better off just shutting up and going away. If they had just let it slide, I don't think most people would have seen the picture anyway."[48]

Another area worth assessing following a crisis is how the spokesperson performed. A review of the coverage can identify whether the spokesperson stayed on message, demonstrated confidence, and came across as articulate and trustworthy. If it is decided that the spokesperson did not perform well, it is up to the communications team to evaluate whether a new spokesperson should be identified or if more training is needed. In addition to reviewing how official company spokespersons did, the communications team should assess whether any unauthorized employees released or leaked information to the press or on social media, as we saw in the BC Place roof collapse. If this has occurred, it needs to be addressed immediately by reminding employees of company policies and procedures on speaking with the media or of using social media to disseminate company information.

Thinking Like a PR Practitioner

1. Choose an organizational crisis you have read about and imagine you had to prepare a statement for the CEO. Craft this statement to express compassion, conviction, and optimism.

2. Identify two criteria you might use to evaluate the various aspects of the crisis.

CASE STUDY GREYHOUND CANADA

Serving over 1100 Canadian communities through ice, sleet, and extreme weather conditions, Greyhound Canada has plenty of practice in crisis response. From the potential for traffic accidents to targeted crime and disgruntled passengers, there are many foreseeable issues that could affect a national bus company like Greyhound. Probably the most famous crisis that affected Greyhound in recent years was the tragic incident in which one passenger was decapitated by another on board a Greyhound bus in Manitoba. In this case study we will examine a similar crisis that involved a hostage situation.

As Della Smith, principal of Q Workshops, attests from her experience working with the organization as an agency partner on its crisis response, Greyhound's team was able to become expert responders because they recognized the potential threats to their organization and were committed and diligent in their crisis preparation.

Della and Greyhound's intense preparation was certainly put to the test when an elderly woman was taken hostage in a Greyhound bus terminal. The incident lasted for several hours and challenged the preparation and training of employees. By having well-prepared and trained staff, Della and Greyhound were able to release a statement to the media in under an hour and keep them informed with regular updates until the situation was resolved. Thankfully, the woman was not injured, and her captor was arrested and taken into custody.

One of the challenges of preparing an organization like Greyhound for a crisis, such as a hostage taking, is the vast number of scenarios that could affect the organization. Each potential scenario needs a crisis plan. Training a large and geographically diverse workforce can also be difficult. Della believed that including the drivers as an essential part of the crisis team was of the utmost importance, as they were often the first, and sometimes only, Greyhound employees on the scene of a crisis.

Della confesses that crisis response was not always as smooth for Greyhound. "In the first crisis I worked on with them there was a severe lack of systems and processes. But we learned from that first event and from each issue after, and refined our response until it was practically seamless," Della says. Della and Greyhound applied their experiences from each situation to their preparation work and challenged themselves to become faster and more efficient.[49]

Questions

1. What do you think were five key components that Della would have worked on with Greyhound in their crisis preparation?

2. How would Greyhound's crisis preparation and response be applied in the social media age?

3. What would be some of the challenges of providing crisis response training to the Greyhound bus drivers?

Preparing for the Worst, Hoping for the Best

Some PR practitioners specialize in issues and crisis management. They are experts not only at preparing organizations for the worst, but also at dealing with situations if the worst does come to pass. They can swoop in on a moment's notice, organize a war room, and help organizations cope with the issue or crisis. Not only are they experts at managing a crisis, they love it. Pulling all-nighters, camping out in a coffee-filled war room, dealing with the stress, and feeling the energy all exhilarate them. We worked with one such individual on occasion. He perked up when it was action time. It was his calling, and while we would not say that he rejoiced in his clients' calamities, he certainly enjoyed getting them out of trouble.

We, on the other hand, were very capable but reluctant crisis and issues managers. The last thing we wanted was to deal with a client catastrophe. Luckily, we dealt with lots of issues but never a true crisis. With a little preparation and lots of luck, issues never escalated. One of the first steps that we took with all new clients was to make sure they were prepared. If they did not already have one, we prepared an issue and crisis manual for them. The manual included a list of scenarios of what could go wrong, as well as templates for media releases. We knew exactly how we would respond, no matter the situation. We also media trained spokespersons to be able to answer difficult questions calmly and with composure. Additionally, we participated in mock exercises during which we enacted our PR response to a potential crisis such as a food recall. As Alexander Graham Bell said, "Before anything else, preparation is the key to success."

post-crisis evaluation
revision of materials
danger start practice & preparation again

response
CCO template
rebuilding reputation
changing the conversation

prevention
media/ environmental scan
seat at the table

CRISIS

crisis
fire
smoke

build relationships

suppliers
first responders
community partners
media
public
trust

issues

management

social media
changing landscape

opportunity

crisis team
spokespersons
CEO
PR agency
communications team

preparation

crisis plan

practice
APP template
key messages
spokesperson training

Key Terms

bottleneck An obstruction or constraint in the flow of production resulting in an unanticipated delay.

crisis An unusual event that puts the typical operations of an organization in jeopardy.

crisis management The process of averting a crisis from happening and managing a crisis once it has occurred.

crisis plan A detailed manual on how to respond in a crisis situation. This plan may be for specific crisis scenarios.

issues management The management of an emerging problem that has not yet developed and may never develop into a crisis.

legitimacy The right in the eyes of the public for an organization to operate because the organization shares the same values and beliefs as its key stakeholders and the public.

mock drills Simulated crisis scenarios, with the purpose of practising crisis response.

Weblinks

Center for Risk Communication
www.centerforriskcommunication.com/

Domino's Pizza Apology Video
www.youtube.com/watch?v=uFiXWboPD5A

Maple Leaf Foods Apology Video
www.youtube.com/watch?v=zlsN5AkJ1AI

Endnotes

1. Linda Bilben, interview with the author.

2. F. Schultz, D. Utz, and A. Goritz, "Is the Medium the Message? Perceptions of and Reactions to Crisis Communication via Twitter, Blogs and Traditional Media," *Public Relations Review*, 2011, 20–27.

3. G.V. Howell and R. Miller, "Organizational Response to Crisis: A Case Study of Maple Leaf Foods," *The Northwest Journal of Communication*, vol. 39, no. 1 (2001), 91–108.

4. S.D. Ferguson, "Strategic Planning for Issues Management: The Communicator as Environmental Analyst," *Canadian Journal of Communication*, vol. 18, no. 1 (1993), 33.

5. Christopher Meyer and Julia Kirby, "Leadership in the Age of Transparency," *Harvard Business Review*, April 2010, 38–46.

6. Peter Harrison, "Never Waste a Good Crisis, Clinton Says on Climate," *Reuters.com*, March 7, 2009. Accessed March 2, 2013, http://in.reuters.com/article/2009/03/06/us-eu-climate-clinton-idINTRE5251VN20090306

7. Ibid.

8. J.E. Massey and J.P. Larson, "Crisis Management in Real Time: How to Successfully Plan for and Respond to a Crisis," *Journal of Promotion Management*, vol. 12 (2006), 63–97.

9. Ferguson, "Strategic Planning for Issues Management."

10. Meyer and Kirby, "Leadership in the Age of Transparency."

11. M.W. Seeger, "Best Practices in Crisis Communication: An Expert Panel Process," *Journal of Applied Communication Research*, vol. 34, no. 3 (August 2006), 232–244.

12. Alyssa G. Millner, Shari R. Veil, and Timothy L. Sellnow, "Proxy Communication in Crisis Response," *Public Relations Review*, July 30, 2010, 74–76.

13. Ibid.

14. Ibid.

15. Seeger, "Best Practices in Crisis Communication."

16. Ibid.

17. Kristin Laird, "Crisis Talks," *Marketing*, July 14, 2010. Accessed February 5, 2013, http://www.marketingmag.ca/news/pr-news/crisis-talks-3885

18. Ibid.

19. Massey and Larson, "Crisis Management in Real Time," p. 69.

20. Ibid.

21. Ibid.

22. Ibid.

23. Linda Bilben, "BC Place Case Study: Reputations," Reputations.com, 2007. Accessed February 5, 2013, http://www.reputations.com/cs_bcplace.shtml

24. Millner et al., "Proxy Communication in Crisis Response."

25. Maurice Bridge, "Beer May Be Flowing Again by Next Week," *The Vancouver Sun*, May 14, 2004. Accessed March 4, 2013, http://search.proquest.com.proxy.lib.sfu.ca/docview/24233899 1/13C9488180877E7E410/3?accountid=13800

26. V.D. Covello, "Core Slides: Risk Communication," Centre for Risk Communication, May 2007. Accessed February 27, 2013, http://www.gchd.us/ReportsAndData/Presentations/ PublicHealthWeek2007/Dr_Covello_Risk_Communication_presentation.pdf

27. Ibid.

28. Ibid.

29. Gordon Pitts, Iain Marlow, and Greg Keenan, "What I've Learned," *Report on Business*, July/ August 2011, 26–35.

30. J. Greenberg and Charlene Elliott, "A Cold Cut Crisis: Listeriosis, Maple Leaf Foods, and the Politics of Apology," *Canadian Journal of Communication*, vol. 34, no. 2 (2009), 189–204.

31. Howell and Miller, "Organizational Response to Crisis."

32. Ibid.

33. Ibid.

34. Greenberg and Elliott, "A Cold Cut Crisis."

35. Seeger, "Best Practices in Crisis Communication."

36. R.S. Levick, "Domino's Discovers Social Media," *Bloomberg Businessweek*, April 21, 2009. Accessed March 2, 2013, http://www.businessweek.com/managing/content/apr2009/ ca20090421_555468.htm

37. Covello, "Core Slides: Risk Communication."

38. Ibid.

39. Greenberg and Elliott, "A Cold Cut Crisis."

40. Howell and Miller, "Organizational Response to Crisis."

41. Bilben, "BC Place Case Study."

42. Laura Petrecca, "Offended Moms Get Tweet Revenge over Motrin Ads," *USA Today*, November 19, 2008. Accessed March 1, 2013, http://web.ebscohost.com.proxy.lib.sfu.ca/ ehost/detail?sid=db818737-a5b3-4301-ae1f-816dd0cf00c5%40sessionmgr11&vid=4&hid=23 &bdata=JnNpdGU9ZWhvc3QtbGl2ZQ%3d%3d#db=aph&AN=J0E256858842008

43. Lisa Belkin, "Moms and Motrin," *The New York Times*, November 17, 2008. Accessed February 5, 2013, http://parenting.blogs.nytimes.com/2008/11/17/moms-and-motrin/

44. Laird, "Crisis Talks."

45. Ibid.

46. S. Muralidharan, L. Rasmussen, D. Patterson, and J.-H. Shin, "Hope for Haiti: An Analysis of Facebook and Twitter Usage during the Earthquake Relief Efforts," *Public Relations Review*, vol. 37, no. 2 (June 2011), 175–177.

47. Josh Rubin, "Labatt Abandons Threat to Sue The Gazette over Magnotta Photo," *TheSpec.com*, June 5, 2012. Accessed February 5, 2013, http://www.thespec.com/news/article/738002–labatt-abandons-threat-to-sue-the-gazette-over-magnotta-photo

48. Ibid.

49. Della Smith, interview with the author.

How Do I Network Effectively?

One of the subjects students often ask about is networking. How do I network? Where should I network? What are some networking tips? Most students know that networking is important but find it intimidating. While some love it and others see it as a necessary evil, others would rather do anything else than walk into a room where they do not know anyone and start up a conversation. It is really not as scary as it seems. Plus, there are so many benefits that come from networking that it is well worth the investment in time, effort, and money (for those membership and event fees). Networking's numerous benefits include job leads, professional support, and the expertise of others to help you solve problems.

Here are some tips that might help:

- Practise being friendly to everyone. The word *networking* makes being social seem more formal than it is. It is really just about meeting new people and talking to them. Talk to people in line at the grocery store or in the elevator. The more you practise making small talk, the easier it gets.

- Read the paper, watch the news, and make sure you are up on current events. PR practitioners tend to be heavy media consumers. Impress them by knowing what is going on in the world and being able to comment intelligently on it.

- Join your local associations. The Canadian Public Relations Society (CPRS) and the International Association of Business Communicators (IABC) provide fantastic opportunities for networking with other PR practitioners. These groups also provide support, guidance, and contacts for budding PR practitioners. They also have mentoring programs, award opportunities, and scholarships that are available to students. They host regular meetings with leading practitioners speaking on emerging trends in our industry. They also provide volunteer opportunities, which are a great way to meet people and gain experience. Most associations have student membership fees that are reasonably priced.

- Volunteer. Walking into a room where you do not know anyone is hard. By volunteering, you will have the ability to meet people in the industry so that when you go to the events you will recognize some friendly faces of people who can help introduce you to others. It is also a great way to build your resumé and portfolio and contribute in a meaningful way.

- Be bold. At the end of the day it does take a bit of courage to be a successful networker. Take some chances. Take a deep breath, smile, and introduce yourself to someone new. You never know where it might lead.

- Start with your classmates. Look at the people around you, from other students to faculty and staff. They each have their own network you can tap into. Also, as you and your classmates find jobs within the industry and develop your skills, you will be able to help each other find new jobs, solve problems, and make connections.

- Consider joining the organizations in your community. These include chambers of commerce, boards of trade, business owners' groups, and women's networks.

Chapter 12
Other Areas of PR Specialization

Peak Communications is using community relations, government relations, media relations, and Aboriginal relations to garner support for the Montana–Alberta Tie Line. Source: © volyk/Fotolia

LEARNING OBJECTIVES

❶ Identify what additional training is needed and who the audience is for each of the PR specialties.

❷ Understand the principles of how public affairs incorporates government and community relations to create a more favourable operating environment.

❸ Compare and contrast the different PR specialties, including audiences and tactics.

❹ Outline the tactics that are available to investor relations practitioners.

Charged Communities: Using Public Affairs to Gain Community Support for a Cross-Border Power Line

In 2006, Montana Alberta Tie Ltd. approached Shael Gelfand, vice president of Peak Communications Alberta, because the company's management knew they needed his help. The privately owned power line company was working on getting its newest project off the ground: a 345-kilometre, 300-megawatt power line that would run between Lethbridge, Alberta, and Great Falls, Montana, tying together the two respective power grids. The company needed to convince both the government and the community of the need for this controversial project to gain their support and move forward.

Gelfand's team sprang into action, engaging in community, government, Aboriginal, and media relations for Montana Alberta Tie. The company had to go through a series of approvals, including National Energy Board and provincial approval, and also win over residents and the city and town councils of the communities that were on the proposed power line's route.

While there definitely was a need for the power line, as ruled by the Alberta Electrical Systems Operator (AESO), in order to prevent brownouts or a drop in electrical voltage, there was a lot of misinformation among the public. This misinformation included the perception that living near the power lines could cause cancer. Gelfand said that deflecting and combatting this misinformation was one of the biggest challenges his team faced. While the opposition could make outrageous claims with few repercussions, Montana Alberta Tie needed to stay truthful, factual, and transparent. To try to counteract the misinformation, the company stuck to its key messages: the line was needed, the line would ensure the security of the energy supply, and the line would create employment. The company also needed to educate the public about power. According to Gelfand, "While we all use electricity every day, the public knowledge about how energy works is very low."[1] To better educate the public on its power supply, Peak Communications and Montana Alberta Tie held open houses, made presentations to town councils and chambers of commerce, wrote letters to the editor and opinion editorials, and distributed informational newsletters. It was important that the community stay abreast of all new developments and of the organization's point of view. They also formed a citizens' advisory panel to hear feedback from the community in the form of written and oral submissions.

"One of our most successful tactics was the development of the citizens' advisory panel," says Gelfand. "This panel was chaired by the former president of the University of Lethbridge and reviewed submissions from the community. The panel would then make recommendations to Montana Alberta Tie based on these submissions. The panel was made up of well-respected, high-integrity community members who didn't have any conflicts of interest. It provided a forum where people felt heard. It also gave us important insight into the largest pain points for the community, so that we could rectify them." The company also engaged the local First Nations community, asking them to review the proposed power line route to ensure it would not disturb any sacred land or burial sites.

Gelfand's team's efforts proved effective in the Canadian market. Following a successful Supreme Court of Canada ruling, deals were reached with all the affected landowners and the power line received permission to go ahead in Alberta. Montana Alberta Tie is still working to reach a similar resolution on the U.S. side of the border.

PR Specializations ❶

The term *public relations* is a broad umbrella that encompasses a variety of specializations and areas of expertise. As we just saw in the opening vignette on Montana Alberta Tie, a PR campaign can encompass several specialties in order to meet its objectives. This specific campaign focused on community relations, government relations, media relations, and Aboriginal relations.

While many communicators start their careers wearing many hats, as they gain more experience they often develop areas of focus and begin to specialize. All public relations specialties share the same fundamentals of building relationships, raising awareness, and managing perceptions among audiences and stakeholders. However, in some instances the stakeholders are so distinct that special training is needed. These areas of public relations require more specialized training outside the area of communications.

The areas of specialization that we will examine in this chapter include public affairs, which encompasses government and community relations; communicating to distinct audiences such as multicultural audiences, including French speakers, international

Table 12.1	PR Specialties	
Specialty	**Audiences/Stakeholders**	**Additional Training That May Be Needed**
Investor relations	Analysts Shareholders Business media	Financial training: e.g., Canadian Securities Course, master's of business administration
Community relations	Geographic communities/residents of a specific community	Community engagement training
	Psychographic communities/members with a common experience	Community development training
Government relations	Government/elected officials	Political science
International PR	Citizens and media in other countries	Cross-cultural studies Language studies
Aboriginal relations	First Nations communities First Nations bands	First Nations studies

audiences, the LGBT community, and Aboriginal groups; and investor relations. We will elaborate on the roles and responsibilities of these functions and their audiences. However, because we will just touch on each area, if you are interested in pursuing any of these focuses, you will need to do more research and investigation. See Table 12.1 for a comparison of the different specialties, their target audiences, and additional education that may be required for those fields.

Public Affairs ❷

Public affairs is a communications specialty that encompasses government relations and community relations. A public affairs department may practise both or specialize in one area. Public affairs departments try to influence the outcomes of civic decisions that help their business environment. The Montana Alberta Tie Line campaign featured in the opening vignette relied heavily on public affairs, incorporating both government and community relations to push projects and agendas forward. Government relations is needed to obtain the required approvals, zoning, and permissions. As governments pay attention to the concerns of their constituents, community relations is also often needed in order to secure the approval and support of the greater public.

To better understand public affairs, it might be helpful to examine the Public Affairs Council's definition of this communications specialty: "Public affairs represents an organization's efforts to monitor and manage its business environment. It combines government relations, communications, issues management, and corporate citizenship strategies to influence public policy, build a strong reputation and find common ground with stakeholders."[2] In other words, public affairs uses public relations tactics to ensure the environment it operates in is favourable. For example, a group of pub owners might band together and engage in public affairs to convince governments and voters that tougher drinking-and-driving laws are not needed because they will hurt the food service industry, just as Mothers Against Drunk Driving (MADD) might engage in the same tactics in hopes of the opposite outcome. Two examples of organizations that often have sizable public affairs teams include banks and universities.

GOVERNMENT RELATIONS

A large component of the public affairs specialty is **government relations**. Government actions can affect an organization's goals and profitability.[3] Therefore, companies employ or contract government relations practitioners to assist them in swaying governments' decisions in their favour on certain issues that are important to their financial or operational viability. It is important to note that government relations is not solely the domain of business or for-profit companies. A charitable organization such as an anti-cancer group might lobby the government for stricter regulations around what chemicals or additives can be included in beauty products. In the case of the Montana Alberta Tie Line campaign featured in the opening vignette, government relations included making presentations to town councils, hosting open houses, and working with local governments to address any concerns.

Successful government relations practitioners understand the political system and know how to operate within it to sway key influencers in the government in ways that will benefit their organization. Government relations practitioners develop relationships with key influencers in political parties and political staff and are the bridge between these influencers and their organizations. It is important for government relations practitioners to understand the different needs of government employees and politicians, both of whom might be their audience. Naturally, politicians will be motivated by different factors than will civil servants. Brent Sauder is the director of strategic initiatives for the Office of Research and Partnerships at the University of British Columbia. He is also a former assistant deputy minister for British Columbia. He notes that, at its most basic level, government relations is about identifying influencers in government and building relationships and trust between them and the organization. The organization needs to have a clear understanding of the government's priorities and expectations, and needs to communicate to the government the organization's priorities and issues. Sauder's advice to new practitioners interested in government relations is to gain some experience in civil service, as it is difficult to understand how government operates from the outside.

Rob Lowe promoting the movie *Thank You for Smoking,* which showcased a satirical view of lobbying.

Some of the tactics government relations practitioners may engage in are constituency building, media relations, and lobbying. They also pay close attention to shifts in political sentiment and potential changes in legislation. Similar to performing environmental scans, discussed in Chapters 4 and 11, government relations officers are always monitoring changes at the political level. It is also important for them to have a gauge on voters' political leanings, as a change in government may affect the business environment. At the same time that Montana Alberta Tie was trying to get approval on its power line, another larger, extremely unpopular power line was also trying to get approval. The unpopularity of the other power line made it more difficult for Montana Alberta Tie to sway public opinion and, as a result, government officials were reluctant to support the project publicly.

Lobbying

A somewhat notorious activity that falls under the government relations umbrella is **lobbying**. This practice was made famous by the 2005 dark comedy *Thank You for Smoking*, which portrays lobbyists from the tobacco, gun, and alcohol industries (who call themselves the "Merchants of Death"). In the film, these lobbyists go to great lengths to protect their industries' business environments.

In reality, lobbying is not sinister—it is simply representing special interests to government decision makers. If you have ever signed a petition, you have been involved in lobbying. The PR agency Hill & Knowlton produced a brilliant YouTube video, titled "Billy Wants a Dog," that explains lobbying in a fun, informative way. In it, the PR firm explains that if Billy wants a dog, he has several options, including trying to get his mom to convince his dad on his behalf, thereby lobbying his parents.[4] Similarly, if a company, charity, or coalition wants the government to do something, such as decrease a tax or change a regulation, the company needs to lobby the government.[5] It is the government relations practitioner's job to develop strategies to help the organization convince the government of its position.

Depending on the size of the firm, its resources, and the policy or regulations it supports, an organization may want to lobby itself, band together with similar organizations in the industry, mobilize supporters or suppliers, or lobby with companies across sectors.[6] For example, for many years in Canada, companies in the organics industry across various sectors lobbied the government for a Canadian organic certification process similar to the United States' USDA organic certification. The Canadian organic certification was finally implemented in 2010. Because the companies banded together, the cost was much lower per firm, and the collective approach had a greater impact in getting the government's attention.

Lobbying can be direct or indirect.[7] An indirect method of lobbying is educating citizens and convincing them to help lobby the government on the issue by employing tactics such as writing letters to elected officials, signing petitions, or staging protests. However, sometimes the citizens are not as arm's-length from an organization as they are made to appear. This is called astroturfing.

As we saw in Chapter 2, **astroturfing**, which got its name from Astroturf, the fake grass, occurs when fake grassroots organizations are formed to lobby the government or public so that it does not look as if a particular organization is tied to the lobbying. Astroturfing also makes it seem as though there is a mass movement behind a particular initiative when there is not. In 2010, the communications team for Toronto mayoral candidate Rob Ford created a fake Twitter profile of a woman with the Twitter handle

Becoming a Government Relations Practitioner

Greg Owen from PathFinders Counsel has this advice for new practitioners trying to break into the industry:

- Be interested in politics. This is not a career path most people fall into. Usually those who are successful are passionate about government and how it works.

- Start in an entry-level position in a government office. You will learn things about how government works and how decisions are made that you could never learn anywhere else.

- Get involved in government at some level. Pick your level, municipal, provincial, or federal government and volunteer.

- Or, if you are interested in partisan politics, pick your party and volunteer.

- Be persistent. It is easy to get a first meeting with an official, but how do you get a second? Also, have the facts and data needed to support your argument. You need a well-researched, well-thought-out case that provides solutions.

@QueensQuayKaren and tweeted supportive comments about the mayoral-hopeful without disclosing that the woman's identity was fabricated.[8] Rob Ford won the election to become mayor. This is astroturfing in the social media age, an activity that is considered unethical for government relations practitioners. The ethical issues arise because, by its very nature, astroturfing is dishonest and misleads the public.

One of the most famous examples of astroturfing occurred in 1991, when Iraq invaded Kuwait.[9] In an effort to convince the U.S. public to support the Iraq War, Citizens for a Free Kuwait, which was positioned as a grassroots group, put forward Nayirah, who was supposedly a 15-year-old Kuwaiti refugee. She testified before a congressional hearing that she had seen Iraqi soldiers go into a hospital and throw babies from their incubators.[10] It was later revealed that Nayirah was the daughter of the Kuwaiti ambassador to the United States and that the incubator story was a lie.[11] The Kuwaiti government in exile had hired Hill & Knowlton and paid the agency $10 million to create the Citizens for a Free Kuwait astroturf organization, prepare Nayirah's testimony, and convince Congress and the American public to support a war with Iraq.[12] Astroturfing runs in stark contrast to community relations, where genuine community support is built by creating a dialogue between the community and the organization.

COMMUNITY RELATIONS

In **community relations**, organizations create a two-way dialogue between themselves and the community to build a relationship and to gain their support. The community can be geographic, meaning the place where the company operates, or psychographic, meaning a group that has a defining interest or cause. In the opening vignette, Montana Alberta Tie illustrated how community relations practitioners built ties to a community by employing strategies and tactics to educate, engage, build understanding, and develop goodwill. According to the PR team, one of the most successful tactics they implemented was the creation of a citizens' advisory panel to receive community feedback because it provided a forum where the public could feel heard and the company could better understand the issues.

A useful breakdown of community relations was conducted at the Great Lakes Regional Community Relations Conference, where it was broken into three parts: serve, sell, and socialize.[13] *Serve* refers to giving back to the community through tactics such as community donations and sponsorships.[14] For example, a Niagara Falls quarry employs a community relations program where it builds goodwill with future business and community leaders through donations to Brock University.[15] The quarry also allows the local Scouts to use parts of the quarry as a camping ground and has donated playgrounds and built walking trails for the community.[16] *Sell* speaks to promoting the company and the activities it does for the community. This could be through applying for awards or sending out press releases and employing media relations. Lastly, *socialize* refers to interacting with the public through tactics such as hosting community open houses and public forums, and responding to customer complaints.[17]

Farm Credit Canada (FCC) is a financially self-sustaining federal Crown corporation that provides financing and other services to primary producers, value-added operators, suppliers, and processors along the agriculture value chain. FCC operates from 100 offices located primarily in rural communities across Canada. In 2004, a community relations program called FCC Drive Away Hunger was launched. The food drive brings together customers and employees to help Canadian food banks help those who go hungry. It has grown to become the largest employee-led food drive in Canada. It's a perfect fit for FCC as an organization in the business of agriculture, which is the business of producing food.

The target audiences are customers and potential customers, corporate and community partners, employees, and the public. The objectives of the FCC Drive Away Hunger are to support food banks by raising food, cash, and awareness of hunger across Canada; enhance FCC's reputation as a good corporate citizen with its stakeholders; and create a

Farm Credit Canada was able to support food banks by raising food, cash, and awareness of hunger across Canada with FCC Drive Away Hunger.
Source: Greg Huszar

positive experience for employees, the majority of whom reported being proud of FCC's continued community involvement.

To achieve its objectives and reach its target audiences, FCC organizes an annual tractor tour through five provinces, including an additional tour in Regina, Saskatchewan—home of the FCC corporate office. The tractor makes frequent stops at schools, community groups, and local businesses to collect donations. On each leg of the tour, media events are organized, including live radio updates along the tour. Employees and community groups are involved locally in handling logistics and engaging the public.

Each year, the tour results in food and cash donations that have exceeded targets, meaning fewer people go hungry in Canada. Positive local, provincial, and national media coverage has resulted in an increase in awareness of FCC's role as a good corporate citizen and employee participation in FCC offices across the country. This, in turn, has resulted in the strengthening of collaboration and positive community relations in more than 100 communities in Canada.

Community relations does not just need to include geographic communities. It can include communities that share something in common, such as a disease. For example, LifeScan Canada, a Johnson & Johnson company that manufactures blood glucose monitors, connects with the diabetes community by sponsoring Juvenile Diabetes Research Fund walks, seeking advice from health care practitioners who specialize in diabetes, and conducting targeted media relations aimed at this population segment. Good community relations, whether geographical or experience based, helps create a better, stronger company and community by finding areas of compromise and support. It also helps both the company and the community meet their goals.

The Tension between Internal and External Audiences

One of the biggest challenges for community relations practitioners is the internal battle for resources and organizational change. To illustrate this point, envision a situation in which a community relations practitioner works for a mining company in a marginalized community. The community relations practitioner meets with the public and listens to their "pain points," or areas that need improvement, regarding the practices of the company. The community has suggested solutions that are viable but expensive and time-consuming for the organization. Even if the community relations practitioner believes these remedies should be implemented, how does he or she convince management of this and explain it in a way that shows a return on investment? To be taken seriously, the community relations practitioner needs to speak in a way that management will understand. On the other hand, if the practitioner tries to convince the community that they should accept the status quo because it is better for the company's balance sheet, he or she will alienate the community. As one community relations practitioner for the mining industry says, "We've learned from experience that it's a balance. In the past we've turned our attention internally too much and lost touch with the community.

When we've turned our attention too external, we dropped the ball with management and lost their support."[18] It is the community relations practitioner's job to bridge the perspectives of management and the community and facilitate solutions that are mutually beneficial.[19]

Thinking Like a PR Practitioner

1. Describe why astroturfing might be considered unethical.

2. Name two challenges that community relations practitioners face and some ways to mitigate these challenges.

Public Relations for Specialized Audiences ❸

In addition to public affairs, various areas of public relations target specialized audiences. These include international public relations, multicultural and diversity relations, and Aboriginal relations. All these specialties focus on learning about and embracing cross-cultural differences and diversity and building relationships with other cultures or nations.

INTERNATIONAL PUBLIC RELATIONS

International public relations involves building relationships across borders and building or enhancing an organization's reputation in other countries. It also involves conducting PR campaigns on the ground in these foreign markets. Many Canadian companies conduct business in the United States or across the globe. Each country has its own distinct economic and political climate, customs, language, and culture.[20] Part of international public relations is learning about the country your organization is doing business with and learning about how the media operate in that company. It is important to remember the PR fundamentals and apply them to the new country and culture. For example, whether they be local or international, you must understand your target audiences.

If the country is significantly different culturally, if the way its media operate is quite different, or if a foreign language is spoken, local PR practitioners can be hired to provide advice and to implement the tactics. They know the local customs and have the key relationships with local media. They know their markets best, just as you know yours.

PR in Global Markets

When Canadian organizations want to conduct PR in foreign countries, they generally seek out on-the-ground local practitioners for the reasons we mentioned above. This can be accomplished in a number of ways. The first way is to work with the large global PR agencies, such as Fleishman-Hillard Inc., which has 80 offices all over the world including in Canada. Several such multinational agencies exist. These large agencies can mobilize their teams in whatever country the client needs support in. The second way is to hire a Canadian PR agency that has opened offices in other countries. National PR, for instance, a Canadian PR agency, has opened additional offices in the United States and the United Kingdom. The third way is to go through international networks of independently owned PR agencies, such as the Worldcom Group, which has 108 partner agencies throughout the world including in Asia Pacific, North America, South America, Europe, the Middle East, and Africa. When the clients of one partner want to conduct a campaign in another country, that partner works in collaboration with the partner in the other country. For instance, when the PACE Group, a Canadian PR agency, wanted to generate media coverage for its clients with the international media visiting Vancouver for the 2010 Olympics, it created an international media database in collaboration with partners in New York, Los Angeles, Philadelphia, and Chicago. This effort helped generate international media coverage with media outlets such as NBC, BBC, *USA Today*, and FoxTel Australia.[21]

Like Canada, most countries have professional PR associations that can provide support and counsel for PR practitioners looking to conduct PR in their country. Some examples include the Public Relations Society of America, the Public Relations Institute of Australia, and the Shanghai Public Relations Association. International professional associations also exist, such as the International Public Relations Association, the European Public Relations Confederation, and the African Public Relations Association.

International PR in Canada

International PR may also involve conducting a PR campaign in Canada for a foreign organization. In some cases, an existing campaign is **localized**, or adapted for a local market, and in other cases it is created from scratch for Canada. An example of the former is the work that the Canadian PR team, both in-house and agency, does for Cathay Pacific Airways. The organization is headquartered in Hong Kong, and the PR team in that country leads all the international PR efforts, writing media releases and sending them to the company's PR teams all over the world, including Canada. The media releases are then localized, meaning that some information is adapted to suit the local market. Localization can also include translating the media release into the local language and adding the contact information of a local PR practitioner. In other cases, the Canadian PR team for Cathay Pacific Airways will plan and implement a campaign strictly for Canada.

Another example of international PR conducted in Canada is the work that the PR agency AHA Creative did for its client Tourism New Zealand. AHA Creative implemented a PR campaign for New Zealand's annual tourism trade show TRENZ (Tourism Rendezvous New Zealand). Organizers feared that many Canadian travel trade media and travel industry professionals would not be able to attend the trade show because of the downturn in the economy and fears over H1N1. The objective was to generate interest in and participation from the key target audiences who usually attended the show.

With social media, AHA was able to reach the target audiences directly and interactively engage the public. In partnership with Tourism New Zealand, AHA developed an interactive blog called TRENZblog, which enabled tourism professionals and media who could not attend the trade show to participate by reading information on tour operators, commenting on what they viewed, and emailing their questions.

New Zealand tourism benefited from AHA Creative's promotional international public relations campaign.
Source: Tupungato/Shutterstock

AHA partner Ruth Atherley attended the trade show to blog about new and interesting tourism-related products being showcased. To add a visual component to the blog, Atherley toured New Zealand's South Island a week before the start of the trade show and wrote about her travel experiences. A media release on the blog was distributed globally to English-speaking travel trade media, travel professionals, and other target audiences to help promote the launch of the blog. A Twitter account for TRENZblog was also created. Atherley blogged several times a day for 12 days and updated the Twitter account with photos and links to the blog.

As part of the campaign and to create compelling content for the blog, Tourism New Zealand requested and received an interview with the prime minister of New Zealand (who also holds the portfolio for tourism). Atherley became the first travel blogger to interview New Zealand prime minister John Key. It is important to note that AHA strategized the best ways to reach the target audiences when carefully crafting each social media tactic.

Tourism New Zealand considered this pilot project a success. The campaign met its PR objectives and delivered results. Readership of the blog was high, while consumer and travel media provided coverage about the blog, providing links to it in their print and online articles. Many of the trade journalists who attended the trade show requested that Atherley's blog be kept online for a few more months, so they could link to it in their articles. In addition, several other bloggers picked up the content, generating even more visitors to the blog. Daily visitors to the blog continually increased from its launch through to the last post, with many people writing in for travel advice. At TRENZ, a strong buzz developed among the tour operators that heightened the excitement around the blog. As a result, Atherley was frequently sought out by tour operators who asked to be profiled.

MULTICULTURAL PR

Another specialized PR function is multicultural PR. This area of public relations is expanding as Canadian society experiences dramatic demographic changes. According to Statistics Canada, the country's ethnic and cultural makeup is undergoing rapid change, especially in our most populous cities. The increase in the number of immigrants whose first language is neither English nor French, members of visible minority groups, and people whose religion is non-Christian has enhanced Canada's cultural diversity in recent decades.[22]

In Toronto, one in two residents was born outside Canada and, in Montreal, one in three. In Richmond, British Columbia, that number is three out of five residents.[23] Plus, these numbers are on the rise. It is projected that half the population of Toronto and Vancouver may be represented by visible minorities by 2017.[24]

What does this mean for public relations? First, this demographic change raises the question of how, as public relations practitioners, we are going to communicate to these audiences and build relationships with these communities. Second, it prompts the question of how public relations will change and adapt as more multicultural Canadians join the industry.

Communicating with Multicultural Groups

In his book *Multicultural Public Relations: A Social-Interpretive Approach*, author Stephen P. Banks emphasizes the necessity of communicating in a cultural style that is consistent with the audience's expectations. He also states that, because of cultural differences, there are challenges in communicating with these target audiences.[25]

Public relations practitioners must take cultural differences into consideration when deciding on the key messages they want to communicate, as well as the tactics they will use in reaching these audiences. As with all audiences, success can be achieved only by getting to know these groups well. PR practitioners cannot make any assumptions, especially when targeting audiences that are different from themselves.

Questions that need to be addressed include: What language is appropriate? What are some of the issues facing these audiences? How does this audience like to be communicated to? Where does this audience get their news and where do they share information? Who are the key influencers?

In order to reach these audiences, PR practitioners work with the hundreds of people who represent the multicultural media across Canada that cater to these audiences, including newspapers, radio, television, and websites. (See Chapter 6 for more information.)

Multicultural PR is an emerging specialty. PR professionals and other marketing experts are just beginning to develop this expertise. *Marketing* magazine holds a yearly conference on multicultural marketing that attracts practitioners eager to learn more about reaching these specialized groups.

Examples of multicultural groups targeted by public relations practitioners in Canada include Chinese and East Indian communities. For example, Home Depot hosts special in-store events targeting multicultural groups. In British Columbia, the company has organized Cantonese events with all the campaign collateral in that language to forge a closer relationship with this group, while in Ontario it has targeted the East Indian community with a similar campaign in Punjabi and Hindi.[33] The multicultural breakdown of Canadians is different from that in the United States, where communicators are placing more emphasis on reaching African-American and Latino communities.

Public Relations for a Francophone Audience

One of Canada's unique aspects is that it has two official languages, French and English. Almost 8 million Canadians consider French their official language and close to 10 million speak it.[26] In Quebec, 80 per cent of residents speak French as their first language.[27] Outside of Quebec, there are French-speaking communities across Canada, from British Columbia to Newfoundland, with the majority living in New Brunswick and Ontario.[28]

A large number of French communities have their own media, including newspapers, TV, and radio provided by Radio-Canada, the French-language CBC network. When Lison Ouellette, a B.C. French speaker, launched her design boutique LisonArtFurniture in Vancouver, she was featured on the local French radio station.

Conducting public relations in Quebec is sometimes similar to conducting public relations in a foreign country. Even if a PR campaign was launched in the rest of Canada, because of the language and cultural differences in Quebec the campaign will need to be either customized for Quebec or created from scratch to appeal to the province's target audiences and media. Many companies find that if they run the same campaign in Quebec as in the rest of English Canada but just change it to French, it does not perform as well because campaigns need to be tailored to Quebec's distinct culture.

Quebec has its own full spectrum of media and bloggers in French. There are some English-language media in the province, but they reach only a minority of the population. Customs and traditions are also different in Quebec. For example, July 1 is moving day in Quebec. Every year up to 700,000 people move on that day; in the city of Montreal alone, 225,000 households move each July 1.[29] You can imagine the pandemonium of so many people trying to secure moving supplies and trucks. To help with the problem, Ikea created a fun PR campaign tailored for a Quebec audience, giving out 18,000 cardboard boxes around Montreal in the days surrounding July 1. An Ikea truck delivered boxes around town, and the company provided real-time updates on Facebook and Twitter on where the truck could be found.[30]

In another example, Michaels, the craft retailer, has been commended for how it handled communications surrounding its Quebec launch. In September 2012, Michaels opened seven stores in Quebec with impressive special events that featured local celebrities, media, and the who's who of the crafting world. Marie-Josee Gagnon of the firm Casacom, which handled the communications leading to the store openings, comments,

> This successful launch did not happen overnight; in fact, the process began three years prior, when Michaels decided to invest in an impressive cross-cultural communication program. It is common to see foreign businesses come to Québec and make only the minimum effort to adapt to Québec's culture. Michaels truly invested in Québec.[31]

These efforts included extensive research through focus groups and a survey, translating all its written materials into French, developing a French tagline, and hiring a local Quebec managing director who was trained as a spokesperson. A local influencer in the craft world was also selected to be the Michaels ambassador for Quebec.[32]

Multicultural PR Specialists

Some public relations professionals have expertise in working with certain groups or belong to those multicultural groups. Because of their deep understanding of the specific audience, they have insights that go a long way toward making a campaign a success.

Organizations are beginning to put resources into reaching multicultural audiences. Some are even establishing in-house positions that focus exclusively on multicultural communications, such as Bell Mobility's specialist role, multicultural marketing communications, and Telus's multicultural marketing manager role.

There are also agencies that specialize in multicultural marketing communications, such as Focus Communications (Chinese relations), Balmoral Communications (East Indian relations), and Indigenous Corporate Training (Aboriginal relations).

In addition, curriculums in PR studies are offering classes on multicultural PR. The First Nations Technical Institute, for example, offers a public relations certificate to train emerging Aboriginal practitioners. These efforts to strengthen multicultural communications will enhance the public relations profession by making it more adept at defining and communicating with niche markets. Long gone are the days when a single message was communicated to the masses. In today's PR world, PR practitioners must truly understand whom they are speaking to and the most effective way to do so.

The LGBT community is another audience public relations practitioners must consider in their communications plans.

Source: © Queerstock, Inc./Alamy

PR for the LGBT Community

Like multicultural audiences, the lesbian, gay, bisexual, and transgendered (LGBT) community is a significant audience that needs special consideration. Around 2.8 per cent of Canadians self-identify as LGBT, which is just under a million people, and this group represents millions of consumer dollars. Savvy companies often communicate directly to these groups.[34]

One of the earliest brands to advertise directly to the LGBT community was Absolut Vodka in the 1980s. The company recognized that this group encompassed trendsetters whom young people might emulate.[35] Since then, it has become more accepted for brands to support and sponsor pride parades and queer festivals across the country, as well as conduct media relations with LGBT publications, such as *Xtra*. In 1995, the PR agency behemoth Hill & Knowlton announced that it was creating a group within its agency that would specialize in communicating to the gay community.[36] While many small boutique agencies were already targeting this consumer, the fact that such a conventional institution would create a group to target this market signals the growing importance of this minority within mainstream culture.[37]

On the flip side, sometimes LGBT associations or businesses need to conduct media relations with publications that will reach a mass audience and build awareness or understanding of issues affecting their community. Montreal's award-winning Rae Spoon, a transgendered indie electronic musician, has used strategic media relations to garner widespread coverage in both the mainstream and LGBT press. Also, sometimes government relations is needed to affect legislation in support of gay rights. PR on behalf of or to the LGBT community is growing in Canada and will continue to gain more prominence in the coming years.

ABORIGINAL RELATIONS

BC Hydro, a Crown corporation and one of the largest electric utilities in Canada, has facilities on 168 First Nations territories.[38] In order to continue to do business on the land, the hydro company must develop and sustain positive relationships with each of the

BC Hydro has facilities on 168 First Nations territories, necessitating a strong Aboriginal relations program for this organization.
Source: © Ken Gillespie Photography/Alamy

bands. To support its relationship building with First Nations communities, the company relies heavily on educating its staff. Over 4700 of its employees have attended a half-day cultural-training program.[39] The organization also involves First Nations communities in the early stages of new projects in order to receive input and foster an open, two-way dialogue.[40] The company gives back to the communities with scholarships and economic development programs.[41]

BC Hydro is a good example of a company that is successfully implementing **Aboriginal relations**, a public relations specialty that involves building relationships with First Nations and Inuit communities. This specialty is imperative for companies that operate in or near First Nations bands or Inuit communities or that do business with bands.

When PR practitioners think of cross-cultural communications, they are probably more likely to envision conducting PR overseas than engaging with First Nations bands.[42] However, with 1.2 million First Nations citizens in Canada, and 630 First Nations bands, this audience can't be ignored.[43] Saskatchewan's PotashCorp, a fertilizer producer, views the province's First Nations as a vital community to engage from a recruitment perspective. In order to further this objective, the company provides two-day Aboriginal awareness training to all employees, practises community relations with targeted First Nations communities, uses facility tours and career fairs to raise awareness about the company, and works to support and develop potential First Nations suppliers.[44]

The Montana Alberta Tie campaign discussed in the opening vignette also conducted Aboriginal relations. The organization consulted with any affected First Nations communities and had them review the plans to ensure the power line route would not affect burial grounds or sacred areas.

Unfortunately, the current relationship between First Nations and the rest of Canada is haunted by a tumultuous history and current land-claim negotiations, which have caused enduring mistrust and misunderstanding.[45] This wariness between First Nations and the business community is illustrated by a comment made by Chris Scott, chief operating officer of the Osoyoos Indian Band Development Corporation: "Some companies view First Nations as easy to take advantage of, and that has, in part, created the trust issues that hinder relationship-building. One hundred thirty years of damage to Aboriginal people means that corporations should be prepared to go over and above the normal commitments they would make in other business relationships."[46]

In 2012, Enbridge and the Wet'suwet'en nation had a communications misunderstanding regarding the Northern Gateway Pipeline. An elder blew eagle down on an Enbridge representative for the pipeline, which the company interpreted as an act of hostility, even a potential death threat.[47] The Wet'suwet'en declared that this blowing of eagle down was, in fact, a well-known act of peace, and this misunderstanding illustrated the gulf between the two cultures. The company also misspoke by speaking of the nation's "northern gods" instead of "spirits."[48] Much of the cultural misinterpretation was caused because Enbridge used Alberta-based consultants who were unfamiliar with the culture of the B.C. band, according to Roger Harris, who once conducted Aboriginal relations for Enbridge.[49]

To overcome the misunderstandings and negative history and build a new, strong relationship, practitioners must be every bit as diligent in educating themselves on the cultural differences between First Nations communities and other Canadian cultures as they would be when entering another country; otherwise, they will suffer the potential consequences of poor communication and distrust.[50]

The Vancouver Olympics provided a unique opportunity for Aboriginal public relations and raised awareness of First Nations people on a world stage. Four of the tribes on whose ancestral lands the games took place coalesced to form the Four Hosts First Nations Society.[52] This group negotiated unprecedented Aboriginal participation in the Olympic games, marking the first time anywhere in the world that Aboriginal people were an official Olympic host.

One of the strategies that was employed to raise awareness of First Nations groups was a media relations and social media campaign. A communications department was created that issued regular media releases. This initiative resulted in a decrease in the number of negative stories about Aboriginal people in the mainstream media and an increase in the number of positive stories. An Aboriginal Pavilion that hosted special events and exhibitions was opened to the public during the Olympics, as well as an Aboriginal artisan village and business showcase. Other initiatives undertaken included a website with a media section, downloadable ring tones, posters of up-and-coming First Nations athletes, and videos posted on YouTube.

Thinking Like a PR Practitioner

1. What would be the challenges in targeting a multicultural group of which you know very little? How can you overcome these challenges?

2. Find an example online or in the media about a multicultural PR campaign and explain why it was or was not effective. What group did it target?

Investor Relations ❹

Investor relations (IR) is a public relations specialty that bridges the finance world with communications. It might be the right profession for you if you have a passion for financial markets, balance sheets, and income statements. Investor relations officers are employed by public companies or agencies hired by corporations to build relationships among investors, financial analysts, and financial media. The interest in this public relations specialty has increased as companies recognize how vital investor relations is to stock prices. Corporate scandals have also led to the need for increased emphasis on investor relations. Recent controversies include the 2009 global financial crisis and

Corporate scandals have led to the need for increased emphasis on investor relations.
Source: Golf Money/Shutterstock

several Canadian corporate scandals including Nortel, Sino-Forest Corporation, and Mega Brands.[53]

Investor relations officers are among the highest-paid PR practitioners. However, to practise in this field, some level of financial training is typically required. Investor relations practitioners need to be able to understand company financials and be able to effectively communicate with financially literate audiences around topics such as share prices and balance sheets. In fact, many investor relations practitioners come from financial backgrounds as opposed to communications backgrounds. A survey by the National Investor Relations Institute (NIRI) found that of investor relations officers, 49 per cent had a financial/accounting background, 23 per cent had a communications/public relations background, and 19 per cent came from marketing and sales.[54]

THE ROLE OF INVESTOR RELATIONS PRACTITIONERS

To better understand what investor relations is about, it is helpful to examine its history. This specialization developed in 1953, after the chairman of General Electric created a department that focused on building and growing relationships with the company's shareholders.[55] Several tumultuous years ensued as companies tried to achieve the right mix of employees on their investor relations teams. They found that public relations practitioners who had no financial training were not trusted by Wall Street, whereas employees with a financial background failed to satisfactorily build key relationships and communicate to investors in a simple, direct manner.[56] By combining the two distinct talents in investor relations, a new discipline was born.

The main areas where investor relations officers deliver value to an organization or client include developing relationships with investors, securing analyst coverage, helping ensure stocks are **liquid** (easy to sell), and helping to maintain a high share price for a company's securities.[57] Developing relationships with investors is vital because investors, whether individuals or institutions, are more likely to be longer-term investors if they have a relationship with the company.[58] A longer-term investor is valued because too many short-term investors can increase a stock's **volatility**, or price swings.

PRACTITIONER INTERVIEW

Kristina Knopp: Investor Relations

Kristina Knopp is manager of investor relations and corporate development for Red Cloud Mining Capital, an advisory firm that offers strategic planning, capital markets support, and marketing solutions to mining companies. Knopp's responsibilities include managing social media relations, organizing special events, managing websites, writing and creating presentations, and marketing communications such as trade show booths.

Question: What is a typical day in investor relations?

Answer: The beauty of the IR profession is that there are no typical days. In reality, there are no typical IR jobs either, as IR means different things to different companies. There is an immense amount of variability in what the role entails and responsibilities can range from building a corporate PowerPoint presentation that demonstrates the investment opportunity to potential investors, to presenting that story to an audience of hundreds in an effort to raise capital for the company you represent.

Question: How does it differ from a general PR job?

Answer: In many ways, IR and PR are similar. In both professions, the goal is to effectively bring awareness of a company to a specific target audience. The biggest difference between IR and PR is the audience itself. The investment community's singular motivation is making money and it's my job as an IR professional to communicate the money-making potential of my company. For that reason, an understanding of economics and finance can be very important.

Question: What is the biggest challenge in investor relations?

Answer: The biggest challenge IR professionals face is fluctuations in the global economy. We, and the companies we represent, are often at the mercy of the global economy. When economic conditions are poor, a company's market value can decrease significantly, causing the share price to drop without reason. When financial losses are involved, shareholders can become emotional and even angry, and you as an IR professional are the point of contact for those shareholders. In these situations, it's important to never take things personally and to always remain positive while communicating optimism to investors.

Question: What is your favourite part of the job?

Answer: There are so many aspects of the IR profession that I love, but what I love most about my career is the adaptability. Because there is so much diversity in the definition of investor relations, I've had the unique ability to define my own IR role based on my skills and aptitudes. IR professionals who love public speaking can find themselves travelling around the globe presenting the company's story to investors and shareholders at intimate luncheons or in large auditoriums. Others with a knack for visual design may focus on branding

(Continued)

Kristina Knopp: Investor Relations

by developing logos and building the company's PowerPoint presentation, fact sheet, website, and annual report. Still others with an aptitude for sales may find themselves pitching potential investors over the phone and arranging meetings for senior management. What's great about the profession is that it can be exactly what you want it to be.

Question: What do you recommend if students want to join this industry?

Answer: My best advice to students who are interested in becoming IR professionals is to learn

how to leverage your network. This is a skill that is exceedingly important in investor relations and in life. Investor relations is a relationship business. Your ability to build and connect with your network will land you your first IR job, get you that all-important investment analyst coverage, and allow you to raise that $10 million in share capital your company needs to advance its projects. Don't burn bridges. Always be professional. Your reputation is paramount to your success as an investor relations professional.

Securing analyst coverage is similar to general media relations, as discussed in previous chapters. Investor relations practitioners must build relationships with key analysts and assist in managing their perception of the company. Investor relations practitioners also ensure analysts have access to required information and company spokespersons. They guarantee transparency and access to the company's management team.[59] Figure 12.1 illustrates the different audiences that investor relations practitioners target. Some specific tactics that investor relations professionals execute include:

- Issuing press releases
- Conducting media relations
- Preparing investor presentations, speaker notes, and Q&As
- Holding in-person meetings with investors

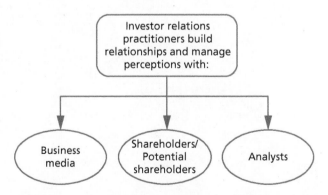

Figure 12.1 Audiences That Investor Relations Practitioners Target

- Developing the corporate social responsibility report
- Updating websites and fact sheets
- Performing media monitoring
- Organizing shareholder meetings
- Drafting the company's annual report

While engaging in these tactics, the investor relations practitioner needs to be conscious of two very different audiences: shareholders and stakeholders.[60] **Shareholders** own shares or a financial stake in a public company.[61] Usually their main concern is the company's stock price. A Canadian company that has come under fire from analysts and communications experts for its communication with shareholders is Research In Motion (RIM). Long criticized for its dual-CEO structure and cerebral announcements, when RIM's shares started to greatly decline in 2012, the company launched a large-scale public relations campaign to assuage investors' fears. The new CEO, Thorsten Heins, conducted many interviews and wrote an opinion editorial that was sent to various newspapers. Alan Middleton, a marketing expert from York University's Schulich School of Business, argued in the *Toronto Star* that having Heins conduct interviews exacerbated the situation, leading analysts to downgrade the shares to a "sell" recommendation.[62] Middleton said, "This is bad PR advice. Very bad. It boggles the mind. Unless you've got something specific and positive to announce, just shut up."[63] The situation continued to worsen when Heins was quoted on the CBC as saying that RIM wasn't in a death spiral. This led to the term *spiral* trending on Twitter in association with the company.[64] Ultimately, despite the massive PR efforts, the markets reacted to the lack of confidence they had in the ability of RIM and its new CEO to turn things around, causing the share price to drop.

Stakeholders can include shareholders but involve a larger group of publics that have an interest in the company. This may include employees, retirees, suppliers, customers, and so forth. Stakeholders have a wide range of sometimes conflicting concerns.[65]

Research in Motion CEO Thorsten Heins.

Source: © epa european press-photo agency b.v./Alamy

It can sometimes be hard to balance the needs of both shareholders and stakeholders. For example, imagine you are the senior investor relations officer for a large packaged goods company. If your management team decided to invest in new, expensive, more environmentally friendly manufacturing equipment, many of the stakeholders, including employees and the community, might be delighted to hear this news. However, your shareholders might not be if you are unable to prove that this investment will increase shareholder value by increasing profits. Shareholders need to be told this news in terms of its potential return on investment or increase in the share price.

Investor relations practitioners need to be familiar with and follow a concrete set of rules that are decreed by the Canadian Securities Act and the Toronto Stock Exchange. These rules govern issues such as timely disclosure and transparency. For example, posting media articles online is discouraged because if a company posts only positive news articles it is seen as biased. If you post a positive article, you need to also post a negative one to show a balanced story to potential investors. The Richard Ivey School of Business at the University of Western Ontario offers an Investor Relations Certification Program in partnership with the Canadian Investor Relations Institute (CIRI). The course covers material such as corporate disclosure policies and securities law.

Some companies see the advantages of doing more than just the minimum requirements of disclosure. For example, in 2004 Petro-Canada (now Suncor Energy) launched an entire website dedicated to transparency around its corporate governance because it believed that this would lead to higher investor confidence.[66] On their website the company also posted information on its ethical policies and code of business conduct. Another benefit of having this type of information available online, in addition to increased confidence, is that investor relations officers can spend less time answering questions related to these issues from investors, since the information is readily available to them.[67] This level of candidness can be especially important during a crisis, such as a hostile takeover.

HOSTILE TAKEOVERS

Sometimes investor relations is similar to crisis communications, as discussed in Chapter 11, such as when there is an unwanted takeover bid. As in crisis communications, the need for speed and transparency is paramount. In February 2000, Air Canada's investor relations team won the Investor Relations Magazine Canada Award for best investor relations during a takeover.[68] This attempted takeover occurred when Onex, a holding company, wanted to buy and merge Air Canada with then airline rival Canadian Airlines, making it the largest attempted takeover in Canada at the time.[69] Through strategic investor relations and media relations, Air Canada was able to stimulate investors' patriotism and halt the takeover.

The director of investor relations at Air Canada said of the company's investor relations strategy during the attempted takeover, "We tried to make everything as clear and timely as possible and to use every resource available. It was definitely an effort that had to be made on all fronts: the Canadian public had to be kept informed, the government had

Air Canada had to engage in investor relations to fend off a takeover by then rival Canadian Airlines.
Source: © Bayne Stanley/ Alamy

to be worked with and the investors had to be kept up-to-date on a fairly complex story."[70] To tell its story, the company ran 57 full-page ads.[71] It also made heroic efforts to contact shareholders individually, calling 23,000 shareholders in four days.[72] Shareholder news was updated daily on the company's website. Even so, the company knew there was misinformation among its shareholders and worked hard to educate them and the public. In the end, its shareholders and the public backed Air Canada. Not only was Air Canada able to fend off Onex's takeover, but the company was able to purchase Canadian Airlines itself.[73]

Like the Montana Alberta Tie case study in the opening vignette, the Air Canada example shows how often more than one PR specialty needs to be used in an integrated communications strategy. Though Air Canada's main focus was investor relations, it also had to engage in media relations and community relations to achieve its objectives.

ADVICE TO NEW PRACTITIONERS
Getting Started in Investor Relations

Here are four tips for young practitioners just starting their careers in investor relations:

1. Confidence and great presentation skills are vital. In IR you deal with senior management regularly. If you don't have confidence in your ability or stammer or look nervous when you present, they won't have confidence in you or your ideas.

2. Brush up on your business knowledge. Read the business section of the newspaper every-

day and have an active curiosity. Also pay attention to politics. What happens in that arena will also affect your company and the investment environment.

3. Don't be afraid to make mistakes, but when you do, be sure to learn from them and ensure you don't repeat them.

4. Pay your dues in a consulting firm. The learning curve is steep, but you will develop your skills quickly.

Government relations was also needed to convince the Canadian government that the merger of Air Canada and Canadian Airlines did not transgress any anti-monopoly regulations. As government decisions affect the business landscape, investor relations practitioners need to be aware of their implications.

Thinking Like a PR Practitioner

1. Name two skills investor relations professionals need in order to be successful. Why are these important?

2. Name two similarities between a hostile takeover and crisis communications.

3. Describe the advantages of having a greater level of transparency in investor relations.

CASE STUDY BARRICK GOLD

Since acquiring its North Mara, Tanzania, mine in 2006, Canada's Barrick Gold, the world's largest gold producer, has experienced challenging government relations and community relations issues.[74] The seven villages that surround the North Mara mine are mostly poor and populated by the Kuria people, who were traditionally cattle farmers.[75] With a community relations budget of $2 million and a community relations team of 50 at its North Mara mine, the company has made efforts to repair its local reputation.[76] However, making inroads in public affairs can be a long and laborious process.

Barrick's predecessors made some of the mistakes that resulted in alienating the North Mara community. However, the company's own mistakes after it took over the mine reinforced the barrier between it and the local community. One of these mistakes was an acidic water spill in 2009, and shooting deaths by security guards and police have been reported at the mine for the last six years.[77] These shootings are in response to trespassing by artisanal miners who invade the mines in search of small amounts of gold. There are also reports of land disputes and of sexual assault allegations against the security guards and police.[78]

In a report published by the South African Institute of International Affairs it was noted that "the company has acknowledged that not only does it now not enjoy a social licence to operate the North Mara mine, but that the very viability of the mine is under threat."[79] It is this social licence that Barrick must work toward in the coming years through its community relations efforts.

On the government relations front, in 2010, Liberal MP John McKay proposed Bill C-300, which would have created oversight on the human-rights abuses and environmental disasters caused by Canadian companies while overseas.[80] Barrick lobbied strongly against the bill, and it was eventually defeated.[81] Despite this defeat, many activists are still highly critical of Barrick's North Mara operations and vow to play the role of watchdog if the Canadian government will not.

Barrick maintains that the North Mara mine has huge potential. However, in order to gain both the North Mara community's and the international community's support for the mine, Barrick will need to re-evaluate how it conducts business in Tanzania. For the moment, the company has not won over local villagers or impressed activists around the globe through effective community relations.

Questions

1. Do you believe Barrick took the right approach when it lobbied against Bill C-300? Why or why not?

2. Do you believe Barrick will be able to overcome its community relations obstacles? Why or why not?

AUTHOR'S OWN EXPERIENCE

Pacific Coast Terminals and Community Relations

Pacific Coast Terminals (PCT) had a problem. Though the company was a great corporate citizen, contributing to the community in numerous ways, the sulphur terminal was considered an eyesore, and residents had the misconception that the yellow pollen that appeared on their cars and decks every summer was sulphur blown up from the terminal. The terminal also occupied what some local developers and real estate agents saw as prime waterfront real estate.

In order to maintain a good relationship with the city of Port Moody and maintain its ability to operate, PCT had to change residents' perception. It needed them to see the organization as an integral part of the community. To do this, PCT hired the agency I was working for at the time to provide a comprehensive community relations strategy. Part of our recommendations included an education strategy because many residents were misinformed about the terminal. To implement this strategy, PCT mailed out newsletters to residents that educated them about the terminal and about the fact that the yellow specks they saw on their cars were pollen and not sulphur.

Another way PCT worked to educate residents was through the local school system. We helped the terminal set up school tours and developed a curriculum that was provided to local schools for teachers to use. Finally, every second year, we assisted PCT in hosting a large community event at the terminal, where residents could come and tour the facility, eat, and enjoy entertainment. This event was vital to helping residents better understand the operations of the terminal and meet the people who worked there.

In addition to education, we recommended that PCT employ tactics to build local goodwill through donations and sponsorship. Senior managers were active volunteers in the community, sitting on boards and committees, and PCT offered scholarships to local students.

To evaluate if these efforts were moving the public opinion needle, we did regular community surveys and found that, over time, the terminal's efforts were delivering success. This type of focused, strategic engagement of community relations is incredibly effective, especially for a controversial organization, like PCT, that is dependent on community support for its right to operate.

other areas of specialization

- government/elected officials
- lobby groups
- public affairs

government relations

specialized training

- geographic community residents
- psychographic communities

community relations

specific audiences/ shareholders

investor relations

- analysts
- shareholders
- business media
- bridge between finance and public relations

aboriginal relations

- need to overcome traditionally negative relationship
- first nations bands

international relations

- international media
- citizens of other nations
- need to learn culture/media/customs

Key Terms

Aboriginal relations A public relations specialty in which practitioners build and sustain positive relationships with First Nations communities.

astroturfing Creating fake grassroots organizations for lobbying efforts.

community relations A public relations specialty in which practitioners build relationships and dialogue between a community and an organization.

government relations A public relations specialty in which practitioners work to build relationships between organizations and government officials.

investor relations A specialty within public relations that promotes public companies among investors, financial analysts, and financial media.

liquidity The ease with which a company is able to find buyers and sellers for a stock.

lobbying Representing special interests to government officials and decision makers.

localization The adaptation of a written piece or campaign for a local market.

public affairs A communications specialty that uses government and community relations to ensure a favourable business environment.

shareholder An investor who has purchased a financial stake, meaning a stock, in a company.

stakeholder Someone who is vested in the performance of an organization.

volatility Stocks changing price often and quickly. Volatile stocks are considered riskier than stable stocks.

Weblinks

Biily Wants a Dog (An Introduction to Lobbying) by Hill & Knowlton
www.youtube.com/watch?v=MjY5Zkt51wY&feature=youtube_gdata

CBC's *Spin Cycles*
www.cbc.ca/news/background/spincycles/

Inside Investor Relations
www.insideinvestorrelations.com/articles/17177/winning-good-fight/

Ivey Investor Relations Certification Program
www.ivey.uwo.ca/executive/our-programs/ivey-ciri-investor-relations-certification-program.htm

International Public Relations Association
www.ipra.org/

Public Affairs Association of Canada
www.publicaffairs.ca/index-reg.html

Sedar Public Securities Documents
www.sedar.com/

Worldcom Public Relations Group
www.worldcomgroup.com/

Endnotes

1. Shael Gelfand, interview with the author.

2. "FAQ," Public Affairs Council. Accessed March 4, 2013, http://pac.org/faq

3. Aidan Vining, Daniel Shapiro, and Bernhard Borges, "Building the Firm Political (Lobbying) Strategy," *Journal of Public Affairs*, vol. 5, no. 2 (May 2005), 150–175.

4. Hill & Knowlton, "Billy Wants a Dog (An Introduction to Lobbying) by Hill & Knowlton" (video), November 25, 2009. Accessed March 4, 2013, http://www.youtube.com/watch?v=MjY5Zkt51wY&feature=youtube_gdata

5. Ibid.

6. Vining et al., "Building the Firm Political (Lobbying) Strategy."

7. David Topping, "Rob Ford's Team Created a Fake Twitter Account and This Is It," *The Torontoist*, October 31, 2010. Accessed March 4, 2013, http://torontoist.com/2010/10/rob_fords_team_created_a_fake_twitter_account_and_this_is_it/

8. Ibid.

9. Ira Basen, "Episode 5: Spinning War," *Spin Cycles*, CBC Radio, July 3, 1997. Accessed March 4, 2013, http://www.cbc.ca/news/background/spincycles/

10. Ibid.

11. Ibid.

12. Ibid.

13. "Toronto Conference Provides a Forum for Solid Public Relations Strategies," *Pit & Quarry*, vol. 87, no. 7 (January 1995), 182–208.

14. Ibid.

15. Ibid.

16. Ibid.

17. Ibid.

18. Deanna Kemp, "Community Relations in the Global Mining Industry: Exploring the Internal Dimensions of Externally Oriented Work," *Corporate Social Responsibility and Environmental Management*, vol. 17, no. 1, 1–14. Accessed March 6, 2013, http://onlinelibrary.wiley.com/doi/10.1002/csr.195/abstract

19. Ibid.

20. Judy VanSlyke Turk and Linda H. Scanlan, "The Evolution of Public Relations: Case Studies from Countries in Transition," Institute for Public Relations, 2008. Accessed March 4, 2013, http://www.instituteforpr.org/topics/evolution-of-pr-third-edition/

21. "Pace Group/2010 Winter Games Media Relations," Worldcom Public Relations Group. Accessed March 4, 2013, http://worldcomgroup.com/files/Microsoft%20Word%20-%20Client%20Success_AMERICAS%20Region%20Pace%20Group%201-2.cfm

22. Alain Bélanger and Éric Caron Malenfant, "Ethnocultural Diversity in Canada: Prospects for 2017," *Canadian Social Trends*, no. 79 (Winter 2005). Accessed March 4, 2013, http://www.statcan.gc.ca/pub/11-008-x/2005003/article/8968-eng.pdf

23. Statistics Canada, "Ethnic Diversity and Immigration," *Canada Year Book*, 2011. Accessed March 4, 2013, http://www41.statcan.ca/2008/30000/ceb30000_000_e.htm

24. Bélanger and Caron Malenfant, "Ethnocultural Diversity in Canada."

25. S.P. Banks, *Multicultural Public Relations: A Social-Interpretive Approach*. Ames: Iowa State University Press, 2000.

26. Statistics Canada, "Table 1: Number of People and Proportion of the Population Reporting French by Selected Language Characteristic, Canada, 2006 and 2011," *2011 Census*, January 9, 2013. Accessed May 31, 2013, http://www12.statcan.gc.ca/census-recensement/2011/as-sa/98-314-x/2011003/tbl/tbl3_1-1-eng.cfm

27. Statistics Canada, "Number of People and Proportion of the Population Reporting French by Selected Language Characteristic, Quebec, 2006 and 2011," *2011 Census*, January 9, 2013. Accessed May 31, 2013, http://www12.statcan.gc.ca/census-recensement/2011/as-sa/98-314-x/2011003/tbl/tbl3_1-2-eng.cfm

28. Statistics Canada. "French and the *Francophonie* in Canada," *2011 Census*, January 9, 2013. Accessed May 31, 2013, http://www12.statcan.gc.ca/census-recensement/2011/as-sa/98-314-x/98-314-x2011003_1-eng.cfm

29. Chris Powell, "Ikea Makes It Moving Day in Quebec," *Marketing*, June 26, 2012. Accessed May 31, 2013, http://www.marketingmag.ca/news/marketer-news/ikea-makes-it-moving-day-in-quebec-56167

30. Ibid.

31. Marie-Josee Gagnon, "Adapting Your Brand to Enter a Foreign Market: 5 Tips from the Michaels Stores' Introduction in Québec," Casacom. Accessed May 31, 2013, http://casacom.ca/en/2013/05/13/adapting-your-brand-to-enter-a-foreign-market-5-tips-from-the-michaels-stores%E2%80%99-introduction-in-quebec/

32. Ibid.

33. K. Laird, "Home Depot Begins First Campaign for Chinese Canada," *Marketing*, January 20, 2010. Accessed March 4, 2013, http://www.marketingmag.ca/news/marketer-news/home-depot-begins-first-campaign-for-chinese-canada-796

34. Terry O'Reilly, "L.G.B.T. Advertising: Chasing the Pink Dollar," *Under the Influence*, CBC Radio, June 2, 2012. Accessed March 4, 2013, http://www.cbc.ca/undertheinfluence/season-1/2012/06/02/lgbt-advertising-chasing-the-pink-dollar/

35. Ibid.

36. Stuart Elliott, "The Media Business: Advertising; Hill & Knowlton Forms a Unit to Direct Public Relations Efforts toward Gay Men and Lesbians," *The New York Times*, June 23, 1995. Accessed March 4, 2013, http://www.nytimes.com/1995/06/23/business/media-business-advertising-hill-knowlton-forms-unit-direct-public-relations.html

37. Ibid.

38. Charles O. Holliday, Stephan Schmidheiny, and Philip Watts, *Walking the Talk: The Case for Sustainable Development*. Sheffield, UK: Greenleaf, 2002.

39. Ibid.

40. Ibid.

41. Ibid.

42. Kathryn (Kylie) McMullan, *Flying with Ravens: Building Better First Nations–Corporate Partnerships*. Faculty of Business Administration, Simon Fraser University: Summer 2008.

43. Bernd Christmas, "Native Wisdom," *Canadian Business*, vol. 80, no. 20 (August 10, 2007), 121–124.

44. "Aboriginal Engagement," PotashCorp. Accessed March 4, 2013, http://www.potashcorp.com/sustainability/key_focus_areas/aboriginal_engagement/overview/

45. Christmas, "Native Wisdom." See also McMullan, *Flying with Ravens*.

46. Laureen Whyte, *Making the Grade: A Guide to Success for Corporate Aboriginal Initiatives*, Industry Council For Aboriginal Business, May 10, 2010. Accessed March 4, 2013, http://fnbc.info/making-grade-guide-success-corporate-%E2%80%93-aboriginal-initiatives

47. Nathan Vanderklippe, "The Language of Eagle Feathers Trips Up a Pipeline Promoter," *The Globe and Mail*, August 8, 2012. Accessed March 4, 2013, http://investdb4.theglobeandmail.com/servlet/story/GAM.20120808.RBENBRIDGEGATEWAYVANDERKLIPPEATL/GIStory/

48. Ibid.

49. Ibid.

50. McMullan, *Flying with Ravens*.

51. Deborah McGregor, "Aboriginal/Non-Aboriginal Relations and Sustainable Forest Management in Canada: The Influence of the Royal Commission on Aboriginal Peoples," *Journal of Environmental Management*, 2009, 300–310.

52. "The Four Hosts First Nations," Government of Canada. Accessed March 4, 2013, http://www.canada2010.gc.ca/invsts/hnationsh/030401-eng.cfm

53. L. Lahey, "Top 5 Business Scandals of 2011," *Yahoo Finance*, January 6, 2012. Accessed March 4, 2013, http://ca.finance.yahoo.com/blogs/insight/top-5-business-scandals-2011-174754706.html

54. S.K. Kelly, Alexander Laskin, and Gregory Rosentein, "Investor Relations: Two-Way Symmetrical Practice," *Journal of Public Relations Research*, vol. 22, no. 2 (2010), 182–208.

55. Ibid.

56. Ibid.

57. Alexander V. Laskin, "How Investor Relations Contributes to the Corporate Bottom Line," *Journal of Public Relations Research*, vol. 23, no. 3 (2011), 37–41.

58. Kelly et al., "Investor Relations."

59. Laskin, "How Investor Relations Contributes to the Corporate Bottom Line."

60. Josiah McClellan, "Stakeholders vs. Shareholders: Making an Uneasy Relationship Work," *The Public Relations Strategist*, Spring 2011. Accessed March 4, 2013, http://www.prsa.org/ Intelligence/TheStrategist/Articles/view/6K-021103/1028/Stakeholders_vs_Shareholders_ Making_an_Uneasy_Rela

61. Ibid.

62. Joss Rubin, "BlackBerry-Maker RIM Battles Death Spiral, Sparks Twitter Surge," *Toronto Star*, July 3, 2012. Accessed March 4, 2013, http://www.thestar.com/business/article/1220972– blackberry-maker-rim-fights-the-death-spiral-sparks-twitter-surge

63. Ibid.

64. Ibid.

65. McClellan, "Stakeholders vs. Shareholders."

66. Vanessa Theiss, "Northern Disclosure," Inside Investor Relations.com, May 1, 2004. Accessed March 4, 2013, http://www.insideinvestorrelations.com/articles/corporate-governance/16692/ northern-disclosure/

67. Ibid.

68. Jeff Cossette, and Adrienne Baker, "Winning the Good Fight," Inside Investor Relations.com, June 1, 2000. Accessed March 4, 2013, http://www.insideinvestorrelations.com/articles/case- studies/17177/winning-good-fight/

69. Ibid.

70. Ibid.

71. Ibid.

72. Ibid.

73. Ibid.

74. Geoffrey York, "Barrick's Tanzanian Project Tests Ethical Mining Policies," *Report on Business Magazine*, September 29, 2010. Accessed March 4, 2013, http://www.theglobeandmail.com/ report-on-business/rob-magazine/barricks-tanzanian-project-tests-ethical-mining-policies/ article559188/?page=all

75. Ibid.

76. Ibid.

77. Ibid.

78. Ibid.

79. Ibid.

80. Ibid.

81. Ibid.

The Fight For Social Media

While many different functions seem to be claiming ownership over social media, the three main contenders are PR practitioners, advertisers, and customer service departments. All have legitimate claims as to why it should fall under their responsibility. PR practitioners argue that social media is similar to earned media with the "mass" in mass media simply capitalized and bolded. They argue that the lines between reporters, bloggers, and citizen journalists become more fuzzy and ambiguous by the second. Advertisers claim that social media provides the perfect vehicle for ad campaigns ready to go viral and guerrilla marketing, and to extend the reach of traditional advertising campaigns. Customer service departments argue that, instead of responding to customer concerns over phone or email, there is value in answering complaints and queries in real time in the public sphere, so that others who might have asked the same question no longer need to bother. There is also a level of transparency to this consumer response method that allows companies to show how "authentic" they are (a marketing buzzword that is even hotter than social media at the moment). And while all the arguments from these different factions for owning social media are valid, and each department should definitely apply its strengths to the tactic at various times for various reasons, it is our opinion that the use of the medium should absolutely stem from a communications platform.

This is because communicators, at least good ones, develop the key messages and are scanning for and ready to respond to a crisis, like the Domino's Pizza YouTube fiasco, where rogue employees made our stomachs turn by tampering with customers' pizzas, or the Motrin viral video "oops" that brought on the wrath of mommy bloggers. They are also trained in providing fast, timely interviews and information to journalists, whether they be professional or citizen reporters. Most of all, PR practitioners are used to being unable to control what is said about their organization, and they know that earned media is risky in a way that paid media is not, no matter how edgy it is. Social media is just communication in its sexiest form (at least for the moment), and just as no one wants to be advertised to while reading their favourite columnist in *The Globe and Mail*, they also do not want to be bombarded with ads while on Twitter or Facebook or while reading their favourite blog. Sure, we tolerate ads around the content, but we like to think the conversation is ad free and that companies have earned, not paid for, their right to be a part of it. So while ad agencies may sell social media services and it makes sense for customer service to tweet when a flight is delayed, the social media direction and strategy need to come from the public relations department. And while no one seems ready to let go of the social media baby just yet, it is just a matter of time before clients and senior management teams recognize who its real mother is.

Glossary

Aboriginal relations A public relations specialty in which practitioners build and sustain positive relationships with Aboriginal communities.

account A term PR agencies use to refer to their clients, as in "I am working on the Westjet account."

ad value The assessment of the value of PR coverage by determining what it would have cost to purchase an ad of the same size.

advocate To push for a certain issue or provide support to an organization.

assignment editor An individual who selects stories to cover and assigns stories to other reporters.

astroturfing Creating fake grassroots organizations for lobbying efforts.

audience The population for which the communication is intended.

B-roll Rough footage PR practitioners provide to news stations to try to secure coverage.

backgrounder A media material that provides additional context and information on a person, product, process, or organization.

beat A journalist's area of specialization or the topics and subjects he or she covers. Beat examples include police, health, transportation, business, and lifestyle.

benchmark A marker that you choose to measure other results against and that provides context to the results.

blog roll A list of all the blogs another blogger follows.

body language Nonverbal communication and all the ways people express themselves without using words, including eye contact and facial expressions.

boilerplate A short paragraph at the end of a release that provides more information on the organization issuing the release.

bottleneck An obstruction or constraint in the flow of production resulting in an unanticipated delay.

brainstorm A creativity-generating technique in which a group of people come up with ideas and build upon them.

brand ambassadors People who are loyal to a brand and tell their peers about it. These people can be employees, may be paid in kind, or may simply be fans of the brand.

breaking news stories Events and stories that are currently developing and are receiving coverage in the news media; often refers to unexpected stories such as natural disasters, corporate crises, or scandals.

bridges Phrases or words that enable you to smoothly jump from one topic to another. Bridges are used in interviews to go from the subject a journalist introduces in a question to the topic the spokesperson wishes to address.

business-to-business (B2B) An organization that targets other businesses and professionals, rather than general consumers. An example would be a maker of cardboard packaging that sells its products to appliance manufacturers.

campaign An overall planned course of action.

cause PR PR efforts that are conducted for social, charitable, and environmental reasons.

communications audit A research method to determine the effectiveness of the public relations programs of an organization.

community relations A public relations specialty in which practitioners build relationships and dialogue between a community and an organization.

competitor analysis An investigation of the strengths and weaknesses of the competition.

consumer-facing Any communications or marketing piece or event that the end consumer will see.

copywriting A writing style that is used for advertising and other forms of marketing such as direct mail.

corporate social responsibility (CSR) An organization's responsibility toward its community and the planet, and its overall corporate citizenship. CSR can include many elements, such as a company's waste management, the number of women and minorities on its board, measures taken to avoid or decrease pollution, and the organization's social and charitable contributions.

counselling The expertise and advice PR practitioners provide and the way they guide and direct their organizations and their spokespersons.

crisis An unusual event that puts the typical operations of an organization in jeopardy.

crisis management The process of averting a crisis from happening and managing a crisis once it has occurred.

crisis plan A detailed manual on how to respond in a crisis situation. This plan may be for specific crisis scenarios.

crystallize an attitude A communication strategy designed to strengthen an existing belief.

CSR report A document that is released on a consistent basis (quarterly, annually, etc.) that informs an organization's stakeholders of its CSR goals and its performance in meeting these goals.

deadline (media) The time by which a journalist must have a story submitted.

deadline (PR) The time by which a tactic or campaign must be completed.

debriefing session A meeting at which team members review how an event went and discuss any key learnings.

demographics Information that can be deduced and researched about a target audience, such as income, education, age, or interests.

earned media Media coverage that has been earned through public relations instead of being purchased.

editorial All written articles and other features, except for advertising, that are found in newspapers and magazines; also refers to an opinion piece written by the editor.

email blast An email message sent to a large mailing list at the same time.

employee engagement A measurement of employees' attachment and feelings of satisfaction regarding their organization and their job.

environmental scan Collecting and analyzing internal and external sources to identify public perception on a particular topic.

evaluation The judgment of the results and the worth of a campaign.

event listing Free listing of events offered by local media.

fact sheet A bulleted media material that provides facts about a company or product.

first draft The preliminary form of a writing project. It will be rewritten and edited to produce further drafts until a final draft is reached.

flagging A media technique by which the spokesperson verbally draws attention to an important key message.

focus group A group of individuals representing a target audience who are brought together and asked questions by a moderator.

front groups Activist groups that are formed to hide the identity of their main beneficiary.

ghost writing Writing on someone else's behalf, where it is agreed that he or she will receive the credit.

government relations A public relations specialty in which practitioners work to build relationships between organizations and government officials.

greenwashing The attempt to make companies that are not environmentally friendly seem as though they are.

hometown release A release that targets the local community.

hooking A media technique by which the spokesperson entices the journalist to ask a follow-up question about a topic the spokesperson would like to discuss.

hyperlocal Extremely local communities.

hyperniche Extremely targeted audiences.

implementation Executing a plan and putting tactics into practice.

impressions The number of people who may have seen a story in the media and in social media outlets.

in-kind donation A donation of products or services instead of money.

influencers People who are influential and whose opinion is trusted.

informal communications Communication among employees that is not disseminated from the internal communications team or management, such as water-cooler chatter.

informal sounding A casual conversation held with members of the target audience to determine their thoughts or feelings on a certain topic.

information-pull technology Tools that allow employees to take information as they need it—e.g., the company intranet.

information-push technology Tools that deliver information to employees that they have not asked for—e.g., company emails.

integrated marketing Many or all marketing activities working together to ensure consistency of messaging.

internal communications Communication that occurs within a company or organization where the main audience is the employees and board members.

interview A research method in which verbal questions are asked of individuals.

investor relations A specialty within public relations that promotes public companies among investors, financial analysts, and financial media.

issues management The management of an emerging problem that has not yet developed and may never develop into a crisis.

jargon Industry-specific language that is not used by the general population.

key messages Concise main points and thoughts to communicate with target audiences. These messages are elaborated in all communication vehicles, such as speeches, media materials, and social media initiatives. The main ideas the PR practitioner wants to convey to the audience.

keynote speech A speech given by a presenter who is the main draw.

lead The most important and attention-grabbing information in a story.

lead times The lapse of time between when a story is prepared and produced and when it is printed or broadcast and presented to the public. Lead times vary enormously and can be as short as an hour or as long as six to eight months.

legitimacy The right in the eyes of the public for an organization to operate because the organization shares the same values and beliefs as its key stakeholders and the public.

liquidity The ease with which a company is able to find buyers and sellers for a stock.

live feed Live broadcast of a television or radio segment from a location outside the studio.

LiveStream A video delivered or streamed live over the Internet.

lobbying Representing special interests to government officials and decision makers.

localization The adaptation of a written piece or campaign for a local market.

marketing communications A public relations role that combines elements of traditional marketing with PR.

media advisory A cross between an invitation and a media release, a media advisory lets journalists know about an important upcoming announcement or event.

media content analysis The study of media coverage that an organization or topic has received.

media coverage Stories covered by media outlets that are sometimes generated by media relations.

media deskside briefing An event consisting of a spokesperson visiting a journalist in the newsroom or office to present information in person.

media interview A meeting either in person or by telephone during which a journalist asks questions of an individual. The answers are recorded or written down and used by the journalist in a story.

media kit A package for the media in which the information they will need is compiled in one place.

media landscape The scope of media and the types available in a specific market or location, including all the print, broadcast, and digital media available there.

media list A database of carefully researched and selected journalists and media outlets, with their contact information, who will be targeted in a media relations campaign.

media materials Written documents, such as press releases, backgrounders, or fact sheets, that outline story ideas and information and that are distributed to the media.

media mix A combination of different media.

media monitoring Keeping track of stories and other media content produced by print, broadcast, and digital media on a certain topic, industry, or organization. Copies of all the stories are collected and presented in media-monitoring reports.

media pitch Direct contact with journalists or editors via email or telephone in an effort to persuade them to cover your story. Pitches are usually brief and customized to the media outlet.

media relations Activities that build or maintain an organization's relationships with media. Also refers to PR practitioners providing information to journalists at news organizations in the hope that they will be interested in the story and cover it. The goal is to generate coverage in media outlets such as newspapers, radio, television, and digital news channels.

media release A document that announces the news about the story that is at the heart of a campaign. Also called a news release or press release.

media scrum A spontaneous media conference during which journalists surround the spokesperson with their microphones and ask questions. It generally takes place following an important meeting.

media tour The media outlets and journalists a spokesperson meets during a campaign. This can involve travelling to different markets.

media training The process in which the spokesperson is taught how to work with journalists and how to manage media interviews.

methodologies Techniques used to conduct research and collect data. In PR they involve such methods as surveys, interviews, and media coverage analysis.

metrics Tools or techniques to measure a campaign that can help PR professionals see if they are meeting their objectives.

mock drills Simulated crisis scenarios, with the purpose of practising crisis response.

muckraking journalism A style of investigative journalism that exposes the wrongdoings of people or companies.

new media influencers Social media users whom others follow and who influence others.

news agencies Organizations that employ journalists and sell the stories they produce to other media outlets that subscribe to their service.

news conference An organized media event at which a spokesperson makes a scripted statement in front of journalists, followed by a question-and-answer (Q&A) period.

news values An angle employed in a release or pitch to make it newsworthy.

news wire A service that delivers content to news organizations.

newsjacking Using news headlines to gain publicity for your organization.

newsworthy Deemed by the media to have the qualities needed to make it into the news. Newsworthy stories contain several news values.

nonprofit organizations (or not-for-profits) Organizations created for social or charitable reasons in which all revenues earned must be used by the organizations and not distributed as profits.

objectives The desired results of a PR initiative or campaign and the goals to be achieved in the future, usually within a specific timeline.

opinion leader Someone whom others look to in order to help form their opinion on a particular topic.

organizational culture The shared values, beliefs, and learned behaviour of an organization's employees.

paid media Media placements that are purchased, such as advertorials or an ads.

persuasive message A communication designed to influence an audience.

photo advisory A media advisory that lets photo editors know about a photo opportunity.

photo opportunities An event, or a period during an event, at which media take photos that have been staged and arranged for them. Also describes the people, setting, and objects that the media will be able to photograph at the event.

photo release A media release in which a photo is sent to the media for publication.

pitch calendar A calendar that maps out when you will pitch your story to which publications, depending on their lead time.

positioning Telling a story from a particular angle or perspective to make it appear in a certain light or to emphasize certain parts of the story. Positioning of a story is done by both PR practitioners and journalists.

PR value Capturing the value of PR coverage by determining what it would have cost to purchase an ad of the same size and then multiplying the ad value by three to account for intangibles such as increased credibility.

press secretary A person who works for a public figure and handles his or her public relations.

prewritten article An article that is written by a PR practitioner in a journalistic style and can be used as is by the media.

primary research Conducting new, first-hand research.

pro bono Work that is done for the public good without pay or compensation.

proactive media relations A publicist's taking the initiative to contact a journalist with a story idea. The action is part of a plan or campaign with the goal of generating media coverage for organization.

propaganda Biased information disseminated to promote a position.

public affairs A communications specialty that uses government and community relations to ensure a favourable business environment.

public opinion A prevailing opinion or a popularly held belief.

public relations plan A written document that outlines all the actions you will be taking and the rationale for them over a predetermined period of time.

publicist The person in a PR agency or in-house communications department who focuses on generating media coverage through media relations.

questionnaire A research method using written questions to gather information from individuals.

quote A brief statement or extract from an interview that is used in a story because it is newsworthy.

reactive media relations An organization's responding to media inquiries that it did not initially contact the journalist about. This tends to occur when there is a breaking story about an organization or during issues or crises.

refresher session A media-training session that is conducted with someone who has already been trained. The goal is to remind the spokesperson of the principles of media relations, provide an additional opportunity for practice, and introduce new key messages.

release A document that describes the information, text, or photo an organization plans to use and make public. It is signed by the individual who is granting permission.

return on investment (ROI) A measure of whether a campaign is profitable. ROI looks at the cost of a program and compares it to the results.

rules of engagement Practices and behaviours expected of social media participants.

secondary research Conducting research by using pre-existing materials, such as research reports.

shareholder An investor who has purchased a financial stake, meaning a stock, in a company.

situation analysis The first section of a PR plan, which outlines the challenge(s) facing an organization and all the factors that influence it.

social capital The worth of a social network with regards to influence and sharing.

social media news release (SMR) An interactive media release that is posted online and includes such elements as live links, pull-out quotes, photos, and video footage.

social media Digital media that are both created and consumed by users.

sound bite A quote delivered specifically for radio or television.

sources People who provide information to journalists which is used as research or to generate stories. PR practitioners account for a large percentage of sources.

speakers bureau A roster of speakers who are available for hire.

spin A negative term, sometimes used to describe what PR practitioners do, to denote taking a negative story and twisting the truth so that it seems more positive.

spokesperson A person who represents an organization to the public or media.

stakeholders The publics to whom an organization is accountable.

strategic thinking The thought process that enables PR practitioners to assess situations and deliver business solutions.

strategies The articulation of the specific actions that will be undertaken to achieve an objective.

streamlining messages The process of honing and simplifying key messages to get rid of superfluous words and ideas.

survey A data-collection method in which individuals are asked predetermined questions. A small group is surveyed and their answers are considered to be a representative sample of the larger population.

tactics The activities or actions taken to accomplish objectives.

talking head A person talking on camera with only his or her head and upper body visible. It is one of the most common shots for television news segments.

target audiences The publics and groups a PR campaign is trying to reach and for whom the key messages are designed. These publics can be affected by or interested in an organization.

template A model that outlines which information must be included and in which order. It is preformatted and is used as a starting point in creating a document.

third-party endorsement A positive story about an organization appearing in the media and bestowing credibility upon it.

timeline The chronological order in which the plan is implemented and the different tactics are carried out.

tone The attitude that the writer projects toward the audience and the subject matter.

touch points Communication channels where audiences interact with brands or information.

town hall An internal meeting where employees are able to ask questions and share ideas with senior leaders.

trade media Media outlets that cover specific industries and cater to professionals in that industry, rather than the general public.

trade show A business event at which many companies in the same industry display their products or services.

unique selling proposition The qualities that make a product or service stand out from the competition; the reason why a person will choose it over others.

user-generated content Information that is created by social media users.

viral campaign A popular campaign that is quickly and widely shared among viewers through social media.

volatility Stocks changing price often and quickly. Volatile stocks are considered riskier than stable stocks.

Index

Note: Key Terms and their page numbers appear in bold face. Page numbers followed by *f* or *t* indicate figures or tables, respectively.

definitions of public relations (PR),
4–5
Degrassi: The Next Generation TV
series, 317
Delicious.com, 226
Deloitte and Touche, 272, 342
democracy, 39
demographics, 77, 132, 202
change in, 370
journalism and, 169
Desman, Shawn, 142
DeSmogBlog, 59
Digg.com, 221, 226
digital age, 205
challenge of fragmented
audiences for public
relations (PR), 215
challenge of issue confronta-
tion for public relations
(PR), 216
challenge of message loss for
public relations (PR), 215
crisis management in, 343
gaining market intelligence
for public relations (PR),
214–215
global opportunities for public
relations (PR), 213–214
opportunities for public relations (PR) in, 213
public relations (PR)
perspective in, 205–206
digital media, 176, 177–178, 203
outlets, 179f
Dion, Celine, 135
Domino's Pizza, 346, 349, 390
Donoghue, Jack, 55
Dove Campaign for Real Beauty, 80–81
Drabek, Kyle, 188
Drake, 135, 294, 296
Duckett, Stephen, 261, 262

E

e-newsletter, 129
e-Talk TV show, 308
Early Edition radio show, 177
Early Psychosis Initiative public
relations campaign, 10–11, 29–30
earned (unpaid) coverage, 163
earned media, 6–7
Earnscliffe Strategy Group, 51
Earth Day, 88, 154
East Coast Music Awards and
Conference, 300
Eaton's Centre, Toronto, 22
Edelman public relations agency, 2
education, 52
public relations (PR) strategy,
384
Eisenhower, Dwight, 51
Ellen TV show, 81

Elliott, Meredith, 200
email blasts, 129, 269
email, 174
internal communications
and, 278
pitch, 183–184
emotions, 43
employee engagement, 276–277
employees,
as stakeholders, 269
buy-in functions of internal
communications, 270–271
face-to-face meetings and, 281
informal internal communications
and, 275, 280
internal communications and,
270–271, 283
newsletters for, 282
organizational structure and,
274
two-way communication for,
283
younger, 275–276
Enbridge, 345, 375
Encyclopedia of Public Relations, 59
Enron, 274
Enterprise Canada (prev. OEB
International), 55
Environment Canada, 88, 303
Environmental Communications
Options, 76
environmental public relations (PR),
75, 83–85
discrediting, 86–88
greenwashing and, 88–89
issues facing, 85–86
relating the issues and, 86
environmental scans, 45, 107, 362
as prevention crisis tool,
336–337
usage of, 108
EPTECH trade show, 296
ET Canada TV show, 317
ethics, 17–18, 43
astroturfing and, **60–61**
codes of conduct, 17–18
definition, 17
example of unethical
behaviour, 18
reputation of public relations
(PR) and, 61
ethnic media, 176, 178
targeting, 193–194
European Parliament, 336
European Public Relations
Federation, 368
evaluation, 8, 9, 27–29
public relations (PR) plan
component, 110, 116–118
special events, 316
surveys, 316

Evans, Kenneth, 43, 348
event listing, 322–323
external communications, 269, 271

F

Fab Four of public relations (PR),
9–10
face-to-face communications, 146,
271, 275, 280–281
Facebook, 2, 27, 45, 74, 83, 109, 130,
148, 202, 203, 205, 209, 211,
213, 215, 217, 221, 222, 224,
226, 228, 302, 324, 346, 348,
350, 390
fact sheets, 131, 142–144, 183
Fairchild TV, 194
Fairmont Hotel, 35
Fairway Divorce Solutions media
relations campaign, 162–163,
165, 167, 171
Fallis, Terry, 212
familiarization (FAM) tour, 192
Farewell to Featherwagons, A (Halton
Region Health Dep't), 90
Farm Credit Canada (FCC) Drive
Away Hunger program, 365–366
Fashion TV, 208
Financial Post newspaper, 162
first draft (of a speech), 145
First Nations peoples, 359
media relations to raise
awareness, 376
public relations (PR) and,
374, 375, 376
relationship to Canada,
375–376
social media to raise
awareness, 376
First Nations Technical Institute,
373
First World War, 49
Fisher, John, 58
flack (as derogatory term), 5
flagging, 248
Flaherty, Jim, 59, 60
Flare Magazine, 227
Fleischman, Doris, 50
Fleishman-Hillard Inc., 60, 368
Flickr, 226, 227, 228
flogging (fake blog creation), 18
FM96 radio, 194
Focus Communications, 373
focus groups, 45, 51, 106
advantages of, 106
in Quebec, 372
internal communications
plan and, 285–286
social media as, 214
usage of, 106
Foodsafe certificates, 310
Ford, Rob, 256, 363, 364